Flagstaff Bay

Barn Ledge

Deadwood Plain

Rose Point

Prosperous Bay Plain

Gill P.t

Scale of Latitude and Distance

Scale of Longitude

Scale of Feet

Longitude 5º 40' West from Greenwich

Engraved by Weller & Addison

1771

NAPOLEON'S
GARDEN
ISLAND

NAPOLEON'S GARDEN ISLAND

Lost and old gardens
of St Helena, South
Atlantic Ocean

Donal P. McCracken

Kew Publishing
Royal Botanic Gardens, Kew

First published in 2022 by Royal Botanic Gardens, Kew, Richmond, Surrey, TW9 3AB, UK
www.kew.org

ISBN 978 1 84246 748 0
eISBN 978 1 84246 749 7

Distributed on behalf of the Royal Botanic Gardens, Kew in North America by the University of Chicago Press, 1427 East 60th Street, Chicago, IL 606037, USA.

British Library Cataloguing in Publication Data
A catalogue record for this book is available from the British Library.

Design: Nicola Thompson, Culver Design
Project Manager: Lydia White
Production Manager: Jo Pillai
Copy-editing: Michelle Payne
Proofreading: Matthew Seal

Publication of this book was supported by a grant from the Stanley Smith (UK) Horticultural Trust.

Cover illustration: The Jamestown trench, 1812. Wathen, *A Series of Views Illustrative of the Island of St. Helena*, 1821.
Endpapers: Detail from Admiralty chart of Island of St Helena, South Atlantic Ocean, 1922.

Printed in Great Britain by Bell & Bain Ltd, Glasgow

For information or to purchase all Kew titles please visit
shop.kew.org/kewbooksonline or email publishing@kew.org

Kew's mission is to understand and protect plant and fungi, for the wellbeing of people and the future of all life on Earth.

Kew receives approximately one third of its funding from Government through the Department for Environment, Food and Rural Affairs (Defra). All other funding needed to support Kew's vital work comes from members, foundations, donors and commercial activities, including book sales.

DEDICATED TO

Seamus O'Brien
Custodian of Kilmacurragh Gardens,
County Wicklow, Ireland

Contents

List of tables, figures and illustrations

TABLES

FIGURES

INTEGRATED ILLUSTRATIONS

COLOUR PLATES

COLONIAL REPORTS—MISCELLANEOUS.

No. 38.

REPRINT

OF

A REPORT

(Written in 1884).

UPON THE

PRESENT POSITION AND PROSPECTS OF THE AGRICULTURAL RESOURCES OF THE ISLAND OF ST. HELENA.

BY

D. MORRIS, Esq., M.A., F.L.S., F.G.S.,

Director of Public Gardens and Plantations, Jamaica.

NOTE.—This Report was written by Mr. Morris (now Sir D. Morris, Director of Agriculture in the West Indies) in January, 1884. There have been many recent requests for copies, and the report is consequently reprinted.

Presented to both Houses of Parliament by Command of His Majesty.
November, 1906.

LONDON:
PRINTED FOR HIS MAJESTY'S STATIONERY OFFICE,
By DARLING & SON, LTD., 34-40, BACON STREET, E.

And to be purchased, either directly or through any Bookseller, from
WYMAN AND SONS, LTD., FETTER LANE, E.C.,
and 32, ABINGDON STREET, WESTMINSTER, S.W.;
or OLIVER & BOYD, EDINBURGH;
or E. PONSONBY, 116, GRAFTON STREET, DUBLIN.

1906.

[Cd. 3248.]   *Price* 3½d.

1. St Helena report, 1884/1906. Sir Daniel Morris, the assistant director of Kew Gardens from 1886 to 1898, visited St Helena in July and August 1883. He then compiled a report for the Colonial Office discussing what might be suitably grown on the island. This was not published until 23 years later when, with the garrison's withdrawal, the economic situation on St Helena was desperate. *Colonial Reports: Miscellaneous. No.38*, HMSO, London, cd. 3248, 1906. Provided by Donal P. McCracken.

Foreword

St Helena's flora today

The remote South Atlantic Island of St Helena has a rich and tumultuous history. We see the impacts of this island history on today's landscapes and their constituent flora. Early colonists introduced species and over-exploited many native ones, so today we see a melange of native and non-native plants across the island and there is no doubt that today's landscapes look very different to those the first colonists experienced. This important new study narrates the story of the public and private gardens on the island and the plants which were associated with them, native and non-native. This saga is integrally bound up with the island's botanical history, pointing to where we are ecologically today.

The flora has been relatively well studied and our collective knowledge of the plants benefits enormously from early plant collectors whose specimens are still available for study in the herbaria of Kew, the Natural History Museum, Oxford University, and others. These specimens are important records that provide the evidence that a particular plant with a particular name grew in a particular place at a particular time. These historical specimens supplemented by modern collections allow us to build up a picture of plant introductions and losses over time and enable us to interpret what we see in today's landscape and to prepare a modern-day flora.

Today, St Helena's flora is dominated by non-native plants, many of which are invasive and harmful to the remaining native flora. Recent estimates suggest that more than 80% of vascular plants have been introduced by man, and in terms of total biomass it is closer to 99% (Lambdon, 2012). Nevertheless, the remaining native flora is both precious and fragile, and the focus of many conservation initiatives. Determining the native status of species is challenging and we think between 69 and 81 species comprise today's native vascular flora plus more than 100 species of mosses and liverworts (non-vascular plants). Significantly, 45 of these vascular plants and 26 of the non-vascular plants are endemic to St Helena and can be found growing naturally nowhere else in the world (Lambdon, 2012; Wiggington,

2012). It is these species unique to St Helena that have been the focus of much conservation attention over the last four to five decades. New discoveries are still being made. The tiny, neglected sedge (*Bulbostylis neglecta*) thought extinct since the last documented collection in 1806 was rediscovered by local conservationists in 2008. Two new endemic species of grass (*Eragrostis episcopulus* and *Panicum joshuae*) were formally described as new to science in 2012 (Lambdon et al, 2012; Lambdon, 2012). Sadly, we have also seen at least six species extinctions, five in recent history and one this century. The most recent loss to the flora is the St Helena olive (*Nesiota elliptica*) which was last seen in the wild in 1999 and declared extinct in 2003 when the last individual in cultivation died despite last-gasp attempts to get material into *in-vitro* cultivation at Kew. The only living remains of this species is a sample of its DNA stored at -80°C in Kew's DNA bank. A further two species are extinct in the wild, remaining only in cultivation and as part of re-introduction programmes: *Lachanodes arborea* (she cabbage tree) and *Trochetiopsis erythroxylon* (St Helena redwood). The future for many of St Helena's endemic species remains precarious and 34 species are currently listed as threatened on the IUCN Red List of Threatened Species (IUCN, 2021). Most of these species are confined to the species-rich cloud forest communities and adjacent natural habitats of the central ridges of the Peaks National Park. St Helena's cloud forest, now restricted to an area of less than 40ha along the crescent-shaped Central Ridge is a global conservation priority.

Unfortunately, early colonists saw the verdant communities on St Helena as a source of commodities useful to their development and progress, and exploitation continued apace. Timber resources were extracted from the forests which declined dramatically such that by the turn of the 19th century few if any large gumwoods or ebonies survived. In the absence of any concerns or knowledge of the importance of biosecurity and the devastating impact invasive species can have on island communities, plants and animals were regularly brought into St Helena, either intentionally or accidentally. Many non-native species became well established with goats in particular having massive negative impacts on the plant communities, as they have done around the world. Islands are particularly susceptible to the impacts of invasive species. Early introductions that are still negatively impacting St Helena's native flora include whiteweed (*Austroeupatorium inulifolium*), bilberry (*Solanum mauritianum*), Bolivian fuchsia (*Fuchsia boliviana*) and trailing fuchsia (*F. coccinea*). More recent introductions continue to impact native species and much of today's conservation efforts are focussed on good biosecurity to prevent new invasions and the removal of invasive weeds from natural habitats to try and push the pendulum back towards thriving, healthy native plant communities. Recent introductions of concern include *Pennisetum setaceum* (African fountain grass), *Nephrolepis cordifolia* (Pheasant-tail fern) and *Asparagus densiflorus* (foxtail asparagus). Collectively, non-native invasive species present the greatest threat to the long-term future of St Helena's unique flora. The latest assault is from non-native plant diseases causing various die-back symptoms of many trees including black cabbage trees (*Melanodendron integrifolium*) and he cabbage trees (*Pladaroxylon leucodendron*), both endemic and restricted to small, fragmented populations on the Peaks central ridge. The final blow may come from climate change. It is precisely these cloud forest habitats that modelling suggests may disappear completely within the next 50 years.

Conservation activities on St Helena effectively started with the amazing efforts of local Saint, George Benjamin who was a forest guard who rediscovered the extinct she cabbage in 1976 and St Helena olive in 1997. George eventually became St Helena's first Conservation Officer, heading the newly established government conservation section. George spent time at the Royal Botanic Gardens Kew honing his conservation and horticulture skills, establishing an institutional relationship that has continued for more than 40 years of conservation partnership and support. Working closely with Quentin Cronk, St Helena's conservation programme grew and our understanding of the current status of the endemic plants flourished and strategies for conservation of these unique species developed (Cronk, 2000; Lambdon, 2012; Lambdon & Cronk, 2020). George was instrumental in establishing the St Helena Endemic Nursery at the Agriculture Station in Scotland, now ably led by Vanessa Williams who graduated from the Kew horticulture apprenticeship scheme and maintains the strong conservation, horticulture and outreach links between our two institutions.

Seed banking is a valuable, cost-effective, long-term means of safeguarding plants *ex situ*. Seed banks ensure that seed of suitable provenance can be stored for long periods and available for reintroductions and restoration of degraded landscapes. Kew's Millennium Seed Bank is the world's largest *ex situ* wild species seed bank and includes seed collections from the UK Overseas Territories, a programme started in the mid-1990s. Seeds from St Helena were amongst the first UKOTs seed batches to be stored and the St Helena Government is part of the Millennium Seed Bank Partnership, a worldwide partnership working towards long-term conservation through seed banking. Today, the Millennium Seed Bank holds 42 of St Helena's 45 endemics species of vascular plants (Clubbe et al, 2020). Species not in safe storage include she cabbage tree (*Lachanodes arborea*), now extinct in the wild, which cannot be stored in conventional seed banks due to its recalcitrant seeds. Research is underway to explore alternative options for long-term storage such as cryopreservation, but for now these seeds must be germinated rapidly to retain their viability to create seed orchards on St Helena to retain genetic diversity.

Seed banking is an important tool in our conservation toolbox, but the real challenge remains *in situ* conservation via habitat protection and restoration. The Peaks central ridge has been the focus of many conservation interventions since the early 1990s because of its global importance for plant and invertebrate endemism. Diana's Peak National Park, formally declared in 1996, and expanded into the Peaks National Park in 2016, is one of St Helena's 23 National Conservation Areas which identify the most important sites on St Helena for conservation. After a full public consultation, The Peaks Management Plan, an ambitious 5-year programme to conserve and restore the Peaks for biodiversity, water security and public engagement, has been approved by the St Helena Government. With a generous grant from the UK Government, the first phase of implementation of this plan and the beginning of a bold restoration programme for the Peaks cloud forest habitat got underway in July 2021. Kew is part of a consortium led by the RSPB supporting the St Helena Government to implement this plan inaugurating a new and exciting chapter for the conservation of St Helena's unique biodiversity.

Colin Clubbe
Senior Research Leader (UK Overseas Territories and Islands)
Royal Botanic Gardens, Kew

References

Clubbe, C., Ainsworth A. M., Barrios S., et al (2020). Current knowledge, status, and future for plant and fungal diversity in Great Britain and the UK Overseas Territories. *Plants, People, Planet* 2: 557-579. https://doi.org/10.1002/ppp3.10142

Cronk, Q. C. B. (2000). *The Endemic Flora of St Helen*a. Anthony Nelson, Oswestry, UK.

IUCN. (2021). The IUCN Red List of Threatened Species. Online: https://www.iucnredlist.org/. Accessed 12 October 2021.

Lambdon, P. (2012). *Flowering Plants & Ferns of St Helena*. Pisces Publications, Newbury, UK.

Lambdon, P. & Cronk, Q. C. B. (2020). Extinction dynamics under extreme conservation threat. *The Flora of St Helena*. Frontiers in Ecology and Evolution. 8:41. https://doi.org/10.3389/fevo.2020.00041

Lambdon, P., Darlow, A., Clubbe, C. & Cope, T. (2012). *Eragrostis episcopulus* – a newly described grass species endemic to the island of St Helena, its ecology and conservation. *Kew Bulletin* 68: 1-11. https://doi.org/10.1007/s12225-012-9413-1

Wiggington, M. (2012). *Mosses & Liverworts of St Helena*. Pisces Publications, Newbury, UK.

2. Napoleon and step-daughter, Hortense, at Malmaison, 1815. It was to the magnificent garden at Malmaison outside Paris, created by the Empress Josephine, that Napoleon came after his defeat at Waterloo in 1815. He spent several days here reading novels. These were his last days of freedom, before leaving for the coast where he presented himself to the British, asking for permission to reside in Britain. This request was not countenanced and he was shipped off to the remote island of St Helena.

19th century engraving drawn by Henri Philippoteaux. Provided by Donal P. McCracken.

Preface

It is a curious fact that the most enthusiastic gardener St Helena ever had was the Emperor Napoleon Bonaparte. The challenges he had to face in constructing his garden on the 'desolate windswept plain' of the East India Company's Longwood estate make for poignant reading. Many years after the drama of Napoleon on St Helena had become a distant memory, Betsy Balcombe recalled of Longwood in his time:

> Before terminating our visit, Napoleon took us over the garden and grounds which surrounded his house. Nothing could exceed the dreariness of the view which presented itself from them; and a spectator unaccustomed to the savage and gigantic scenery of St. Helena, could not fail to be impressed with its singularity.[1]

But elsewhere on the island, for a generation before, miniature country estates worked by the enslaved population had showcased, if not formal gardens, at least a fairly standard layout of the grounds around the attractive Georgian farmhouses. In 1821, when visiting St Helena, the Indian nabob Henry Russell recorded:

> In the country the houses are generally built on the side of the hills; many of them on declivities so steep as to look, when seen from a distance, as if the house with all its appendages were sliding down into the chasm below.[2]

And the following year, J. Kerr commented:

> The appearance of St. Helena from the sea is most desolate and repulsive, but there are some pretty spots in the interior, and some scenes, particularly from Sandy Bay Ridge, that are extraordinary and romantic. The enclosures and plantations surrounding the white houses of the Colonists, with farms and gardens in the sheltered nooks and recesses, form a pleasing contrast with the rugged and tremendous rocks, which in some places overhang them.[3]

Both were correct. Invariably perched on a ridge or small plain were elegant whitewashed, straw-roofed farmhouses. To their sides and behind lay what were essentially arboreta: avenues of trees, imposing in their own way, which – even well into the 20th century – gave the island a quaint 18th-century feel. In the early 1930s St Helena's colonial secretary, Charles Kitching, wrote in his excellent but unpublished handbook and guide to St Helena:

> Today the ruins of public buildings, of vast fortifications, and of large and beautifully situated country houses, are all, excepting its climate and scenery, that remain of its former glory.[4]

The same might be said of St Helena's old gardens, both public and private. Few remain. What was the island's old botanic garden, once curated by the young William Burchell (1806–1810), one of the world's finest 19th-century botanists, is now the site of two blocks of flats. Further down the Jamestown Valley, the older established British East India Company garden is greatly reduced in size and has become a public park called the Castle Garden.

It was to Jamestown and these gardens that Captain Bligh brought his famous breadfruit. More significant in impact was the fact that the great East India Company fleets from China and India made St Helena a depot for revictualling. So the Jamestown gardens were in a sense the *raison d'être* for Britain to retain St Helena – but their significance went further.

Even though St Helena was an 'island fortress', especially during the 22-year war period with France, the spirit of the Enlightenment affected a series of governors who effectively established St Helena as a botanical hub. In the age of sail only a small proportion of plants survived lengthy sea voyages so plants being transported north were rested in these gardens before the final leg of their voyage. In this way, Jamestown became an entrepôt for plants coming in from the east and south Asia, which rested in the gardens before being shipped on to botanic gardens and wealthy collectors, or being trialled for horticultural or agricultural economic potential. Some of these plants remained, giving the 47-square mile (122 sq. km) island today a controversially globally diverse flora.

The decades following Napoleon's captivity and the end of the East India Company's trading monopoly effectively left St Helena without a role in the empire. Even its key link in the process of introducing ornamental and economically valuable plants was overtaken by two great developments that helped the 19th-century plant revolution flourish. Firstly, the advent of steamships dramatically cut the time taken to transport plants across the globe. For example, a journey between the Cape of Good Hope and Britain, which had taken about 120 days in 1800, was by 1870 cut to about 30 days. The second innovation drastically cut the death rate among plants being transported onboard ships. This was the invention by Dr Nathaniel Ward of the Wardian case, a simple wooden-framed structure with glass sides and sometimes a glass roof. It will be discussed later in this book.

Not surprisingly and quite appropriately, in recent years botanists who have studied St Helena have focused on the island's indigenous flora, what Joseph Hooker, the future director of the Royal Botanic Gardens, Kew (1865–1885), termed 'a fragment from the wreck of an ancient world'. However, remarkably little has been written about the 17th and early 18th-century plant hunters who stopped off on their voyages into the unknown, or more likely on their way home.

As will be seen, only a trickle of plant specimens from St Helena came into Britain in the late 17th and early 18th century. There was then a hiatus until the late 18th century and early 19th century, when the scientific exploration of St Helena's flora was established properly, although little publicised. Why there is this gap of two or three generations is difficult to explain precisely. Two factors need to be considered. The first is simply that there were very few governors who were much interested in science, their position essentially being a military one, so there was no encouragement to the planters to botanise. Equally important was that back in Britain Philip Miller and the Chelsea Physic Garden did not have the imperial political clout which Kew Gardens was to acquire in the dawning Age of Enlightenment, when botany became fashionable.

For good or ill, what strikes the visitor to St Helena today is the extraordinary variety of subtropical vegetation from across the globe. The island has in effect become an international botanic garden in itself. This was in no small part due to the role played by the island's gardens, both public and private.

None of the old private gardens have retained their former glory. The old, landed class has long gone. A few of these properties have been renovated or had new houses built on the estates. These include Glencot, Guinea Grass, Knollcombes, Mount Pleasant, Myrtle Gove, Pear Tree Farm, Rock Mount, part of Rock Rose, Rural Retreat, Seaview, Southens, Terrace Knoll, Trapp Cottage, Virgin Hall, West Lodge, Willowdene, Windy Point Cottage and Woodlands.

But many of the old St Helena country houses and cottages now lie in ruin or have been demolished. These include Arno's Vale, Bates, Bradleys, the Briars [old house], Broadbottom, Chestnut, Cleugh's Plain, East Lodge, Fairyland, Friar's Lodge, Half Moon Cottage, Harpers, Mosquito Cottage, New Longwood, Old Luffkins (near Horse Ridge), Poplars, Rock Cottage, the main section of Rock Rose, Rock Mount, Rosemary Hall, Sane Valley House, Scotland, Vaughans, Warbro, Whites and Willow Bank.

And yet, as Thomas Moore wrote about the time when the old St Helena order was vanishing: 'You may break, you may shatter the vase, if you will, But the scent of the roses will hang round it still.'

John Charles Melliss, in his superb natural history anthology of St Helena published in 1875, observed on occasion that a plant species survived 'where gardens previously existed'. It was through these gardens, in their many forms, that most new plant arrivals made their way, for better or worse, into the island's ecosystem. If one digs deep into Melliss's book and analyses the locations of plant species then found on the island, one discovers that of 1,058 species listed about 47 per cent were in the wild, 32 per cent in identified gardens and 21 per cent in unnamed gardens. This means that just over 50 per cent of the island's plants were to be found in present or previous garden locations, an extraordinary fact, especially when one considers the 500 or so plants in the wild included the mosses, lichens, ferns and grasses.

FIGURE 1
Location of plants listed by Melliss, 1875

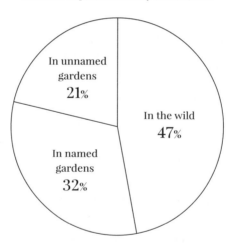

As an entrepôt for plants during the late 18th and early 19th centuries, St Helena was a kind of 'botanical Dubai'. Much was introduced by accident, among grain, in fodder, on the boots of soldiers and the hooves of horses. Then there were the plants purposely introduced onto the island for aesthetic or economic reasons. These came from the Royal Horticultural Society in London, several East India Company botanic gardens in India, from private individuals, and from the

East India Company's agent at the Cape, as well as from the Royal Botanic Gardens, Kew. While some species survived and flourished, a great many lasted only a while before disappearing. In his anthology of the island, Melliss names 25 species which Kew had introduced in the late 1860s/early 1870s. Today only three of those species are to be found on the island: cinchona (*Cinchona officinalis*), bilberry (*Solanum mauritianum*) and pitch pine (*Pinus rigida*).[5]

Four miles inland from Jamestown is the remnant of a second island botanic garden and a once-great arboretum at Plantation House, the residence of the governor of this British Overseas Territory. Beyond Plantation House little survives of the scattered and frequently ruined homesteads of planters or East India Company officials and their once park-like demesnes and gardens.

It was the old botanic garden in Jamestown which first attracted me to St Helena. Having written *Gardens of Empire: Botanic gardens of the Victorian British empire* and several books on South African botanic gardens, I was curious to explore why St Helena's botanic gardens did not fit the pattern of most other British imperial botanical institutions, which flourished after the restoration of the Royal Botanic Gardens, Kew from the 1840s under the Hooker dynasty. By then, St Helena Botanic Garden was moribund having had its glory days during the reign of George III, when British botany was dominated by Sir Joseph Banks. It was established in 1787, very early for a British colonial botanic garden, and most unusually flourished during Britain's struggle against revolutionary and Napoleonic France, a time of international war. Most botanic gardens suffer due to war, but not the one in St Helena.

The saga of the rise and fall of the island's botanic gardens was an interesting tale in itself, but visits to St Helena in 2006 and 2017, and forays into the East India Company's papers, now housed at the British Library in London, convinced me that there was a wider, interlinked story to be told which would include the unexpected context of the other parks and gardens on this remotest of British territories. Garden history might not seem to fit into the historical narrative of St Helena, with its focus on the island fortress, on Napoleon's period of captivity, or on its emergence from a slave-owning society to a modern territory with the prospect of a thriving international upmarket tourist trade. In fact, the old and the lost gardens of St Helena are an integral part of that island fortress experience.

Recent historians have usually attempted to place St Helena in its wider imperial context and, in particular, in the context of East India Company possessions. Such attention has tended to focus on conservation and/or environmental issues though not, significantly, the military context so much: such review of wider linkages and influences is a healthy development. However, this no-island-is-an-island concept can be taken only so far. There is a danger of viewing St Helena more superficially and making assumptions about how such elements fit a preconceived pattern or plot. There are too few solid comparative studies, considering East India Company island possessions in relation to each other, for instance, or placing the St Helena exemplar alongside that of Penang or Mumbai (Bombay). Even then, the main danger of such an approach is that the uniqueness of St Helena could be played down. Whatever is said of trade linkages and supply and of utopian settlement attempts, which in any case died a rapid death, St Helena was maintained as a British sentry post in the middle of the South Atlantic. It did not pay and, regardless of the desire of some enlightened governors, it was never expected to pay. St Helena was a key military outpost to the west of Africa as Aden was to the east. When St Helena became obsolete in military and navy terms, the British left it to manage as well as it could, keeping it, as it were, under imperial mothballs until the Admiralty and the War Office might need to utilise it again, such as during the Second World War and Falklands War.

This picture of a remote island that occasionally became the focus of geopolitics and scientific attention gives a unique quality to St Helena's garden story. Here, a self-styled gentry, mostly without much lineage, established themselves on small farms with estate gardens, utilising the rolling and often jagged landscape to great effect. They portrayed themselves as a landed class – and perhaps what went on in the gambling hell at Olive Cottage was not that different from the rakish activities of some of the gentry and aristocracy back home. Laurence Sterne could not have invented better.

Apart from recording an untold narrative, my task has been to bring to the consciousness of the island's existing inhabitants, the Saints, the fact that St Helena has a garden heritage, and that they need to think seriously about re-establishing a fully functional and supported botanic garden. Ideally, this would be one that collects the island's indigenous flora and possibly also plants species such as breadfruit, cinchona and coffee that have left a historical footprint. This might be created at the Castle Garden, Plantation House, or at one of the old planters' farmhouses. As an educational, scientific or tourist facility, such an initiative would look both to the future and to the island's past.

In 1868, writing to Kew Gardens, Melliss observed, 'the more one goes into the natural history of this little island the more attractive it becomes'.[6] This is in part because the topography is so strange and varied. Its small space, ten miles long by six miles wide [16 x 8 km], is dissected by a hundred steep-sided valleys with three distinct botanical zones. The concept of the distance a crow flies has little relevance in St Helena, where direct land access is interrupted by valleys, gorges, chasms, slopes, peaks, ridges and plateaus. And despite having an abundance of springs, which according to Percy Teale decant some 5,000 tons of water into the sea every day, the island has experienced periods of acute drought. That the spring at Oakbank House generated 1,200 gallons [5,455 l] of water an hour explains in part the success in laying out the grounds of that old house. This compares to 280 gallons [1,272 l] an hour at Longwood, where Napoleon was admonished for taking baths, let alone watering his remarkable garden.[7]

Another reason this island is so fascinating is because of its variety of flora. Lambdon and Cronk estimate that habitat loss due to the 'continuous onslaught of invasive plants' has eliminated endemic plants from 96.5 per cent of the island.[8] Not unnaturally, environmental focus and concern has been on conserving and expanding the old indigenous plants, something which up to now has not been as successful as might have been hoped. It has been estimated that of the 56 known species of endemic plants on St Helena six are extinct both in cultivation and in the wild, and a further two are extinct in the wild but exist precariously in cultivation. These are:

Trochetiopsis melanoxylon (St Helena ebony tree): Seen by Banks and Solander in 1771; believed by Burchell to be extinct when he was on St Helena (1806–1810).

Heliotropium pannifolium (St Helena heliotrope): Collected by Burchell, February 1810.

Acalypha rubrinervis (stringwood): In 1875 Melliss stated one had grown at Oakbank House 20 years before (*c.*1855).

Wahlenbergia roxburghii (Burchell's bellflower): Last recorded in 1872 when Melliss found a specimen at Taylor's Flat.

Wahlenbergia burchellii: Lambdon and Cronk list last record as about 1880. Lambdon in 2012 lists this species as dubious, being very similar to *W. roxburghii*. Only a poor herbarium specimen survives.

Nesiota elliptica (St Helena olive): Rediscovered on Diana's Peak by George Benjamin in 1977: one cutting survived in cultivation until 2002.

Trochetiopsis erythroxylon (St Helena redwood) and *Lachanodes arborea* (she cabbage tree): both extinct in the wild but cultivated specimens are still in existence.[9]

Of the 48 endemic species surviving in the wild, Lambdon and Cronk cite an endemic plant abundance and distribution survey which records 7 plant species as locally common, 7 as endangered, 9 as vulnerable, 23 as critical, and 2 as not threatened.[10] Occasionally a plant once thought extinct has been rediscovered. For example, the neglected turf sedge *Bulbostylis neglecta* disappeared from scientific view for 130 years between the 1870s and its rediscovery in 2008. Mention also needs to be made of the extinction of those plants which arrived on the island with or without the assistance of human agency.

The issue of island flora exercised the minds of Victorian scientists, not least after Charles Darwin's work on the Galapagos Islands. St Helena, falling as it does so near the equator, posed the obvious question as to which hemisphere or land mass influenced it prior to the 1500s. In October 1878, Darwin sent Joseph Hooker at Kew Gardens an article for review concerning the island's flora and insects. Hooker, who had visited St Helena briefly in 1840 and 1843, replied that there was no relationship whatsoever between the island flora of the north Atlantic and St Helena, but rather that the island's flora 'is very S. African'. Over a hundred years later the argument confirmed Hooker's looking south rather than north. Indeed, one fancies that Hooker would have lauded Ronald Gordon Fennah from the Natural History Museum in London:

> The important point is that these old endemic species in St Helena are not the progeny of miscellaneous waifs and strays, but a recognizable fragment of a biocoenose which is more completely preserved in the mid-Pacific islands.[11]

Hooker looked at plants with a global perspective. He enthused of St Helena that 'the plant that pleased him more than any other' was a South American monkey puzzle, which in 1840 was very rare in Britain. He climbed the spiny trunk and obtained some cones, which he hung up in his cabin on board HMS *Erebus*. No araucarias appear in Roxburgh's 1813/1814 flora published by Beatson in 1816. But the anonymous *Flora Sta Helenica*, published in 1825, does include two species of this noble tree, the monkey puzzle (*Araucaria imbricata*) and the Norfolk Island pine (*A. excelsa*).[12] By 1870, the monkey puzzle had disappeared from the island, the Norfolk Island pine remaining a feature to the present time.

St Helena is also an interesting case study for the nature, range and origins of its alien flora. The central belt of the island has been described as looking like an English county, with hedgerows, gates, fields and sheep. Visitors frequently said that it seemed to be a missing county of England, similar to Wiltshire or Dorset, and likened the Marchland with Wales and even Surrey. But look closely at those luscious hedgerows and you will see that, more likely than not, the trees are not English beeches but African erythrina with arum lilies growing at their damp bases – as before the advent of botanical nationalism on the island the arum lily was the island's floral emblem. In Jamestown the traditional tree of the settlement was the Indian fig, now practically vanished apart from a few noble survivors including one fine specimen in what was the old 18th-century botanic garden at the top of the town. Still there, however, is the sacred peepul tree (*Ficus religiosa*) outside the Canteen building, where – 'under the trees' – auctions of enslaved people used to be held, and at the old harbour defences. According to Thomas Brooke in 1808, it was Governor Colonel David Dunbar in the 1740s who first planted an avenue of these trees leading up the middle Jamestown Valley to the hospital. It will be a sad day when Jamestown loses those symbols of its international shipping past.

The old and now mainly lost gardens of St Helena, public and private, played a key part in the island's natural history as reservoirs both for the introduction of an extraordinary amount of alien plants to the island in the 18th and 19th centuries and, on occasion, as shelters for the rather sad last stands of indigenous flora, sometimes represented by a single plant. As early as 1727, in a letter from St Helena, the East India Company was informed:

> Red Wood Trees [*Trochetiopsis erythroxylon*] excellent Timber of a good colour and fine scent and much resembles Red Cedar. Yet it was nearly lost to the island, but about five years ago the Govr. [Edward Byfield] got a couple of young plants neither of them above an inch high set them in his garden, took great care of them and they now produce seed in great abundance.

Attempts to save the St Helena redwood were repeated in the 1970s, when the tree was once again on the brink of extinction.[13]

The nature of the manuscript and printed sources are such that very few names of gardeners have survived, but where located, they have been included in the book. Even in the heyday of the St Helena plantation garden, gardeners were never great in number. One should not forget that these extraordinary gardens, which blended the local St Helena flora with a host of plants especially from the Cape and Asia, were maintained by labour which was not free. Some of the gardeners were from Britain or were serving Company soldiers, but most were either enslaved gardeners from Africa or Asia or indentured gardeners from China. That these gardens were a noted feature of the island and were such extraordinary institutions, visited by people travelling the globe, is a memorial to the tenacity of the St Helena gardeners and to their obvious love of plants.

3. School House, Jamestown. 11 August 1810. William Burchell, the eminent botanist, made this sketch as a young man – he was school master in Jamestown from 1806 until 1810. This gave him a small salary and accommodation. From November 1806, he was also custodian of the botanic garden. Both tasks he carried out well, especially under Governor Patton, who treated him with great affection. This drawing was made a few days after Burchell left the school and two months before he left the island for his great adventure in southern Africa. The gardens are beyond the school wall.

Acknowledgements

My special thanks go to Dr Percy Teale, formerly of the University of Natal, historian of St Helena and once head of the Public Works Department on St Helena. I first met him in 1981 at the University of Natal in Durban and his stories and enthusiasm for St Helena were infectious. He also gave me copies of the various books he had produced or reproduced relating to the island's history.

Thanks also to Lorna Cahill of the Archives at the Royal Botanic Gardens, Kew; Colum O'Riordan and the Irish Architectural Archive; and to Karen Henry, Lacosta McDaniel and Tracy Buckley of the St Helena Archives; and Michel Dancoisne-Martineau, the consul honoraire de France on St Helena. Also on the island, thanks are offered to Edward Baldwin, Stephen Biggs, Dr Rebecca Cairns-Wicks, Maureen Jonas, David Pryce, Adam Sizeland, Gail Thorpe, Nick Thorpe and Emma Weaver. I am grateful to Ian Mathieson, president of the Society of the Friends of the St Helena based in Britain, as well as to Colin Fox of the society, an eminent historian of the island. Robin Castell, whose books are a valuable source to those interested in the island's history, kindly showed me his fine collection of prints relating to St Helena at his home on the island at Prince's Lodge. I am also grateful for assistance from Dr Colin Clubbe, William Forgrave, Claudette Kercival, Patricia McCracken, Dr E. Charles Nelson, Professor Mark Nesbitt, Seamus O'Brien of Kilmacurragh Gardens, County Wicklow, Dr David Rae, and Joan Schrecker.

Any modern researcher working on an aspect of the botanical history of St Helena must be indebted to the pioneering work of Professor Q. C. B. Cronk, whose excellent book *The Endemic Flora of St Helena* appeared in 2000, the same year as Philip and Myrtle Ashmole's epic *St Helena and Ascension Island: a natural history*. Also of great value is the first modern flora of the island written by Dr Phil Lambdon of Kew Gardens, *Flowering Plants and Ferns of St Helena*, published in 2012. Three other historians of St Helena also need to be mentioned, Barbara B. George, Professor Stephen A. Royle of Queens University Belfast and the late Trevor W. Hearl, whose papers are now deposited in the University of Oxford.

The following institutions are thanked: Bodleian Library, Oxford; British Library; Irish Architectural Archive; Longwood House, St Helena; Jardin des Plantes, Paris; Muséum National d'Histoire Naturelle, Paris; National Library of Australia; National Library of Ireland; Society of the Friends of St Helena; St Helena Archives; The National Archives, London; Royal Botanic Gardens, Kew; and the University of KwaZulu-Natal.

A special word of thanks is due to Gina Fullerlove, Head of Publishing at the Royal Botanic Gardens, Kew. Also in the publishing team, my thanks go to Pei Chu, Michelle Payne, Jo Pillai, Matthew Seal, Nicola Thompson and Lydia White.

I am grateful to the Stanley Smith (UK) Horticultural Trust for the generous award towards the publication of this book.

This work is in part based upon research sponsored by the National Research Foundation of South Africa and the University of KwaZulu-Natal. Any opinion, findings and conclusions or recommendations expressed in this material are those of the author and therefore the National Research Foundation does not accept any liability in respect thereto.

4. Lichen hanging from gum trees at Sandy Bay. Sketch by William Burchell, who wrote of this endemic plant, 'The gum wood makes a delightful fire', 27 April 1806.

1

St Helena within the global botanical network

Until the opening up of commercial flights to the newly built airport in October 2017, any visitor to the small south Atlantic island of St Helena arrived by ship. Having jumped ashore off a tender onto the dockside, the visitor passed through the old sea wall defence beside the fort and entered a square dominated by the Anglican church of St James. Behind this to the west is the dramatically steep Jacob's Ladder up a cliffside of the steep valley in which Jamestown is situated. About 200 metres inland from the sea wall and on the left just opposite the church is a modest iron gate off the square. It leads to a small park known as the Castle Garden, the main features of which are an old cast-iron fountain, several mature fig trees and a tearoom. This is all that remains of what was once part of the British East India Company's experimental gardens complex. As well as this garden, it included another further up the valley within the town and a third garden at Plantation House, the governor's residence.

St Helena's garden history is interesting because it begins so early in relation to other British colonial processions. It was in many respects a pioneer, growing out of an early concept of having a garden to provide fresh vegetables and citrus fruit, especially lemons, to calling ships of the East India Company. Every year the great Indiaman fleet with its protective squadron would arrive from India and replenish after the long, gruelling and dangerous voyage. At another time the Company's China fleet would also appear in the roadstead off Jamestown to recover and replenish. As will be seen, the Dutch used gardens for the purpose at the Cape.

St Helena also pioneered the formation of an agri-horticultural society in the 1780s, the same decade that the Linnean Society was established in Britain. As was the way of colonial society, such societies came and went, perhaps the most famous being that in existence when Governor Beatson was governor. The archives on St Helena has a minute book of the Agricultural and Horticultural

Society for the years 1823 to 1825. An attempt by the governor of French-controlled Mauritius at that time to establish such a society failed. But the agricultural society on St Helena succeeded, at least for a while, and was the driving force between the establishment of the island's botanic garden in 1787.

This garden was remarkable in that it thrived during the tremulous years of the French revolutionary and Napoleonic Wars, only to become moribund just before Kew Gardens was revived by Sir William Hooker and the great imperial botanic gardens experiment commenced in the 1840s and 1850s. What is perplexing is why St Helena, which had a botanic garden in physical existence, was not drawn into that imperial nexus, not least when it had been or was soon to be visited by such botanical luminaries as Charles Darwin (1836), Dr Joseph Hooker (1840 and 1843) and later Dr Daniel Morris (1883).

By the end of the Victorian era, there were some 350 botanic gardens in the world, of which about 120 were in the British empire. Botanic gardens on small British-controlled islands were not uncommon in the 19th century. Excluding Jamaica, which had four botanic gardens by the 1870s, there were no fewer than 13 in the West Indies, including a notable one on Trinidad (established in 1818). There were botanic gardens on Mauritius (founded by the French in 1768; British from 1815), Hong Kong (1864) and Fiji (1879), Malacca (1886) and the Seychelles (1900). So there was nothing strange about a Crown Colony or an East India Company island having a botanical institution.

ᰥ⁓᠍ The Kew global web ᠍᥀⁓᰿

However, most of these colonial botanical institutions post-dated the revival of the Royal Botanic Gardens, Kew in the 1840s. The St Helena garden had been a much earlier establishment founded in 1787. Its development came not so long after St Vincent (1765); the Jamaican gardens of Liguanea (*c.*1770), Endfield (1775) and Bath (1779); and the Indian gardens at Madras (1778), Saharanpur (1779, re-established 1817) and Kolkata (Calcutta, 1787). St Helena was originally an East India Company garden, along with Kolkata; Penang (1796, re-established 1822); Bengaluru (Bangalore, 1819); and Singapore (1822).[1]

Kew did not own or indeed control these colonial gardens, but from the time of Joseph Banks (*c.*1760–1820) and during the golden age of the Hooker dynasty (1840–1905), the Royal Botanic Gardens, Kew, had an extraordinary hold on the Colonial Office (formerly the War Office), and to a lesser degree the India Office and the Foreign Office regarding, botanical matters. In practical terms, Kew supplied many colonial and foreign gardens with curators it had trained or whom the director recommended. Indeed, Sir Joseph Hooker kept a record book especially for this purpose. Kew was also the centre of a worldwide plant-exchange network. This involved the movement of seeds, roots and bulbs, living specimens, and dried herbarium specimens, what one detractor in parliament described as 'dried foreign weeds'. It has been estimated that Kew despatched on average a consignment of plant material for every day of Queen Victoria's reign. For a period in the late 18th and early 19th century Kew sent out its own plant hunters to collect plants and seeds. Later, Kew would rely on the newly established colonial botanic gardens and on private collectors abroad, many of them settlers in far-flung colonies like St Helena.

Kew also advanced and promoted the publication of a series of botanical works which heavily, or sometimes completely, relied upon exotic plants previously unknown to European science. These included *Curtis's Botanical Magazine* (which frequently had a volume dedicated to a botanist overseas or a colonial administrator who had assisted the advance of scientific botany) and the *Colonial Flora* series. The *Index Kewensis*, the *Kew Guild* and the *Kew Bulletin* also depended heavily on this imperial network. Then there were the annual reports of colonial botanic gardens and herbaria which were sent across the globe in this network of exchange.

Perhaps Kew's most valuable role was in protecting young curators sent abroad to places where local settlers were more concerned with day-to-day survival in the subtropics than with what was regarded as the falderal of botany. And in this endeavour, as in St Helena with Governors Brooke, Patton and Beatson, Kew was frequently assisted by the goodwill and the active practical support of the local governor, military commander or district officer. It is an extraordinary fact that a great number of the colonial officials who were sent overseas were enthusiastic botanisers, their keenness for plant hunting equal only to their desire to shoot any big game which moved.

In the West Indies and West Africa, small gardens serving as agricultural research stations were called botanic stations. Some of the larger botanic gardens such as some in India, Ceylon (Sri Lanka) and Mauritius had satellite gardens which also served as proto forest stations. There was also a number of very fine gardens scattered across the empire that were in private hands but still were very much part and parcel of the botanical linkage system of plant exchange. Perhaps the most noteworthy was that belonging to Dr Kirk on the island of Zanzibar off East Africa. Dr Ludwig's garden in Long Street, Cape Town was another such garden, where James Bowie, the talented and reclusive plant collector for Sir Joseph Banks, was employed.

Kew and St Helena

Kew long dominated the movement of plants, although private nursery firms were becoming increasingly significant in the process, and one cannot underestimate the role of continental European botanic gardens, especially in Germany, the Habsburg empire and France. But it was in the Australian colonies and in the Indian empire that the most impressive botanic gardens were to be found. Given the immediate link between St Helena and India through the East India Company, it is hardly surprising that it should be India and, by extension through the East India Company trade, China and later the Cape of Good Hope that provided St Helena with so many of its exotic plants. This was sometimes in association with Kew, but more often through the Company and its agencies.

That said, Kew had a significant role in the saga of importation into St Helena. As will be seen, Sir Joseph Banks, effective director at Kew from the 1770s until his death in 1820, was an important person in the saga of plant exchange between St Helena and Britain. Banks had visited St Helena when on board HMS *Endeavour* in May 1771. The archives at the Royal Botanic Gardens, Kew, contain handwritten books of exchange for plants and seeds received at the gardens as well as for those sent out by Kew. The earliest consignment recorded was one sent in 1793 from St Helena which included:

Fern trees 4 plants
Camellia japonica fl. Albo 1 plant
Lycium japonicum fl. Plena. 1 plant
China orange 1 plant
Plant from China 1 plant
Plant 1 plant[2]

Interesting as these lists are, they amount only to a fraction of the exotic imports to St Helena. Far greater were those plants, bulbs and seeds which came off the East Indiamen from India and China, and from the regular ships which plied between Table Bay and Jamestown.

Attention to the island's indigenous flora

Environmental degradation and empire frequently went together. When the Marianne North Gallery opened at the Royal Botanic Gardens, Kew in 1882, Sir Joseph Hooker wrote in the preface of the first gallery guidebook:

Very many of the views here brought together represent vividly and truthfully scenes of astonishing interest and singularity, and objects that are among the wonders of the vegetable kingdom; and that these, though now accessible to travellers and familiar to readers of travels, are already disappearing or are doomed shortly to disappear before the axe and the forest fire, the plough and the flock, of the ever advancing settler or colonist. Such scenes can never be renewed by nature, nor when once effaced can they be pictured to the mind's eye, except by means of such records as this Lady has presented to us.[3]

It is difficult to track the decline of the native vegetation on St Helena except through general sweeps. We know that as early as the late 17th century, British officialdom was concerned with the rapid decline in wooded vegetation, traditionally attributed to the activity of large numbers of goats but also probably due to felling timber for firewood, building, fencing, tanning, smelting, working lime kilns and creating pastureland. In the 1680s it was also recorded that timber was used in distilling spirits from potatoes, a form of poteen which was outlawed in 1700.[4]

Then there were occasional references in what are now regarded as the standard contemporary historical texts on the island, with passages such as this from Brooke's 1806 *History of the island of St Helena*:

The summits and sides of most of this interior heights are wooded with the cabbage-tree of the island, the red-wood, string-wood, dog-wood, and other indigenous trees and shrubs; and in situations less elevated, the gum-tree was formerly to be found in great abundance; but at present few trees of this kind are left standing, except at Long-Wood, where they have been protected by the injunctions of the Company, and cover unequally a surface of nearly 1500 acres.[5]

In the early 18th century Longwood, which included Deadwood Plain, was Company-controlled and used as what today would be called an agricultural research station, with imported timber trees, shrubs and fruit trees, apple, peach, mulberry and quince showing promise. Governor John Roberts and subsequently the rough and brutal old seadog Governor Isaac Pyke were particularly energetic in trying to reverse environmental degradation and encouraging tree planting. This included a law decreed in 1709 which not only enclosed the Great Wood but also laid down that landowners should plant one acre of trees for every ten acres possessed, at a density of 888 trees per acre. However, as with so many such schemes on St Helena, intention and practice were very different. There was not a great deal of success in this venture, and a decade later it was said:

All the hill between Long Wood, Flagstaff, and Halley's Mount, and from thence to the alarm house, had within the recollection of several persons living in the year 1718, been an entire forest.[6]

By 1724 the law was a dead letter. Under Governor Edward Byfield, in 1728 about 150 acres were enclosed on the Longwood estate. The remains of 'the Great Wall of St Helena' can still be seen today. It was Byfield who also set out to tackle the problem of the island's large flocks of sheep and especially goats, supporting a planter demand for their destruction or attempted eradication in a ten-year period starting with an ordinance in 1731. The result is recorded by Thomas Brooke in his history:

The law was in consequence confirmed, and was followed by the expected success. The indigenous trees shot up spontaneously in great numbers. An inhabitant who died in the year 1805, at the age of eighty-three, informed the author that many parts of the island where no trees had grown for many years before became covered with wood.[7]

As A. T. Grove has discussed, the environmental degradation caused by the destruction of forest and woodland on St Helena was exacerbated by a cycle of droughts and floods from 1682 through to 1797. These caused considerable damage and removed exposed topsoil.[8] The Company was not oblivious to this. On 7 March 1794, Governor Brooke received the following imperative from his masters in Leadenhall Street:

We are of the opinion that encouraging the growth of wood is of the utmost consequence to this island not only from the advantages to be derived from it as fuel but because it is well known that trees have an attractive power on clouds especially when they pass over Hills so high as those on your island and we are inclined to believe that the misfortunes the island has been subject to from Drought might in some measure have been averted had the growth of wood been properly attended to. We have been uniform in our directions for keeping Longwood securely fenced ... Should there be any parts of this enclosure that are not at present planted we direct that you immediately order the Gardener to plant as many young trees there as possible.

L'hôpital des marinaux

In 1825 a list of St Helena plants carried an anonymous preface, probably written by Alexander Beatson, containing the following insightful comment, 'St. Helena has been termed by the French L'hôpital des marinaux [seafarers' hospital] – and, it is equally well adapted as a place of recovery for plants.' This had been the case since the 1760s.[9] Even then, the survival rate on the trip on to Britain from St Helena was small. After Sir Hudson Lowe left St Helena in July 1821 and before Governor Walker arrived in March 1823, the entourage guarding Napoleon returned to Britain, with crusty old Brigadier-General John Pine-Coffin remaining on at St Helena for a short time as commander-in-chief living at Knollcombe House. He despatched a small consignment to Kew on the *Vansittart*. It is recorded at Kew as containing the following plants from St Helena and China:

I Box 1 ft sq directed to Thomas Downes Esq plants all dead

2 large tubs 2 ft diamt plants all dead

1 cask 1 ft d. plants all dead

I Box 8 in square containing a Passiflora dead

1 box 72 in squ containing a Camellia alive but in a very sickly & doubtful state.

1 Tub containing Dicksonia arborescens in tolerable good cond.[10]

Things, however, were soon to change. In the late 1830s and early 1840s a new invention, the Wardian case, revolutionised the transportation of plants across the globe, coupled as it was with the arrival of steamships, the invention of curvilinear glass for conservatories, the abolition of the glass tax and improved methods of producing iron frames with curved surfaces.[11]

In about 1829 Dr Nathaniel Bagshaw Ward, a medical doctor and keen naturalist in the East End of London, invented a terrarium in which plants, placed in damp soil in a sealed glass case, could survive the terrible London smog pollution.[12] By the 1840s, this invention was also widely used to transport plants on board ship. By this time, St Helena's importance as a botanical entrepôt had passed due to the island's transfer in the mid-1830s from the Company to direct British government control as a Crown Colony and, of course, the reality that the Wardian case meant that plants no longer needed to be 'rested' when being transported from the East to Europe or the West Indies. These cases were, however, used to export specimens of St Helena's endemics and introduce ornamentals and forest trees.

Designs of Wardian cases varied, from the elegant to the utilitarian, with many being simple wooden frames, sealed with green glass and putty and covered in chicken wire. They came in all sorts of shapes and sizes. Some were tall to fit cycads and tree ferns, others smaller and squatter. The volume of glass also differed from case to case. George Bennett on St Helena was given a case by his mother, Eleanor. Writing to William Hooker at Kew Gardens on 22 May 1843, George commented:

> I have had a suitable case constructed and glazed and am sorry to perceive on summing up the expenses that they so nearly trend upon the limit you had fixed – and these arise to on merely fitting up a case which was made a present to me by my mother. It required some alterations inasmuch as it had no glazed roof and just supplying this deficiency has cost the sum, a memoranda of which you will find annexed. Our mechanics wages here are very high indeed.

The cost of this joinery and glazing was:

Nails		2s	3d
Glazier		3s	0d
Paid carpenter		20s	0d
30 squares glass		15s	0d
Paid man conveying a basket of plants from Diana's peak		3s	6d
Total	£2	3s	9d

On top of this Bennett had to pay three shillings and six pence (3/6) to arrange boat hire at the harbour and twenty-one shillings and six pence (£1-1s-6d) to freight the case from St Helena to London. This came to the not inconsequential sum of three pounds eight shillings and nine pence (£3-8s-9d).[13]

There were various mechanisms for transporting plants on board sailing ships. Seeds and bulbs had a greater chance of survival than living plants. These were stored in as dry a place as possible, bulbs sometimes in sawdust or dry sand or even wrapped in newspaper; seeds usually just in bags.

Before the Wardian case was invented there was a not dissimilar box-shaped container for transporting plants, which had solid wooden sides and a sloping roof like a house, one side of which could be opened to let in light and for watering. But more common were pots, large and small tubs or ordinary wooden boxes. There are several paintings of the famous mutiny on HMS *Bounty* in 1789 which depict the mutinous crew throwing the 1,015 pots containing breadfruit plants overboard after Captain Bligh and his 18 crew were set adrift in the longboat.

Salt water and the lack of light in the hold were the great killer of plants on board sailing ships but there were other dangers, such as rats, ships' cats and indeed human beings who tore off plant leaves or broke branches. It was said that many ships' captains disliked having plants on board and cared little for their welfare. There were, of course, notable exceptions and sometimes the captain would give up his cabin so that cases of plants could be stored there. In the 1825 printed list of St Helena plants, Beatson included the following instruction from Roxburgh relating to transporting plants at sea:

Particular care, if not placed in a cabin, must be taken that they are kept covered during stormy weather, or such as raises the least saline spray into the air; for the chief danger plants are liable to at sea, is occasioned by the saline particles with which the air is then charged. These, falling on the plants, quickly evaporate, but leave the deadly salt behind: every care must therefore be taken, to guard against salt water, and the spray at sea.

During moderate weather, it will be proper to keep boxes open – for plants cannot long exist without air and light – also during moderate rain; for rain is much better for the plants than water from the cask. A moderate degree of moisture is sufficient. When the weather is dry, it will be necessary to give them a little fresh water, now and then – the periods and quality cannot be pointed out in any Instructions, as the state of the weather must be the guide.

Directions where to place the chests cannot be well given; as that will in a great measure depend on the size, structure, etc. of the Ship. In our Indiamen, round the capstan, on the quarter deck seems the best, on many accounts. The greatest danger, in such a situation is, while the deck is washing in the mornings, the boxes must then be shut and covered with a piece of canvas, or something to prevent the salt water getting in between crevices.

When plants from a cold climate get into a warm one, they shoot most luxuriantly and often kill or choke one another; the larger shoots must therefore be frequently shortened, and as many of the leaves thinned as will give the rest air and room. Insects, particularly caterpillars, often make their appearance about the same time – they must be carefully picked off.

Baskets with roots (such as potatoes,) or succulent plants, may be hung up in any cool airy place – such, for example as the projecting part of the desk which covers the wheel of an Indiaman, or hung over the stern; but in that case, they must be covered with a tarpawling, or painted canvas.

SEEDS are to be kept in a cool dry place, and never put below the gunroom, hold, or lower deck.

Roots ought to be packed in dry sand, after being moderately dried, and dispatched in any ship that sails about the close of the year.[14]

The other means of transporting plant material across the oceans was as herbarium specimens. This involved drying, pressing and often poisoning specimens to prevent them from being eaten by insects. Some plant collectors were experts at this procedure despite having to adapt to difficult circumstances. Newspapers were (and are) frequently used in the pressing and drying process. Blotting paper was in fashion for a time, though Robert Brown in the Botanical section of the British Museum was hostile to this in the tropics as the blotting paper tended to ferment.[15] Nonetheless, herbarium specimens were essential to formally describe plants previously unknown to European science, and they remain the core of taxonomy even to the present.

Not surprisingly, the mortality rate among plants transported across the oceans was very high. But some plants did get through, and St Helena played its role in what was an increasing number of plant species coming into Europe. As illustrated in Table 1, John Claudius Loudon highlighted the dramatic increase in plant introductions into Britain in the period when the St Helena Botanic Garden was at its peak:

TABLE 1

Introduction of exotic plants into Britain[16]

Monarch	Dates of reign	Number of years	Approx. number of exotic plants introduced into Britain	Average per year
Henry VIII	1509–1547	38	47	1.2
Edward VI	1547–1553	6	7	1.2
Elizabeth I	1558–1603	45	533	11.8
James I	1603–1625	22	20	0.9
Commonwealth	1649–1659	10	95	9.5
Charles II	1660–1685	25	152	6
James II & William & Mary	1685–1702	17	298	17.5
Anne	1702–1714	12	230	19.1
George I	1714–1727	13	182	14
George II	1727–1760	33	1770	53.6
George III	1760–1820	60	6756	112.5

Although the St Helena Botanic Garden became renowned as a 'convalescent home for sickly plants' arriving from the East Indies, the survival rate of plants shipped into St Helena is difficult to estimate. One consignment in 1818 is summarised in Table 2.

TABLE 2

Survival rates of plant consignments entering St Helena, 1818[17]

Trees	Received	Healthy	Doubtful	Dead	Unaccounted status
Apples	74	61	4	6	3
Apricots	9	–	–	9	–
Nectarines	9	–	9	–	–
Plums	9	–	–	9	–
Pears	9	6	3	–	–
Deserts	6	–	6	–	–
Poplars	9	–	–	–	9
Sycamores	6	6	–	–	–
Aspens	6	–	–	6	–
Oaks	6	6	–	–	–
Filberts	6	–	6	–	–
Willow cuttings	12	–	–	12	–
Horse chestnuts	6	6	–	–	–
Total	**167**	**85 (51%)**	**28 (17%)**	**42 (25%)**	**12 (7%)**

A survival rate of 50 per cent for living healthy plants was above the norm. Governor Walker in a letter to the St Helena Agricultural and Horticultural Society dated 16 August 1824 set out the reason why the consignment sent to the island by Sir Stamford Raffles had arrived:

> in a state of perfect preservation. This was owing to the judicious manner in which they were arranged in the cases; and protected from the spray of the sea, while air and light were sufficiently admitted.[18]

Like Governors Brooke and Beatson before him, Walker was keenly aware of the hazards facing the transportation of live plants in and out of St Helena. Walker was also aware of the immediate dangers of landing plants at a harbour such as Jamestown which had no docking facilities, or only the most primitive kind. Removing boxes, chests or tubs over the sides of pitching sailing ships and then manhandling or craning them onto the harbour wall could expose plants directly to sea spray or even a drenching. To try to prevent this, in April 1825 Walker instructed William Brabazon, the redoubtable harbour master, the following:

> A variety of plants are expected to be sent to this Island in different Ships from Sundry parts of the world, you will therefore comply with such applications as you may from time to time receive from either the company's Gardeners for Boats or other assistance either for landing these plants or for embarking such as may be deemed expedient to ship for England. You will also please to afford every facility to either of the Gardeners visiting Ships for the purpose of ascertaining what plants may be obtainable for this island by purchase or otherwise.[19]

⤳ St Helena as a pioneer in colonial forestry ⤳

On St Helena the word forest is probably misleading for this period. What were considered indigenous forests were mainly woodland rather than dense forest in the more common meaning of the word. And, indeed, woods was the word often used. In 1686, rewards were handed out to those who had captured Richard Hancock who, 'had lived in ye woods twenty-two months and was a principal agent in the late Rebellion'. The Longwood–Deadwood plateau area was, at least from the 1670s, referred to as the Great Wood. However, when the drive to plant trees began on St Helena in earnest from the 1780s onwards, it was forests and forest trees which would dominate the enterprise.

Forestry involves two fundamentals, the scientific management of indigenous forestlands, which involves conservation as distinct from clear felling, and afforestation, planting new forests or renewing old forest and woodland. The saga of forest and woodland under empire was by no means simple nor was it a uniform development either geographically or in time. It cannot be denied that there was extensive forest exploitation, restricted initially only by technology, transport and access. What is sometimes overlooked, however, is the extraordinary drive in the 19th century to conserve forestland, albeit sometimes for self-serving purposes. There was often recognition, especially among the ruling colonial administrators, that deforestation led to a decrease in rainfall. There was also the feeling that forests served as catchment and containment areas for water supply and soil retention. Then, where one had a white settler population, as in St Helena, matters were complicated by the ever-growing demand for fuel, building material, lime smelting, leather tanning, and fencing. Added to this was the impact of cattle, sheep and especially goats stymying forest and woodland regeneration.

The British Indian forestry service became the gold standard for imperial forest management.[20] Initially, its foresters were trained for two years and eight months at the École Forestière at Nancy in France before going out to India. The Imperial Forestry School at Dehradun in northern India commenced in 1878. Foresters were still trained in Europe for India, however, and from 1885 forestry candidates attended the Royal Indian Engineering College at Coopers Hill near Windsor. Here candidates underwent three years of rigorous instruction, including practical visits to German or French forests.[21] Later, what was being undertaken in India was also attempted in many other parts of the empire, be it in the Australian colonies, Malaya, Mauritius, Natal, the Cape or British Guiana [Guyana].[22] Underpinning all this was the notion of forestry and forest conservation. However, all this practical application in the empire really dated only from the 1850s and 1860s, with forest ordinances and legislation mostly commencing from the 1870s and 1880s. What is extraordinary is that so much time and effort was put into such a concept on St Helena from the early 1700s, with decrees, laws and instructions all relating to the preservation of forest or woodland. Nearer the end of the 18th century would come the push for afforestation on the island.

There is no doubt that the more enlightened early Company governors on St Helena were concerned both by deforestation on the island, and by the gentry's primitive and lackadaisical approach towards agriculture. To counter both problems, they introduced various species of agricultural plants as well as timber tree species. While some did threaten the native species, it can be argued that many of the invasives on St Helena came onto the island by accident rather than by design, and indeed some of the introductions, such as trees, helped relieve the pressure on the last enclaves of indigenous plants, at least until the late, 19th-century onslaught from New Zealand flax. However, the truth was that too little was done too late and by the time that officialdom sought to protect native plants, they were already well on the retreat. Added to this was St Helena's perennial problem of different policies being pursued by different governors. A lack of administrative continuity bedevilled the island during its history.

In the 1740s, Governor Colonel David Dunbar, like several of his predecessors, was enthusiastic about promoting agriculture. He is an interesting example of the rough-tough colonial governors of the day. Many of those of who served in St Helena were there as an end-of-career sinecure because they had caused trouble elsewhere, like Governor Pyke, or because of advancing penury. Dunbar ticked both those boxes, but that is not to say that he was without ability or drive. He had extensive colonial experience, including knowledge of the natural environment. He had earlier served in a swashbuckling fashion in Maine and New Hampshire in British North America. He was a frontiersman and as such not very popular with many of the white settlers. For a period he was lieutenant-governor of New Hampshire, in which post he made a bitter enemy of Governor Belcher, who in 1732 engineered his dismissal. Ironically, as governor of St Helena in 1747, it was Dunbar's deputy Charles Hutchinson who eventually managed to engineer Dunbar's removal and then replace him as governor.

One of the principal reasons for this Irishman's downfall in North America was that he held the post of surveyor-general of his majesty's woods, 'the nursery of royal masts'. This position carried a stipend of £200 a year and a proportion of the value of timber recovered. Dunbar took his responsibilities very seriously, acting with great vigour and 'little respect for justice', raiding sawmills and confiscating and marking what he regarded as illicitly felled lumber. After his removal, Dunbar retreated to his farm at Belvidera Point, 'a habitation which he also beautified by a contiguous well-cultivated and tasteful garden'. Returning to London in 1737, he was imprisoned by his creditors for a while. Then, in 1743, he agreed to give up his surveyor-general's position which he still held in North America and accepted the East India Company's offer of £2,000 as governor of St Helena.[23]

So Dunbar was interested in plants and forestry long before he came to St Helena. But then so was his enemy and successor. Governor Charles Hutchinson's 18-year rule witnessed the introduction onto the island of 'scotch pine' (*Pinus sylvestris*), 'spruce fir' (*Picea* spp.) and oak (in the form of acorns).[24] Hutchinson also made the first serious attempt to grow coffee on St Helena, which met with 'several disappointments' because of successive annual droughts, something which may also have affected many of the island's once-famous lemon trees. They started dying and were all but gone by the late 1740s.

By 1777, under Governor John Skottowe, it was said that there were more trees on the Longwood estate than on the whole of the rest of the island, a reflection on the overall deforestation on the island despite the earlier conservation attempts by Governor Roberts. Yet again an attempt was made to enclose Longwood's 800 acres. Extensive planting was undertaken, the whole costing some £8,000. This included, in 1778, planting large numbers of gumwood trees at Horse Point, a substantial, fairly level part of the estate. Along with this new programme came extensive planting of furze or gorse (*Ulex europaeus*), which along with brambles or blackberries (*Rubus pinnatus*) were seriously invasive although their use as fodder and firewood might have been a factor in preserving some indigenous species from eradication.[25] In 1787 maritime pine (*Pinus pinaster*) made its appearance. This hardy and fast-growing Mediterranean tree grows well in poor soils and is still a feature of the island.

From the scant records which survive, it seems that with the passing years Longwood became a provider of firewood rather than a controlled forestry concern. This was despite an admonishment from the East India Company in 1795 that:

> On perusing the minute of the Lt.-Govr. and the Gardener's report on the Estate of Longwood we lament the want of attention not to say total neglect that has prevailed for more than 70 years past with respect to an object of the highest importance to the welfare of the island, namely the cultivation of wood, and if a steady perseverance is not observed to promote it in future the present inhabitants will afford their prosperity as just a reason for condemning their conduct as they have now to deplore that of their ancestors.[26]

Later Governor Beatson recognised this and chose to advance cultivation on part of the Longwood plantation. He also opened up a tree nursery at Plantation House to farmers in his drive to encourage commercial afforestation.[27] A decade later when Governor Brooke assumed his position in 1787, Longwood was still being used to raise trees. It was, however, under the enlightened dispensation of Governor Patton (1802–07) that the Governor Roberts regulations of 1709 were amended, whereby a tenant of Company land had to plant 60 trees for every 10 acres (4 ha), a rate of 6 trees per acre, wherever the tenant wished. To encourage this measure, automatic lease renewal on previously held terms was offered under certain conditions.[28] The new century brought with it yet more attempts to increase the tree coverage of the island. As will be seen, this persistent theme of Company administrations slowly began to pay dividends for the island's economy. By the time of Governor Walker's tenure from 1823 to 1828, afforestation was well under way. In 1823, the Company's penultimate governor asserted at a public meeting in Jamestown, 'The pursuit of agriculture, however, should go hand in hand with the planting of trees and with all those measures of improvement or of ornament, which, within these few years, have made so many great advances on the island of St Helena.' As will be seen, Walker practised what he preached and, emulating his much-maligned predecessor Governor Lowe, planted 60 acres (24 ha) of wasteland with forest trees.[29] Sadly, the end of Company rule stymied for a century any hope of regreening St Helena.

Ordered that the following Letter be written to Captain Bligh by the Secretary

To Capt. W. Bligh
Commanding His Majesty's Ship
Providence

Sir /

I am directed by the Governor and Council to acknowledge the Receipt of the following Trees and Plants —

10 Pots and 1 Tub of Bread Fruit Plants very fine
12 D° sickly —
2 Pots containing 2 Plants of Avees / Apples
1 D° —— 4 D° of Rattah / Chesnut
2 D° —— 3 D° of Ayyah / Jambo
1 D° —— 1 D° of Muttee / Frees
1 D° —— 4 D° of Etow
2 D° —— 2 D° of Peah, besides Roots
                    Timor Plants
1 Pot containing 4 Plants of Nanche / Soursop
1 D° —— 1 D° Lemon / China
1 D° —— 2 Jambo mare
1 D° —— 4 Jambo armiriah
1 D° —— 2 Mango
1 D° —— 2 Penang — Beetle nut /
1 D° —— 2 Long Pepper
1 D° —— 2 Black Pepper
1 D° —— 1 Barbarina Banana —

The Governor & Council were greatly obliged and highly gratified by a View of the Delightful Scene onboard your Ship, which impressed their Minds with the warmest and most animated glow of Gratitude towards his Majesty for his Royal Goodness and Benevolent attention shewn to the Welfare of his Subjects here and in the West Indies Islands, and it also raised in them an inexpressible degree of Wonder and Delight to Contemplate a Floating [...]

5. Captain's Bligh's St Helena plant schedule. When Captain Bligh and HMS *Providence* visited St Helena (17 December 1792 to 23 January 1793), Bligh donated to the island plants in 40 pots and one tub, which included 500 breadfruit plants. Writing to Bligh to thank George III for this gift to St Helena, Governor Brooke commented upon the 'Wonder and Delight to Contemplate a Floating Garden'.
© St Helena Archive

Section I

EAST INDIA COMPANY DAYS

2

East India Company gardens

For 177 years, generous subsidies in cash and kind from the British East India Company kept St Helena running effectively and eventually prospering. In the early days, interest in botany, horticulture and forestry tended to be confined to the Company and its servants rather than planters on the island. A scattering of St Helena herbarium specimens which came into Britain at the late 17th and early 18th centuries can be found in British herbaria. Oxford University has some but most are housed in the herbarium at the Natural History Museum in London, among a collection from Hans Sloane. These include collections containing St Helena specimens purchased by Sloane, such as the collections of Dr Leonard Plukenet (bought in 1710), James Petiver (1714) and the collection of the extraordinary taxonomist and 'top of all the moss-croppers', Rev Adam Buddle (bequeathed 1715).

6. The damp and humid Castle Moat at Jamestown, complete with ferns and banana plants (*Musa acuminata*), sketched by Burchell on 12 January 1809.

James Petiver ran an apothecary shop in Aldersgate in early 18th-century London. But he was far more than this, taking a keen interest in plants, plant collecting and the medical use of plants. To obtain plant specimens, he actively sought out ship's surgeons, one of whom, Alexander Brown, had been to St Helena in 1697 and collected plants. Petiver may well have also received plants from St Helena from other sources. Not all of these were endemics. For example, he obtained from St Helena specimens of sassafras and balsam tree, both from America, an early example of the island serving as an entrepôt in plant distribution. We know that Petiver also received specimens from the Scottish surgeon James Cuninghame, including the 'Wild Rosemarie-tree' (*Phylica polifolia*) and the attractive mossy fern (*Elaphoglossum furcata*). From Surgeon Stonehouse, Petiver received specimens of the island's endemics the sickle fern (*Asplenium platybasis*); the veined tongue fern (*Elaphoglossum nervosum*); the tooth tongue fern (*E. dimorphum*); the mossy fern (*E. furcatum* syn. *Microstaphyla furcata*) and the large bell flower (*Wahlenbergia linifolia*).

Dr Plukenet received various specimens of St Helena endemics, probably from George Stonestreet, whose brother Rev. William Stonestreet was also a plant hunter. These included gumwood (*Commidendrum robustum*), scrubwood (*C. rugosum*), black cabbage tree (*Melanodendron integrifolium*), mossy fern (*Microstaphyla furcata*), St Helena redwood (*Trochetiopsis erythroxylon*) and St Helena ebony tree (*T. melanoxylon*).

Hans Sloane himself, at a meeting of the Royal Society held on 10 February 1697, exhibited an oil extracted from the seed of a castor oil plant (*Ricinus communis*) obtained from St Helena which he had received from Cuninghame, who had recently returned from the East Indies: 'Ye same Mr Cuningham related yt ye Governor's wife usd it for a purge, taking abt. 3 spoonfulls of it for a dose.'[1] This governor was Captain Stephen Poirier, a Huguenot who had arrived on St Helena with a French entourage in January 1689. He was immediately placed on the island's ruling council, a reflection in itself of the lack of talent on the island. When the embattled Governor Kelinge suddenly died, Poirier took over and remained in office until his own death on 8 September 1707.

Poirier was described in April 1689 as 'an honest man living formerly in great plenty upon his own land in France where he made 200 or 300 hogsheads of Wine and Brandy per annum'. He did not have the happiest governorship, one suspects because he was a pleasant individual and not the usual no-nonsense type who kept order with a rod of iron – although treatment of the enslaved population was not improved under Poirier. There is some evidence that the much-abused Poirier found diversion from the problems he faced with the 71 planters on the island and the 'bickering and backbiting' officials by taking an interest in botany and agriculture. The island's main crops were yams and potatoes with some plantains, bananas and lemons, the last described as 'very large and fine'. Also grown and sold to passing ships were 'delicate herbs'. These were also used as a curative for sick sailors who were brought ashore to recuperate. In 1691 the one-time pirate turned Royal Navy captain William Dampier noted of St Helena:

> For the island affords abundance of delicate herbs, wherewith the sick are first bathed, to supple their joints, and then the fruits, and herbs, and fresh food, soon after cure them of their scorbutick humour. So that in a week's time, men that have been carried ashore in hammocks, and they who were wholly unable to go, have soon been able to leap and dance.

Under Poirier's dispensation cotton, indigo and sugar cane were attempted, as well as vines at Horse Pasture. It had been hoped in London that Poirier would not only create a wine industry on the island but also possibly distil brandy.[2] None of this came to pass, though in 1709 a sugar cane plantation at Sandy Bay was said to be doing 'extraordinary well'. But, as seen in Table 3, a host of other garden fruits and trees also came onto the island, some of which thrived.

TABLE 3
Newly introduced economic plants at the turn of the 17th century

Plant		Plant	
Apple	Thrived	Gooseberry	
Apricot		Medlar	
Barberries		Mulberry	Thrived
Cherry		Nectarines	
Chestnut		Peach	Thrived
Coconut	Thrived	Pear	
Currant		Plum	
Cypress	Thrived	Quince	Thrived
Filbert		Walnut	

The topography and strange climate were against St Helena becoming a second West Indies, and the potato and the yam remained king and queen. Potatoes were the base for distilling arrack, which supplied the notorious and numerous punch houses in Jamestown. Arrack generally brought down the tone and sobriety of the settlement to such an extent that the authorities were keen to deter soldiers from boarding with planters and thereby being induced to excessive drinking. This distilling involved burning large amounts of indigenous timber. In 1701 Poirier introduced a fee of a shilling per hundredweight on firewood collected, but this did not ameliorate the problem of either deforestation or excessive distilling of spirit.[3]

Despite attempts from the 17th century to introduce plants of possible economic value to St Helena, by the turn of the new century it was said with some justification:

> But though several trials which have been made, with different sorts of exotics, have completely succeeded, they have hitherto tended rather to ornamental than utility.[4]

Poirier continued Governor Kelinge's work in constructing the seaward defences and moat, which included a 12-foot (3.6 m) wall around part of what was then a much larger Castle Garden. Goat hunts with dogs and guns were permitted every Wednesday in an attempt to lessen the damage done by what were considered to be wild animals. A drought in 1698 and bad storms in 1701, 1705 and 1706 did not help Poirier's efforts at improvement.[5]

Poirier was interested in St Helena's plant life and sent some dried specimens back to Europe. These included the now-extinct large buck's-horn (*Huperzia saururus* syn. *Lycopodium saururus*), which ended up in the Sloane herbarium. The mossy fern (*Elaphoglossum furcatum* syn. *Acrostichum bifurcatum*) sent from St Helena by Poirier in 1701 ended up in Oxford University's herbarium, where another specimen sent in 1697 by Alexander Brown is also housed.

The saga of the island's land settlement and occupation is confusing and byzantine. But increasingly over the course of the 18th century, a landed class developed which either leased Company estates or acquired them. The Company's possession of St Helena eventually drew to a close in February 1836.[6] By then it was very much a minority landowner, with only 22 properties. Its holdings in the 1820s and early 1830s were approximately as follows:

> The East India Company retained ownership of the large Longwood (623 acres/252 ha) and Deadwood regions area (not given). The company also owned three properties just to the west: Alarm House (2 acres/0.8 ha), Hutt's Gate (3 acres/1.2 ha) and (from 1827) the Briars (55 acres/22 ha).
>
> In the low ground was Francis Plain (31 acres/12.5 ha).
>
> The Plantation House complex of 396 acres (160 ha) included the house/ garden/arboretum/farm (176 acres/71 ha), mulberry plantation (5 acres/2 ha), the Triangle (195 acres/97 ha) and the New Ground to the north (20 acres/8 ha).

The Company also ran a series of estates near Plantation House. These include Bearcrofts/Rock Cottage (34 acres/14 ha) to the north-west; and to the south of the Plantation complex were Kaunjee Hill (8 acres/3.2 ha), Pounces (area not given), Hardings (52 acres/21 ha) and Carsons (15 acres/6 ha).

Finally to the west was High Peak (46 acres/18.6 ha).[7]

In 1903 Governor Gallwey castigated a predecessor who, when petitioned 200 years previously 'to remedy the evil' of the vast quantities of goats destroying the indigenous flora, responded that the goats were of more value than the ebony trees.[8] This is not strictly fair as the Company's officials in the early 18th century, or at least the more enlightened ones, were well aware that the island was being rapidly deforested, mainly through the ravages of goats and collecting fuel for houses in Jamestown. Much has been made of the good intentions of the regulations introduced in 1731 to exterminate the goat population. But this was a slow process. In 1744 it was recorded, 'Govr. reports that Peak Gut hath heretofore produced great quantities of Ebony and would still produce the same but the goats bark the growing trees.'[9]

Building must also have accounted for significant timber exploitation, especially during the period when the Georgian farmhouses and adjacent properties were being constructed. Wood was required for doors, window frames (when eventually glazed), rafters, lintels, staircases and floorboards. Professor Cronk has an interesting section in his *Endemic Flora of St Helena* on 'Old houses and ruins of St Helena and their timber'. He writes that five species of endemic trees were used for construction: gumwood, she cabbage, he cabbage, black cabbage and redwood. But clearly most of the timber extracted from old or ruined buildings was from exotics, in part a reflection in some areas of the destruction which had previously been wrought on buildings by white ant infestation.[10] In addition to this, the discovery of lime deposits at Sandy Bay from 1709 meant that much of the local indigenous ebony was by the 1740s being destroyed.

There was an awareness, which grew as the 18th century progressed, that deforestation affected both the climate and the retention of water and soil. Even earlier there had been periodic attempts to enclose woodland and protect indigenous trees on Company lands. For example, in 1683 an attempt was at least planned to enclose the Great Wood, that is, the areas today known as Deadwood and Longwood. At the same time the Company gave instructions that exotics were to be sent from India to assist in reconstituting this woodland.[11] In other words, protecting the wood was seen as safeguarding a timber resource rather than an indigenous conservation measure. Nonetheless, the concept of keeping that area for woodland persisted.

In 1709, under the rule of Governor John Roberts, instructions were once again given to fence in the Great Wood. As mentioned in the opening chapter, that was when the famous order was given that one acre in ten should be enclosed to protect tree growth, 'otherwise you shall have no benefit of our Wood or Common'. To try to enforce this ruling, it was announced that the Company would not pay an owner of enslaved people for work by any privately owned enslaved person, until that owner 'could certify that his land was fenced, and planted with a due proportion of wood'.[12] Moreover, no wood was to be cut until 'the vast quantity of deadwood that lays in the Company's woods be first used'. The destruction continued unabated, however, and it is doubtful whether the order was actually carried out to plant 15 acres of Plantation House grounds with gumwood and 500 lemon trees. The problem was essentially one of a lack of regeneration of timber. As the island council observed in 1709, if the trees which were meant to be planted were not, in 20 years' time there would be 'utter ruin for want of wood'. A year later that same council lashed out at poor dead Governor Poirier as regards wood preservation, 'Whatever service that gentleman had done is a Secret to every soul upon the island.' In a letter to the Company's directors in London dated 1 December 1710, the council asserted that Poirier never laid a single stone to fence the Great Wood. They went further, stating that when he took possession of Plantation House, no fence was erected, with disastrous results:

> In the wood round about him which was so thick that they could hardly find their way to the place and now they can hardly find a tree.[13]

In the Consultation documents for 16 October 1716, when Governor Pyke was in command, it is stated:

> The Great Wood in a flourishing condition and full of young trees. But miserably lessened and destroyed within our memories and is not near the circuit and length it was, but we believe it does not contain less than 1500 acres of Fine Wood land and good ground. But no spring of water but what is brackish which is the reason why that part was not inhabited when the people first chose out settlements. But if wells could be sunk we should think it the most pleasant and healthiest part of the island. The 'Wood's End' was formerly at the huts but the Wood is so destroyed that the beginning of the Great Wood is now a whole mile beyond that place.[14]

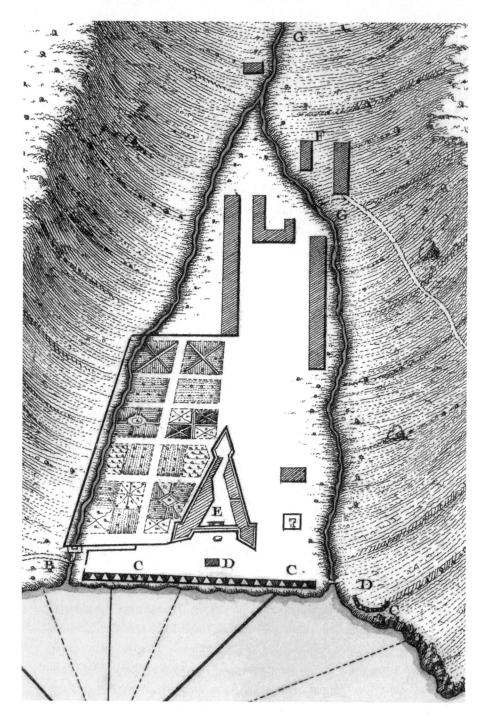

7. The position of the British East India Company garden beside the fort at Jamestown (marked E) is clearly seen in this Plan de la Forteresse et Bourg de l'Isle de St. Helene, dated 1764.

Bellin, *Petit Atlas Maritime*, t.3, no.124. Provided by Donal P. McCracken.

Four years later some young gum trees were planted in a vain attempt to prevent further destruction, but as Governor Beatson later observed, by 1724, 'the old trees had mostly fallen; and, as goats and hogs were at that time suffered to range, all the young trees were devoured'. The land was subsequently colonised by wire grass (*Cynodon dactylon*). Beatson was of the opinion that the Great Wood not only extended from Hutt's Gate to Deadwood but also across the flat ground in front of Longwood down to the sea, which must have been about Horse Point. This meant the Great Wood must have covered some 2,000 acres (809 ha).

The introduction in the early 18th century of gorse or furze (*Ulex europaeus*), possibly by Governor Pyke, in part assisted in augmenting the firewood supply and creating quick-growing hedges, but soon led to a new problem as the plant colonised large areas. Both Brooke (1824) and Lambdon (2012) speculate that gorse might, however, have served to save the last stands of native trees from 'total extirpation'.[15] But there was more policy drift and only in the mid-1720s was any meaningful attempt made to make further progress. This entailed building a 'great wall' on the Company lands to keep out cattle and allow for regeneration of gumwoods. The exercise lasted from 1723 to 1727, in the face of opposition from local inhabitants who regarded the plateau lands as commonage for their domestic beasts.[16] Progress was slow and patchy. A memorandum dated July 1725 from the island's rulers to the Company's directors recorded:

> That part of the Great Wood called the Horse Point we acquainted your Honours in our 5th Para by the Maclesfeild [ship] was compleated on 15th of May last, and that the Overseer had received Orders to begin at one Corner of the upper end of the Enclosure in order to ffence all round the wood, in which for the Benefitt of the Pasherage [Pasturage] as well as for the preservation of the Trees.[17]

By 1728, some 64 acres (26 ha) of this land had been enclosed and 'appropriated to wood'.

Back in 1739, the Great Wood was valued at £4,500 but this did not prevent continuing destruction of St Helena woodlands. By the late 1770s, it was said that there were more trees at Longwood than in the rest of the island. Instructions were sent from London to plant gumwoods at Horse Point.

The Company's garden

There is evidence that an earlier East India Company garden existed on St Helena before the 1780s botanic garden was established at Jamestown. The older garden extended from near the waterfront deep up into the valley in which the island's only town now nestles. The earliest reference we have to this garden in what became the lower Jamestown Valley was an account written on 8 June 1588 by the Elizabethan explorer and adventurer Captain Thomas Cavendish of *The Desire*:

> There is also, over and against the church, a very fair causeway, made up with stones, reaching unto a valley by the sea side, in which valley is planted a garden, wherein grows a great store of pompions and melons ... The valley is the fairest and largest low plot in all the island, and is exceedingly sweet and pleasant, and planted in every place either with fruit or with herbs. There are fig-trees which bear fruit continually, and very plentifully; for on every tree you may see blossoms, green figs, and ripe figs, all at once, and it is so all the year long.
>
> The reason is, that the island standeth so near the sun. There is also great store of lemon-trees, orange-trees, pomegranate-trees, pomecitron-trees, and date-trees, which bear fruit as the fig-trees do, and are planted carefully and very artificially, with pleasant walks under and between them; and the said walks are overshadowed with the leaves of the trees; and in every void place is planted parsley, sorrel, basil, fennel, aniseed, mustard-seed, radishes, and many very good herbs. The fresh-water brook runneth through divers places of this orchard, and may, with very little pains, be made to water any tree in the valley.[18]

This was undoubtedly the predecessor of the later garden near the fort. On 16 January 1682, Major John Blackmore – governor from 1678 to 1690 and formerly a Cromwellian army officer – approved the raising of the garden's stone wall to 11 or 12 feet (*c*.3.6 m) to protect it by acting as a windbreak against the 'blast', though it is doubtful if this was completed.[19] A map by Bellin in his *Le petit atlas maritime* dated 1764, although inaccurate in some respects, clearly demarcates a large set of allotments next to the old fort on the north-east side of the valley.[20]

That such garden-cum-allotments existed even before the 1680s is not surprising, as we know that ships called at St Helena earlier than this to pick up water, vegetables, herbs and, when available, lemons to protect the crew from scurvy. In many respects, this reflects the saga of the old Company Garden in Cape Town, established by the Dutch in 1652, with the primary purpose of the settlement being to provide fresh vegetables and fruit for ships' crews as well as for the Table Bay fort. Indeed, Bellin's 1764 atlas plate of Cape Town shows the fort and the large garden, which stretched up the lower slope of Table Mountain.[21] This garden also had an up-and-down existence, finally being developed into a botanic garden in the 18th century, only to go into decline before being resurrected as a botanic garden again between 1849 and 1892. Then, as with the St Helena Botanic Garden, it became a public park.[22]

The East India Company was, of course, well aware of what the Dutch had achieved outside their fort at the Cape. The St Helena garden was similarly a curious mixture of indigenous plants scattered among the provisioning fruit trees, vegetables and herbs. In December 1703, during Poirier's governorship, the following paragraph was contained in a letter sent from the British East India Company's headquarters in London:

> We observe what you write about the Garden. You will see by our Letter of the 18th January sent by Captain Tollatt, We resolve – not to debarr our own Country Men, that come in our Ships the privilege of walking in the Garden, but since you say you have another and better Garden designed for that use we are content – that the Garden you have leased out be for the reasons you mention continue as it now is, and hope you will take care that we have Thirty pounds a year for it at the Expiration of ye present Lease as you give as reason to hope for.[23]

The lot of the St Helena Company garden was not always easy, not least because of regular drought followed by torrential rains. In 1707, Governor Poirier was reprimanded for completing a 12-foot (3.7-m) high wall at the seaward end of the garden, probably completing the work begun by Blackmore a quarter of a century before. Poirier pleaded that the wall added to the defences of the settlement. The first known alienation of this Castle Garden land was in 1709 when ground was used to build a barracks. This complex later became the courthouse, police station and the library.

More serious were the antics of Governor John Roberts' successor, Captain Benjamin Boucher (1711–1714), who was considered to have neglected the Plantation House estate where he kept a large stud of donkeys. These he rode for many hours every day, for reason of his health.[24] Down in Jamestown, it was reported:

> He [Boucher] made alsoe a level riding place of about 400 feet long and 12 foot wide in the garden of the Fort by raising it five foot with stone work at one end and by digging five foot into the ground at the other end that His horses (for Asses were ordered to be called so) might not tire by carrying him up and down the Hill. The rest of the garden at the Fort were made into a field for these Horses to graze in, only some plantain trees growing therein.[25]

Governor Isaac Pyke succeeded Boucher in 1714 and devoted much energy in promoting agriculture on the island, including introducing new plants. Reporting to London on 19 May 1716, Pyke recorded that he had received a letter from Captain Richard Holden of the *Mary*. In this, Holden stated that he had been instructed by the government of Madras to deliver to St Helena 'garden seeds from the Cape and sheep, arrack [distilled spirit] as the island is in short supply'.[26] Less than a year later, an official despatch from Pyke, dated 12 January 1717, to the directors of the East India Company in London contained the following observation concerning the devastating denudation of vegetation on the island:

> For example when the mountains at the Upper end of this [Jamestown] valley where the Fort stands were covered with Trees the valley itself abounded with most kinds of fruit usual in such latitudes so that you[r] garden in the valley which for six years past has been entirely barren was then lookt upon by most people to be as fruitful a spot of ground as any in the whole world. Large groves of Lemon trees etc, grew so close and thick as to yield a shade from the Sun on the hottest days and all the branches bending down with fruit, but since the wood was suffered to be cut down and that Frogs have not been defended from the gardens and the winds which rage impetuously from the hollows of breakings of the mountain topps have not been restrained from those trees which used to be a shelter to this valley all the Fruits have been blighted and destroyed, or if any few have grown they have been encrusted over with a black and unwholesome Scurfe as if covered with soot which is occasioned by the frogs that fall down the valley but which used to be kept off by the shade of Trees above the Hills.[27]

A year later Pyke expanded the Company garden and erected a high wall along the north-east side of the valley, in effect enclosing the garden as well as the hitherto open back areas behind the houses. This created windbreaks and it was said that occupants of these houses cleared the ground of stones and planted fruit trees. The water run that Governor Pyke had constructed dissected these back areas, creating a useful water supply for both homes and gardens.[27]

There is a record of a second Company garden well up the Jamestown Valley, an 'Upper Garden and Concord House', being let to Margaret Cotgave in October 1701 for £10 a year during the governorship of Stephen Poirier.[28] After the arrival in the 1730s of seven enslaved or pressed labourers – five men, one woman and one boy – presumably from the Maldives, this was renamed Maldivia House in 1735. The first hospital, constructed in 1741, was also on this site. By the 1760s, there were extensive yam, fruit and vegetable gardens at Maldivia.[29] A memorandum dated

NAPOLEON'S GARDEN ISLAND

23 December 1774 stated that 'the island is in so very plentiful and flourishing a condition' that it would be able to supply five or six ships returning from the East, 'the inhabitants and Planters being perfectly enabled to answer their demands'. It also claimed that they had 'been lately overstocked with [vegetable] Garden Seeds' and pressed each ship's captain to limit to £5 their purchasing such seed for the island's use.[30] In 1792 it was recorded that £9–12–0 of 'extra produce' was sold from this garden. There were two houses on the property, one of which was later occupied by Major Charles Hodson, the notable town major and later judge advocate. When this famous St Helena property moved into private ownership is unclear, possibly with Hodson.

Captain Cook visited St Helena twice on the *Endeavour*; first from 1 to 5 May 1771 and then again from 15 to 21 May 1775. On his second stay he commented on the extensive garden at the governor's country residence, Plantation House.[31] He also noted the cabbage trees and, lower down the island, the gum trees but observed that the ebony, used for tanning, was nearly extinct.[32] Of the Company gardens in Jamestown, Cook's botanist Johann Forster noted on 16 May 1775, 'A small garden, at the back of the governor's house [in Jamestown], contains a few shady walks, and some curious East Indian trees, among which is the Barringtonia.'[33] The shady walks later provided a good refuge during the army mutiny on St Helena on 1 December 1811; the night guard hid in the Company garden, 'to prevent the mutineers taking them, or being murdered upon refusing to join them'.[34]

In the post–Napoleonic period the remnant of the old Company garden was referred to as the Public Garden, what is now the Castle Garden. A detailed 1839 map of Jamestown shows the park, which extended down to the harbour and up to the Sisters Walk. Some of the serpentine paths are as they remain today. Illustrations from the period show how lovely this garden appeared then, with large trees with varying shades of green leaves as well as high palms, all giving the impression of a lush tropical garden. Many illustrations of Jamestown which were drawn from ships out at sea looking up the valley show the neat yellow and grey-painted houses with their green verandas and wooden shutters, but also invariably show great clumps of trees and palms where the Castle Garden is situated. Twelve years after the map of Jamestown was drawn, the following description of the Castle Garden was written:

Emerging from the Castle yard we pass a large banian tree, a centry box, and a bench for the idlers to lounge upon, pass two archways, and find ourselves under the shade of two trees which partially screen the 'Supreme Court' and the Police Office from sight ...

Facing the east end of the church is the Public Garden, and I suppose may be called the grand promenade of the towns-people, whenever they are disposed to indulge in the luxury of a gentle stroll, especially when by chance the regimental band may happen to play there, on which rare occasions some half dozen people assemble to listen to their ravishing strains.

A centinel used to guard the entrance of this little Elysium, with orders to keep out dogs and puppies, which orders were strictly enforced, till on one unfortunate occasion, a young recruit made a grievous mistake and stopped his colonel – so the report goes – who, not liking to be confounded with the canine species, removed the guardian, to prevent the recurrence of such a calamity in the future; the centry box is empty, the gates open, so walk in and fear no interruption. Those who are fond of flowers will not find many to gratify their taste, nor is there much fruit to please the eye, or tickle the palate. It is laid out in a style suitable to the place, and that is saying a great deal; there are straight and crooked walks, some up hill, some down hill, and others beautifully zigzagged for the gratification of those who are partial to the serpentine line of beauty, here you may enjoy yourself under the shade of clumps of lofty reeds, admire the 'Margossa' with its lilac like flowers, and bunches of clustering berries – the Cotton tree with its flowers, and snowy plumes – Date, Palm, and the graceful Olive, its oily fruit and pretty yellow flowers, reminding one of sunny Spain and Italy. The greater part of the ground is covered with thriving beds of Guinea Grass, a little Oasis of verdant green, in which the eye loves to rest, and seek repose from the sunny glare of the streets, white-washed walls, and painted houses. In the centre of the garden stands a plain Tuscan column of Marble surmounted with an Urn, erected to the memory of the men and officers of the Water Witch man-of-war, who died during her career in the African waters, while cruising for the suppression of the slave-trade, in which cause she rendered very efficient service, no name being better known on the coast than that of the Water Witch. Ascending a rather steep path up the side of the hill overhanging one side of the town, we reach the 'Sisters Walk,' an avenue of banian trees.[35]

The Company also had a series of plantations scattered across the island. Many of these grew yams which were used to feed the very poorest, including the enslaved population, who had been on the island since the 1660s. The problem was the length of time it took the root to mature to a state where it could be cooked. In 1725 it was estimated that 18 months was the minimum time.[36] Other crops were tried with limited success. Coffee was introduced about 1729 and was certainly growing on the island in 1733. Considering that Java coffee was only introduced into Europe from 1719 and that the first Martinique coffee plantations were only established in 1720, with Brazilian plantations following in 1727, this St Helena introduction is very early. However, it would be wrong to try to claim a continuous crop since then. Coffee growing came and went, occasionally reappearing in accounts, such as when in 1792 Governor Brooke recorded, 'However the coffee Tree has lately been cultivated with better success & a bale of Coffee was this year sent to the Honbl Court of directors.'[37] It is also important to distinguish between the growing of a few coffee bushes as a curiosity and establishing a whole plantation. The reality was that coffee was essentially an early 19th rather than an early or mid-18th century phenomenon on St Helena.

Governor Brooke toyed with the idea that 'a beautiful situation might be chosen in the Company Gardens to build a Government House in'. The old castle would become a session house with facilities for the occasional assembly and public balls. Fortunately, he did not follow up on this idea of occupying the Castle Garden and the ramshackle set of buildings known as the castle remains to this day the seat of government in Jamestown.[38] The point needs to be made that this old Company garden continued to have horticultural and botanical uses into the early 19th century. Saint-Vincent, who is mentioned elsewhere, recorded in his travel book around the islands of Africa, published in 1802:

> It is in the company garden, located on the square and opposite the church, that the newly arrived plants are familiarized with the aridity of the soil: they find there a fairly good source of land.[39]

❧ The Plantation House garden ☙

The site of the Plantation House estate appears to commence with John Prowd's lemon garden of 1645,[40] though planting lemon trees on the site may well predate this. The first we hear of the early Plantation House garden is its destruction. Governor Benjamin Boucher (1711–1714) – who has generally gained a bad reputation, not least through the pen of Thomas Brooke – is said to have 'laid waste' the garden and, as stated elsewhere, converted it to 'pasture for the Governor's asses, of which he kept a numerous stud'. Boucher also took it upon himself, to the dismay of the Company, to buy up on the Company's behalf any plantation which came on the market thereby, no doubt deliberately, reducing the troublesome landowning sector of society.[41] In 1728, under Governor Edward Byfield, five acres (2 ha) of the Plantation House grounds were enclosed with a stone wall, and a proper nursery established. It was here that the governor brought two plants of the endemic redwood (*Trochetiopsis erythroxylon*). The tree was known to be endangered as early as 1694, with the sale of redwood timber for private use being prohibited in that year.[42]

In volume three of Bellin's *Le petit atlas maritime*, published in Paris by Buch in 1764, there are two engraved maps which show two different gardens on St Helena. As discussed earlier, the first is in the Jamestown Valley with a garden adjacent to the castle, laid out in formal style, and running up the valley beside the water course. The second map, entitled 'Plan de L'Isle Ste Helene', has a substantial garden marked to the south-west of Jamestown. A caption below reads, 'Jardins de la Campagne'.[43] This would suggest that two gardens existed on the island at this time. If this is the case, the situation would suggest the location of Plantation House.

Such a garden attached to the governor's residence was neither surprising nor unique. In the early 18th century, Peter Kolbe wrote of the Dutch East India settlement at the Cape of Good Hope:

> Several beautiful Country-Seats, Vineyards and Gardens are to be seen on almost every Side of the *Table*-Hill. The Company has here Two very spacious, rich and beautiful Gardens. In one of 'em Stands, erected at the Company's Expense, a noble Pleasure-House for the Governor, and near it a beautiful Grove of Oaks, call'd the *Round-Bush*, from which this Garden takes its Name, being call'd *Round-Bush* Garden. The other Garden, which is at some Distance from this, is called *Newland*, because but lately planted. Both these Gardens are finely water'd by the Springs on the *Table*-Hill; and the Company draws from 'em a very considerable Revenue.

These were separate Company gardens from the main one in Cape Town, which, Kolbe considered, grew 'the noblest and most beautiful Curiosities in all Afric'.[44]

By the early 18th century, the area around Plantation House was all but destitute of timber and the garden on the farm was said to contain only plantains. It was ordered that the valley be planted with gumwood.[45] We know a garden of sorts did exist here because, in 1723, Plantation House had the following nine enslaved gardeners working there:

Ben (aged 29)	Good
Scipio (27)	Good
Dan'l (32)	Indifferent
George (18)	Good for nothing

Peter (17)	Indifferent
Lime house (20)	Indifferent
Dick (20)	Poxed
Mercury (25)	Good
Cato (24)	Indifferent
Dan'l (35)	Indifferent
Joney (20)	Indifferent[46]

Another list, dated the year before and probably referring to the Jamestown Company garden, names five enslaved gardeners:

Benjamino (aged 42)	Good
Harry (24)	Indifferent
Monrow (26)	Indifferent
Tom (24)	very lame
Antony (42)	Sickly[47]

Some of these names are repeated in a list specific to the Fort Garden, though the given ages are slightly different:

Benjamin (44) Head Gardener	Good
Harry (26)	Indifferent
Antonio (44)	Sickly

Jumping 30 years, an illustration in J. Sewell's *European Magazine* of 'The seat of Governor Brooke at St Helena' shows Plantation House before its rebuild. The hill behind the mansion is bare and the whole surroundings have a bleak appearance. But in front of the house, where there is now pasture, distinct areas are laid out either for a formal garden or at the very least allotment plots. However, a slightly earlier drawing of the house in the 1780s gives a somewhat different and probably more reliable backdrop to the old house. This was by a J. Corneille, who must have been a relative of Daniel Corneille, who was governor from July 1782 to June 1787 and who laid the botanic foundation on which Governor Brooke was to build. This drawing shows a series of formal gardens, on the left side when viewing the house from the front.[48] It also shows that the garden and house were enclosed within a stout and reinforced compound wall, a reflection of the precarious nature of existence on the island even before the French revolutionary wars.[49]

Brooke himself left the following account describing Plantation House as adorning a 'Beautiful and Romanic situation':

The Plantation House Grounds and farm adjacent are excellent Land and great Expense has been gone into from time to time to fence them well and render them productive, but persons unknown have these 10 years past made it a Practice to break down the Gates and destroy the Walls and the Ditches, and altho' rewards have been in every Government offered for finding out the offender no discovery whatever has yet been made, however latterly near the Plantation House such care has been taken not much damage has been done, and the Company having sent out a Gardener on purpose the place begins to improve fast, and there are already collected on the spot a greater variety of Trees, Plants and Flowers of various Climates than perhaps can be found in any other situation of equal extent.[50]

Nearly a decade later, in 1801, and with the enlightened Governor Brooke now departed the island, Francis Duncan compared the Plantation House garden favourably with the new botanic garden in Jamestown, as being 'still more extensive and various, as the climate here was found to favour the productions of almost all other countries'.[51]

Conjecture about a garden at Plantation House was replaced by certainty during Brooke's residence and from then on the governor's establishment had its own garden as well as allotment plots. With time it included what might be termed an arboretum of exotic and indigenous trees. Indeed, on Lieutenant Read's famous 1816/1817 map of St Helena the area behind Plantation House is clearly marked 'Botanic Garden'. That year a military surgeon called Henry Walker recorded of the utilitarian part of this remarkable garden:

Next morning, before breakfast, I walked about the grounds of Plantation House, and was very much pleased and interested to see the vegetable natives of a dozen different countries and climates thriving here harmoniously together. The tea-shrub and the English golden-pippin, the bread-fruit tree and the peach and plum, the nutmeg overshadowing the goose berry; with many other dendrological contrasts. Whilst the rich Brazilian passion-flower, a common creeper in the island, expanded its blue cruciform petals, and wove its luxuriant tendrils around the stems of all alike; in imitation of the religion, whose catholic embrace of all races and climates it thus happily represented.[52]

This garden was in no small part due to the exertions of Governor Beatson and subsequently Governor Wilks. The garden also flourished because of its moderate climate, away from the windswept heights, and its situation – at 1,700 feet (518 m) it was away from the humidity of the Jamestown Valley, yet with an annual rainfall of some 30 inches (760 mm).[53] Sir Hudson Lowe had found on arrival at Plantation House in 1816 that 16 indentured Chinese labourers filled the water cisterns once a week, with two or three of them daily carrying water from the spring to the kitchen of the big house. That year Lowe saw to it that a water pipe was laid between Luffkins Farm and Plantation House, which must also have assisted the garden and plantation.

This was confirmed by island council member, and nephew of Robert Brooke, Thomas H. Brooke (b.1774)[54] in his history of St Helena, which first appeared in 1808 with a second enlarged edition in 1824:

> Here [Plantation House] a considerable fund of amusement is afforded to the botanist. Not only the indigenous productions of the island, but plants and trees from distant and opposite climes have been introduced within the inclosure. The mimosa of New South Wales, the pine of the North, and the bamboo of India, seem to outvie each other in the luxuriance of their growth.[55]

Botanic gardens adjacent to governor's residences were very common in the British empire. Botanic gardens in Accra, Cape Town, Hong Kong, Melbourne, Udhagamandalam (Ootacamund), St Vincent, Sydney, Trinidad and Zomba all had this arrangement.[56] The raison d'être was simple enough. These adjoining gardens were expected to provide vegetables for the governor's kitchen and flowers for his residence. But matters went beyond that. In some botanic gardens, the governor had his own private and discreet entrance to the botanic garden and could stroll around them after closing hours for the general public, or on days when the public were excluded. This arrangement might mean extra duties for the curator but generally it acted in favour of the gardens, which were more likely to be supported and protected when under threat when the governor resided adjacent to them, rather than elsewhere.

In the case of St Helena, there was not even the inconvenience to the governor of having the public visit during weekday opening hours. There was, however, still a drawback in broader terms. If the governor had his private botanic garden, it also had to be cared for and supplied with interesting and unusual plants. With resources so limited on the island and the head gardener having to attend to both botanic gardens, this meant inevitably that the Jamestown botanic garden suffered.

Arboretum and tree nursery

It is clear that at times the Plantation House grounds were used as a tree nursery in the frequently emerging effort to reforest those parts of the island which until the late 17th century had been covered with woodland. Indigenous trees were looked upon as a curiosity, and at times efforts were made to sustain certain species, but their significance was not fully understood, and they did not feature prominently in the reforesting programmes. Indeed, there were those who were hostile to at least the native gum tree. The Russian representative on St Helena from 1815 to 1820, Count Alexander Balmain, made no bones about the plant: 'Longwood is only a hovel, surrounded with gum-trees (a dreadful tree which gives no shade) and very windy.'

Governor Alexander Beatson (1808–1813) did much to improve the Plantation House gardens. This was hardly surprising given his enthusiasm for all things horticultural and agricultural. Both he and his successor, Governor Colonel Mark Wilks, worked with the Company's agent at the Cape, Pringle, to import into the island good-quality wheat, vegetable and possible timber trees. For example, in 1814 and with Cape Governor Cradock's cooperation, Pringle sent to St Helena from Plettenberg Bay seeds of assegai (*Curtisia dentata*), white pear (*Apodytes dimidiata*) and stinkwood (*Celtis africana* or *Ocotea bullata*). In addition, and also from the southern Cape, a supply of yellow wood (*Podocarpus* spp.) planks was sent to the island.[57]

Kitching records that in 1824 J. C. Melliss released into the grounds of Plantation House thrushes, linnets and goldfinches, an experiment in introducing birds of the English countryside which failed then and again under Governor Sterndale.[58] As the aviflora of the island well illustrates, though, many other releases were successful, whether the 16th-century partridge, the Java sparrow in the 1790s or the mynah in the 19th century. The last species was introduced on at least three occasions, in 1815, 1829 and 1885, a saga not unlike the introduction of certain plant species.

The departure of Governor Dallas (1828–1836) from Plantation House to Longwood began the long decline of both the house and the garden. The transfer of the island from the Company to the Crown merely continued that process, with the house being rented out to the island's military commander. By 1877, Plantation House had 'not quite escaped the infection of general decay'. Governor Janisch lived in his modest home, Palm Villa, just above the old botanic garden in Jamestown, and Plantation House was occupied by army officers, officials and visitors – in 1877 visitors included Isobel and David Gill, the famous astronomer. Isobel noted then that:

Below the [Plantation House] park are the famous gardens, containing fruit trees and tropical and sub-tropical plants in such wonderful variety, that all our time in St. Helena, and more, would have been needed to examine them thoroughly.[59]

Only in 1889 did Governor Grey Wilson move the governor's residence back to Plantation House, and some effort was then made to resurrect the old garden.

3

St Helena's old private gardens

A large ledger exists in the India Office Records in London's British Library. Anyone glancing across its lined entries is soon in no doubt that the British East India Company was a large enterprise which thought and acted on a grand scale, not flinching at a lavish annual expenditure of £2 million and more. On its 'homeward' island base of St Helena it was equally lavish, with the directors thinking nothing of an annual expenditure of £100,000. Here arrived the great company fleets and their naval escorts that had sailed from India or from China, making good use of the south-east trade winds that swept them up to St Helena from the Cape of Good Hope. If ever the principle that to make money one must spend money existed, it was in this global parastatal. The Company's officials on St Helena and their suppliers benefited from this 'artificial condition'. Many years later Governor Grey Wilson, who cared greatly for the then 'ruined island', looked back to the days of the Company and observed that nearly all the island's public servants were 'engaged in farming and other speculative ventures', all of which crashed around them when the Company withdrew from its custodianship in the mid-1830s.[1]

The gentry class

For the East India Company, St Helena was a difficult mix of settlers, enslaved people and soldiers. Of those, the gentleman farmers were the most truculent. They differed from the artisans who had arrived in the 17th century through several plantation schemes to be allocated tiny farms – 'a commonwealth of market gardeners' – to start what was hoped would be a utopian society.[2] Instead, from a settler society under mild subjugation there developed something of a cowboy, free-booting, slave-owning society. As the 18th century progressed, the gentry were composed in part of serving, full-time or part-time, army or navy officers. Alongside them were members of the militia establishment, businessmen, adventurers, those stranded on the island by circumstance and a good sprinkling of those climbing the social ladder. Few were island born, even fewer were originally farmers.

The county houses of St Helena occupied by the gentry fell into two categories: substantial farmhouses, sometimes double storeyed; and smaller cottages. Given the peculiar nature of St Helena society, there was not necessarily any class differentiation between these two. The reason for this, apart from the obvious one of availability, was that officers posted to St Helena were quite content not to have the expense of a larger establishment over the limited period of their posting and were happy to occupy a relatively humble abode. St Helena was not India with its cantonment system. What was important on the island was to be within the orbit of either what might be termed the greater St James Valley or of the governor's country domain, Plantation House. Indeed, one may make a rough division of gentlemen's houses in relation not so much to their size as to their location.

The most desirable residences were obviously those which adjoined or were within reasonable walking or riding distance from Plantation House. As this central region was also the most fertile, there was an added incentive to farm here. The upper Jamestown Valley–Sane Valley–Longwood corridor was also desirable not only from the point of view of social cachet but also farming land, though some of this region was not as appealing in that regard. Many of the older established St Helena families – such as the Dovetons, Alexanders, Greentrees and Knipes – had properties beyond these prestigious node areas, literally and figuratively on the fringe in the Sandy Bay region and the western segment, areas which today are the most attractive and unspoilt parts of the island.

8. Burchell's sketch of Brooke Hill farm with High Knoll fort in the background. Despite the efforts of several governors to improve farming practices, the enslaved labourers and gardeners here are using picks rather than a plough (18 October 1809). Enslaved gardeners worked in St Helena gardens up to the 1830s.

From the start, there was an artificiality about the St Helena gentry. This was due to the simple fact that their estates were actually relatively small farms. They also fluctuated greatly in size with the passing years as adjoining land was acquired or, more likely, sold to pay off or relieve mortgages. In the 1880s, Prospect, the well-known property of the former colonial secretary and historian of the island Thomas Brooke, was described as containing '15 acres of arable ground wherein corn, mangold wurzel, potatoes, vegetable, and fruit of all kinds are produced'. Admittedly, Prospect had more land than this under timber and later, when much of that was cleared, flax, but at its height the estate cannot have been more than 50 acres (20 ha). The engraving of Prospect as the frontispiece to Brooke's second edition of his *History of the Island of St Helena* (1824) gives the impression of magnitude and affluence, thanks to its long drive up to the two-storey and short double-winged Georgian building with its typical grand St Helena backdrop of exotic trees. The existence of an English park-like garden emphasised this image, though in fairness, the emerging fascination with science and in particular botany impacted upon such landowners.

The St Helena gentry's behaviour and the style in which they laid out the grounds around their elegant yet modest farmhouses aped those in the shires of England. The gentry were frequently mortgaged and trapped in rolling debt. Colin Fox in his *Bennett letters* mentions that in 1823 Major Hodson of Oakbank was carrying a staggering mortgage of £3,600 on the property.[3] When he finally retired to England in 1845, he sold the Oakbank estate to George Melliss, the island's colonial surveyor, for only £1,600.[4]

This unstable prosperity depended on two fundamentals: the East India Company, which poured vast sums into this strategic replenishment station for the journey home from the east, and on the occurrence of visiting ships This prosperity was particularly noticeable at times when Britain was at war, and the era of Napoleon's captivity can be viewed as an extension of that. Along with the other factors frequently cited for St Helena's decline in the Victorian era was, ironically, the protracted era of international peace for Britain which followed the Napoleonic Wars.

The gentry – and indeed the whole island population which was not military – was frequently regarded as being disinterested, careless and lazy. This reputation bred on itself and was quickly picked up on by visitors such as Joseph Banks and Captain Cook. Shortly after visiting the island in December 1792, Captain Bligh wrote to Banks praising Governor Brooke whom he said would:

> take every measure to secure to the island so great a blessing [breadfruit], but I am told Yamstocks (as the people born on the island are called) care little for what I have brought them with such pains & trouble.[5]

While there was something to the criticism of the gentry by officialdom, the truth was that the gentry of St Helena were frequently an annoyance to the Company, albeit a necessary one as long as the infantry and artillery militia were required, and ships were to be supplied. As mentioned elsewhere, in the reign of Queen Anne, Governor Benjamin Boucher tried to settle matters by buying up as many plantations as possible which came on the market, releasing a howl of protest by doing so. That these St Helena planters were owners of enslaved people merely added to their feelings of self-importance and frequent truculence.[6]

This planter population varied in number, probably reaching its peak about the time Napoleon was on the island. Then there were 3,500 whites, excluding the military establishment. This was some 45 per cent of the island's total population, not all of them planter families. Most planter families were, perhaps inevitably, frequently related to each other. This situation if anything increased as the 19th century developed. The crisscrossing familial relationships between the Bennetts, Dovetons, Knipes, Hodsons, Pritchards, Solomons/Gideons and Thorpes was little short of byzantine.

Today the visitor to St Helena is struck by the colourful gardens that many islanders maintain around their homes. They are not unlike those which a traveller in 1817 called 'small and neat'. References to domestic gardens in 18th- and 19th-century St Helena are few and far between, and one must be cautious that such references to gardens are not instead using the South African usage as plots for crops, vegetables, yams or potatoes. Enslaved labourers and peasant farmers lived hand-to-mouth without the luxury of flower beds. Even the grounds of the better-off planters and of the transitory army and naval officers showed more the 18th-century passion for the vista and the tree avenue than the Victorian passion for the flower garden. St Helena's plantation houses and gardens were best seen from afar, taking advantage of the often-spectacular borrowed view. The steep and undulating topography well suited this framing. In certain cases, even from the sea these elegant Georgian plain-fronted white-painted farmhouses and surrounds could be admired.[7] In 1792, William Hickey commented:

> St Helena is much more beautiful and picturesque in sailing from it than in approaching towards it, as in departing you have in view the rich and fertile valley with a remarkably neat and handsome town as well as a variety of country houses and gardens in different directions, forming an interesting and agreeable appearance of verdure or capacity of cultivation.[8]

In St Helena's transient social scene, much depended on the personality of the governor. In 1801 Francis Duncan, an East India Company army surgeon who visited the island, felt that St Helena lacked the 'gay and cheerful scenes of the East Indies' and that island society 'seems dull and irksome'. More to the point, perhaps, he also observed that country houses were separated by 'crags, precipices, and chasms' which 'preclude the opportunity of easy and frequent intercourse'. He went on to describe the island's landscape and houses in terms of the gothic and romantic views then popular in art and literature:

> The garden-houses are situated on different parts of the island, especially on the south side, towards SANDY BAY, which is full of the wildest scenery imaginable. The situation of these houses is very striking and curious, being placed here and there on gentle slopes, or little platforms, which jut out at different heights from the sides of the hills, and surrounded with small clumps of trees and shrubs. From DIANA'S PEAK, we observe them on each hand, stuck up in corners like bird-cages, and hanging in elevations so different, that the distance in height between the highest and the lowest, cannot be less than two thousand feet. The small tufts of trees and evergreens with which they are decorated, are heightened and enlivened in their effects by the rude and desolate scenery of the intermediate hills and rocks.

When the India and Chinese fleets of Indiamen arrived, however, Duncan observed:

> They quit their gardens, flock to James Town, open their houses [in Jamestown] for the accommodation of the passengers, and entertain them with play, dances, and concerts.[9]

This phenomenon was noted 110 years before when William Dampier observed of Jamestown, 'the houses in the town before mentioned stand empty, save only when ships arrive here, for their owners have all plantations farther in the island, where they constantly employ themselves. But when ships arrive, they all flock to the town, where they live all the time that the ships be here; for then is their fair, or market, to buy such necessities as they want, and to sell off the produce of their plantations'.[10] These rural retreats were boltholes from the hothouse of Jamestown society and occasionally for those recovering from the 'unbound hospitality' they had endured in India. An 1817 description of Fisher's Valley near Longwood gives a good picture of these working farms with their picturesque orchards:

This beautiful vale is watered through its whole extent; and in it, and along its gently sloping acclivities, are several pretty rural dwellings, more particularly that belonging to Miss Mason; presenting an agreeable assemblage of farmhouses and cottages, with pasture land, yam plantations, and well cultivated gardens. The latter abounding with fig trees, which bear fruit so continually and abundantly, that blossoms, green figs, and ripe ones may be seen on one tree at the same time; and this throughout the year. In these gardens are also lemons, oranges, pomegranates, citrons, and peach trees, bearing almost abundantly as the fig trees; and upon the estate of Miss Mason good apples are extensively produced. The beauty of these grounds is preserved by the attention that is paid to laying them out, so as to produce a pleasing effect by the arrangement of the trees, and afford agreeable and shady walks among them.[11]

The eccentric Miss Mary (Polly) Mason was one of St Helena's chief landowners, who died in July 1859 at the age of 83. She was known locally for her habit of riding around on the back of an ox.[12]

Many of these early St Helena residents, like Polly Mason, remain largely unknown to us in more than name, because so few family papers have survived. That is why the Bennett letters are so important. Indeed, the principal obstacle facing the botanical historian of St Helena is the scarcity of sources relating specifically to plant usage in Company, and especially private, gardens. There are some exceptions, and even official reports and letters can be valuable sources. Occasionally William Burchell mentions private houses on St Helena in his draft manuscript 'Flora Heleniana'. For example, for 17 May 1810 he lists *Ranunculus repens* as being at Bramin's House. Near the waterfall at the Briars on 23 February 1810, he found *Alyssum maritimum* which he also included in the manuscript flora.[13] But such sources are all too few.

❧ The smaller gardens ☙

In the 18th and 19th centuries, St Helena was scattered with a large number of small cottages distinct from the substantial farmhouses. These were not occupied by those rising up the social scale but by those in that fascinating societal mix which made up the bulk of the population, some with the disparaging nickname Yamstocks. These included the remnants of the artisans sent out to St Helena after the Great Fire of London; those who were called 'free blacks'; later the descendants of indentured Chinese workers who had arrived in the early 19th century; and those whose ancestors had been brought ashore by fate at some time in the past and who had by desire or necessity remained. Melliss's map of 1825/1835 marks villages as Brooke's, Dallas's and the Briars. These were not truly villages in the English sense but a community scattered between a grouping of cottages, each with its own flower, fruit and vegetable garden. Some were very attractive, such as that in Lemon Valley below the Rosemary Hall estate:

> It may safely be asserted that the lanes and hedgerows in this vicinity remind one most forcibly as being counterparts with their congeners in the rural parts of Devon and Cornwall, but having the additional charm of masses of geranium, fuschia, rose, buddleia, mallow, nasturtium, &c., growing in the wildest profusion and tended only by the hand of Dame Nature.

Half Tree Hollow was 'literally studded with cottages'. The Sandy Bay community had something of a feudal air about it with interconnected families living within sight of each other in the upper valley. Then there was what in Ireland might be termed a clachan, such as at Hutt's Gate where two or three houses were in proximity to each other – 'a sort of happy family. Coffee, cotton, elder, plantain, and other fruit and forest trees, all thrive well here.'

Scattered among this diverse population were cottages occupied by elderly whites living in genteel poverty off Company or military pensions. And no doubt there were also what might be termed St Helena's own Sunday gentlemen, those confined to the island for fear of encountering creditors in Britain or India. The enslaved population tended to live close to their masters, sometimes in rooms under the farmhouses or in nearby huts or cabins. Many of the indentured Chinese workers, who arrived in the early 19th century and were technically free, lived in huts in the upper part of Jamestown, in an area later cleared and beautified by Governor Janisch, who lived in the adjacent Palm Villa, a small regency-style, double-storey house.[14]

As might be expected, what had been backyards in Jamestown sometimes developed into flourishing gardens. How far back these go is uncertain, but Council Record for 21 October 1678 records:

> Mr John Greentree and Mr John Coleson desiring to have an Order for the Houses they have builded in Chappell Valley above the ffort, and Companies Great Storehouse, with a Garden adjoyning to each of them.[15]

These early urban gardens were essentially vegetable plots with some fruit trees and with a little market gardening in the upper valley. Frequently such small garden allotments were interspersed with a palm or a larger tree and often some

9. A 1795 view of Rosemary Hall from a drawing by J. Walker. Four miles from Jamestown and famous today for its coffee, this was the residence of William Wrangham, who died in 1819. During most of Napoleon's captivity, it was occupied by Baron and Baroness Sturmer as well as by Count Balmain. A young Hungarian botanist called Welle established a botanic gardens here but was expelled from the island by Governor Lowe. The French courtiers pressed that Napoleon be allowed to move from the windswept Longwood plain to this more attractive setting but the idea was blocked by the British on the grounds of security. This engraving is rather stylised but the fundamentals of the house with pasture in front flanked by avenues of trees and a plantation behind are correct. The house no longer stands. The house to the right among the trees is Rosemary Hall Cottage.
European Magazine, October 1797, opp. p. 222. Provided by Donal P. McCracken.

shrubs and the occasional flower bed. Jamestown had a significant number of large trees, both as street planting and as garden shade trees. These might be quite formidable, such as the margossa mahogany also known as the neem or Indian lilac (*Azadirachta indica*). There were also the Indian figs or banyans (*Ficus benghalensis*), which were such a feature of the botanic garden and surrounding area. Two fine specimens were outside the old military hospital up the valley from the botanic garden. It was said that these had numerous names carved on them, presumably by sick soldiers and sailors. The oldest date was 1765, when John Skottowe was governor. The third conspicuous tree in Jamestown was the peepul tree (*Ficus religiosa*). This was first planted in the area down from the hospital in the 1740s by Governor Colonel David Dunbar, who was interested in the welfare of the Great Wood.[16] Later, more peepul trees would be planted beside the military lines at the bottom of the Jamestown Valley. Some care was taken with these trees, the young ones being both staked and roped off to protect them in early growth. Planting of banyan trees also took place in front of the Supreme Court/Post Office complex.

Then in upper Main Street, or High Street as it was sometimes called, were the famous three peepul trees in front of George's Dispensary and the Lower Bazaar, where public auctions, including those of enslaved people, were held. These should not be confused with the other and possibly earlier 'under the tree auction', which was at the famous Indian almond tree (*Terminalia catappa*) at the gate to the Castle Garden, what Governor Beatson held to be and continued to be for many decades, 'the resort of idlers'. This site was banned by the authorities as an auction site in 1821 after new iron railings were erected at the Castle Garden frontage. The old tree, however, survived and by the 1880s was six feet (1.8 m) in circumference at eight feet (2.4 m) off the ground though badly destroyed by white ants. There were also large trees in the old Lower Churchyard as well as along the side of part of Market Street.

There was a cluster of cottages with attractive gardens in the Maldivia area. These included St John's Villa ('a pretty house with a small garden'); Cambrian Cottage ('pretty gardens'); and further up Chubb's Spring ('had a very good garden where grapes grew profusely'). George Brooks Bennett, who was born in 1816, recalled when young and living at Chubb's Spring with his mother Eleanor:

> tripping along the garden path, armed with long-handled flower scissors, snipping off the roses which clustered about that well-remembered walk. It led from the house to the spring head. She was dressed all in white, and with a large sun-bonnet of straw.[17]

These and many other gardens, particularly on the eastern side of the Jamestown Valley, were either devastated or destroyed by the great flood which swept down the valley on Monday 14 April 1878.[18] Of Chubb's Spring garden it was said, 'this once noble garden ... the best part of it is literally covered with stones, and a large stream of water running over it. Up to the flood this garden was enclosed by a high wall, but is now level to the ground.' The Escourt Cottage garden was also partially carried away in this torrent.

Out in the country were a lot of attractive cottages. Their gardens were not, however, of the stylised William Robinson type. Instead, what was extraordinary about them was the exotic and diverse nature of their plants, mainly from China, India and the Cape. In some respects, they were miniature versions of what existed around the big farmhouses. This is not altogether surprising. Many of these plants, primarily from Africa and Asia, were disseminated through the Company's nurseries, and whether five plants or fifty plants were of no concern to the gardener Henry Porteous, his subordinates or successors. This explains the at times strange distribution profile of plants on the island. For while many of these old cottages with their gumwood beams fell into decay as the island decayed in the early 20th century, the plants sometimes survived untended as symbols of a fading glory.

In 1824 a fruit and flower exhibition was held on the island which appears to have been a great success. Governor Walker praised this event as proof of the 'great inherent power' of the island's climate 'and the attention of the proprietors of Gardens ... The Flowers afforded some beautiful specimens, but were mostly the productions of Asia.'[19]

Of the Hermitage, its new owner George Bennett, wrote in the 1840s:

I think it could not have been long after this that I sold my little Estate [Southens] and removed to the Hermitage, a most charming spot. It is in the same valley but much higher up. The dwelling house, which was somewhat of the Indian bungalow style, was most picturesque in appearance and in situation. It stood under a high bank and was overshadowed, in part, by Cork Oaks which would occasionally drop their acorns upon the roof. Flowers abounded and flourished in the greatest profusion and luxuriance. The road leading up to the house was bordered for some 100 yards or more by a hedge of the St. Helena fuchsia (the most graceful of all the fuchsias) of such a thickness that when riding by I have often measured its width by stretching my riding whip over it, and could just reach the tip of the shoots on the other side. Pelargoniums were in great profusion, and variety; it was a very paradise of flowers and I soon found plenty of congenial employment ... The Hermitage was a delightful place for rats; they swarm in this part of the Island and it certainly was amusing to see the games they would play. It is a curious fact that they often build their nests in the trees. At the adjoining property 'Rosemary', many such nests were to be seen.[20]

In his quaint wander through St Helena in the early 1880s, Benjamin Grant, the printer and one-time newspaper proprietor, frequently commented on what was growing in various cottage gardens, a great deal of which seem to have been characterised by flowering buddleias and fruit trees. Here are some examples:

Cambrian Cottage with neat walks adorned with flowers, stately cocoa-nut and date (Arabian) palms, peach, loquat, guava, fig, rose apple, orange (Seville and Mandarin,) plantain (3 kinds), mulberry, acacia, oleander and laburnum trees; and a very productive little vegetable garden in front, and cactus trailing along the boundary wall. Here a Brazilian almond tree is to be noticed growing, as it were, on the top of the roof of a horse stable recently erected; but on closer examination it will prove a delusion. Not wishing to destroy so scarce a tree, the proprietress of the estate, when the stable built around the tree was being roofed, caused the iron to be so cut as to allow the upper part of the trunk and branches full scope to enjoy existence in this mundane sphere. We wish all would have as much thought for the well-being of their trees instead of ruthlessly cutting them down and thus injuring their estates, as well as depreciating their value.

Constantine's cottage ... where are excellent flowers and pretty evergreen trees and coffee.

Long's cottage: 'we notice a few pineasters, Cape yew [yellowwood/ Podocarpus sp.], and pear trees, moon plant [Ipomoea alba], and buddle[i]a, on the right a hedge of thorn trees'.

Mosquito Cottage with young cypress, pear, guava, peach, poison peach, and fir trees, and moon plant; and beyond beds of rushes and plantain trees.

Rose Bower is seen basking in the midst of diversified vegetation, including Norfolk Island pine, Bermuda cedars, oak, thorn, coffee and many others. Bordering the lawn are fine oleanders, cedars, privet and a good specimen of the double white hibiscus. This genteel cottage residence is the country seat of the highly respected and benevolent Mrs. NOBLE, the wife of our worthy Postmaster.

Walbro' Cottage, with small, well-kept lawn in front, whereon stand two grand specimens of the Norfolk Island pine. These grounds are celebrated for the fine bergamot pears and that curious shrub, called locally the 'Bottle Brush,' they produce.

Willow Cottage and enclosure, which is surrounded by a wall and contains a few trees – Cape yew, date, and margossa.

The mention of Norfolk Island pines (*Araucaria heterophylla*) at Rose Bower, where there were actually six specimens, and at Walbro Cottage were not isolated examples as these trees developed into something of a status symbol. Other specimens were to be found at the Benevolent Society's School at Sandy Bay; two at the civil hospital in Jamestown; two at the entrance to Rose Bower and a further six 'hand-some young' ones around the house; two at the attractive estate of Fairy Land; two at Mr George's; two 'grand specimens' in the 'well cultivated grounds' of

Teutonic Hall (Masons); two at Varney's; three at Woodlands; and single specimens at the Briars, Knollcombe vicarage and Mount Pleasant. The small arboretum at Napoleon's tomb had five 'fine' Norfolk Island pines. Two of the finest, upwards of 80 feet (24 m) high, were to be found on the front lawn of Rock Rose Cottage and at Plantation House, where the specimen in the early 1870s was said to rise 'as straight as an arrow from the ground to a height of one hundred and ten feet (34 m), tapering from ten feet three inches (3 m) in circumference near the bottom to a few inches at the top'. In the 1880s, it was also noted that a 'healthy young Norfolk Island pine and a few willows are growing among the indigenous trees' at Diana's Peak.[21]

Few of the country houses or parks on St Helena were without a palm tree and occasional palms could be found scattered around the island. A 'very fine' date palm stood in Rupert's Valley in the opening years of the 18th century. But these were isolated, forlorn sights. Invariably appearing in the 18th- and 19th-century etchings to denote the exotic and supposed Robinson Crusoe nature of the island in the middle of nowhere, there were actually surprisingly few palm trees let alone palm avenues. This fact was touched upon by Francis Duncan in 1801, who saw the plant as a source of sustenance in times of need:

> But the various sorts of Palms, which would afford a more certain resource, because they are less subject to suffer from drought, seem wholly neglected. Yet there can be little doubt that they would grow in the valleys.[22]

ᏯᏇ Melliss's map and the old order ᏯᏇ

George Melliss's 1820s/1830s map provides a picture of land tenure on the island at that period.[23] In his 1972 thesis, Percy Teale states that the original map was in an extremely fragile state. He and L. W. Shepherd made a copy from which the historian can work. This is about 100 x 150 centimetres (40 x 60 inches) in size. Around its edge are lists of reference numbers relating to principal springs, a list of properties in private hands including the name of each proprietor and estate as well as the acreage, several indices to remarkable places, and expired leases to Brookes, Dallas's and Briars villages and the East India Company properties. There are a total of 89 family names, with quite a few different members of a family owning different properties. The largest property discernible on the Melliss map is Longwood, with 477 acres (193 ha), and the largest in private hands is Richard Bagley's 157 acres (64 ha) at Thompson's Wood. There are, however, areas of the map where numbers should be located but the original was too destroyed to copy, leaving the facsimile blank. The researcher must be aware of these omissions.

The named private estates number 216 in total, compared to 22 belonging to the East India Company. There are also gaps on the map for 85 estate names, so the map in its original state would have had information on 301 private properties in total. These gaps are presumably either where the writing was illegible or where there are fragment gaps missing from the large sheet. The information on the 22 East India Company estates have no estate name gaps, but two acreage gaps, these being Deadwood and Pounces.

In addition, the map has five proprietors' names missing, though it is possible in some instances to know who they are by the estate names which are still present. Finally, there are 46 gaps relating to the acreage of estates. So overall the information gained from Melliss's map must be taken as approximate. Table 4 sets out the position in relation to private properties.

TABLE 4

Private properties on the Melliss map

	Surviving	Obliterated/missing	Total
Proprietors' names	296	5	301
Estate names	216	85	301
Acreage	4,822	46 entries missing	

The average property of known acreages consisted of 22 acres and the total property in private hands in the 1820s/1830s must have been in the region of 6,622 acres. As illustrated in Table 5, there were families who owned multiple properties. This table also lists the leading families and the names of any notable houses on the property.

TABLE 5

The largest properties indicated on Melliss's map

Name of the family	Number of properties owned	Acreage owned by family	Notable house/ garden on property	Acreage of domain
Alexander	17	565 (+ 1 unknown acreage)	Bamboo Grove (1808)	15
Seale	17	313 (+5 unknown)	Deadwood Southin [Southens?] Rock Rose Hill Wranghams Horse Pasture	? ? 22 57 100

Name of the family	Number of properties owned	Acreage owned by family	Notable house/ garden on property	Acreage of domain
Brooke	12	243 (+ 2 unknown	Prospect Alarm Hutt's Gate	9 5 17
Doveton	12	220 (+4 unknown)	Mount Pleasant Bay House Rose Cottage	? 47 8
Greentree	12	248 (+4 unknown)	Fairy Land	?
Beale	9	27 (+1 unknown)	Terrace Knoll	?
Lambe	9	71 (+4 unknown)	Bamboo Hedge	21
Samson	8	395	West Lodge Luffkins Myrtle Grove	119 90 60
Blake	7		Woodlands	29
Wright	6	205		
Scott	5	96		
Craig	3	58		
David	3	6		
Desfountain	3	223	Peake Dale Prospect Place	105 90
Heathorn	4	96		
Knipes	At least 4. Possibly 8	Only one acreage survives, Half Moon	Half Moon	53
Pritchard	4	17 (+2 unknown)	Knoll House	2
Harper	3			
Leeche	3	82	Oaklands Woodcot	40 42
Masons	3	69	Teutonic Hall	7
Young	3	57	Rose Bower	23

The map also marks those proprietors who owned only one or two properties, but which were of a large acreage. These include:

Richard Prince, who owned both Farm Lodge (60 acres) and Knoll Cottage (28 acres)

The famous 'fine looking' Oakbank (83 acres), the country house of Sir Charles Hodson

Richard Bagley's estate Thompson's Wood (157 acres), the largest privately owned estate on St Helena

John Bagley's Rock Mount (139 acres)

Finally, there were notable properties on small or medium-sized plots such as Ann Haymes's Rosemary Hall (41 acres) and McIntosh's (31 acres), as well as Woodlands/Blenkin's (29 acres). Of these Woodlands had a particularly interesting range of fruit trees, Cape and Eastern exotics and an extensive coffee plantation:

apple (English and Cape), orange (Mandarin and sweet), cherimoya, quince, peach, pear, loquat, fig (2 kinds), red plum, white mulberry, numerous plantain, and about 2,000 coffee trees which yield abundantly; also pandanus [screwpine], calodendron [Cape chestnut], cedrela [mahogany], ailanthus [tree of heaven], aralira papyrifera [*Tetrapanax papyrifer*], acacias, pineasters, oaks (African and English), cypress, Norfolk Island pines (3), cork, with several others, besides canthium, box, bamboo (3 kinds), and flowers. Fine vegetables, especially cabbages, are produced in the grounds of this estate.[24]

A generation later George Melliss's son, John Charles Melliss, in his celebrated and very valuable 1875 book *St Helena*, set out the land use of St Helena in acreage. It is noteworthy that this information largely dovetails into the information on George Melliss's map. In particular, the total land which was economically viable – which could be used for pasture, hay production, forestland, cultivation, orchards and gardens – was in the region of 8,000 acres (3,300 ha).

John Charles Melliss's later information is summarised in Figures 2 and 3.

Several things strike one about land use in St Helena. The minuscule amount of land under cultivation was nothing new. It is worth noting that it was not until the 1740s that Governor Dunbar introduced the plough to St Helena.[25] Governor Beatson was concerned in 1808 that only 88 acres (36 ha) on the island was under the plough, with the result that a population of 3,600 inhabitants were 'living almost wholly upon the public stores'. He asserted:

Lands formerly in cultivation were abandoned and overgrown with weeds; and few traces of industry were to be seen. Under such circumstances, the increase of population, that is, of planters and their slaves, had been of no advantage to the island; for in the year 1717, when the total of those inhabitants was only 833, there were 1765 cattle on the island; and in 1812, when the same class of inhabitants had increased to 1732, their stock of cattle was no more than 1494.[26]

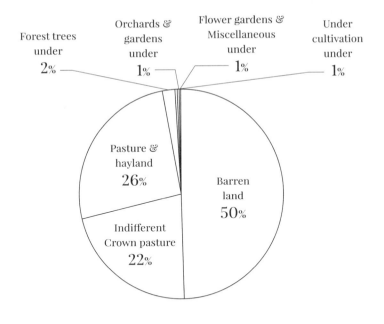

FIGURE 2
St Helena land use (1875): By percentage

Forest trees under 2%

Orchards & gardens under 1%

Flower gardens & Miscellaneous under 1%

Under cultivation under 1%

Pasture & hayland 26%

Barren land 50%

Indifferent Crown pasture 22%

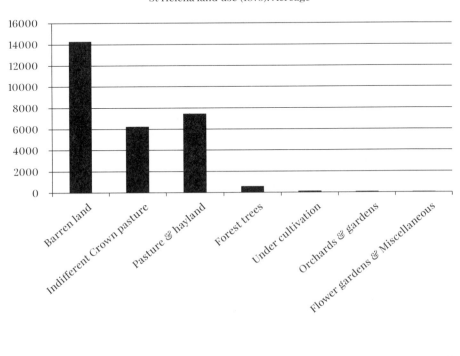

FIGURE 3
St Helena land use (1875): Acreage

The most striking thing about Melliss's 1875 figures nearly 70 years later was the amount of land which was regarded as being of little or no use. Nearly 50 per cent (14,283 acres/5,780 ha) of the island was considered barren, with only 13 per cent of such barren land being privately owned. Another 6,233 acres (2,522 ha), according to Melliss, was described as indifferent Crown pasture. Therefore, nearly two-thirds of St Helena – more than 20,000 acres (8,100 ha) – was regarded as fairly useless agricultural land. Useful land was broken down as follows:

7,450 acres (3,015 ha) of pasture and hayland
575 acres (333 ha) of forest trees
144 acres (58 ha) of cultivated roots and crops
65 acres (26 ha) of orchards and gardens
50 acres (20 ha) of flower gardens and miscellaneous

These 50 acres of gardens formed only 0.17 per cent of the whole island and a mere 0.6 per cent of its usable land. Even if one adds the orchards and cultivated gardens these proportions increase only to a mere 1.3 and 0.4 per cent respectively, suggesting that gardens were not a feature of old St Helena.[27] Yet if gardens are in their broadest sense to include what in Britain and Ireland could be termed the demesne around the house then the picture is different. Flower beds were a rarity but shrubs, and especially trees, many from distant and exotic corners of the globe, set off the landed estates of the St Helena gentry. These plants frequently arrived with the annual visits of the great East India Company fleets from China and India.

St Helena was remote from the world but even internally the farmhouses were remote from each other, thanks to the island's many steep valleys and steep hills. One officer out hunting partridges remarked that the birds need fly only a short distance over a valley in seconds, but it would take him very much longer to go down and up to reach them again. Added to this was the lack of roads. Travelling along such tracks as existed required frequently dismounting to open gates across the thoroughfare, not unlike the situation which existed in South Africa into the 20th century. During the period of Napoleon's imprisonment, Basil Jackson asserted:

We found tolerable bridle-roads, zig-zagging up and down the hills, but only two real highways, such as wheels could roll on; one, as before mentioned, leading to Longwood from the town, the other to Plantation House, the country residence of the Governor; but at the period I am scribbling about, the only carriage ever seen was a very ancient one, drawn by four bullocks, which at rare intervals carried Lady Lowe between the Governor's town and country houses.[28]

Two farms that might on the map seem adjacent, often were separated by a gorge, or one was in the valley and another on the apex of a formidable hill.

In the 1930s Kitching calculates the number of known rural gentlemen's residences then on St Helena at 62, excluding Plantation House. Leaving aside the condition of these houses by then, this was a drop in actual numbers from what had existed a century before. As mentioned, these were not palatial mansions but essentially farmhouses very much of a plain Georgian design. The estates had prospered during the 18th century when there was a regular turnover of occupation and ownership, with military, naval and colonial officials coming and going. Other owners and occupiers include men who had been in colonial or Company service and who did not quite make it home to Britain, living the life of a gentleman on St Helena rather than in genteel poverty back home. The estates were invariably worked by enslaved labourers who cultivated the gardens and agricultural land.

By the time of Napoleon's captivity, most of these residences had some form of established garden, including the ubiquitous arboretum framing the house at the back and sides, interspersed with shrubberies and invariably an open grass area at the front. These were fields rather than lawns but the effect was the same, often affording dramatic vistas from the homestead. Fortunately, a number of engravings of such residences appeared in books and magazines in the late 18th and early 19th centuries. Though St Helena had its economic woes during the Company's days and was especially affected when drought hit hard, the plantation economy and lifestyle survived into the 1830s and the abolition of enslavement.

ᜒᜒ Plant lists ᜒᜒ

Several lists and editions of lists of plants survive from the 19th century. These include the works of William Burchell, William Roxburgh, Stephen Pritchard with James Bowie and John Charles Melliss. The most complete is the last of these. Melliss's epic work, *St. Helena: A Physical, Historical and Topographical Description of the Island, Including the Geology, Fauna, Flora and Meteorology*, was published by Lovell Reeve of Covent Garden, London, in 1875. It devotes 162 pages or 40 per cent of the book to this botanical list of 1,085 species, both indigenous plants and exotics, whether introduced or naturalised by current, birds or wind. The following table is a breakdown of Melliss's list in relation to garden location.

TABLE 6

Location of plant species in Melliss's *St Helena*, 1875

Garden	Plant species	Acreage	Occupied in 1830
Not specified as in gardens	662	–	–
Gardens (unnamed)	183	–	–
Plantation House (includes governor's, ladies', kitchen gardens and arboretum)	79	176	EIC: the governor
Oakbank	32	83	Charles Hodson
Maldivia	23		
The Briars	10	55 (14½ acres planted with mulberries)	East India Company from 1827/ Crown 1836. Early 20th century: Eastern Telegraph Co.
Longwood	9	569	EIC
Terrace Knoll	9		Anthony Beale. Now ruined.
The Hermitage	8		
Oaklands	8	40	Miss E. Leech.
Castle Garden (Public)	7		
Mount Pleasant	7		Originally Matthew Bazett. Doveton family from 1786.
Rosemary Hall	7	41	William Wrangham, then John De Fountain from 1819. EIC for a short period. Estate of Ann Haymes widow of Ensign Haymes. The Wranghams also owned the house known as Wranghams in Sandy Bay, which had perhaps the finest flower garden on the island.
Botanic Gardens (Public)	5		
Fairyland	5		
Lowe's Garden	4		
Prospect	3		Thomas Brooke 1820s. Good illustration of the house as frontispiece of the 2nd edition of Brooke's *History of St Helena* (1824).
Rock Rose Hill	3	22	Built as a secondary house for Governor Brooke in the 1780s. Later occupied by Major Robert Seale, whose family remained there until 1967.[29]

Garden	Plant species	Acreage	Occupied in 1830
Rose Cottage	3	8	Doveton/Greentree
West Lodge	3	119	Charles Samson. Previously occupied by Porteous (1804) and Cocks (1811).[30]
Luffkins	2	90	Charles Samson
Myrtle Grove	2	60	David Leech, assistant accountant and from 1820 John Samson of West Lodge.[31]
Sydenham	2		
Arnos Vale[32]	1		Had belonged to the Doveton family.
Bamboo Grove	1	15	William G. Alexander. House built 1808.
Farm Lodge	1	60	Richard Prince. Had been the home of Col Smith, artillery commander who died in 1819.
Half Moon	1	53	William B. Knipe
Ladder Hill (Officers' garden)	1		
Picket House	1		
Southens	1		Francis Seale. Described by George Bennett in the 1840s as a 'nice little property' and 'devoid of trees'.[33]
Wallbro	1		
Woodlands	1	29	George Blake

These figures are useful as they reflect those properties which had either an interesting garden or, at least, an interesting arboretum and shrubbery. Of the 240 plants in gardens according to Melliss's list, 144 (60 per cent) are in four gardens: Plantation House, Oakbank, Maldivia and the Briars. Plantation House was the governor's country residence. Chapters 2 and 10 have sections specifically devoted to this interesting garden.

The enslaved and 'economics'

The old gardens of St Helena were worked by enslaved gardeners and other gardeners who were poorly paid, including indentured Chinese labourers. Contemporary accounts and records paint a bleak picture of a rather vicious slave-owning society, which was quick to inflict severe punishment on those unfortunate enough to be their property. Whether they were any more or less extreme in their attitude to the enslaved population than planters on the West Indies is a matter of conjecture, but whether it was through fear or lack of enlightenment or both, St Helena was no bastion of compassion. In 1792 Governor Brooke wrote of this plantation population:

> The White Inhabitants are in general tall & well shaped, and althro' so near the line [equator], have as fair Complexions as those of great Britain; the women have ever been particularly admired by strangers.
>
> Both sexes are naturally sensible and ingeneous, but a want of Education, a confined Situation and the misfortune of being connected with Slavery renders it difficult for them to become blessed with Liberality or humanity of Disposition, several however, do rise superior to those Obstructions and thereby become Characters truly worthy of Admiration.[34]

We have few stories relating to enslaved gardeners. By definition, enslavement was a dehumanising matter. Anyone wishing to read about the lot of enslaved people on St Helena and the painfully slow moves towards their emancipation, including the bizarre regulation that some enslaved people had to purchase their own freedom, should read Colin Fox's recently published book, *A Bitter Draught: St Helena and the Abolition of Slavery*. But for the sheer brutality of enslavement on St Helena, one need only consult Governor Janisch's *Extracts from the St Helena*

10. Hunting with dogs on St Helena was a leisurely business as there was little to hunt, but life at Prospect House was pleasant with its shrubberies and arboretum. The residence of the island council's secretary, Thomas Henry Brooke (1774-1849), he used this illustration as the frontispiece to the second edition of his *History of the island of St Helena* (1824). Provided by Donal P. McCracken.

NAPOLEON'S GARDEN ISLAND

Records, published after his death in 1885. This is full of instances of prolonged floggings, mutilations and execution.

Several things strike the historian of the island in relation to enslavement. The first is that it extended over a long period, from a few individuals in the 16th century, increasing in numbers from the mid-17th century and through until the trade in enslaved people was stopped in 1792. As ships carrying enslaved people frequently called at St Helena enroute across the Atlantic to America, sometimes individuals were left on the island. This meant that the composition of the enslaved population was varied and was not homogeneous. Perhaps most came from Africa and its islands: West Africa including what would become Ghana (Gold Coast), Mozambique, Madagascar, Zanzibar. But there were also enslaved people from the Maldive islands, India and Indonesia. As will be seen, later St Helena was used as a home base for the British Royal Navy squadron operating along the West African coast against vessels engaged in shipping enslaved people. This resulted in St Helena becoming a destination, sometimes permanently, for those Africans freed from captured vessels carrying enslaved people.

The second observation relates to numbers. Because of the small size of the island, the numbers of enslaved people was never vast, with perhaps 10 to 20 enslaved people being landed at Jamestown at any one time. By 1802 the black population numbered 1,256, half the island's population of 2,511. Of that number 1,029 was enslaved people and 227 were described as 'free black'. The military garrison numbered 892, the Company's officials and family 241, and planters and others were 241.

As will be seen, Napoleon had poignant encounters with the enslaved gardener Toby at the Briars. The celebrated Dr James Barry (*c.*1792-1865) was on St Helena from 1836 to 1838. Born in Ireland as a woman, Barry successfully defied the norms of the age by self-identifying as male and protecting gender identity throughout medical training at Edinburgh University and at St Thomas's Hospital, London, and during a significant number of colonial medical appointments, which included holding senior army and civil medical appointments at the Cape, St Helena, Jamica, the Windward and Leeward Islands, Corfu and Canada. He is remembered in particular for carrying out a caesarean operation in 1826 where both mother and child survived. Lord Charles Somerset, the Cape's governor and possibly Barry's lover, described him as 'the greatest physican I ever met, but absurd in everything else'. While fulfilling his tasks as principal medical officer on St Helena with remarkable energy, Barry was also dragged into a series of disputes and rows. As in his other postings, these altercations on St Helena were frequently caused by his prioneering attitude to hygiene and health.

On one occasion Barry took up the case of a jailed Chinese cook called Acho. He had been arrested as an accessory to burglary and had been condemned to death in 1835, but had been in the St Helena jail since because his case was under review in Britain. Writing to the authorities in July 1837 Barry asserted:

I have the honour to inform you that the Chinese Convict Acho, who has been long under sentence of Death and whose case has again been referred to England, in consequence of repeated illness arising from the state of his mind, more than his body, has been several times a Patient in the Civil Side of the General Hospital under my Superintendence.

On his last admission, I found him in so weak and desponding a state that I feared for his intellect and therefore thought it fit to remove him into my own residence close to the Hospital, to have him more immediately under my own eye and to give him advantage of air and exercise in my little garden, I being personally responsible for his safety and also that he should be paraded or mustered when required by any of the authorities. I notified to the Government that such were my intentions and gave orders to the Hospital Sergeant that the Convict Acho should be presented to any person authorized to see him by the Authorities.

Judge of my surprise to hear that this forenoon, William Weller, the Civil Provost, came to the Hospital without any written authority and there insisted on having the patient delivered up to him, which of course could not be complied with as I was not in the Hospital to authorize his dismissal. I have only further to state that this unfortunate man, being subjected to the taunts and observations of Prisoners or even Patients, will in my judgement drive him to despair or madness.

I therefore earnestly and respectfully submit that the Convict Patient Acho be permitted to remain under my professional superintendence until his case be finally decided, I being of course personally responsible as I am for others.[35]

For a time Barry was able to continue this prison-leave for Acho so he could walk in Barry's little garden near the hospital in the upper valley, which contained a rare mango tree. Eventually the death sentence was repealed, but sadly, and despite Barry's strong determination to protect him, in October 1837 Acho was taken off St Helena in a convict ship and transported to New South Wales.[36]

A poignant note appeared in an 1851 account of the island relating to a derelict set of cottages in Lemon Valley. It is not clear who had lived there, but clearly it had been poor people, most likely black labourers:

There are one or two ruinous cottages near the middle of the valley, placed in the midst of what once have been thriving gardens, which are now, however, totally neglected, run wild, and choked up with weeds and shrubs, the boundary walls of which are lined round with formidable hedges of the prickly pear, from amongst which several fine fig trees show their glossy leaves, and display their luscious fruit, as if to shew what could be done in such a place with a little care and cultivation ...

There are one or two cottages inclosed in little gardens, which are more or less cultivated, while at the extreme end of the valley is a little forest of plantains, with here and there a fruit tree peeping from their broad green leaves, and under the lee of a bank of rocks.[37]

At different times, there was a series of Company plantations across the island, mostly lemon or yams and sometimes gumwood. For a while in the early 18th century, sugar cane was tried down at Sandy Bay. These were, of course, not flower and shrub gardens. The one exception was the Maldivia Garden, which shifted between being yam and vegetable plots supplying the nearby military hospital and a residence for various officials, civilian and military and included one of the few vineyards on the island.

In 1836 four gardeners, presumably recently liberated from enslavement, worked at Maldivia. In part they were paid in wine, a dop system no doubt borrowed from the Cape. The head gardener received nine shillings (9/-) a week, plus nine bottles of wine a week and board and lodgings. Of the three other gardeners, one earned twelve shillings (12/-) a week without wine; one earned nine shillings a week (9/-) plus six bottles of wine, and one earned six shillings (6/-) a week and six bottles of wine. That totalled one pound and sixteen shillings (£1-16-0) in cash wages a week, plus twenty-one bottles of Cape wine.[38] The Company's plantation was worked by enslaved labourers, and William Burchell's diary shows us a small number worked as gardeners. By 1827, one enslaved woman and about 20 enslaved men were listed as gardeners on St Helena, at least for part of their working time. And some 14 indentured Chinese also worked in the Company's gardens.[39]

It was the hope of many governors of St Helena that a new crop might be introduced which would thrive in the climate and soil and be adopted by the planters. The Company nurseries, which fell under the person who attended to the Company's gardens, were the vehicle for such introductions to the farming community. The historian of St Helena must beware asserting too confidently the date on which a certain species of plant was introduced to the island, however. Multiple introductions of a species were common and little evidence exists of early plantings actually naturalising. Equally, one must be wary of statements of intent. As will be seen, the resolve in the 1680s to enclose the Great Wood of St Helena in fact never materialised fully. Table 7 gives some of the recorded dates of plant introductions aimed at creating a profitable agri-economy run by enslaved labour. Such plants were sometimes referred to as 'economics'.

TABLE 7

Approximate dates of introduced plants of possible economic value to St Helena

Approximate year introduced	Crop
1672	Indigo
1678	Cotton
1678/1708	Sugar cane
1684	Rice
1697	Tobacco
1708	Mulberry
1708	Yam
1708	Potato
1718	Vine
1729/1733	Coffee
1749	Oaks (acorns to feed pigs); scotch pine; spruce fir
1775	Blackberry
1789	Guinea grass
1792	Breadfruit
1853	New Zealand flax

ৡঌৢ The jewels in St Helena's floral crown ৡঌৢ

Many of the plants which grew on St Helena in the 17th and 18th centuries survived into the colonial era after the Company's departure. Indeed, some of the old gardens became reservoirs where endangered indigenous and rare exotic plants survived when their old habitat was being destroyed, not least by the one successful economic, New Zealand flax. An interesting example of this was the attractive St Helena rosemary, *Phylica polifolia*, a shrub with leaves not unlike the herb but no relative. Melliss recorded in 1875 that 'not more than 100 specimens now exist'. He cited the still-famous dozen or so bushes growing near the top of the Lot rock pinnacle, 'which seems to thrive without any soil'. But he also stated that the plant grew at Fairy Land, Plantation House, Rosemary Hall, Oaklands and Oakbank.[40]

A number of private houses on St Helena may be singled out as having particularly interesting gardens in what many consider the golden age of Company rule. Some of these were or would become Company-owned, a fact in itself which points to the transient nature of colonial society on the island. Below are some of the Georgian houses which constituted the golden age of gardens on St Helena.

Maldivia

Maldivia, which has been mentioned in the previous section as being an important Company plantation in the 18th century, was foremost among the island's gardens. As will be seen, it was later to temporarily become the island's botanic gardens.

The original Maldivia, with its elegant single-storey residence, occupied a considerable site and held a yam plantation and a working farm. These stretched up the valley to a damp area covered with rushes, and down into what is now part of Jamestown, including land later occupied by the botanic garden. In the 1790s, three plots were alienated from the original Maldivia.[41] These included land for the island's Company secretary, Thomas Henry Brooke. Later the land immediately adjacent to the homestead was divided again and occupied by the hospital, originally including what became Blundens, Cambrian and Villa le Breton.[42]

The town's hot and sultry microclimate made Maldivia an obvious place to grow interesting exotics. From the time it was called Concord, until well into the 19th century, Maldivia had a lush and special feel about it. And because of this, sometimes it was referred to as the Upper Garden, a title which was to lead to confusion once the botanic garden was established a little way down the valley, yet still in the upper part of Jamestown.

In June 1823 two acres (0.8 ha) were alienated by Major Charles Hodson to Captain James Bennett, who was living on the adjacent Chubb's Cottage property. In February 1826, Bennett, having sold Chubb's Spring and with a mortgage of £1,000, purchased Maldivia and its eight acres (3.2 ha) from Hodson. To this he added those two adjacent acres (0.8 ha) he had already acquired from the major, making the property 10 acres (4 ha) in total. It is interesting to note that when James died in 1835 the property was valued at £1,500.[43]

James Bennett was, as were so many on the island, a self-made man who had started life as a soldier. The property supplemented his generous government stipend with its crops and legendary fruits, including the only mangos grown on the island. Bennett also held public office, ran a theatre in Jamestown until it burned down on 14 July 1831, educated his children back in Britain, and, possibly because of that, lived one step ahead of his creditors. Though frequently stretched for money, the Bennetts maintained the magnificent garden with its abundance of fruit trees, roses, myrtle and geranium hedges.[44]

After James's death in 1835, Maldivia passed to his widow Eleanor. She was burdened with James's debts and was forced to rent out some rooms to a succession of people. Colin Fox, through meticulous scrutiny of surviving farm papers, has shown how she survived financially. He reproduces in *The Bennett Letters* an inventory of Captain James Bennett's Maldivia estate. Under 'Garden and outer premises' this includes: tool chest, garden tools, four pairs of steps, two ladders, four large shells, wheelbarrow, garden pots, watering can, grindstone, cow and calf, poultry, wheelbarrow, crowbars, tools, handbarrow (broken), two gongs and two goats. All this was valued at £41.[45]

On her death in August 1860 at the age of 80, the property passed then to her daughter Lady Eliza Ross, so Maldivia remained in the family's hands. Ten years before, when Eliza was living in Plantation House, George Bennett wrote to his brother Charles in England:

> The Governor still is on the sick list; he doesn't get well. One day better, the next worse but no material change either way. I hear today he is dressed and is in the library — last week he kept his room — he is seriously thinking of trying a change of air to a warmer and drier situation. Plantation [House] at this season of the year is very cold and he feels it — it is proposed to bring him down to Maldivia which he likes the idea of much but would not go to the castle – he has a great antipathy to that place ... the place has no comforts and loads of mosquitoes.[46]

Sir Patrick survived only a fortnight longer, dying on 28 August 1850 and leaving Eliza a widow. She lived in Maldivia from 1860 until her own death in 1890, keeping up the now well-established old garden. After that the property was owned by Mrs Eliza Lloyd, daughter of Rev. George Bennett. What if any the relationship there was between these branches of the Bennett family remains unclear. In 1891, Rev. J. H. Daine was living at the property. Unclear also is the saga of Maldivia passing into official ownership. The property was used for a couple of years from 1893 to house King Dinuzulu kaCetshwayo and the Zulu royal exiles after they were moved from Rosemary Hall, which they complained was damp and unhealthy. Maldivia was purchased by the government of the Colony of Natal for this purpose. Then, in 1898, the property was sold by Natal to the St Helena government for £391.[47]

Despite the relative genteel poverty of the Bennetts, they had maintained Maldivia and its garden in splendid state. Joseph Hooker, the future director of Kew Gardens, described Maldivia during his visit in 1843 as the best garden on

PLATE 1 Off St Helena. The forbidding cliffs of St Helena created the popular myth of 'The Rock' in the middle of the wild South Atlantic Ocean. They certainly made a natural barrier around much of the East India Company outpost, but St Helena's magical interior contained its botanical treasures, both indigenous and introduced, in Company and plantation gardens as well over its wild valleys and ridges. Sketch by William Burchell (12 December 1805).

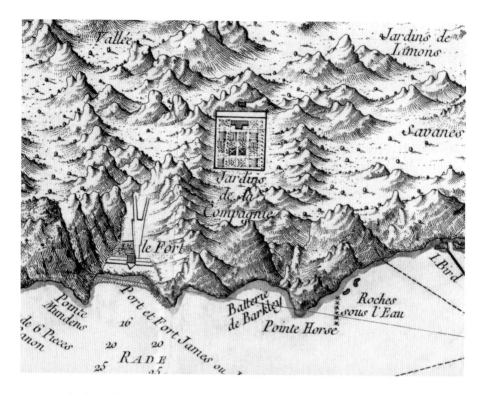

PLATE 2 The formally laid-out Company garden, *Jardins de la Compagnie* at Plantation House is clearly marked in this Plan de l'isle Ste Helene published in 1764 when John Skottwe was governor.

Bellin, *Petit Atlas Maritime*, t. 3, no.123. Provided by Donal P. McCracken.

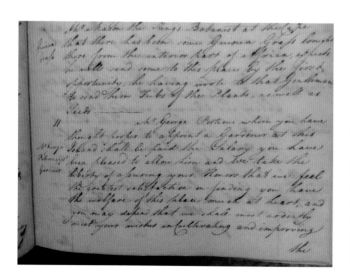

PLATE 3
Letter dated 28 May 1787 from St Helena to the East India Company concerning the appointment of a gardener. SHA, Letters to England, 1785–1789; 1789, item 10.

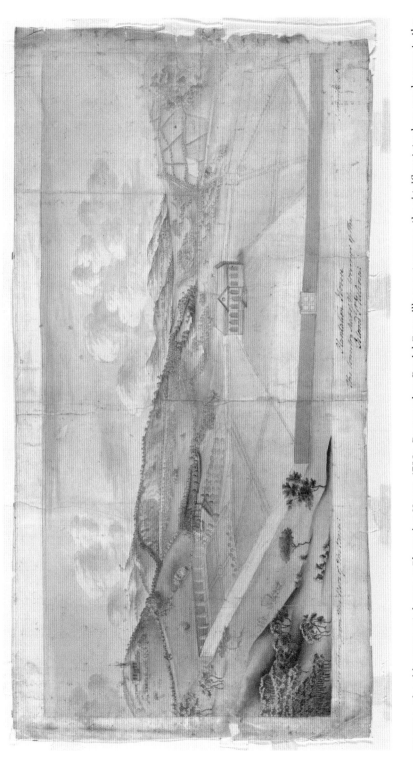

PLATE 4 The old governor's house at Plantation House, 1780s. Drawn when Daniel Corneille was governor, the significant gardens can be seen to the left. The whole compound is surrounded by a reinforced stout wall, indicating how precarious was the existence of successive governors.

IAA Guinness Collection 98/68.6/2. © Irish Architectural Archive

PLATE 5 Governor Robert Brooke. A successful East India Company soldier and a disastrous industrial speculator, Robert Brooke (1744–1811) was probably St Helena's best Company governor (1787–1801). Moderate in opinion and pleasant in character, his reforms regarding the enslavement of people, improvement of the island's economy and the island's safety in time of international war earned this Irishman a good reputation.
Courtesy of Joan Schrecker

PLATE 6 "There's a famous big one there, Charles". "Yes Sir, I'll soon have that down". Self-portrait by Burchell of his plant hunting with Charles, who was the enslaved servant of Lieutenant John Barnes who commanded the artillery batteries at Powell's Valley and who also joined the botanical exploration of the south-east part of the island on 8 December 1807.

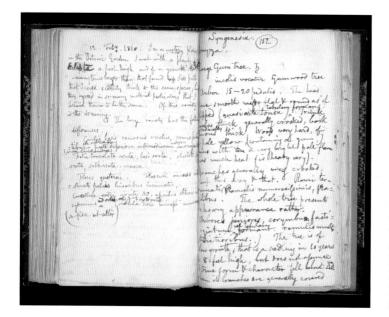

PLATE 7
Burchell's plant collecting book with Botanic Garden entry, February 1810, Burchell Flora Heleniana mss, f.151b.

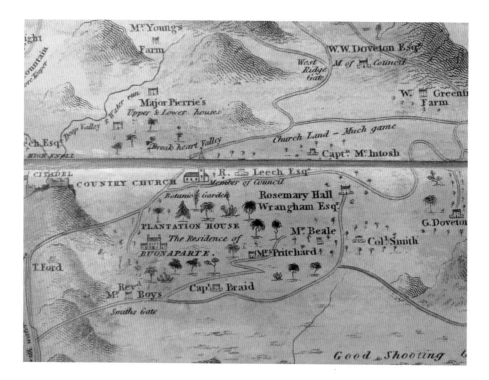

PLATE 8 Map incorrectly showing Plantation House as the residence of Napoleon Bonaparte (corrected in later edition). Note the use of the term 'Botanic Garden' behind the house. This geographical plan of the island & forts of Saint Helena ... by Lieu. R.P. Read.

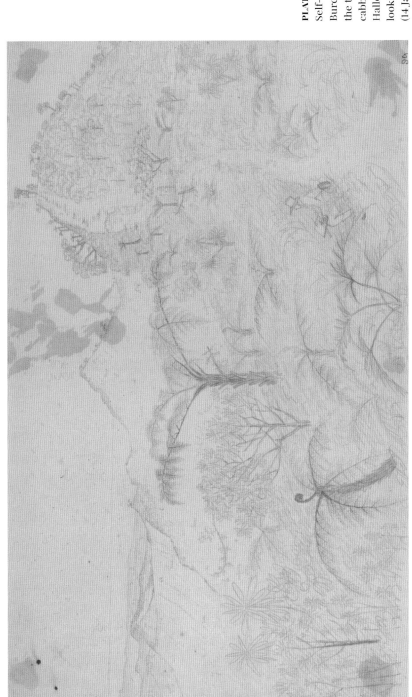

PLATE 9
Self-portrait of
Burchell among
the tree ferns and
cabbage trees on
Halley's Mount
looking north
(14 January 1808).

PLATE 10

The Briars in the post-
Napoleon period. Though this
lithograph from a drawing
by Lieutenant F.R. Stack was
made 30 years after Napoleon's
death, the buildings, including
the sentinel cypress trees
beside the main house and
the remnants of the garden
and tree avenues survive.
Having been used as a
brewery, a mulberry farm
and later a cable and wireless
communication station, the
original planter's house was
demolished and replaced by
a utilitarian building. Only
in 1959 was the property
donated to the French nation,
ensuring the preservation of
the Pavilion where Napoleon
had lived from 10 October to 10
December 1815.

Souvenir of the Emperor Napoleon,
1851. Provided by Donal P.
McCracken.

the island. This situation was assisted by the active correspondence that George Bennett maintained with Sir William Hooker, Joseph's equally famous father. George was not slow to assist Kew when asked, but equally he was not slow in respectively requesting a quid pro quo:

If you wish for more plants from St. Helena I shall be glad if you will return me the case with the grandilla and other species of Passiflora bearing a yellow fruit about the size of an egg known in the West Indies as water lemon or Belle apple. Also the Cape zante currant, Musa cavendishii, star apple, Sapodella or any other of the genus, Annona except cherimolia which we have, any of the ornamental plants such as petunia would be acceptable – we have no orchideous plants on the island. Any of them would also be acceptable. I think the misty woods at Diana's peak would suit the epiphytes.[48]

In her account of her brief visit to St Helena in 1877, Isobel Gill, wife of the famous astronomer, recorded what might well have been Maldivia:

After a short stiff pull, we left this motley crew [of townsfolk] behind, and a shady lane soon led us into a lovely garden where palm and pomegranate trees shaded the rich luxuriance of sweet-smelling roses and scarlet geraniums. A low-roofed verandahed cottage formed the centre of this little Eden, and here we found a comfortable home during our stay.[49]

A generation after Hooker's sojourn on the island, Benjamin Grant's description of Maldivia, written about 1881, is the most detailed we have of this grand old St Helena garden:

Maldivia garden, by the back entrance to which stands a fine eucalyptus. This fine garden contains a great variety of fruit and ornamental trees, and shrubs, viz :--mango (3 kinds), orange, guava (3 kinds), loquat, peach, Brazil guava, bananas (various), rose apple, Kei apple, papau apple, ohirimoya, pomegranate, fig, a Fruit (Xanthochymus Dulcis) from Malacca Islands, date palm (2 kinds), Kaffir date, tamarind, litchi, shaddock, Spanish mulberry, Otaheite gooseberry, granadilla, oleander, myrtle (2 kinds), - hibiscus (4 kinds), bougainvillea (2 kinds), rose (white, and China), splendid ginger or cardamom plant, ginger (yellow and white), star-shaped lily (white flower), strelitzia (3 kinds), plumbago, China box, raphia palm, acacia, margossa, thorn, Indian fig (Ficus Indica), cotton, cypresses, bamboo

(2 kinds), Madagascar creeper, and Cereus triangularis, which is to be noticed trailing along the wall.

Arriving opposite a cottage we discover Maldivia residence surrounded with beautiful flowers and flowering vines. Maldivia and Cambrian Cottage estates are, at the present day, the best fruit and vegetable gardens in James' Valley, producing, amongst others, excellent lettuces, radishes, brinjals, cucumbers, capsicums, and chilies. A visit to these fine estates would prove highly satisfactory. Above Maldivia residence is another building belonging to the estate, and beyond it a productive garden called Maldivia Upper Garden, the walks in which are bordered by fruit trees—such as pomegranate, orange, (Seville and Mandarin), peach, mango, pear, rose apple, guava, date palms, red plum, fig, loquat, plantain (4 kinds), mulberry, and acacia trees; also granadilla, sugar cane, farinha, chili (4 kinds), and numerous clumps of reed. The orderly arrangement of the beds of vegetables demonstrate considerable care and perseverance on the part of the Tenant. A glance above this garden will reveal a few beds of dark green rushes, which are exceedingly picturesque on the red and brown rocks.

Grant's 1883 plant list for Maldivia is contained in Table 8. It is more horticultural than botanical and, in that sense, less interesting than Melliss's.

TABLE 8

Grant's; plants at Maldivia, 1883

Scientific name	Common name
Paritium tiliaceum	Gamboge
Citrus aurantium	Orange
Citrus vulgaris	Seville orange
Mangifera indica	Mango
Nephelium lappaceum	Litchi (Rambutan of China)
Erythrina corallodendron	Coral tree
Bauhinia kunthiana syn. *Bauhinia rosea*	
Carica papaya	pawpaw
Bignonia tecoma	Yellow bignonia
Thunbergia alata	Black-eyed Susan
Phyllanthus acidus syn. *Cicca disticha*	Otaheite gooseberry
Ficus indica	Banyan
Cocos nucifera	Cocoa nut
Corypha umbraculifera	Fan palm

Scientific name	Common name
Phoenix dactylifera	Date palm
Agave variegata	(Spiky-leaved succulent)
Cycas revoluta	Sago palm

Oakbank

In 1806, a visitor to St Helena commenting on Plantation House in its 'pleasant little valley, with small plantations and gardens' added the thorny rider: 'however, the situation does no credit to the taste of the person who first pitched upon it, as it is much inferior to many places which we afterwards saw: its proximity to the town, was probably the cause of its being preferred'. One such place, in its time the crowning jewel of St Helena, was Oakbank House and grounds. From the sketch by Fowler in the 1860s, this was certainly a grand establishment. It should be noted that Oakbank, at an elevation of 1,700 feet, had one of the highest rainfalls on the island, with Kitching giving it 46.60 inches per annum.

In 1877, Isobel Gill considered Oakbank the 'most beautiful of all St. Helena's beautiful homes'. This, she asserted:

> ... is the queen of pocket landscapes, but in every gully here, little gems lie hid that
> would delight a painter's eye, and the variety of scenery within so small a compass
> is indeed wonderful. Grand rugged rocks, gentle, grassy slopes, tilled fields and
> hedgerows, gardens of palms and pomegranates, beds of violets and mignonette,
> clumps of pine trees, waysides of gorse, and everywhere the sea.[50]

Oakbank, sometimes referred to as Bowman's, had been built around 1742. It replaced an earlier house which appears in the 1680s to have belonged to a man called Hoskinson, who was involved in the 1684 mutiny. At the time of Napoleon's captivity it was occupied by the town major, Major Charles Hodson (1779–1858) of the St Helena Regiment. He was well over six feet tall and referred to approvingly as 'Hercules' by Napoleon.[51] Hodson was an influential figure on the island, who until 1826 had also owned Maldivia. He had a sizeable mortgage on Oakbank House. This property later became the residence of the Melliss family, and then, in the last quarter of the 19th century, that of the Anglican bishop of St Helena.

Oakbank contributes 32 species to Melliss's 1875 list of plants. As will be seen in Table 9, in Grant's 1883 plant list Oakbank has 24 species, exceeding the 17 named plant species at Maldivia. These Oakland plants included St Helena rosemary, the North American burr oak, a stone pine and the Australian bottle brush.

TABLE 9
Plants at Oakbank listed by Grant, 1883

Scientific name	Common name
Magnolia fuscata	Magnolia
Mimosa australis	
Phylica polifolia syn. Ramoissima	Rosemary
Virgilia capensis	Sophora
Acacia verticillata	
Eucalyptus globulus	
Begonia glauca	
Serissa foetida	Stinkwood/snow rose
Eupatorium pallidum	
Chrysanthemum	Listed as camphor
Plumbago capensis	
Thunbergia alata	
Olea fragrans	Sweet olea
Banksia speciosa	Bottle brush
Poinsettia pulcherrima	
Quercus oliviformis	Mossycup [burr oak] RARE
Pinus pinea	Stone pine
Strelitzia capensis (reginae or alba?)	
Ixia monadelpha	
Ixia patens	
Trichonema ochroleucum	
Watsonia rosea	
Narcissus biflorus	
Ananassa sativa	Pineapple

The Briars

The Briars and its adjacent Pavilion are the houses famously associated with the hapless Balcombe family and their temporary guest, Napoleon. Two marquees were pitched at the Briars for Napoleon Bonaparte, one beside the Pavilion or summer house and another in the garden.

The Briars had been an East India Company yam plantation in the early 18th century. Like so many St Helenian properties, its ownership changed frequently from its first incarnation in 1678 as Parsley Bed Hill or Purslane. By 1739, it was called the Bryers. It was with the Balcombes' occupation from 1811 that its glory as a garden came into its own. As well as the Briars, other planters' houses which passed in and out of Company ownership or occupation included Bearcrofts/Rock Cottage, Cason's, Francis Plain and Unity Cottage (Society of Gentlemen).

The Briars possessed the open stretch of grassland in front of the property that was a feature of so many such residences on St Helena. There was also an avenue of trees which were not maintained and where individual trees were not replaced when they died, also an all-too-common aspect to St Helenian country houses. The shrubbery, garden and small arboretum were to the side and back of the house, a miniature version of what existed at Plantation House.

After the Balcombes, the land adjacent was used as a brewery. Moving back into Company hands in 1827, a commercial mulberry plantation was established in a forlorn attempt to create an island silk industry. That ended with the demise of the Company's authority over the island in the 1830s. The Briars passed through the hands of the famous island entrepreneur and trader Saul Solomon and then on to George Moss. By the early 1880s it was said:

> The grounds of this estate are very productive and contain thorn, cypress, Cape yew [yellowwood], Norfolk Island pine, black-fruited olive, wild olive, banyan, blackboy, cassia, acacia (Kaffir thorn), pineaster, cherimoya, mango, rose apple, Kei apple, peach, fig, wild fig, orange, lemon, pear, China gooseberry (a 3-cornered fruit) the only tree of its kind in the Island, guava, loquat, pomegranate, shaddock, mulberry, Bussorah date, and plantain trees, bottle brush, and flowers.[52]

The Briars ended up as the site of the Eastern Telegraph Company, which admirably maintained the Pavilion which Napoleon had occupied but allowed the rest of the old homestead and garden to fall into ruin.[53]

Oaklands

Further down the list of notable gardens on St Helena was Oaklands. Like so many of the old St Helena country houses, little is known about it. The reason for this generally is probably twofold. First, many of these houses changed ownership frequently somewhat like officers' houses in the Indian cantonments. Second, they had their heyday in the late 18th and early 19th centuries after which many of these old houses fell on hard times and deteriorated along with the fortunes of the island. In the case of Oaklands, the house was the home of the cantankerous Robert Leech during Napoleon's captivity and, after Leech's death in 1818, the home of David Kinnaird, the officer commanding the St Helena Artillery. By 1830, it was in the hands of Miss E. Leech.[54] In 1883 Oaklands was described as a fine residence 'with porch and good lawn, bordering which are two handsome stone pines, several eucalypti and hedges of pepper bushes. A neat flower garden is also to be observed in front of the house. This estate contains pineasters, oak, pear, coffee, and other trees.' By the 1930s, all the oak trees had gone.

Rock Rose

Also on Melliss's list of interesting gardens was Rock Rose in Deep Valley, built about 1783, once one of the great houses of St Helena with its fine St Helena ebony staircase. Its garden was noted for a giant Norfolk Island pine and its red, white and variegated camellias. It also possessed several 'fine eucalypti, Cape yews, oaks, Chili fir, white ash, evergreen oaks, willow (3 kinds), numerous chirimoyas, apples, rose apples, pears, plums, and fir trees. In these tall trees the white (sea) bird builds its nest and hatches its young!' The birds referred to were the fairy terns, which still often come inland to roost and nest, sheltered from the Atlantic gales. The Chilean pine or monkey muzzle (*Araucaria araucana*) at Rock Rose was possibly the monkey puzzle tree Joseph Hooker climbed on his visit to St Helena in the 1840s.

Terrace Knoll

Terrace Knoll was one of the great houses of St Helena, with an equally superb garden complete with conservatory. In Grant's plant list of 1883 it ranks second to Plantation House. Grant's comment on the property runs as follows:

> A little further on the fine residence Terrace Knoll, embosomed in coffee and other valuable trees, attracts the eye. A great improvement has been effected here by the Rev. J. C. LAMBERT, F.R.G.S., who has erected a Greenhouse and has already planted out 90 trees, including coffee, grapes, mulberries, &c., since he became proprietor. This enterprising resident is daily expecting a consignment of mangoes from India and an assortment of grapes from America, (Since writing this the grape cuttings have arrived and are thriving excellently well). having engaged the services of Mr. F. E. GRANT, of Boston, (who is only too willing to lend his valuable aid in advancing the material interests of his native home,) to superintend the selection and exportation. In the grounds of Terrace Knoll may be seen a very fine collection of the Lily tribe, gathered from all parts of the world, some handsome specimens of the indigenous 'Redwood,' now a very scarce tree, and one of the only two curious plants called 'Traveller's Joy' (Urania specosa) growing on the Island.[55]

Mount Pleasant

Overlooking Sandy Bay, Mount Pleasant was to be immortalised when Napoleon
and his entourage turned up on Sunday 4 October 1820 to have a picnic breakfast
on the lawn followed by a convivial encounter with the affable and island-born
Sir William Doveton and his family in the old farmhouse. Henry Russell described
it as 'quite an English box in an English garden' and having 'the air of a country
seat'. Russell talks of the house elsewhere in his account of the island as 'more
in the ordinary manner of the island, [Mount Pleasant] is built on the face of a
high steep ridge and stands upon a little terrace of turf of which, though the
residence may have been natural, the chief part seems to have been artificially
constrained'.[56]

Fairy Land

A once very attactive property, Fairy Land, became down at heel before being
eventually demolished. Situated rather remotely on the island, it was described
in 1882 as follows:

> Fairy Land, a beautiful spot, whence a pretty view of most of the several fine
> estates and groves, and fertile spots in Sandy Bay can be obtained. Fairy Land is
> well wooded and contains several handsome trees, among which are magnolias,
> camellias, a fine large eucalyptus about 90 feet high by 12 feet in circumference,
> Norfolk Island pines (2), stone pine, mimosas (numerous), willows (2 kinds),
> pineasters, Cape yew, thorn and other forest trees; also fruit trees—such as
> bergamot pear, common pear, peach, mulberry, &c., —bamboo and privet.
>
> A Dairy was erected on this estate some 30 years ago by the late Honble
> GEORGE W. EDWARDS, for several years Colonial Auditor of this Island, who
> also planted most of the trees along the walks (4), but it is out of repair. This
> must have been a pretty place a few years ago—in fact its beauty is but slightly
> tarnished even at the present day. Here may be seen the raspberry trailing
> along the ground with its red berries shining brightly in the rays of the morning
> sun, and excellent flowers. Having enjoyed a good view of this enchanting place
> and the delightfully romantic and rural scenery about it, the Tourist leaves
> Fairy Land.

West Lodge

A house which declined more rapidly after the Company's departure was West
Lodge. Mentioned three times in Melliss's 1875 list of plants, by 1877 it was
described by Isobel Gill as:

A gloomy, half-ruined and haunted house is West Lodge, but all around it is bright, and smiling vistas of wooded knolls and flower-clad dales stretch far away among the hills. Beautiful ferns embellish every nook of the half-wild garden, and here and there along the paths are stationed great camellia trees with a stately burden of crimson and white flowers.

To this she added significantly:

But this was only one of the many pretty country residences which we observed tenantless and in a state of ruin.[57]

But only a few years later we find Benjamin Grant writing the following about West Lodge:

West Lodge estate, which is enclosed by a wall and trees, and is 150 acres in extent. In this fine estate are to be seen apples, sweet oranges, pears, peaches, rose apples, handsome camellias (with red and white flowers), magnolias, white olives, Cape yews, oaks, pineasters, willows, and a fine cedar; also granadillas, privet, balm of Gilead, moon plant (numerous), bamboo, buddleia, hydrangea, cabbage rose, multiflora, heliotrope, fuchsia, and other flowers along the walks. Several dead pineasters are to be observed in the upper part; of West Lodge.[58]

Other gardens also existed, some merely for the lifetime of a particular occupant, others preserved over several generations. In the 1790s, a special garden belonged to Dr John Charles Dunn, who 'from the midst of rocks and stones has to the surprise of every person formed a Garden which is at once useful and ornamental to the Valley and that he still proceeds to further improvements undismayed by the trouble he has been at'. For his endeavours Dr Dunn was awarded a silver cup by the East India Company. He retired as head surgeon to the island in March 1814.

Looking back from the 1930s, Charles Kitching in his excellent typescript gazetteer on St Helena comments that 'the number of large houses still in occupation has decreased very considerably, but the ruins of those abandoned, and once the scenes of such generous hospitality, still stand as silent witness to vanished glories'.[59] Sadly, what there had been in the way of grand private gardens – and, indeed, more so, the arboreta which so frequently were to the rear of the house – have also gone, remembered only in contemporary and often over-dramatised prints.

11. Payment to Henry Porteous, East India Company gardener, 1793. As well as becoming superintendent of gardens and plantations, Porteous owned a large house beside the Castle Garden. The interior of the house was clean but rather poky, with small rooms that were rented out to Company officials, members of the armed forces and visitors to the island. Arthur Wellesley, the future Duke of Wellington, stayed here in 1805, as did Napoleon himself when he arrived on the island in 1815. The house was destroyed by fire in 1865, the gutted remains being demolished only in 1937.

© St Helena Archive

4

The St Helena Botanic Garden

The plant craze came early to St Helena. The intellectual plant craze that swept through Britain's ruling elite had a disproportionate impact on St Helena compared to most other colonial possessions because the island's population was divided between a peasantry and a gentry/officer class but had very little in the way of a middle class. Sadly and ironically, by the time that the middle class in Victorian Britain had begun embracing the plant craze, St Helena was in decline. Unlike the rest of the settler empire, few on the island maintained an enthusiasm for plants.[1]

The last quarter of the 18th century was a period of change in the relationship of the Company to the British establishment in London. The British public's attention was focused on the activities of the Company by the Regulation Act (1773), the East India Act or Pitt's India Act (1784) and the Warren Hastings trial (from

12. St Helena Botanic Gardens. In light pencil, Burchell marked the following plants on this sketch: bamboo; banyan (*Ficus benghalensis*); *Cocos nucifera* (coconut); cotton (3 plants); Datura metel (fastuosa) (Indian thornapple/devil's trumpet); olive (2 plants); Robina (species indecipherable), (*black locust tree*?); and on the wall the spectacular sea bean (*Entada gigas*). Drawn on 16 April 1810, the day Burchell resigned as St Helena's naturalist.

1788). But parallel with this was the new age of Enlightenment, bringing with it notions of defined imperial benevolence. Such benevolence was frequently seen in terms of agricultural improvement, moral rectitude and a dislike of enslavement. These phenomena created an ethos in the Company establishment at Leadenhall Street which was conducive to moderate and limited change.

Two caveats need to be made as regards such change in St Helena. First, the gentry on St Helena were either unwilling or incapable of reforming rapidly, especially while benefiting from the various direct and indirect subsidy systems on the island. Many were also, it must be said, not from the same rank in society as those who had embraced wholeheartedly the new ideas. Furthermore, the harsh slave-owning set-up on St Helena was not typical of other East India Company-controlled territories. Studies which have looked at the nexus between imperial governance (including Kew Gardens) and the plant world in this period have included books by Lucile Brockway, Richard Drayton, Richard Grove, Donal McCracken and David Mackay.[2] Though this late Georgian and Regency period has been seen as something of a golden age in the island's history, there were problems and tensions on the island that were exacerbated by a serious drought, alcoholism, a decline in military disciple and a mutiny. Beatson recorded, 'The roads leading to the country were often stewed with drunk men, laying insensible, both white and black.' The anonymous note announcing the 1811 army mutiny on St Helena specified, 'if they [Council] do not immeadatly soply this garrison with liquor and provisions, in the same manner has Governor Brooks did ...'[3]

But the key factor was the Company's representative on the island. St Helena has tended to succeed when it had an active and enlightened governor. As will be seen, Robert Brooke was certainly both. Perhaps he is best remembered for his attempts to improve the treatment of the island's enslaved population, as well as taking the important step of banning any future importing of enslaved individuals.[4] In establishing the St Helena Botanic Garden, Brooke was influenced by both Joseph Banks at Kew and Colonel Robert Kyd, who in 1787 was also establishing the botanic garden at Calcutta.[5] Without Brooke, it is doubtful whether the botanic garden project would have got off the ground.

The St Helena Planters' Society

It is no real coincidence that the St Helena Botanic Garden was established in 1787, the same year as *Curtis's Botanical Magazine* began publication in Britain. The Royal Academy of Arts was a mere nine years old, and the Linnean Society would soon be established in 1788. Intellectual endeavour, both in the arts and the sciences, was being firmly established among the upper classes. It was hardly surprising then that there was an impact in the colonies, not least in the establishment over the next few decades of agricultural and horticultural societies.

According to Francis Duncan, the island's first historian, the St Helena Planters Society emerged in 1787/1788 and as such was a pioneer in emulating what was coming out of Europe. This was exactly when the island's botanic garden was being established. Both were very much a reflection of St Helena's position in the trans-global activities of the East India Company. But it also reflected the quality of officers and officials present at that time on the island. The establishment of a similar society was discussed on the French island of Île de France (Mauritius) but this came to nothing, though that island had a botanic garden established in 1768, with origins dating back to as early as 1737.

Of St Helena, Duncan writes:

> The only attempt towards a more general improvement of the island was made about seventeen years ago [1787/1788], when some of the inhabitants formed themselves into a society for this laudable purpose. The subscribers to this scheme were to contribute, according to their circumstances, towards raising a fund; the object of which, was to excite a spirit of industry, and an ardour for botanical experiments. For by the distribution of small pecuniary rewards, and honorary premiums, it was their purpose to advance and encourage planting, gardening, farming, and every sort of improvement, of which the grounds are capable.

The society initially had 53 members, including Governor Brooke. They were divided into two classes or ranks of membership. One could be a life member, or a first-class member paying an annual subscription, or a second-class member paying one shilling (1/-) a week (£2-16-0 a year). Life membership was a hefty £50, which, as the society did not survive, was a bad investment. There were 22 life members, 24 annual first-class members and 6 second-class members. The secretary was the energetic Dr David Kay (1749–1833), who arrived on the island in 1774 and was the island's surgeon and later secretary to the governor.[6] What is significant is that 42 per cent of the membership held military rank, albeit some of those as members of the local St Helena Regiment.

One gets the distinct feeling that without pressure from the military and civilian establishment on the island, most planters would have been quite content to meander along much as usual, a fact picked up on by both Joseph Banks and, especially, Captain Cook when the *Endeavour* anchored off Jamestown from 1 to 5 May 1771. Indeed, Cook got into trouble with the locals for being quoted as implying that they did not even use that essential garden tool, the wheelbarrow. The blunt-speaking Yorkshireman also described Jamestown as having ill-built houses and resembling a 'large trench'. On his second visit, between 15 and 21 May 1775, it is said that several wheelbarrows were placed pointedly outside his lodging house.[7] However, Cook was wined and dined by Governor Skottowe and his wife Margaret, a Greentree from the island. This was in part because James Cook's father had worked for John Skottowe's back home in Yorkshire in Great Ayton. Cook subsequently recanted and praised the island.

Certainly the much-vaunted Planters Society soon became in reality Governor Brooke and Porteous, his superintendent of improvements,[8] under a convenient nomenclature.

Robert Brooke

The link between the Royal Botanic Gardens, Kew and St Helena was given a firm foundation by a relatively unknown civilian governor, Daniel Corneille, who served in the post from 1782 to 1787, a period which included the 1783 army mutiny on the island. Before becoming governor, Corneille was the lieutenant–governor under Governor John Skottowe (1764–1782). Skottowe in his turn had been lieutenant-governor under Governor Charles Hutchinson (1747–1764), who in turn had been lieutenant-governor to Governor David Dunbar (1744–1747). Such a succession plan meant there was great continuity in the running of the island, perhaps too much so.

Daniel Corneille sent plants from St Helena to Sir Joseph Banks, Kew's effective director. Corneille also introduced coffee, cinnamon, clove plants and various trees and shrubs to the island.[9] The first sack of St Helena coffee beans was sent to the directors of the Company in 1792, the date that should be taken as the real birth of the St Helena coffee industry.[10] Despite these progressive moves, in reality the botanic garden was successfully established and survived its early years thanks to the enlightened 14-year governorship of Lieutenant-Colonel Robert Brooke (1787–1802), an unusual man who had a see-saw career.

Brooke was born in Rantavan House near Mullagh in County Cavan, Ireland in 1744.[11] His father Robert was an artist, his Uncle Henry – a 'literary patriot' and friend of Dean Swift – was the first editor of the *Public Register* which became the *Freeman's Journal*, and his cousin Charlotte (d.1793) was a literary figure whose achievements included translations from Irish manuscripts. Her most noted work was *Reliques of Irish poetry* (1789).[12] Brooke joined the East India Company's Bengal Army in 1764 and served with distinction as an officer under Robert Clive and then

Warren Hastings in India, where he had for a period been in charge of Corah. He made a name for himself in the campaign against the Mahrattas.

Returning to Ireland, in 1775 Robert Brooke married Anna Maria Mapletoft, the widow of William Wynn. She was the daughter of Rev. Robert Mapletoft, an assistant chaplain to the Company in Calcutta.[13]

The following year he bought Killybeggs House and 88 acres in the townland of Curryhills in County Kildare. Near there, in the 1780s, he established the model village of Prosperous, where he launched an ambitious but unsuccessful business manufacturing cotton. As the *Asiatic Journal* was to note, 'the means of Captain Brooke were not co-existensive with his benevolent views'.[14] This failure necessitated Brooke's return to the service of the East India Company. In September 1786 he published a pamphlet defending his record. It was entitled *A letter from Mr. Brooke to an Honourable Member of the House of Commons*. At the conclusion of his defence, he added the following:

> P.S. since I wrote the above, I have been appointed by the Court of Directors, Lieutenant Governor of St. Helena; this will just afford that part of the family I take with me an Honorable subsistence. I would have obtained my rank again in India, but that I had struggled too long there, I leave part of my family behind, depending upon the generous support of my Country.[15]

All this did not bode particularly well for the island of St Helena. But Brooke turned out to be arguably the finest governor the island has ever had, before or since. He was on the island from May 1787 until his departure due to ill health in March 1801, nearly 14 years later.[16] Anna accompanied him to St Helena, where their infant son was born in March 1788 but may have died shortly afterwards. In August 1790, Richard Wogan Brooke was born to the couple, followed by John Michael Brooke in September 1792. James Kelly states that the Brookes had two sons and a daughter.[17]

In the early 1780s, Robert Brooke had been a benefactor of the Dublin Society, from 1820 the Royal Dublin Society, during his aspirational, though doomed, attempt to introduce cotton manufacturing into Ireland following his successful career in India. He was therefore very familiar with the activities of such an improvement society.[18] It was also the era of Grattan's parliament and colonial nationalism in Ireland, so Brooke was also well aware of the thinking of a settler population. As early as 1785, when Brooke was still in his native Ireland, a proposal was being discussed in the Irish House of Commons to establish a public botanic garden in or near Dublin. Though the Dublin Society Botanic Gardens was not formally established at Glasnevin until 1796, the idea of such an institution was well established during Brooke's time in Ireland.[19] The Trinity College Botanic Garden at Ballsbridge did not follow until 1806.[20] So Brooke was ahead of Dublin in his endeavour, in establishing on St Helena three acclimatisation gardens at different height locations:

High Peak (High vegetation zone)
Plantation House (Middle vegetation zone)
Jamestown (Lower/coastal vegetation zone)

Founding the botanic garden

The Jamestown garden was some two acres in extent and was soon being referred to as the St Helena Botanic Garden. At the top or south end of High Street was the Canister, an old army storehouse with the famous peepul auction tree outside.[21] To the left forked out Cock Street, now named Napoleon Street. To the right of the Canister ran Southwark Street, which now has the utilitarian name Market Street. The botanic garden was up Southwark Street on the left beyond a military barracks. This area, which included the hospital, had once been part of the Maldivia estate but by the 1780s was largely wasteland.

The St Helena government was involved in developing the garden from the start. In a detailed report on the island written in 1792, Governor Brooke recorded:

And it was observed that the Grounds both below and above the Barracks were rocky and uneven a receptacle for filth and of course noisome and disagreeable, to obviate this and if possible to get the Hospital a supply of Vegetables a plan was fallen upon to give the Soldiers condemned for Petty Crimes the option of working in lieu of being flogged; by their labour Gardens have been formed on these Grounds a parade has been made opposite the Officers Barracks, and a space has been cleared on which Houses have been built, in short the upper part of the Valley begins to wear a pleasing appearance and proof has been afforded that grounds deemed utterly incapable of vegetation can be made wonderfully productive, this Discovery has led to further improvements and Individuals have begun to form Gardens and improve the Grounds on their own account.[22]

The records show that in 1787 £64-2-9 was expended to 'make a Garden above the Barracks'. This was the new botanic garden, which stretched from what is now a public school, then a military barracks, up to and including what is referred to as the Brick House, a former nurses' home. This is just below the strangely shaped house which was the home of that admirable and only island-born governor, Hudson Ralph Janisch.

The date for the establishment of the garden is sometimes given as 1792,[23] when Captain Bligh was at the island with his famous cargo of breadfruit. The matter of starting a garden was linked to the West Indies, but started earlier. On 6 February 1785 Alexander Anderson pressed the British Secretary of State for War, Sir George Yonge, to encourage the British East India Company to establish a botanic garden on St Helena. Then on 13 January 1787 Colonel Robert Kyd in Bengal, writing to Sir Joseph Banks, also advocated a botanic garden for the island. As Richard Grove has pointed out, this was prior to Kyd becoming superintendent of the proposed new botanic garden at Calcutta. Grove also points out that Kyd approached Patrick Russell, the naturalist at Madras, for support for the idea of a halfway station for plants on St Helena. On 31 March 1787, Yonge was able to confirm in a letter to Anderson that he had succeeded in prevailing upon the East India Company to establish the garden on St Helena. He also stated that he had given instructions for 'seeds and plants of all kinds which may be useful in medicine and commerce to be brought and cultivated therein and to [have them] from thence conveyed in a favourable state to St Vincent'.[24] So from the start, the idea was that St Helena should be a staging post for plants, especially to supply the West Indies.

In June 1787, Kyd advised Banks that a deposit of European plants should be made at St Helena. Banks had been on St Helena for four days in early May 1771, when he complained about the lack of fruit and vegetables available to ships and the 'extravagant prices' for what articles were for sale. He was also scathing about the local gentry, denouncing them as lazy and exploitative both of their enslaved labourers and visitors to the island. Now Banks actively supported the idea of this halfway house, making the East India Company hierarchy amenable to the idea. The excitement generated by the Bligh expedition to Tahiti, which sailed in December 1787, was part of this halfway house plan.[25]

⧼⧽ Staging post for the West Indies ⧼⧽

In Robert Brooke, Joseph Banks had a governor who was only too keen to assist in setting up a functioning botanic garden. Indeed, Brooke invited Banks to send his plant collector Francis Masson 'to explore our Cabbage tree lands (as we call them). I think he may find some plants worthy of notice'.[26]

Tradition has it that the botanic garden was laid out by soldiers who had been found guilty of various misdemeanours and were given the choice of undertaking labour for the Company or being flogged.[27] Thomas Brooke, Robert's nephew, writing in 1806, confirms this, but as mentioned above points out that the work these soldiers carried out extended to much of the upper part of the Jamestown. Brooke noted:

> By the labour obtained in this manner, tracts of waste ground, offensive to the eye, and receptacles of filth, were converted into a handsome parade for the soldiers, and into gardens, highly ornamental to the town, and beneficial to the hospital.[28]

This is confirmed by an interesting short account by Surgeon Arthur Smyth in 1789, written on his return from New South Wales where he had gone with the First Fleet. We know from this that the botanic garden was established by then. Writing about Thursday 20 May Smyth observed:

> There is one singular circumstance deserves notice, as it reflects great merit on the Governor [Brooke] & at once serves to show his great biass to Humanity to Delinquents as well as regard for improving this little Island – it is a large Garden just above Town (wh they emphatically nominate Botany Bay) wh in its original state was little more than barren Rocks wh here & there a small patch of soil, & it is now a very handsome & fertile Garden, & the work was begun & is carrying on by Soldiers or others who have committed faults wh in the Army are punished by flogging – They are tried & if convicted to receive such a No. of lashes as their Crime merit wh punishment they can evade by working in this Garden, some for a fortnight others for a week 3 days etc etc accordg to the heignousness of their offence & if they quit their work but a single day before the Expiration of their term they receive the lashes wh were first ordered them.[29]

The site of this 'Botany Bay' botanic garden is sometimes confusing because of the ambiguity in many documents as to what is being referred to – the old Company garden beside the fort or the new garden further up the valley, which came to be known as the botanic garden. The two were, in fact, one and the same institution. Indeed, the Castle Garden was the primary garden, and the botanic garden was for a time essentially an extension half a kilometre up the valley.[30] However, as mentioned in a previous chapter, this matter is complicated by Lieutenant R. P. Read's 1817 plan of St Helena which, while marking the Maldivia Gardens, places the Botanic Gardens behind Plantation House, the governor's out of town residence. There is no doubt that several governors did pay special attention to the Plantation House garden at the cost of those in Jamestown. Perhaps if St Helena had had only one botanic garden that institution might have been more successful.

One of the major problems with these gardens was the water supply. Both gardens in Jamestown were serviced by the stream, or Run as it was and is still called, flowing down at the north side of the steep Jamestown Valley. The gardens in the upper valley, especially Maldivia and the new garden, obviously siphoned off water to the detriment of the lower Castle Garden and that of the lower town inhabitants. As early as October 1787, a system was introduced by Brooke to try and ensure that enough water was supplied to gardens and households in the lower valley so that not all the water went to those properties which the stream passed in the upper part of Jamestown.

ᠵᠥᡒ Layout of Jamestown's 'Botany Bay' ᠵᠥᡒ

We know that in the 1830s St Helena Botanic Garden stretched 342 feet [104 m] along the length of Market Street. The boundary at the Run would have been slightly longer as it curved. The garden's lower end between Market Street and the Run was 140 feet [43 m] wide, with the upper end narrower at 112 feet [34 m]. That would make the garden about one acre [0.4 hectare] at that date. The original garden was, however, larger, with at least part of the sizeable garden attached to Palm Villa above, as well as part of what became a parade ground below, having fallen within the original garden. The layout was complicated by the drop in the level from the road down to the Run. To obviate this, it was terraced with a steep flight of 12 stone steps leading from the upper level to the lower in the middle of the gardens, and a second flight of steps at the lowest coastal-side of the gardens.

The botanic garden was on two parallel levels running down the valley, each with a network of paths with square blocks for plants. Later a stout retaining wall ran between these two sections. This appears to have been constructed during the curatorship of William Burchell (1806–1810). This layout saved the gardens during the two disastrous floods of 1873 and 1878 when a torrent came down the Run, destroying only part of the lower section of the gardens, the upper section being protected by the retaining wall. A tall external wall, possibly in the region of 12 to 15 feet [3.6 to 4.6 m] in height, closed off the gardens from Southwark (Market) Street. The entire garden was enclosed with a wall, including down at the Run. A large iron gate of equal height existed at the bottom end of the Market Street wall. There was also possibly a second entrance from Market Street just before the Palm Villa property. A large, covered iron water-tank was positioned near the Market Street entrance at the lower end of the gardens.[31]

13. Old botanic gardens wall and street planting in Jamestown, *c.*1910. Street planting in Jamestown started about the mid-18th century. Here in Southwark (Market) Street were the sacred peepul trees and a few Indian fig trees. On the left is the old botanic gardens wall, which was more than four metres high, with well-established trees behind. Street lighting dates from 1888, with each lamp being run on paraffin.

Provided by Donal P. McCracken

Brooke showed a keen interest in exchanging plants with East India Company officials in India, and in particular corresponded with the surgeon-general of Madras (Chennai), Dr James Anderson (1738–1809), who in 1778 established the botanic gardens near Fort St George in Madras.[32] On 19 February 1790 Anderson sent Brooke 'wine chests filled with poorsa Ellapa Jaunbolifera mango Jack Guiava and custard-apple trees'. The 'Kew Nopal' [*Opuntia cacti*], which one day would become an invasive nuisance on the island, was also sent by Anderson for experiment in Brooke's new botanic garden. Seeds of 'Mimosa Odoratissima Mimosa Nilotica Mimosa Catechu and Hibiscus Populneus' followed from Madras as did wine chests filled with young plants of the following for the company's gardener to plant out:

> Sapindus saponaria, Aingi, Laurus ginnamon (of Ceylon), Billi, Gardenia enneandria, Dyospyros ebenum, Tunbali, Malli bundi, Artocarpus integrifolia or Jack, Gossypium or cotton of the finest grain, Kulki, Bignonia adoratissima, Bassia Longifolia or [??] Tecktonia or Indian Oak, Banyan bearing the largest Fig, Tamarind Crescentia Cujete or Calabash, Milla Poindoo a strong Creeper used as Rope, Nerium Tinctorium, Thespesia Populnea and three sorts of Mulberries.

Other plants despatched from Madras to St Helena included seeds of *Caesalpina sappan*, *Giulandina bonducella*, *Pterocarpus santalinus*, Venga and *Mimosa Madraspatensis* [*M. latispinosa*?]. These last were promised to be covered with 'red Lac insects, and of the wodier with live insects of white Lac, as well as Silkworms'.[33] In 1792, however, Governor Brooke recorded that both mulberry and peach trees were susceptible to insect attack.[34] Another insect species successfully introduced via Dr Anderson was the cochineal beetle, though no carmine production is recorded as having been successful. Of guinea grass, Governor Brooke wrote to Anderson on 13 April 1791 that while the ordinary grass 'is burnt up', the guinea grass at High Knoll looked 'green and beautiful'.[35]

Sir Joseph Banks was kept up to date on this supply of plants to St Helena from India.[36] Banks was also full of praise for what Brooke was doing on the island. From 1787 up to 1807, there is a record of plants coming into St Helena, mainly from Kew, India, and through Robert Lance at the company's factory at Canton, China. Indeed, it was said that Chinese fruit trees grew very well on St Helena.[37] Plants were also sent from St Helena via the Company in London to Kew Gardens and St Vincent Botanic Gardens, which was the oldest British colonial botanic garden, dating from 1765.[38]

In 1792 a pile of 'bad steel' bars, which had been dumped about 20 years previously, were used as railings to add to the appearance of the Company garden. These were replaced with a wall topped with more elegant railings 'at considerable expense' in 1821, when a proclamation decreed that cart drivers were forbidden from drawing up or leaving their carts in the street opposite the garden, under penalty of a five shilling (5/-) fine. Moreover, public sales were prohibited 'under the Almond Tree, or near the said iron Railings'.[39]

A suggestion in March 1792 that run-off water from Chubb's Spring in the valley be diverted into the Company garden was met with obstruction from Mr Newton, the plumber, who said that 'it was impossible to do it, and that it never could be done and that he believes it never has been done [26; 1792] '. Nonetheless, the record volumes for this period in the St Helena Archives show that other work was being undertaken on the garden beside the fort. These included:

30 September 1791: (£2-6-6) work done to the garden (30 September 1791).

26 April 1792: (£5-8-0) 100 days labourers' work at Fort garden at one shilling a day.

15 October 1792: (£4-15-0) work done in the Fort garden plus £5-2-0 for 34 garden rakes, and 18 shillings and 4 pence for four garden shears.

31 December 1792 [During Captain Bligh's visit]: carpenter (£25), mason (£30), and a plumber (£37).[40]

And an additional sum of £10-19-6 was granted for work on the Fort Garden including 40 days smiths (£3); 3 days overseers (6 shillings); 6½ days mason (6 shillings); 5 days carpenter (7 shillings and 6 pence); 6½ days sawyers (9 shillings and 9 pence); and 126½ days labourers (£6-6-6).[41]

Despite the expenditure of 1792, when yet another of Banks's protégés, Captain Edward Cumming, visited the island bringing with him some plants from arid regions sent by Banks, Cumming found the St Helena Botanic Garden in 'a languishing condition'. However, this would change shortly.[42]

In August Brooke wrote a 32-page report on St Helena. This included the following passage on Jamestown:

the Private Houses and Lodging Houses are in general neat and convenient and fitted up in the European Stile, on the whole the buildings intermixed with Trees have a pretty appearance from the Bay ... And it was observed that the Grounds both below and below the Barracks were rocky and uneven a receptacle for filth and of course noisome and disagreeable, to obviate this and if possible to get

> the Hospital a supply of Vegetables a plan was fallen upon to give the soldiers condemned of petty crimes the option of working instead of being flogged: by their labour, Gardens have been formed in these Grounds a Parade has been made opposite the Officers Barracks, and a space has been cleared on which houses have been built; in short the upper part of the Valley begins to wear a pleasing appearance and proof has been afforded that grounds esteemed utterly incapable of vegetation can be made wonderfully productive, this Discovery had led to further Improvements and individuals have begun to form Gardens and improve the Grounds on their own Account.

Henry Porteous

The first regular Company gardener mentioned in records is Thomas Allen who was employed from at least 1786 to 1787, but paid only about £25 a year.[43] It should be noted that this appointment was during the governorship of Daniel Corneille, who had an interest in botanical and agricultural matters.

The gardener who was to make his mark on St Helena was Henry Porteous (1762–1819). Described as 'a person well skilled in Horticulture', he was appointed gardener in May 1787, the month that Governor Brooke landed, with Allen also continuing until the end of that year. Some reports say Porteous came as a gardener from India. He was certainly paid well for a gardener, with a salary of £90 a year, substantially more than Allen, an indication of the growing importance placed on the role of the garden. Governor Brooke was commended by the British East India Company for this appointment, and by January 1791 Joseph Banks was praising Porteous to the Company's directors. That year Kew received 'four more chests of trees and plants ... they are mostly natives of the island and reared in the manner you directed'.[44]

On 1 April 1788, Porteous wrote to Governor Brooke presenting his first and only known report on what he termed his 'Department, Botanical as well as Agricultural'. Part of this ran as follows:

> In executing the business I was directed to have three objects in view, at the same time that I received positive injunctions to put the Colony to as little expense as possible. These objectives were, in the Garden in the Valley to rear plenty of vegetables for the Hospital and try the productions of the warm climate of India. At the Plantation House to attempt an inlarged System of Cultivation for to assist the Yam Plantation in feeding the Honble Company's Slaves, and at the High Peak where the moist and cold atmosphere seems favourable to try all the productions of Europe.

To enable me to execute all this at little or no expense, I have always been provided with as many of the Honble Company's Slaves as could be spared, assisted with the labour of those Europeans who were permitted to work instead of receiving the Punishment allotted by a Court Martial for petty crimes. I have also made good use of the Honble Company's Oxen trained by Order for that purpose.

Conformable to my instructions I am now naturalising all the trees and Shrubs which come from India in the Garden in James's Valley when in a short time I trust there will be a fine collection, as those already procured and planted grew very well as the Mangosteen, Mango tree, Baseen Plantain Jambo Malac Coffee etc but We soon hope to propagate a much greater varietys of trees and shrubs here, as the Soil and Climate seem so peculiarly well adapted to eastern productions. The Garden which consists of about 2 Acres of Ground now nearly in a state of perfect Cultivation was ten Months ago to all appearance nothing but a Mass of rocks and Stones laying confusedly one over the other so that the change already accomplished makes a pleasing difference in the appearance of the Valley above the Town. Vegetables begin to grow luxuriously, The Hospital has just commenced a receipt of some benefit from this place which will soon I think be as well provided with all kinds of wholesome roots and Grasses as could be wished.[45]

Porteous established and ran the botanic garden, which was also a vegetable allotment for the hospital. He grew yams and potatoes at Plantation House to feed the Company's enslaved population, at the Company's Sandy Bay plantation he raised more yams, and at the High Peak garden, where insect attack was less of a problem, he raised 400 stone pine and Scotch fir seedlings, as well as experimenting with growing root crops and vegetables including mangel-wurzel. As early as June 1790, Porteous was complaining to Banks that he was unable to pay much attention to botany because of 'his duties at a distance from the Botanic Garden'.[46] Be that as it may, Porteous' appointment certainly had an impact. Of Plantation House, Governor Brooke wrote in 1792, 'the Company having sent out a Gardener on purpose the place begins to improve fast, and there are already collected on this spot a greater variety of Trees, Plants and flowers of various Climates than perhaps can be found in any other situation of equal extent'.[47]

At various times Porteous was described by different titles such as Botanist or Gardener. Then in 1808 John Mason, the paymaster on the island, was given the following instruction:

I am directed by the Board to impress upon you Mr Porteous's name is not in future to stand on the books as Gardener; the designation of his appointment being changed to 'Superintendent of the companys Lands & Inspector of Fences' at a Salary of £200 per annum.[48]

The pressure of work was exacerbated by Porteous himself, who combined his onerous job with keeping a large and successful boarding house adjacent to the Company fort garden. In 1787, we also find him marking out and surveying 12 acres (4.8 ha) of Clough's Plain to be planted with trees because of the lack of firewood in the settlement. It was later said (in 1817) that 'Mr Porteous knows nothing of farming', but he was certainly involved in the Company's farming enterprise. We know very little about him personally, save that he kept his job when many did not, even though he was no stranger to disputes on the island. He assisted and sometimes went on botanising trips with any botanists who turned up on the island, such as Francis Masson (May 1795). Later, as the king's botanist at the Cape, Masson provided the guinea grass from the Cape which grew luxuriantly at Plantation House.[49]

Porteous married the 21-year-old islander Mary Knipe on 15 June 1808. He was then 47.[50] and it was his second marriage; his first wife, Mary Goudy, had died in May 1805. This first marriage had produced two daughters, Sarah and Mary. The second marriage produced James Edward (born April 1809), Henry William (July 1811) and William Bevill (July 1813). Henry and William both married daughters of Baron von Ludwig (Magdalena and Geertruyda), the famed owner of the three-acre (1.2 ha) Ludwig's-Burg private botanic garden in Kloof Street, Cape Town.[51]

Porteous first appeared on the St Helena government payroll in 1787 and was still receiving payments 31 years later in 1818, having held several government positions. In 1818, his salary was £500 per annum. He died on 23 June 1819, aged 58.[52] He was succeeded as superintendent of the Company's lands by A. A. Seale.[53]

෴ Maldivia ෴

The link between the Maldivia plantation and the St Helena Botanic Garden was very close, and at times in the 1790s they were probably practically undistinguishable, with plants being laid out in either garden depending upon space and circumstance. From this upper valley location, some plants were sent on to the West Indies or to Kew. These included sea poison tree (*Barringtonia speciosa* [*B. asiatica*]).[54] We also know that tree ferns were prepared for shipment. In 1791, a proposal was made that part of the Maldivia garden should be rented out for a year under strict conditions as a money earner. It also appears that some of this land was sold for building.[55] It was also proposed that the walks and trees of the garden part not used as allotments be retained and opened to the public. The allotments would produce a profit that could assist the island's Widows Fund. However Governor Brooke felt that any profit should be returned to maintain the gardens:

> a pleasant place for strangers to walk and drink Tea in, a nursery for plants from Warm Climates & assists in spreading useful ones on the island, or sending Curious ones home etc and the Experience of keeping it to the Company would never exceed 20 or 25 Pounds an annum.

On 22 September 1794, it was recorded that the yam plantations at Maldivia were to be rented out.[56] As will be seen, 46 years later the portion of the Maldivia garden devoted to leisure was again under threat.

໌↴ Captain Bligh's 'floating garden' ໌↴

In December 1792, Captain William Bligh arrived at St Helena from Tahiti, on his second and more successful voyage to fetch breadfruit for experimental introduction to the West Indies, where it was hoped it to provide a cheap and nourishing food source for the enslaved population. Bligh had two ships, the 406-ton sloop *Providence* and its 110-ton tender HMS *Assistant*, under the command of Lieutenant Nathaniel Portlock. Both ships were laden with plants, together forming a 'floating garden'. The authorities at St Helena had been forewarned a whole four years earlier that a ship had been sent to the South Seas to gather breadfruit and other plants which might be of use in the West Indies as well as being of interest to Kew Gardens. Writing to Governor Brooke on 31 December 1788, Sir Joseph Banks had said:

> She [HMS *Bounty*] had orders to leave you with some of all her usefull plants & in return I trust that you will order some of all such as you have & which are likely to be Either usefull to the West Indian Island or acceptable to his Majesties Botanic Garden at Kew.[57]

The famous mutiny on the *Bounty* had occurred on 28 April 1789 and it was not until 2 August 1791 that Captain Bligh, still favoured by Sir Joseph Banks, set out a second time to finish the task. It was on his return from this adventure in Tahiti that Bligh arrived off St Helena. Once again the governor had been advised that plants from the island must be collected to be shipped on the onward voyage to the West Indies.

Bligh was at St Helena from 17 December 1792 until 23 January 1793, having been at sea for the previous ten weeks. The visit is famous for his donating perhaps about 500 young breadfruit plants, which were intended, as they were in the West Indies, to provide a cheap food crop and bring economic prosperity to the island. It is worth noting that the botanic garden on St Vincent also received plants from this second voyage.

From the following entry in Captain Bligh's log, we know that Bligh's plants were taken to the new botanic garden at the top of the town:

> On the morning of the 24th we began to land the plants. A number of negroes carried the pots on their heads to the Botanic Garden which is about 2 miles distant from the beach; and on returning they brought back in the same manner the plants that Dr. Anderson had got ready for His Majesty's Garden at Kew.[58]

That same day Governor Brooke, on behalf of the East India Company, acknowledged the following as having been donated to the island:[59]

10 pots and 1 tub of bread fruit plants very fine
12 pots of bread fruit sickly
2 pots containing 2 plants of avoes/apples
1 pot containing 4 plants of rattah/chesnut
2 pots containing 5 plants of ayah/jambo
1 pot containing 1 plant of mattee/trees
1 pot containing 4 plants of ettow
2 pots containing 2 plants of peach, besides roots

In addition to these 31 pots were 9 pots of plants from Timor making a total of 40 pots landed. The Timor plants included:

1 pot containing 4 plants of nanche/soursop
1 pot containing 1 plant of lemon/china
1 pot containing 2 plants of jambo mare
1 pot containing 4 plants of jambo armiriah
1 pot containing 2 plants of mango
1 pot containing 2 plants of Penang/beetlenut
1 pot containing 2 plants of long pepper
1 pot containing 2 plants of black pepper
1 pot containing 1 buhgnna kanana

14. Burchell's sketch of *Calla ethiopica* [*Zantedeschia aethiopica*], 18 October 1809. The arum lily was, for a period, the national flower of the island. It was introduced from the Cape and has been a feature of damp habitats on St Helena since at least the 1770s.

We know that 'the principal plants' Bligh donated were transported inland to grow at Plantation House.[60] Major Robson, the lieutenant-governor, and William Wrangham, the first member of the island's council, were also each given a breadfruit plant. In a gushing letter to Captain Bligh thanking George III for this benevolence, the island's governing council commented on the 'Wonder and Delight to Contemplate a Floating Garden'. Governor Brooke supplied Bligh with 'all such Plants and Trees from this island as they wishes for'. In reply the following day, Bligh commented, 'May you live to see a happy result of the labours to serve the Island with the inestimable Fruits.'[61]

Because the governor of St Helena had been forewarned of Captain Bligh's arrival and cargo, and of Banks's expectations, he had instructed Porteous to collect 'infant' plants from the island which might be of worth or have ornamental value in the West Indies or at Kew Gardens. In a letter written to the board of directors of the East India Company on 24 December 1792, Governor Brooke mentioned that the trees were planted out under the 'Directions and advice of Captain Bligh and His Majesty's and the Honble Company's Botanists [Christopher Smith and James Wiles]'. Brooke also states that plants and trees from the island have been supplied to Captain Bligh. A short list of nine plants from St Helena for HMS *Providence* survives in the Kew archives:[62]

Fern trees	4 plants
Camellia japonica fl. Albo	1 plant
Lycium japonicum fl. Pleno	1 plant
China orange	1 plant
Plant from China	1 plant
Plant	1 plant

This is an interesting example of St Helena being the resting place and sometimes place of exchange for exotics from the East, brought in by the Company's ships.

As a footnote to this famous episode, within a few years the breadfruit disappeared completely from St Helena and certainly did not become a staple diet, a failure repeated in the West Indies. But another of Bligh's plants, the Tahiti sago palm, caused great interest at Plantation House when Mydiddee and Pappo, two Tahitians who had accompanied Bligh on his voyage north, used the plant's root to prepare a sago pudding for Robert Brooke.[63]

With Bligh's departure, work continued on the new garden, as the botanic garden was still sometimes called, and various sums were spent on the site in the 1793–1794 period. These included £5-3-6 in March 1793 and another, much larger, sum that year of £148-12-7. This was at a time when the Fort Garden down the valley received a one-off grant of only £20-4-6.[64] Professor Cronk states 'the magnificent Indian figs (*Ficus* sp.) below the present hospital in Jamestown still mark the location of the botanic garden'.[65] No doubt these were planted about this time.

ᔰ The work force ᔰ

On 24 February 1792 Governor Brooke issued 42 articles of law relating to the ownership of enslaved labourers on St Helena, of which 19 related to their treatment.[66] Article 39 took the important step of banning the importing of enslaved individuals to St Helena. This enlightened act began a long, slow process of abolishing enslavement on the island. Of the seven botanic gardens run by the East India Company, St Helena was the only one where using enslaved labourers was usual, though such a system was also in use in some of the government botanic gardens in the British Crown Colonies of the West Indies. Punishment labour duty for soldiers on St Helena seems to have been relatively short-lived but soldiers were used in Governor Beatson's time (1808–1813) as labourers on public works, receiving a shilling (1/–) a day on top of their army pay. Later on, convict and indentured labour was common across the 120 botanic gardens of the Victorian British empire, with convicts actually living in Hobart Botanic Gardens in Tasmania.[67] Indigenous cheap or indentured labour was frequently employed. In Natal, for example, both Zulu labourers and indentured Indian labourers were employed in the 1870s and 1880s. At the time of the Anglo–Zulu war, in 1879, all the African labourers vanished from Durban Botanic Gardens, slipping away to join the army of King Cetshwayo.

Like many colonial gardeners, Porteous moved in and out of the governor's favour. This is perhaps because he appears to have had fingers in many pies and his name appears more than once in the endless bickering and disputes which affected the white settler population.[68] After Brooke's decision to send to England various pots containing trees and shrubs was stymied, as most of the plants died before being transferred to a ship, the governor suggested that the plants had been 'taken up too soon after the bad seasons, or not a good time of year'. Not to be defeated, Brooke set about the task anew and it was recorded that 'Mr Porteous is taking new measures for this purpose'.[69]

Porteous was more than a gardener, however. He actively imported plants and seeds from the Cape Colony, and in March 1794 he was reimbursed the substantial sum of £40 for this endeavour.[70] In a travel account published in 1819 in the *Asiatic Journal*, Eleanor Reid recalled her visit to St Helena, mentioning Porteous' collecting endeavours on the west coast of Africa as well as his home on St Helena:

> On the same day the Captain [Reid] had the pleasure to see his old friend and shipmate, Mr H. Porteous, the Company's botanist, who had accompanied him to the Coast of Guinea, when sent thither by the present governor in 1792. This gentleman insisted that I should proceed to his country residence, called Orange Grove, nearly at the extremity of the island. His kind invitation was accepted, and next morning we went on shore. I was mounted on a fine little pony, and proceeded up the zig zag road, called Ladder-hill; whence we had a fine view of the shipping below; they appeared much diminished in size, from our being so high above them. The guns at this place pointed down immediately at the road. We still ascended and passed the governor's residence, called the Plantation house, to the right, after which an immense high peaked mountain opened to our left, called High Knoll, on which it was intended to place cannon. We arrived at Mr Porteous's house about four in the afternoon, and found his lady a most affable pleasant woman; she was born upon the island of European parents ...

We rode over several parts of the island, and were most hospitably received
by the Lieutenant-governor and family; by Col and Mrs Robson, at Longwood;
also by Mr John Thompson, who accompanied my husband to Guinea with Mr P. I
feel much indebted for his great kindness during my stay at this place ...

At Orange Grove I spent nine days very happily in the society of Mrs P., whom
I left with regret. She wished me much to stay with them until the return of the
ship in the voyage home; but this could not be, as my mind was made up to follow
the destiny of my husband.[71]

As Britain was at war with revolutionary France from 1793, Governor Brooke
had to do much to improve the fortifications of the island.[72] His position was greatly
consolidated in 1795 when he took the initiative and risk of releasing garrison
troops on the island to assist in what proved to be the successful British assault on
the Dutch Cape of Good Hope. For this, Brooke received the thanks of George III
and in 1799 was presented with a sword by Arthur Wellesley.[73] His majesty already
knew about the intelligent governor of St Helena because of the plants he had seen
which had been sent to Kew. Writing to the secretary of the East India Company,
William Ramsay, Sir Joseph Banks acknowledged the efforts of Brooke in formal
but clear terms:

I beg you to Return My best Thanks to the court of Directors for the honor they
have done me by Communicating to me their destination of the Curious Plants
sent home by Mr Brooke Governor of St Helena at the Same time to assure them
that the very first time I shall have the honor of attending the King in his Royal
Botanic Garden I will not Fail to Remind His Majesty of the hansome manner in
which the Court of Directors have upon this & Former occasions been pleased to
promote the improvement of a Science at Present Eminently Patronised by the
whole of the Royal Family.[74]

But by the turn of the century Brooke's health was deteriorating and in 1801
he was forced to resign his position and return to Britain, long being remembered
with affection by many on the island. He died in a house in the elegant, terraced
Somerset Place in Bath on 25 January 1811, aged 66.[75]

ॐ Governor Patton ॐ

The new governor, Colonel Robert Patton (1802–1807), was Governor Brooke's
brother-in-law, having in 1772 married Constantia Adriana Sally Mapletoft, Anna

Mapletoft Brooke's sister. There appears also to have also a Mapletoft connection with St Helena. There is a record of a widow, Mrs Sarah Mapletoft, dying on the island in December 1792 during Robert Brooke's governorship.[76]

Like his predecessor, Patton was an educated and able man who had been Warren Hastings' military secretary in Bengal. He came to St Helena out of financial necessity. He was also sympathetic to advancing botanical matters on the island. Patton, supported by Porteous and Burchell, continued to retain the botanic gardens as a restorative depot for plants in transit and, of course, as the years progressed many plants became well established. But this old arrangement did not satisfy all visitors. In August 1802, with Europe temporarily at peace, the amateur botanist George Annesley Viscount Valentia (1770–1844) and his draughtsman, Henry Salt, stopped at St Helena on their way to India. In his diary he recorded:

> The fair daughters of the Governor [Patton] arrived this morning at the Castle drawn in a light carriage by oxen, the only animals adapted to ascend and descend Ladder Hill. They accompanied us to the botanical garden, which, although there is a botanist appointed by the India Company, has no pretensions to that title, as there has not been an attempt to collect even the indigenous plants of the island.[77]

Nonetheless, the usefulness of the botanic gardens was admitted by Valentia in his contact with Joseph Banks when he confirmed that a collection of plants from Indonesia had been repotted and were recuperating in the botanic gardens.[78] Henry Porteous took Lord Valentia deep into the island to the Sandy Bay Ridge where he was delighted to find growing in profusion cabbage trees, ferns, gumwood and tree ferns.[79]

We know that in 1804 the botanist and plant hunter William Kerr sent fruit trees from China all the way to St Helena, though whether these flourished is not recorded.[80] In 1805, there is a rare description of the Jamestown botanic garden in a book published without the author's name but known to be written by Dr Francis Duncan:

> The ground pitched upon in St James's Valley, consisting of about two acres was found to be well adapted to the culture of all Oriental plants, the Mango, Mangosteen, Jumbo Malac, Coffee, Plantain, etc. So favourable was the climate here to these, and a variety of other productions, that this place, which had only been a heap of broken rocks and stones, was, in the short period of 12 or 14 months, covered with a great variety of shrubs and trees; besides yielding a great supply of roots and greens for the hospital.[81]

But by 1806, at the time Governor Patton caused displeasure in London by assisting Sir Home Popham in an unsuccessful expedition to Buenos Aires, the then 19-year-old botanic garden was in a rather dilapidated shape. That year also witnessed the introduction of the island's first printing press and the establishment in September by John Barnes of the island's first newspaper, the *St Helena Gazette*, which appeared irregularly. While this was not a government publication, it had government support in the form of advertisements and announcements. Barnes freely complained about lack of copy – 'a dearth of rich intelligence and entertainment as we might reasonably have expected to furnish our readers'.[82] Barnes introduced an 'Occasional Papers' column 'relative to the improvement of the Island'. The first such opinion piece was entitled 'Botanic Garden'. This lauded the beneficial role of a botanic garden, particularly as a means for raising shrubs and young trees useful to the island. It asserted:

> We must, therefore, conclude that the establishment of a BOTANIC GARDEN at St Helena, must ultimately, be highly beneficial to the settlement, and is an object which must be regarded of no trifling importance. There are few countries in the possession of Europeans which have not established this kind, owing to its obvious public utility. The value of these have chiefly been increased by the liberal communications of those who have had it in their power to add to the collection; and by the current endeavours of those who wish for the improvement of the island, the St Helena BOTANIC GARDEN may be brought to a degree of respectability which shall claim the notice of every passing stranger and offer independent of the advantages a real source of amusement to those who reside here.[83]

There can be little doubt that the writer was a young botanist less than a year out from England, William Burchell.

15. Jamestown. The Square with market and church. The charming Georgian square or main parade in Jamestown is little changed in 200 years. To the left is St James' Church, the present building dating from 1774. To the right, on the site of the old barracks and guard room, are public offices which at times have housed the law offices, court house, the police station, the library and the Post Office. Beside this building is the entrance gate to the Castle Garden, which stretches behind the building down towards the Castle and the Jamestown wharfs. Sketch by William Burchell, 14 April 1810.

Section II

THE NAPOLEONIC ERA

The big three: Burchell, Beatson and Roxburgh

The Napoleonic era proved to be a period of great activity for St Helena as its strategic position increased, culminating in the six years of captivity for the fallen emperor Napoleon. This era also signals the heyday of botanical activity on St Helena. This is in no small way due to the activities of three people who built on the foundation laid by Governor Brooke.

On 13 December 1805, the emotionally fragile 23-year-old William John Burchell arrived on St Helena.[1] He held three positions while on the island. From 1 August 1806 he was the schoolmaster, until he resigned the post in a huff on 9 June 1809.[2] Three months after becoming schoolmaster, in November 1806, Governor

16. Burchell's sketch of tree ferns on Diana's Peak along with the enslaved gardener Jimmy, who had to carry the tin plant-collecting box up the steep mountain side, 14 January 1808.

Robert Patton appointed him to the additional position of superintendent of the botanic garden. Finally, on 12 June 1809, three days after giving up the school position, he was appointed the island's naturalist on the substantial salary of £300 a year, a position which included his existing function as the botanic garden's superintendent. But less than a year later, on 16 April 1810, he resigned as naturalist. So, all in all, Burchell was in control of the St Helena Botanic Garden from November 1806 until April 1810, a period of three and a half years.[3]

Burchell lived in a house provided for the schoolmaster, which was some distance away from the garden, probably in what is now called Napoleon Street. There was a cottage in the botanic gardens, which was possibly what became known as Palm Villa. In 1808 a Major Billinghurst rented this and had the annoyance of having the furniture removed at short notice as it was needed 'for the Service of Government'.[4]

Burchell kept a journal for much of his time on St Helena. But it is incomplete, sections having been removed by an unknown person. In the journal, Burchell gives an interesting overview of his work as superintendent. The gardens are mentioned 74 times in the period from 2 November 1806 to 16 October 1810. He records visiting the botanic garden 51 times: once in December 1806, 22 times in 1807, 19 times in 1808, 5 times in 1809, and 4 times between January and October 1810. Even accepting that this is an incomplete record, what is clear is that Burchell only visited the gardens irregularly, leaving the day-to-day watering and maintenance to an untrained labourer. One of the reasons why the St Helena Botanic Garden did not succeed was that unless Burchell or his gardener was present the high-walled garden was kept locked, excluding the local population who might otherwise have supported it and rallied to its defence.

This is not to say that the garden was without use in these wartime years. One important point to emerge from Burchell's journal is the confirmation that the gardens continued to be used as a plant entrepôt or resting station for specimens being transported from India and China to Britain or the West Indies. For example, in April 1807 when the China fleet anchored off St Helena, sickly plants were taken off the ships and replaced with healthy ones. Next year a consignment of plants was landed at Jamestown which, according to Burchell, appeared not to have had a drop of water all the voyage and were consequently all dead. In July 1809 Burchell was preparing plants from China for onward shipment to England and in September he received plants and seeds from the *Warley*. And so the cycle continued.[5]

Like many plant hunters who were curators, such as Mark McKen in Natal (1851–1868) or William Purdie in Trinidad (1846–1857), Burchell was not one to be confined within a garden, and this sometimes told on the institution. In fairness to Burchell, though, in this period the St Helena Botanic Garden held its own. His absence from the garden can be explained in several ways. In the morning he had his duties as the schoolmaster. He also was ever-keen to get out of Jamestown to explore the island, collecting plant specimens in his green-painted metal box. At his home he assembled an extensive herbarium. Later, as naturalist, he was required to provide the East India Company in London with different-coloured soils and with the guano from wild birds. This was forwarded to William Jacob (1762–1851) who about 1808 conducted successful experiments with the soils and informed Sir Joseph Banks that if utilised fully the coloured soil would 'change the island from a barren to a fertile and productive country'.[6] This was not to be, even as a foundation for an artist's pigment.

While much has been made by biographers of Burchell being jilted by Lucia Green in April/May 1808 and the psychological impact this had on him, this blow did not seem to affect his collecting expeditions. It must also be added that Burchell was constantly dining out and partying on the island. But there was an air of remorse and self-pity about him, and a tendency occasionally to take unnecessary offence and to quarrel, be it with the church organist or even two of the three governors in post while he was on the island.

⁓ Burchell's difficulties ⁓

William Burchell faced four difficulties in relation to the botanic garden in Jamestown. There was the constant threat from wild goats entering and, as in February 1808, eating delicate plants and seedlings. The solution was straightforward enough, and the garden was enclosed with a set of 'great gates'.[7] Then there was the climate. In March 1809 a serious flood washed away two seedbeds and caused a lot of damage.[8]

Labour was also a problem. One gardener, a seconded soldier called Dawson, was the norm. When he was seriously ill, a man named Newton replaced him. Enslaved people sometimes worked in the garden, including occasionally a man named May, who had been allocated to or purchased by Burchell, it is not clear which. In 1806 there were 1,280 enslaved individuals on St Helena and 310 'free blacks', together totalling 1,590, just under 50 per cent of the total population.[9]

Burchell was reduced sometimes to doing manual labour himself, including building wooden seed boxes and watering the ground.[10] He seems to have had a cordial but not close relationship with Henry Porteous, who was occupied during this time by various official duties under the title of nebulous title of superintendent of Improvements, which included running various Company farms. Porteous was also busy elsewhere earning bounties for clearing farmland of brambles.[11] He seems to have kept his distance from the sometimes querulous curator.

More serious than any of these difficulties were Burchell's relationships with the island's governors. Burchell idealised Robert Patton and in return the old governor encouraged the young man as much as possible and especially in opening up regular contact with William Aiton at Kew Gardens. There is some evidence that Burchell was influential in developing the botanical interests of the governor's daughter, Anna Maria Patton (1774–1852). She married George Warren Walker (1778–1843) who eventually became an army general. The pair became notable amateur botanists in Ceylon (Sri Lanka). Several entries in his diary testify to Anna Maria's botanical interests and Burchell's encouragement of this:

> To Miss Patton I sent St. Helena colours [clay], the Tunbridge Fern, with some other ferns and lichen to shew hoe they recover their natural shape and colour after being plunged in water. (11 May 1807)
>
> Mr. Brooke called on me this morning. He had some conversation with me respecting his work and the engravings for it. I offered to give him a letter to Mr. Nottes and to make some drawings for him. Miss Patton having already drawn some. (19 May 1807)[12]

Governor Patton resigned on the grounds of ill health in 1807, and the island's acting governor was the very different character of Colonel William Lane. From the start he alienated the young curator. On 1 August 1807 Burchell recorded:

> In the evening Dawson, my gardener, came to me with much concern to tell me that Col. Lane (the present Governor) had been to the Botanic Garden where he had signified his intention of entirely altering all my plans and of overthrowing all my arrangements. He said that let it cost him what it would, he would have some good pines out of that garden yet. I had just been making a trellace for the different twining exotic plants that I had collected and reared. This he said would just do for him to plant vines against, and it appears that he is resolved to undo whatever the good and excellent Governor Patton strove to accomplish.[13]

On 12 August the governor and Burchell had a row in the botanic garden:

> I refused to agree to his plan of destroying the garden by making it into a vineyard, leaving the plants to shift for themselves between the vines. I parted with him under a threat that he 'would not forget me'.

Two days later holes for the vines were dug and by 25 August they had been planted. The next month Dawson was ordered back to his military barracks, though this order was later rescinded and he returned to work as a gardener. Burchell petitioned the directors of the East India Company to remove Lane from his position. Other more influential figures did likewise, for Lane was quick to make enemies.

Lane's spitefulness or, at least, lack of interest in Burchell and the gardens emerged after he left when the new governor, in July 1808, discovered a letter and seeds from William Roxburgh in India in one of Lane's drawers. We are not told what was in this letter, but in August 1807 Burchell had written to Roxburgh giving him an account of Lane's conduct regarding the botanic gardens.[14] On St Patrick's Day 1808, with a band moving down the main street of Jamestown playing at the door of any Irish officer, Burchell received the news of the removal of 'that wretch Lane' and his replacement by Lieutenant-Colonel, later Major–General, Alexander Beatson, whom one islander described as 'cool, firm, and active ... He reduced useless expenditure, economised the public money, raised many useful buildings, and left a name behind. Yet half his schemes were unmitigated failures.'[15]

Burchell was now facing the personal trauma of being jilted by his betrothed, Lucia Green. She arrived on the island in April 1808 to announce that her new betrothed was the captain of the ship in which she had sailed to St Helena. Feeling abandoned and deeply hurt, Burchell soon found fault with the new governor despite the fact, as will be seen, that Beatson knew about plants and was a keen advocate of agricultural improvement. Alexander Beatson was, however, a very different character from Governor Patton. For Burchell, there was no return to frequent invitations to dine at Plantation House as in the days of Governor Patton. He complained bitterly of a lack of attention bestowed on him, stating that he had been 'left to my own discretion' by Beatson and that the botanic garden had fallen into ruin 'owing to the little notice and support which it receives from the present Government'.[16] In June 1809 Burchell recorded in his journal:

> I proposed that as the Botanic Garden could never come to any good in the Valley,
> it would be best to abandon it altogether as soon as another place could be found
> whereto the plants could be moved. The Governor was of the same opinion and at
> my request ordered that for securing the plants for the present.[17]

Nothing came of this idea and the old garden languished. The Napoleonic War by necessity concentrated the mind of the governor and every ship sighted meant an alarm and call to arms lest it should be an enemy vessel. As one of several security measures, Jamestown was to be secured and a fortified line was commenced at what Burchell described as the 'upper Botanic Garden', an interesting indication that he regarded the Castle or lower botanic garden as part of his domain.

It is difficult to give a picture of how the botanic garden looked during the Burchell era. Though *Pinus pinaster* had been reintroduced to St Helena in 1787 when the botanic garden was being established, there was a perceived need for timber trees.[18] This continued and, coupled with the endless demand for fuel, stripped what was left of the main blocks of indigenous woodland. In 1814 gumwood was selling in Jamestown for half a crown (2/6) a hundredweight (cwt).[19] Over 50 years later, in 1875, the entomologist Thomas Vernon Wollaston complained to Joseph Hooker at Kew:

> The A. Burchellii is so rare that I have been drying you a few specimens, feeling that (as it may soon be gone altogether if we cannot persuade the islanders to spare it fr their donkey-loads of firewood) you might perhaps like some fresh ones ...[20]

In 1787 the East India Company had sent a consignment of 'Plants of Ash and other trees' in tubs from England. These not only arrived safely but prompted Governor Brooke to ask for some more as well as for some fruit trees 'ready grafted, as they answer much better than from seed', none of the tree seed having come up when sown, except for firs.[21] It was under Burchell that seedlings from pine cones were successfully raised and distributed.[22] Indeed Burchell had somewhat of a cavalier attitude to disseminating exotic seeds, walking along the island's roads and paths scattering them willy-nilly. He even ruminated of the *Xanthium orientale* which he so scattered, 'no doubt that it will on some future day be reckoned an indigenous St. Helena weed'. Burchell's journal makes several references to plants growing in the botanic garden,[23] and we know that the following were growing in Burchell's period:

Amaranthus: Eaten by Burchell as part of his dinner

Boxwood: Collected on the island

Clitoria ternatea: Blue flowers. Grows very rapidly and swells its pods

Coconut palm: Leaves up to three metres long

Coffee plants

Cotton plants

Convolvulus nil: goodnight convolvulus; eight flowers open. Covered with flowers 'till sun shines'. Seeds sent to William Aiton at Kew.

M. 5. 1808.

17. Burchell's sketch of bastard gumwood trees, globblegheer, wild rosemary and aloe, 14 May 1808.

Gladiolus

Ipomoea bona-nox 'very handsome'

Ixia

Solanum laciniatum: Tasmania

Ipomoea bona nox: large white flowers

Tree peony

Tricolour: Grows like a weed

Virginian Campion

Malay walnut: First tree Burchell planted in the botanic gardens. When he left St Helena, Burchell asked that it be preserved 'as a memorial of me at St Helena'. It was still there in 1882, but appears to have been cut down when the military took over the Castle Garden during the Anglo-Boer War.

'Everything succeeding except the China plants' (25 July 1807).

Mr Hesse's Cape plants 67 succulent species planted (3 March 1807).

The 'seeds of some wild plants' of St Helena

There are also references to plants and the botanic garden in Burchell's papers held in the archives at the Royal Botanic Gardens, Kew. For example, in his draft manuscript 'Flora Heleniana' the following is noted under *Syngenesia superflora*:

12 Feby 1810 in a watery place in the Botanic Garden I met a plant of Eclissla a foot high and of a growth so-many times larger than that found up Side path that I could scarcely think it was the same species, but they agreed in so many material particulars that I believe them to be the same.[24]

A somewhat more extensive list of plants at St Helena, carefully laid out in columns, is included in Burchell's manuscript at Kew, entitled 'Flora Insulæ Sta Helenæ'. Neither manuscript can be classified as anything approaching a complete flora of the island, indigenous or otherwise. As regards gardens and the grounds of houses, Table 10 illustrates which properties are included.

TABLE 10
Gardens included in Burchell's manuscripts

Habitat	Name of plant	No.	Comment
Alarm House	*Schænus*		By the side of the road under the Alarm House these in sight of Longwood Telegraph.
Botanic Gardens	*Cyperus* *Radixrepens tuberosa*	11	'Knot grass'.
Botanic Gardens	*Eclipta* Var *Aplo major* [in pencil – erecta Roxburgh?]	151	In the Botanic Gardens.
Bottley's	*Salanium Sodomium*		'Brinjal' Above Sandy bay the largest & finest bushes are at Bottleys. 8 feet.
The Briars	*Schænus* *capitulis lateralibus*		In a pond (in some water) under some willows near Mr Balcombe in Swanley Valley.
Mr Brooke's garden	*Poa compressa*		
Bramin's house	*Ranunculus* (Buttercup)	121	Pencil species name with WR [William Roxburgh?].
Castle garden			
Major Denaaffe's	*Cyperus*	6	At Major Denaaffe's in Sandy Bay under the Waterfall.
Major Denaaffe's	*Euphorbia helioscopia*	111	Major Denaaffe's in Sandy Bay. Above South Sea Hall.

Habitat	Name of plant	No.	Comment
By the side of the road, just above Mr Dunn's	*Elensine Egyptiaca*		
Sir William Doveton's garden	*Briza media*		
Doveton's	*Fragaria*	118	
Forbes's	*Euphorbia peplus* (petty spurge)	112	By the side of the road on the ridge over against Mrs Forbes's.
Forbes's	*Conastrium vulgatum*		By the side of the road on the ridge over against Mrs Forbes's.
Forbes's	*Raphanus* (radish)	128	On the valley below Mrs Forbes's.
Forster's	*Juncus radix repens*		In the Run at Forster's. Ditto below Major De Fountains.
Forster's	*Spergula arvensis* [corn spurrey]		About Forster's and bank on side of road.
Forster's	*Fragaria*	118	
Forster's	*Drimyphyllium heleniana*	160	'Whitewood' [Petrobium arboretum].
Above Major Hodsons (Maldivia) plentiful	*Cyperus*		In localities.
Longwood	*Euphorbia peplus*	113	In Longwood towards the sea.
Longwood	*Poa compressa*		In Longwood under the trees and many places both dry and moist.
Longwood	*Digynia Chenspodium* (x2)		
Longwood	`*Commidendrum burchella*	159	Bastard Gum Tree. In Longwood. The largest and most ancient trees are in Shark's Valley below Julio's.
Luffkins's	*Adiantum*	191	By side of road over above Luffkin's. In Swanley Valley.
Above Dr Kay's, in the road about Red Hill House	*Panicum*		A Milii species, cum sequente?
Plantation House	*Elymus Redix repens*		'Bull-grass'.
Plantation House	*Convolulus arvensis*		On the lawn at Plantation House.

Habitat	Name of plant	No.	Comment
Plantation House	*Rubus*	117	At Plantation House.
Porter's Gate	*Frankenia*		St Helena Tea. On the sides of precipices = 'Deep valley' 'Near Lot' Near 'Porter's Gate'.
Rosemary Hall At Mr Forbes	*Bromus*		
Rosemary Hall	*Gnaphalium* (cudweed)	144	About Rosemary Hall K Sowden's.
Rosemary Hall	*Siegesbeckia*	148	Rosemary Hall & Sowden's.
Above Sowden's	*Panicum* (x2)		
Taylor's	*Campanula*		On Sandybay-ridge near Taylor's.
Taylor's	*Aspidium* Var. *Pinnulis arqute incises*	174	On Sandy Bay ridge about Taylor's.
West Lodge	*Commidendrum gummiferum* (cluster-leaved gumwood)	158	Thompson's Wood Hill Under 'West Lodge' Telegraph.
West Lodge	*Panicum*		At West Lodge.
West Lodge	*Mercurialis*	167	At West Lodge. At Swanly Valley.
West Lodge	*Acrostichum*	179	On Diana's Peak and under Westlodge Telegraph on the stems of the Cabbage trees.
West Lodge	*Dicksonia arborescens*	193	On Diana's Peak & Sandy-bay ridge. Under Casons Gate & Westlodge telegraph; towards Sandy bay.
Major Wright's	*Digitaria*		'English Wire-grass'.
Major Wright's	*Cucubulus behen*		On the side of the road between South Sea Hall & Major Wright's.

Yet another, fuller, Burchell list of St Helena plants has survived and is in Kew's archive. This is under the title 'Catalogus plantarum quæ Sta Helena variis hortis inveniuntur' [Catalogue of St Helena plants found in various gardens]. It is dated 10 November 1809, but other dates in the manuscript clearly show it was compiled well into 1810, even after Burchell resigned as curator on 16 April 1810. Although it is a garden list, a great many of the scribbled entries have no location. This said, Figure 4 indicates the gardens and their frequency of mention in the document.

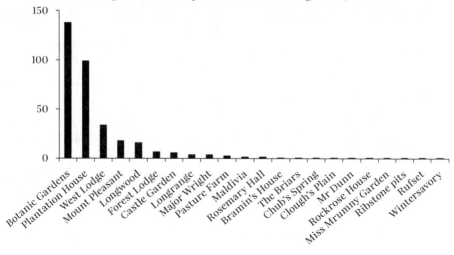

FIGURE 4

Catalogue of St Helena plants found in various gardens, 1809

The full list of those plants within gardens is contained in appendix 4. Table 11 shows those gardens of the 22 listed with the greatest number of plants recorded.

TABLE 11

Largest number of species per garden listed by Burchell

Garden	Acreage	No. species listed
Botanic Gardens	2	138
Plantation House	c. 200	90
West lodge	119	34
Sandy Bay		18
Longwood	633 including common	16
Prospect House	9	9
Forest Lodge	60	7

What is particularly interesting is the range of plants which existed in the St Helena Botanic Garden and its rival at Plantation House at this time. The botanic garden in Jamestown certainly had not declined since the 1780s. The Plantation House list is dominated by tree species and then by South African plants, including proteas, lilies, flaxes of several varieties, aloes, and yellowwood. It also lists a specimen of *Strelitzia reginae*, which is a very early record of its cultivation outside of Africa or Europe. The botanist will observe that the Burchell list also contains many plants no longer growing on the island, itself an indication of the decline that these settler plantation gardens were to suffer in the ensuing decades. The list also assists botanists with pinpointing early introductions which do still exist.

NAPOLEON'S GARDEN ISLAND

For example, the South American purple vervain (*Verbena bonariensis*), appears in this 1809/1810 list, a plant which was previously recorded as first mentioned in Melliss (1860–1871).[25] More significant is the listing by Burchell of New Zealand flax (*Phormium tenax*), as growing at West Lodge, more than 40 years before it was reported to be growing wild in every part of the island the early 1850s.[26]

There is little evidence that Burchell sent much in the way of living specimens back to Britain. But two small consignments did make their way to Kew, via Sir Joseph Banks, in about 1809. The first contained the following:

Borago zelanica	*Clitorex ternatea*
Clitoria ternatea	*Cassia occidentalis*
_____ *ternatea*	*Dracaena australis*
Dolichos sp.	Hibiscus sp. From China
Hibiscus herbacae	*Helitropium indicum*
Heliotropium indicicius	*Ipomaea bona-nox*
Dida cristata	*Melia azidirach*
The second consignment was listed as	*angulata*
seeds:	*Sida cristata*
Asclepias fruiticosa	*Urena lobata*
Borago zeylanica	*Vinca rosce*
Convolvulus from China	The Dogwood tree of St Helena

Short though they are, these lists illustrate the character of the flora growing on this small island, reflecting the geographic spread of the activities of East India Company in two hemispheres.[27]

Burchell resigned, on 16 April 1810, and left the island only six months later on 16 October 1810 to become colonial botanist at the Cape Colony. He noted in his journal that his resignation was because of 'the Governor's selfish and illiberal conduct, and the disgust I have long felt has left me no alternative but that of resigning'.[28] But the fact was, as Burchell had admitted, he was 'left to his own discretion'. Rather than making the most of that and staying mindful of the Lane period, the personal neglect made him brood and encouraged him to be quarrelsome. The island's medical superintendent, Dr Adam Baildon, wished to take over from Burchell after he left, but it is uncertain if this appointment was formalised.[29] In any case, Baildon died in February 1815.

Burchell died by his own hand many years later back in Fulham in London on 23 March 1863, having made his name in South Africa as one of the great plant hunters. His sister donated his collecting books, personal papers (well exorcised), manuscript flora, drawings and specimens to Kew Gardens. Interestingly, in 1866 Kew in turn donated some of Burchell's specimens from St Helena to the Bibliothèque du Phanérogame of the Jardin des Plantes in Paris.[30] In 1867 Joseph Hooker went to the trouble of having tracings made of Burchell's sketches and sent these to the naturalist and St Helena government surveyor, Charles Melliss. Melliss responded by writing:

> I have to thank you also very much for the tracings of Burchells sketches which are very acceptable as I have been rather bewildered with Roxburgh's list of plants, but these drawings form just the key to it. The drawings themselves are perfectly accurate, I do not think that I have ever seen drawings more so; the Ebony being the only one that I have not seen – the other six are still plentiful in the island and I can send you any amount of them.[31]

⁐ Governor Alexander Beatson ⁐

Colonel Beatson's tenure as governor of St Helena lasted from 4 July 1808 until 21 August 1813. He was promoted to major-general in 1810 and to lieutenant-general in 1814 after he had left St Helena to become a gentleman farmer near Tunbridge Wells. He has been lauded for his undoubted enthusiasm in promoting the welfare of the small colony and in particular his advocacy of agricultural and horticultural improvement. It is therefore rather perplexing that Burchell hated him. As seen, Burchell and by default the botanic garden were consequently left to their own devices. In this respect Burchell did no favours for the long-term prosperity of the gardens. That isolation in itself annoyed the sensitive young Burchell. Beatson may have been a colonial 'Coke of Norfolk'[32] in his advocacy of agricultural reform but he was also a hardened Scottish soldier who had fought at the famous bloody battle of Seringapatam in India in 1799. He and Burchell were just clean different.

Governor Beatson was an agriculturalist rather than a botanist, as shown, for example, in his including in his book on St Helena the thoughts of Dr Andrew Berry relating to the island's endemic gumwood woodlands:

> The few gum-wood trees which are said to be indigenous, seem to have so little hold of the ground on the sides of the ridges of Diana and High Peak, as to be of little value either as a wood of utility, or for firewood. It should therefore be cleared away at Long Wood, where it interferes with agriculture, leaving only intermediate rows for shelter, for it occupies at present, ground capable of agriculture without

being of the smallest use, and is not sufficiently elevated to answer the purpose I am recommending: the peaks that should be covered with wood, being elevated far above the level of Long Wood.

As it would be an undertaking of labour and expense, more perhaps than would be given to cover the sides of the ridges towards the summits with wood, I have suggested to some gentlemen, and particularly to Major Hodson, as Arabian dates are sent here for sale (the seeds of which will grow), that if he would put some of these seeds in his pocket on going to these peaks, and make his servants stick them into the rich soil on these elevated ridges.[33]

And yet Beatson could get on with botanists. There is an 11-week overlap between the arrival of the celebrated botanist and superintendent of Calcutta Botanic Garden, William Roxburgh, on 7 June 1813 and the departure of Beatson on 21 August 1813. It is interesting that, unlike Burchell, Roxburgh and Beatson clearly got on well together. Indeed, as will be seen, Beatson promoted Roxburgh's work on the flora of St Helena after the botanist's death in February 1815.

Beatson's legacy rests primarily on journal articles he wrote. Surviving copies of the *St Helena Register* have yet to surface, but fortunately Beatson compiled all his 30 articles in this Jamestown-printed journal into a book. Two of the articles

18. Burchell and his 'poor little faithful dog' below Alarm Cottage looking down on Jamestown. Entitled 'Overlooking Jamestown from Two Gun Saddle' (20 October 1809), it appears that Burchell's gardeners are collecting further down the hill; one of them, the enslaved gardener May, holds Burchell's horse.

date from 1810, eleven from 1811, ten from 1812, four from 1813 and three have no date attached. Those dated run from 20 September 1810 until 20 May 1813. In addition the book contains a substantial and useful 77-page introduction, an 84-page narrative of his version of the December 1811 army mutiny and four appendices, including a 32-page 'Alphabetical list of plants, seen by Dr. Roxburgh growing on the island of St Helena, in 1813–14'. Beatson published the impressive 360-page book with a Pall Mall bookseller in London under the title, *Tracts relative to the island of St Helena written during a residence of five years*. It was dedicated to the directors of the United East India Company and published in 1816 – by which time, of course, St Helena was internationally known for its imperial captive.

Beatson's book has proved to be an invaluable source not only to local historians but to the wider and expanding number of environmental historians of empire. Charles Darwin greatly enthused over this book, though the worldlier Duke of Wellington drily commented of the weighty volume that not so much could have been written about the Garden of Eden.[34]

It should, however, be remembered that Beatson's was a proselytising exercise and that what was advocated was not what necessarily occurred – not least because of the arrival of Napoleon and all that resulted from that, a mere 14 months after Beatson's departure. Beatson had three primary aims: to encourage and cajole the planters to allocate some of their land away from pasture to cultivation; to encourage them to plant trees and to encourage them to create and plant hedgerows.[35] His articles in the *Register* were packed with facts, statistics and advice. He was also a hands-on governor when it came to agricultural matters. Take, for example, his advocacy for the growing of salsola, which he had planted out in boxes up at Plantation House with the hope it could be grown in fields as in Spain, though he was uncertain if that growing on St Helena was the same species of salsola. Some salsola was planted out in desolate spots on the periphery of the island and was still growing in the 1850s, but the experiment as a commercial enterprise was not a success. It was also at Plantation House that Beatson in 1809/1810 carried out an experiment growing mangel-wurzels using three plots, one with pig's dung and ash, another with bird guano and a third without any manure. The guano was a clear winner. An experiment growing barley at Longwood was stymied by the arrival of a flock of canary birds, though the use of protective nets at Plantation House averted disaster there. Beatson reckoned that an acre of land on St Helena could produce 16¼ tons of corn. He had, however, a tendency to extrapolate perhaps to excess, as for example this piece of logic concerning the black-speckled kidney beans he had planted at Plantation House in April 1812:

Now as an acre planted in the above manner, would contain 43560 feet of rows, the extent of 38 feet is the 1320th part — consequently this sum multiplied by 66½ ounces gives the produce 87780 ounces, or 5486 pounds, per acre.[36]

Given the rigour and enthusiasm with which Governor Beatson carried out his drive to harry the recalcitrant planters of St Helena into modernising their farming practices, it is interesting to note the top thirteen planters, including two women, with 'strong conviction' whom the governor considered made the grade: Mr Alesworth, Mrs Alexander, Mr Bagley, Thomas Brooke, John De Fountain, Mr Hayward, Mr John Kay, Mr Samuel Knipe, Mr George Leach, Mr Legg, Miss Mary (Polly) Mason, Mr Sampson and Mr Wright.

William Roxburgh

William Roxburgh arrived on St Helena on 7 June 1813 off the East Indiaman *Castle Huntly* from India with his wife, three children and two servants. They left the island nine months later on 1 March 1814. Beatson and Roxburgh had known each other years before in India, when Beatson was an army major. Roxburgh was to name the sea heath genus *Beatsonia*, now a synonym for *Frankenia*, after his friend.

For many years Roxburgh had been trying to assist St Helena with consignments of seeds and plants, in particular forest species. In 1795 he gave the gardener Peter Good three bags of scutch grass (*Agrostis linearis*, now *Cynodon dactylon*), one of which was for St Helena. Then, in 1808, Roxburgh recommended to Thomas Douglas that he send plants from Calcutta to St Helena 'with every prospect of advantage to that island'.[37] Early in 1813, when requesting permission from the East India Company directors to leave Calcutta and journey to St Helena, Roxburgh reminded C. M. Ricketts, chief secretary to the Bengal government, that in the past he had sent to the island, 'plants, seeds, and roots of the most useful', but that 'hitherto with much less success than was hoped for'. He went on:

Forest trees they want most of all, and I understand they have in general failed in rearing such trees from seed. Permit me therefore to request you will suggest to His Lordship in Council, that it might be advisable to send by each of the companies ships which form the next Fleet, one or two Chests filled with growing plants of all those trees as appear to promise most success. Such as Sissoo Buddam Lundry, Teak, Sumatra Cassis, &ca &ca which the state of the nurseries in this [Calcutta Botanic] Garden can at present furnish. If this idea meet with the approbation of Government have the goodness to oblige me with the order for getting them ready as soon as you can. It is probable that I shall be at that island at the time the plants will arrive, and in that case will with pleasure give the best advice and directions in my power for their planting and future management.[38]

Floras of St Helena

When Roxburgh arrived on St Helena he was not at all well, being 'now reduced to a perfect skeleton and weak in proportion'.[39] But despite this, as the Ashmoles have observed, 'Roxburgh's work essentially completed the discovery phase of botanical work on St Helena'.[40] Roxburgh spent nine months on the island and devoted much time to plant hunting. The result was his famous list or catalogue which identified 388 species of flowering plants and ferns, 58 or 15 per cent being indigenous to the island. As mentioned, this appeared in print in 1816 in Beatson's *Tracts relative to the island of St Helena*.[41] An argument can, of course, be made in support of William Burchell as the pioneer, predating Roxburgh in his scientific study of the island's flora. However, Burchell's work was to remain hidden in manuscript form for many decades.

A reprint of Roxburgh's list appeared in 1815 in an anonymous St Helena-printed pamphlet entitled *Flora Sta Helenica*. This has been attributed to Alexander Watson but it is possibly, if not probably, the scheme of Beatson. The preface gives thanks to William Leycester (1775–1831) who lived on St Helena for a short time and who was 'unwearied in his endeavours to ascertain the various vegetable productions of the island, either indigenous or exotic'.[42] Leycester was a man of some standing, being chief justice of the Sadr Diwani Adalat Supreme Court of Revenue in Bengal. He was also the first president of the prestigious Agricultural and Horticultural Society of India.[43]

Flora Sta Helenica is 20 pages long and contains the names of 581 plants. Of these, 67 (12 per cent) are marked as not being in Roxburgh's list. The preface promises an updated list, in which 'the names of those benefactors of the Island who have introduced the Exotics will be mentioned, so far at least as they can be ascertained; the dates of their importation will be given; and the location of the rarer species will be stated'. Sadly, this does not seem to have materialised, possibly because of the death in 1830 of the 70-year-old Beatson.

Despite the short sojourns of Charles Darwin (8–14 July 1836) and of Joseph Hooker (January–February 1840 and May 1843) on St Helena, it would be another 50 years before an updated flora of the island was published. In 1875 John Charles Melliss lists some 1,048 species for St Helena.[44] According to Cronk, this 'replaced Roxburgh's list as the standard work'.[45] In 1903 Jackson also reproduced Roxburgh's list.[46] It is interesting to note that in Burchell's manuscript list 'Flora Insula St Helena', there are pencil additions frequently with R or WR written beside them.

It was also Roxburgh who in January 1814 first recommended that *Cinchona officinalis* be planted on the island, where it could become established before being transported on to India.[47] In addition, Roxburgh pressed for the resurrection of the botanic garden and the appointment of a gardener or nurseryman. Since Burchell's departure in 1810 the botanic garden had been without a curator and had clearly fallen into a state of decay.

Governor Beatson was less sanguine. Only the previous year he had summed up his attitude to the botanic garden following another proposal for planting a prospective economic. In March 1813, writing from St Helena to the East India Company directors in London, Dr Andrew Berry pressed for the growing of the cactus 'Kew nopal', not only as a foodstuff for silkworms but also as an anti-scurvy vegetable:

> I feel less hesitant in recommending this principal culture in that garden, as its object as a Botanical Garden has been frustrated, and from its limited scale, and the little that is growing in it of a foreign and valuable nature: from the many seeds from many quarters, and particularly from India, that have been forwarded, it would seem badly calculated for the continuance of such an object. But for the culture of the Kew Nopal it will answer well the only thriving plants of this Cactus being there the very few at Plantation house and Long Wood being of so stunted a growth though long in the ground as to show that either the ground or the elevation is not favourable to the luxuriant growth of this esculent plant. There is also another species of Cactus growing in the Botanical Garden of a large size what Dr Anderson called the China Nopal I wish attention to be paid to this distinction in making plantations as the Kew Nopal is alone the object of culture as a vegetable.

Beatson took Berry up on this and on 17 April 1813 instructed even using some of Berry's phrasing:

> I feel the less hesitation in recommending this principal culture [Kew Nopal] in that garden, as its object as a Botanical Garden has been frustrated, and from its limited scale, and the little that is grown in it of a foreign and valuable nature from the many seeds from many quarters, and particularly from India, that have been forwarded, it would seem badly calculated for the continuance of such an object. But for the cultivation of the Kew Nopal, it will answer well, the only thriving plants of the *Cactus* being there; the very few at Plantation House and Long Wood being

19. An evocative sketch of Thompson's Wood Hill in the remote south of St Helena by Burchell, 16 May 1810. He writes, 'I found some Cymose Cabbage Trees so thick in flower as to be quite snowy'. Nearby he picnicked in front of the deserted West Lodge House and ate his German sausage from Fulham (London), 'and hunger made me find it excellent.'

so stunted a growth, though long in the ground, to show that either the ground or the elevation is not favourable to the luxuriant growth of this esculent plant. There is another species of the *Cactus* growing in the Botanical Garden of a large size, which Dr Anderson called the China Nopal ... Due attention shall, therefore, be paid to the appropriation of part of the Botanic Garden as a nursery for the Kew Nopal; from whence, having been naturalised to the climate, it might readily be transported to the sides of the hills on either side of James's Town: which would serve for utility as well as ornament, and would also be conveniently situated for the supply of shipping.[48]

So was a major problem created for the future.[49]

It is little wonder then that, as mentioned, Read's famous 1817 map places the botanic garden behind Plantation House and not in Jamestown, where the public's admission was dependent upon the goodwill and availability of the curator.

A note needs to be added about two other floras. One manuscript, entitled 'Floræ Stæ Helenæ', apparently prepared in 1813/1814, is housed in the Natural History Museum in London. This is among the papers of Robert Brown, librarian to Sir Joseph Banks, who had been given a life-long interest in his library. In 1827 the library passed to the British Museum upon Brown becoming their keeper of Botany. Between 1849 and 1854, Brown was president of the Linnean Society.[50] Robinson writes of this St Helena flora:

> it refers extensively to Roxburgh's work which took place in those years, and so it is possible that Brown relied heavily if not entirely on his friend's notes. Dr William Wright, President of the Royal Society of Edinburgh, wrote to Brown shortly after Roxburgh's death stating: 'Our Friend Dr Roxburgh was worn to a shadow before He died, I never saw any one so exhausted to last so long: and yet he was to the last writing a Flora of St Helena!'[51]

The other flora is a 31-page pamphlet. The title page reads, *An alphabetical list of indigenous and exotic plants, growing on the island of ST. HELENA, complied by Stephen F. Pritchard, Esq. and corrected by Mr. James Bowie, botanist, Ludwigsburg Garden, Cape Town, Cape of Good Hope. Printed by G.J. Pike, 11, ST. George's Street. 1836.* This plant list takes the form of two columns, one giving the Latin name and the other the common name. Of the 317 genera[52] and 484 species listed, 58 species are listed as indigenous. While there is much in common with Roxburgh's list, Pritchard's is not a direct copy of Roxburgh and species are found in the latter which do not appear in the former.

James Bowie was one of Banks's plant hunters who had gone to South America and on to the Cape. In 1827 he returned to the Cape in a private capacity and from about 1835 until about 1842 was superintendent of Baron von Ludwig's famous garden in Loop Street. The link between von Ludwig and Henry Porteous has already been mentioned. Bowie had also called at St Helena on one of his voyages to the Cape. Lieutenant Stephen Frazier Pritchard was of a St Helena family who, like Charles Melliss after him, was also interested in botany. Pritchard had been born on the island in 1802 and was a local civil servant, described either as a Company writer or as assistant to the island's (colonial) secretary, who in 1836 was Major Robert Seale. Pritchard was a lieutenant in the St Helena Regiment and was considered a public-spirited citizen, who involved himself in charity works. This did not exclude him owning, in 1827, three enslaved men and two enslaved women.

Pritchard's boss, Seale, was also bitten by the natural history craze of the time and in 1834 had published *The Geognosy of the island of St Helena, illustrated in a series of views, plans and sections accompanied with explanatory remarks and observations.* When Pritchard's pamphlet was published in 1836, Seale had just been appointed the first colonial secretary under the crown, having served previously as a writer under the noteworthy island Company secretary Thomas Henry Brooke. Seale's first wife had been Harriet Bird Pritchard. He had a complicated and notorious private life and was victimised by the island's new governor, General Middlemore. Seale was dismissed and died in penury in 1838, leaving as his major legacy a spectacular wooden model of the island, for which he had been paid £500, and which sadly was sent to England where it was neglected, attacked by woodworm and eventually destroyed in the basement of a London museum.[53] So ground to a halt for many years any serious natural history work on the island by its inhabitants.

ৼৣ Tree planting in the late Georgian era ৼৣ

Quentin Cronk suggests that in 1502 ebony (*Trochetiopsis ebenus*) and scrubwood (*Commidendrum rugosum*) stretched down to the sea, with thick gumwood (*Commidendrum robustum*) woodland covering those areas between 400 to 600 metres. Cronk divides the island into seven vegetation zones. He also states that it was only under Governor Beatson that tree planting became widespread on St Helena.[54] There is no denying Beatson's determination to promote horticulture, agriculture and silviculture on the island during his five-year tenure. Beatson's *Tracts* included the following sections:

Plans proposed for restoring wood

On planting trees

On pineaster trees

Nurseries of trees established at St. Helena

Mr. Miller's directions for rearing scotch pine are applicable to the pineaster

Further observations on the importance of planting trees at St. Helena

Before Napoleon's arrival, the Longwood government farm was in part utilised to raise young seedlings in a vain attempt to re-establish the old St Helena 'forest'.[55] From 1801 clauses were added to leases compelling the planting of a tenth of the property with trees. This was amended a couple of years later when leaseholders had to plant six trees per acre wherever they wished. In 1813, large-scale tree nurseries were established by Beatson, who was distributing pinaster and oaks. However, it took time before results became apparent. By 1818 Colonial Secretary Seale was observing that there were not '1,500 trees on all the estates [on St Helena], Plantation House excepted'. Planter inertia and the previous ravages of the large goat population had hindered the afforestation enterprise. But things were now changing.

Governor Lowe was zealous in planting trees on the island, with Plantation House and other gardens belonging to the Company serving as the nurseries for his endeavours. Apart from a genuine interest in botanical matters and a recognition that trees brought rain, Lowe's drive to plant trees was motivated by the alarming destruction of St Helena's woodlands for fuel, a demand greatly exacerbated with the largely increased military garrison. A proclamation issued by Lowe dated 25 May 1816 ran in part as follows:

> Whereas it has come to the knowledge of the Governor and Council that certain landholders without regarding the mischievous consequences of divesting the interior heights of the Island of wood, but intent only on present advantage are in the habit of cutting down growing Trees and selling the same for fuel. Said practice is hereby positively prohibited in future and any person who shall be convicted of cutting down/ except for purpose of building/ or otherwise destroying a live tree growing on the interior highlands usually called the Cabbage Tree Lands whether said lands be in their own occupation or not, or of selling, or purchasing green Cabbage Red wood, or of being carriers of the same Such person, or persons shall be subject to a penalty not exceeding ten pounds for each offence, or Corporal punishment not exceeding 200 lashes.[56]

Lowe's efforts included plantings in the Plantation House arboretum behind the house. He cleared three to four acres of unutilised ground at Plantation House which had been overrun with blackberry plants, a growing problem on many farms.[57] Lowe also saw to it that trees were planted elsewhere on Company ground. As will be seen below, others followed his example, especially Major Charles Hodson and George Voteur Lambe, a factor and merchant.

It was under Lowe's watch that premiums were paid for tree planting, an echo of the activities of the Dublin Society back in his native Ireland, where tenant farmers at the time flocked to register their tree planting as an insurance against eviction.[58] Colonel Secretary Seale's estimate of the primary tree planting of this Napoleonic period is summarised in Table 12.[59]

TABLE 12
Tree planting in St Helena, 1816 to c.1820

Area planted	Approximate number of trees	Approximate acreage of afforestation
Plantation House (1816–1820)	81,334	32
Alarm House	59,750	24
Longwood Grounds	5,000	2
By sundry individuals (1822)	92,540	37
Rock Rose House	22,018	9
Others	16,530	7
By sundry individuals	30,000	12
TOTAL	**307,172 trees**	123 acres

This is based on Seale calculating approximately 2,500 trees per acre. This seems rather high but may indeed be accurate because of the fashion in St Helena of planting saplings closely, and then, at least in theory, thinning later in growth. In 1821 Henry Russell noted:

> The trees are generally planted thick, and most of them are firs of various kinds; there are also a few oaks. But timber is all small and evidently stunted for want of depth in the soil. [60]

A second set of figures has survived in the consultation papers of the EIC Factory papers for St Helena.[61] They date from 1816 to 1820. The figure for Plantation House, Alarm House, Longwood and individuals remains approximately the same at 253,128. But omitted from the factory list are 68,548 trees described as Rock Rose House (22,018); 'others' (16,530); and 'by sundry individuals' (30,000). These sundry figures would include those substantial plantings of Charles Hodson and George Lambe.

The value of the Factory list is in its breakdown. For example, of the Plantation House plantings of 81,334 trees, the following is recorded:

1816	In various places/where failed:	7,314
1817	On Blackrock or near Rock Cottage:	7,800
1818	Without the experimental field leading to the stockyard:	17,790
1819	On Merriman's Hill and various other parts of Plantation House Grounds by White gate and the Angles by the church:	26,790

1820	On the upper part of the Princes from green gate:	7,050
	Towards Rock Cottage on the new enclosed ground:	5,400
	On the Clump near the house:	3,300
	Near Red hill where not planted in 1819:	2,290
	On the left of the road leading to Carson's gate:	2,800
	Near Hardings:	800

But the most interesting part of that Factory list is the names of those who planted trees on their private property. This represented approximately 40 per cent of the trees planted between 1816 and 1820. Table 13 lists these.

TABLE 13
Trees planted by private individuals during Napoleon's captivity

Name of planter	Position held	Number of trees planted
Thomas Henry Brooke	Secretary to the island council, senior administrator on St Helena	18,000
Mr Richard Barker	Ran the Longwood farm	14,000
Anthony Beale	Factor	13,000
Captain Charles Sampson	St Helena Regiment	10,000
Captain Francis Seale	St Helena Regiment	10,000
John De Fountain	Merchant	5,000
Charles Blake	Writer for the EIC on St Helena	5,000
Lt. Col. Sir Thomas Reade	Deputy adjunct–general	3,500
Thomas Greentree	Council member; magistrate; storekeeper; farmer; son-in-law Sir William Doveton	3,000
J. Legg	Publican (?)	3,000
Lt. Col. John Alexander Wright	St Helena Regiment	2,500
Henry Seale	Writer for the EIC on St Helena; briefly island Secretary; builder of the wooden model of St Helena	1,500
R. Willis		1,500
Captain Jno. Edward Shortis	Superintendent of public works	1,500

Name of planter	Position held	Number of trees planted
R. Knipe	Farmer [Woodlands West/Horse Pasture Farm?]	1,000
Captain Robert Mason	St Helena Regiment	700
Captain Onesiphorus Beale	St Helena Regiment	600
Joseph Cole	Postmaster/member of Balcombe, Flower & Co, the firm which supplied Longwood	570
William Janisch	Clerk	300
Total	19 private individuals	92,544 trees

A report to the directors of the Company written the following year commented on the link between the Company's afforestation scheme below Alarm House and that on the private property on Prospect Farm:

This forest will in time, with the contiguous Plantation of Mr Brookes, afford a very pleasant prospect from James's Town and the Harbour.[62]

20. Genteel society in the Ladies' Garden at Plantation House, watched by an enslaved gardener. Drawn by Burchell on a short second visit to St Helena while en route between the Cape and back home to Britain, 19 September 1815.

St Helena plants did not become popular in British gardens. As is shown in Table 14, the first edition of *Hortus Kewensis* (1789) contains only five plants listed as from St Helena. *Hortus Kewensis* was a catalogue of plants grown at the Royal Botanic Gardens, Kew compiled by William Aiton (1731–1793), who was 'gardener to his Majesty' at Kew. In the second and enlarged edition (1810–1813) compiled by his son, William Townsend Aiton (1766–1849), also gardener at Kew to the king, only two additional St Helena plants are added, making a total of seven. This was at a time when the plant craze was at its height in Britain and plants, especially from the Cape, were flooding into British nurseries and nursery catalogues, as well as being featured in the botanical and gardening magazines.[63] Nor did the situation improve. Robert Sweet's *Hortus Britannicus* appeared in 1826 with only six plants listed as coming from St Helena, this at a time when St Helena had recently been much in the public mind because of Napoleon's captivity.

TABLE 14

Plants as listed from St Helena in the first two editions of *Hortus Kewensis*

Edition Vol/Page	Plant	Common name	Date introduced to Britain	Comment given
1st 1789 3/234 2nd 1813 5/102	*Cotula anthemoides* [*C. coronopifolia*]	Dwarf cotula [yellow-flowered pagoda]	1732 1696	Stove house plant Cultivated by James Sherard MD In Chelsea garden
1st 1789 2/428–9 2nd 1812 4/175	*Pelargonium cotyledonis*	Hollyhock-leaved crane's bill [old father live forever]	1765	Green house plant John Bush
1st 1789 2/438 2nd 1812 4/146	*Pentapetes erythroxylon* *Melhania erythroxylon* [*Trochetiopsis erythroxylon*]	St Helena redwood	1772	Stove house plant Sir Joseph Banks

Edition Vol/Page	Plant	Common name	Date introduced to Britain	Comment given
1st 1789 3/184 2nd 1813 5/30	*Conyza rugosa* [*C. bonariensis*]	St Helena flea-bane [hairy fleabane?]	1772	Green house plant Sir Joseph Banks
1st 1789 3/469 2nd 1813 5/528	*Dicksonia arborescens*	Tree dicksonia	1786	Stove house plant Anthony P. Hove
2nd 1811 3/270	*Rubus pinnatus* Native of St Helena & Cape	Wing-leaved Cape bramble	1789	Green house plant Sir Joseph Banks
2nd 1812 4/146	*Melhania melanoxylon*	St Helena ebony or blackwood [Dwarf ebony or possibly ebony?]	c.1800	Stove house plant

TABLE 15

Plants listed from St Helena in *Sweet's Hortus Britannicus* (1826)

Part/Page	Given name of plant/common name	Date of introduction	Comment given
1/57	*Melhania erythroxylon* St Helena red wood	1772	Stove shrub
1/220	*Conyza rugosa*	1772	Green house shrub
1/234	*Petrobium arboreum* [whitewood]	1816	Tree. Stove shrub
2/424	*Agave angustifolia* Narrow-leaved agave	1770	Dry stove shrub requiring very little water
2/444	*Cynodon stellatus* [*Cynodon dactylon* var. *stellatus*] Starry cynodon	1823	Stove shrub [grass]
2/464	*Dicksonia arborescens* Tree	1786	Stove shrub

There are several reasons for this lacuna. The fact that St Helena plants were prized by wealthy collectors of exotic species in itself underlines their rarity. But another factor was that St Helena plants were difficult to grow in Britain, so confining their distribution to botanic gardens or wealthy private individuals, both having stove houses or adequately heated conservatories. Writing in his famous *Botanical Dictionary*, published first in 1840, Joseph Paxton observed of *Dicksonia arborescens*:

> A very ornamental genus of fern, containing the tree of St. Helena, which has often been brought in a living state to this country, but rarely survives many months.[64]

The 1840 edition contained only eight plants from St Helena including a mysterious *Pinaster st.heleniea*. And a generation later, in 1873, the London nurseryman and author Benjamin Williams commented of the St Helena tree fern, 'this fine plant is apparently difficult to establish when imported of large size from its native country ... A beautiful stove Fern, at present very rare in cultivation, and singular in being only found in the island of St. Helena.'[65]

Apart from this imposing tree fern, had these St Helena plants been more dramatic in appearance they might have received greater public attention. Their delicacy was not in keeping with the showy nature of many of those plants which dominated this new age of gardening. There are very few early plates of St Helena plants in this age of high botany, and even some of those were mistaken for endemics. For example, there is a *Canna patens* in the 1830 volume of the *Botanical Cabinet*:

> In his magnificent work on MONANDRIA plants Mr. ROSCOE has given a fine representation of this beautiful species. He considers it to be a native of the island of St. Helena.[66]

In fact, it is the *C. indica* or Indian shot, a naturalised plant on St Helena.[67] The one St Helena species which did receive some attention was the St Helena redwood (*Trochetiopsis erythroxylon*). Volume 6 of the *Botanical Repository* (*c*.1803–1807) has the redwood as *Dombeya erythroxylon*, a name used by the nursery trade at the time:

> The handsome plant here represented is a native of Saint Helena, and is known by the name of Saint Helena Red-wood. Although introduced into this country by Sir Joseph Banks in the year 1772, it is at this time one of our very rarest and most desirable of hot-house plants. Mr. Aiton enumerates it in the Hortus Kewensis, but marks no time for its flowering; which therefore, we must suppose, but seldom occurs.[68]

The specimen used by the magazine's publisher Henry Andrews was provided to him in June 1803 by Thomas Evans, who spent his wealth introducing rare plants from East and South-East Asia and growing them in his Stepney garden in London. Evans even had his own private plant hunter whom he sent to collect in Penang. Evans freely distributed plants to fellow gentleman collectors.[69] Andrews also records that he saw the St Helena redwood a month before publication of the magazine, 'beautifully in bloom at the honourable Charles Greville's, Paddington'. Greville was an associate of Sir Joseph Banks, who apart from putting the future Emma Hamilton on the road to fame, was a patron of horticulture and a collector of rare and exotic plants.

Shortly after the *Botanical Repository* illustration of the St Helena redwood appeared a more amateurishly executed plate was included in John Sims' *Botanical Magazine* in 1807 as plate 1,000, now under the name of *Pentapetes erythroxylon*. The commentary for this plate also mentions another St Helena plant:

> Native of St. Helena, where there occurs another species with leaves quite entire at the margin, called Black-Wood or Ebony (PENTAPETES *Melanoxylon, Soland. MSS.*) which is an undoubted congener of our plant, and perhaps the one figured in the Botanist's Repository. Introduced by Sir Joseph Banks, in 1772. Cultivated in the stove. Flowers in May, June, and July, Propagated by cuttings.

The specimen of redwood was supplied to Sims by the veteran London nurseryman Reginald Whitley, who ran his business at Old Brompton. In 1810 he sold this 20-acre site and moved to Fulham, closer to the River Thames. Here Whitley went into partnership with two other men, purchasing Matthew Burchell's nursery where the famous botanist William had been brought up before going to St Helena.[70]

A final factor restricting knowledge of St Helena plants and so their promulgation by British nursery firms was the fact that knowledge of the island's endemic flora was largely a closed book until the last quarter of the 19th century. Much is made of the pioneering work on the plants of St Helena by Solander (1770s), Burchell (1800s) and Roxburgh (1810s). But for whatever reason none of these did much or anything to publicise their work in print. As stated, Solander's collections ended up in the Natural History Museum and Burchell's remained within the family until their donation to Kew Gardens in 1868. The only exception was Roxburgh and the offshoots mentioned above. But, as seen, thanks to the enthusiasm and exertions of Governor Beatson, Roxburgh's 32-page 'Alphabetical list of plants' was reproduced in 1816 in *Tracts relative to the island of St. Helena*.

PLATE 11 Sandy Bay, 1814. Governor R.A. Sterndale observing Sandy Bay in 1900 commented, 'here and there on a grassy knoll, embowered in trees, nestle cosy little houses with fertile gardens'. This was the home of the eccentric and St Helena–born Colonel Sir William Doveton (1753–1843) who lived and farmed here from 1784. It was on Doveton's front lawn that Napoleon came with his entourage and sat and ate breakfast on 4 October 1820, the emperor's last expedition before his death. Beside Doveton's house is Rose Cottage and up the hill is a military outpost. Print drawn by J. Wathen and engraved by J. Clark. Provided by Donal P. McCracken.

PLATE 12

Napoleon's tomb
garden. The site for
the tomb is said to
have been selected
by Napoleon himself,
near a spring which
provided fresh
drinking water for
him every day at
Longwood. Needless
to say, the small
enclosure became a
place of pilgrimage and
remained so even after
the emperor's body
was exhumed in 1840.
Fenced in, with a small
sentry box, it became
an attractive small
arboretum with the
famous willow trees
and araucarias.

Kerr, *Series of Views in
the Island of St Helena*,
London, 1822. Provided by
Donal P. McCracken.

Thunbergia sp.
246 Aristolochia sp.
247 Artocarpus incisa
Fraser St. Helena
248 Dimocarpus sp.
249 Solanum ?
250 madagascarensis Buddlea sp.
Napoleon Willow came in this collection planted where it now is by Smith in 1827 (1851.) J.m.
Chevr. Parmentier
251 Ficus ferruginea
252 —— lutescens
253 —— ceratiformis
286 Bactri
287 Phoen
288 Latan
289 Coccos
290 Thrin
291 Elais
292 Tetra
293 Ochr

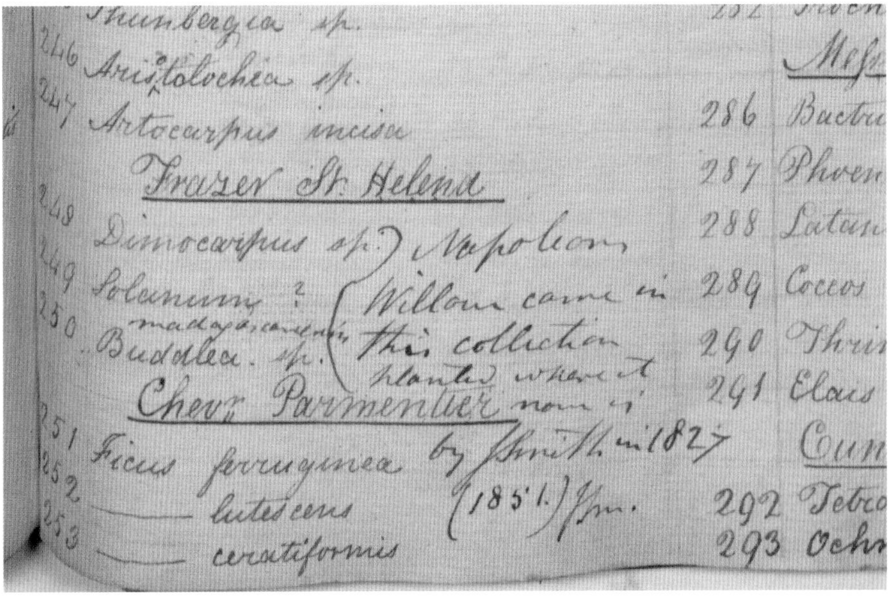

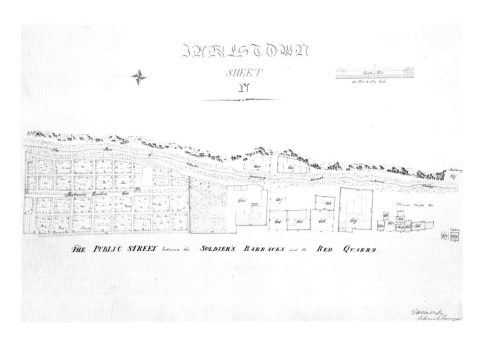

PLATE 13 Kew Gardens accession book entry for 1827 mentioning the famous St Helena Napoleon willow, which was planted out at Kew and for many years was a popular attraction.

PLATE 14 1839 plan of the St Helena Botanic Gardens in Jamestown by G.W. Melliss. This shows the grid layout, the main entrance and the steps dividing the upper and lower levels of the gardens. TNA CO700/StHelena8, sheet N.

PLATE 15 Longwood garden today
© Patricia McCracken

PLATE 16

Indentured Chinese gardeners were much sought after on St Helena and Napoleon had four working for him. These experimental plots are sited in front of Plantation House, with formal gardens on the lower right. Later the garden was relocated behind and beside the governor's residence.

Kerr, *Series of Views in the Island of St Helena*, London, 1822. Provided by Donal P. McCracken.

PLATE 17

View taken from the Road leading Towards the Plantation House, 1816

This fine coloured aquatint by paymaster to the 66th Regiment, John Kerr was engraved by Robert Havell. The scene looks down on plantation land, where the road rises from the Jamestown Valley and Half Tree Hollow. On the right is High Knoll fort and in the background are the flat-topped Barn Mountain and the conical Signal Hill. Exotic tree planting is evident around the modest homesteads, with some hedgerow planting and willows in the damp course on the left.

Kerr, Series of Views in the Island of St Helena, London, 1822. Provided by Donal P. McCracken.

PLATE 18

Georgian plantation gardens and farmland, 1784

'Interior View of the Island of St. Helena' was drawn by James Forbes and engraved by J. Greig. It depicts the upper Sandy Bay valley with five farmhouses, gardens, tree plantings and agricultural land worked by enslaved labourers. The dramatic tops of the peaks of Lot and Lot's Wife can be seen and, on the higher ground on the left, some surviving wild indigenous flora of St Helena.

Forbes, *Oriental memoirs: A narrative of seventeen years residence in India*, 1834, plate 69. Provided by Donal P. McCracken.

PLATE 19
Fairyland House, beautifully and dramatically set at the edge of Sandy Bay with the Lot stone pillar in the background, was the home of the Greentree family. It was laid out, like many St Helena farm houses, with pasture at the front and a shrubbery and arboretum at the rear. Drawn by George Hutchins Bellasis, engraved by Robert Havell. Bellasis, *Views of Saint Helena*, 1815

Provided by Edward Baldwin / Museum of St Helena

Plant lists alone, though, were never going to have much impact on the wider horticultural and botanical world. This is why Melliss's book on St Helena's natural history is such a seminal work. The importance of the work undertaken by Solander, Burchell and Roxburgh rests essentially on providing modern botanists with snapshots of St Helena's endemic flora at various times within a two-generation timeframe. Important as that is, it has led to an incorrect impression of St Helena's plant life entering public consciousness in Britain and elsewhere.

A note has to be added to the record of these early St Helena plant imports to Britain. Professor Cronk has highlighted the caution that needs to be exercised in taking these early names, scientific and common, at face value. In particular he raises and elucidates the confusion swirling around identity as regards dwarf ebony (*Trochetiopsis ebenus*) and St Helenaebony (*Trochetiopsis melanoxylon*). The situation is further confused in more recent times with the alarming cross-pollination on the island between the redwood (*Trochetiopsis erythroxylon*) and ebony (*Trochetiopsis ebenus*), both in cultivation, which has produced the hybrid rebony (*Trochetiopsis* x *benjamini*). *Trochetiopsis melanoxylon* is now extinct and appears to have been so since the late 18th or early 19th century. This was after a long decline. It was recorded in 1709 that, 'nearly all the ebony wood was burnt up in providing 10000 or 12000 bushels of lime (*c.*35–42 tons) for building the castle on Munden's Point'. Melliss did not distinguish between the dwarf ebony and the ebony. In the early 1870s he considered the species to be extinct. He wrote, 'I saw the Ebony once twenty years ago; it was growing in a garden on the high land, one miserable little plant, only six inches in height, and yet it blossomed.' In the true tradition of the classic plant hunters, the dwarf ebony was rediscovered by Charles and George Benjamin and Quentin Cronk at Blue Point, the former famously descending a cliff on a rope to obtain cuttings.[71] Had these St Helena plants been a success in the late Georgian gardens of Britain, the saga of their current struggle for survival might have been very different.

6

Napoleon's gardens

In an uncharacteristic moment of relaxed and candid reflection on St Helena, the Emperor Napoleon admitted to General Gaspard Gourgaud (1783–1852), a member of his court in exile:

> The life that I live here on St. Helena, if I were not a captive, and if I were in Europe, would suit me very well. I should like to live in the country; I should like to see the soil improved by others, for I do not know enough about gardening to improve it myself. That kind of thing is the noblest existence.[1]

Napoleon Bonaparte arrived on St Helena on 15 October 1815 and lasted five years and six months. His unexpected arrival on the 'Rock of St Helena', along with an entourage of 28 people, of course changed everything for the island and,

21. Las Cases and Napoleon talking to Toby, the enslaved gardener at the Briars. Napoleon frequently spoke with Toby during his walks and unsuccessfully attempted to get him his freedom.

Abbott, *Napoleon at St Helena*, p. 50. Provided by Donal P. McCracken.

for a time, brought prosperity. The shadow of the exiled emperor has come down through the years and imprinted itself on the very name of the island. Though St Helena remained part of the East India Company's domains during the 'Captivity', as it has been called, it was in fact a military stronghold, governed by a British army officer with extensive powers and authority. Napoleon's establishment cost the British about £12,000 a year, but the cost of maintaining the garrison of 2,000 troops sent to guard the fallen emperor totalled more than £200,000 per annum. On top of this could be added the cost of the squadrons of naval vessels which constantly patrolled offshore.

St Helena's population more than doubled during the time Napoleon was on the island, from about 3,600 in 1814 to 8,000 in 1820. Along with the garrison, a third of whom were Company troops, were 1,200 enslaved persons, 600 'free blacks', 500 Chinese indentured labourers and about 3,500 whites. For the last of these it was a period of great excitement and, for those with any degree of entrepreneurship, a time when respectable profits might be obtained by supplying this enlarged garrison.

Longwood was the third and last house where Napoleon stayed on St Helena. On his first night ashore (17/18 October 1815), he lodged in a barracks of a building which overlooked the Castle Garden. This was owned by none other than the Company's gardener Henry Porteous. It was a cramped though extremely clean boarding house with small stuffy rooms, obviously designed to squash in as many paying government officials and military officers as possible. Not surprisingly, the conqueror of Europe was not keen for a second night in this strange establishment. He was also not keen on being the subject of curiosity for excited townsfolk.

The Briars

The next morning Napoleon left Jamestown to look at the Longwood property, which was being made ready as his residence. Returning, he noticed the Briars, the small and elegant estate not far from Jamestown at about 870 feet [265 m] above sea level on the Longwood road. It was owned and occupied between 1807 and 1818 by the colourful and controversial William Balcombe (1777–1829), whose former business partner William Burchell, the botanist, regarded him as a scoundrel. The two men's business partnership had shattered not long after they had arrived on the island. Balcombe, as well as farming, owned the Union Brewery. The produce of the Briars garden alone, over and above what the family could consume, brought in annually an income ranging from £500 to £600.

The Briars had its own garden, 'a wilderness of orange trees, myrtles, vines, pomegranates, white roses, fuchsias, geraniums and many other flowers'.[2] One description ran:

> I must plead the same excuse for devoting a few lines to the garden that I have to the cottage, for it was lovely in itself, and the favourite retreat of the emperor during his sojourn with us. It would require the pen of a Scott, or the pencil of a Claude, to do anything like justice to its beauty. I often wander in my dreams through its myrtle groves, and the orange trees, with their bright green leaves, delicious blossoms, and golden fruit, seem again before me, as they were in my blessed days of childhood. Every description of tropical fruit flourished here luxuriantly; various species of vine, citron, orange, fig, shadoc, guava, mango — all in endless profusion.[3]

Napoleon lived in the distinctive garden summerhouse known as the Pavilion from 18 October to 10 December 1815. This still stands, though the original two-storey main house, with its two cypress sentinels and great palm in front, fell into decay and was replaced in 1959 by a utilitarian building for the manager of the Cable and Wireless Company. Fortuitously, the property later became the property of France.

The Briars was not untypical of a St Helena gentleman's rural home, with a tree-lined pathway running up to the house. Napoleon habitually walked along this path for an hour before dinner was served. The gardens to the side were also a favourite place for the emperor to walk with his courtier Las Cases.

On 20 November 1815, during Napoleon's interlude at the Briars, the imposing Major Hudson had an unexpected dinner guest at Maldivia. This materialised after Napoleon discovered an old track in the Briars garden used by enslaved people, which led down to Maldivia and the town. The botanic garden was not much further down from the Hudsons' home. There is, however, no record of Napoleon entering the actual botanic garden, though Count Charles Tristan Montholon (1783–1853) speaks of it as an asset to the town along with Jamestown's fine houses. We do know from Captain Nicholls's record that on 21 November 1818 Count Bertrand walked the considerable distance from Longwood to the 'Company's garden'. At that time the gardener was Edward Charlton.

Because the pavilion was so small and scantily furnished, it was not surprising that the emperor spent much time outdoors or with the Balcombes. Despite all that is written of his friendship with their 13-year-old daughter, Betsy, and, on another level, with Emmanuel, Count de Las Cases, Napoleon liked to be alone for long periods:

The only exception to the emperor's habits of regularity when with us [the children] was in his hour of rising. In the midst of our garden was a very large pond of transparent water, full of gold and silver fish; and near this was the grapery, formed of trellis-work, quite covered with vines of every description. At the end of the grapery was an arbour, round and over which a treillage of grapes clustered in the richest profusion. To this spot, which was so sheltered as to be cool in the most sultry weather, Napoleon was much attached. He would sometimes convey his papers there as early as four o'clock in the morning, and employ himself until breakfast time in writing; and, when tired of his pen, in dictating to Las Cases. No one was ever permitted to intrude upon him when there, and this little attention was ever after gratefully remembered.

Betsy claimed that 'as a privileged person', she was exempt from Napoleon's prohibitions: 'Even when he was in the act of dictating a sentence to Las Cases he would come and answer my call, 'Come and unlock the garden door,' and I was always admitted and welcomed with a smile. I did not abuse this indulgence, and seldom intruded.'[4]

There was someone else at the Briars to whom Napoleon took a liking. He struck up an acquaintance with an old gardener, an enslaved man called Toby, who was described as a Malay Indian. During his walks through the Balcombe garden, Napoleon would stop at Toby's hut and the two would talk through an interpreter. It is said that Napoleon unsuccessfully tried to buy him his freedom. Of Toby, the emperor said:

What, after all, is this poor human machine? There is not one whose exterior form is like another, or whose internal organization resembles the rest; and it is by disregarding this truth that we are led to the commission of so many errors. Had Toby been a Brutus, he would have put himself to death; if an Æsop, he would now, perhaps, have been the governor's adviser; if a Christian, ardent and zealous, he would have borne his chains in the sight of God, and blessed them. As for poor Toby, he thinks of none of this. He stoops and works in tranquillity ... It was a horrible act of cruelty to bring him here to die, under the fetters of slavery.[5]

Toby's attitude to Napoleon is well illustrated by Betsy in her memoir:

Frequently, when the nights were illumined by the splendid tropical moon, would he rise at three o'clock, and saunter down to the garden long before old Toby, the slave, had slept off his first nap, and there he would regale himself with an early breakfast of delicious fruits, with which our garden abounded. Our old Malay was so fond of the man Bony, as he designated the emperor, that he always placed the garden key where Napoleon's fingers could reach it under the wicket.[6]

Napoleon spent only 54 days with the Balcombes at the Briars. As well as the famous friendship with young Betsy Balcombe, there was later some contact between William Balcombe and Napoleon, as Balcombe secured a concession to supply the Longwood establishment with certain provisions. This eventually drew suspicion from Governor Lowe and, as it proved, with reason. In March 1818, three years before Napoleon's death, the Balcombes felt it expedient to leave St Helena. William Balcombe ended up as colonial treasurer in New South Wales and died there aged only 51.

In fairness to Balcombe, it is clear that he behaved in a perfectly civil and hospitable manner to Napoleon during his brief stay at the Briars. The event has been dominated by the Betsy Balcombe saga but without the father's good grace, the stay would not have been as pleasant for the unfortunate captive.

So the eight weeks passed well enough between the Pavilion, residence and garden. General Gourgaud quoted Napoleon, perhaps a little ungraciously, if not inaccurately, saying:

> Posterity will not fail to reproach England for having left me two months at the Briars, in an ill-furnished room, without even the convenience of taking my accustomed bath.

Worse humiliation was to come.

৵৽ Longwood ৵৽

The Longwood farm, situated at 1,763 feet (537 m) above sea level, had already been noted for some interesting botanical specimens prior to Napoleon's arrival. William Burchell, in his draft manuscript 'Flora Heleniana', notes at some length the bastard gumtree he found at Longwood on 19 February 1808.[7] Then in his more extensive manuscript list, 'Flora Insulæ Sta Helenæ', Longwood crops up 16 times with the following species being listed:

Cissus vitiginea	*Psoralæ aphylla*
Hypericum (*monogyrum*)	*Crotalaria incana*
Lathynis odoratus	*Clutia pulchella*

Thuja sp.	*Mimosa odorata*
Mimosa farnesiana	*Cupressus horizontalis*
Stillingia sebifera	*Cucurius sativus*
Furcæa Spanish aloe	*Cotyledon orbiculata* pig's ear
Mesembryanthemrum edule	*Hibiscus rosa sinensis*

Longwood had always been a working farm rather than a gentleman's residence, though in later years the lieutenant-governor had lived in the house. It had a large, fairly flat area around it with adequate soil which made it, unlike much of the island, ideal for farming. In the greater part of the 18th century, it had in part been used as pasture for profitable cattle farming. The decision was then taken to enclose large tracts of land at a cost of between £8,000 and £10,000 and recreate woodland, in part to supply timber to Jamestown for firewood. This led to a reduction in the herd but does not appear to have produced a forest. Later, under Governor Brooke's dispensation, parts of the Longwood pastures were restored, and a trench cut from the hills to bring fresh water down to the cattle. Company 'wasteland' had by that time been considered by the planters to be commonage, so this development had not gone down well with the tough settlers. Indeed, attempts to let out several Company farms met with no offers as these planters basically did as they pleased and used what land they pleased, in particular letting their sheep roam where they wished, be it on their or the Company's land.[8]

Improved methods of growing potatoes were shown to be a great success on Company farms, with up to three crops a year being extracted annually.[9]

⁊ᷱᷧᷴ The problems at Longwood ᷤᷧᷴ

Napoleon's Longwood establishment was a hotbed of gossip, made more so by the sheer boredom of nothing happening and by the restrictions imposed on occasion by Lowe. Some, though not all, of these were petty, bureaucratic and unnecessary. Napoleon added to the atmosphere by being, at least at first, unwilling or unable to accept the conditions in which he had to live and the treatment he had to endure. If ever there were a 'caged man', it was he. The problems encountered with the Longwood setup are important for this study because the garden was essentially a response to them. Those problems were formidable. The picture of Longwood on its fairly windswept plateau was exaggerated by the French but it could be bleak enough. Apart from the underlying annoyance of having been brought to this 'miserable rock', there were three major problems.

22. Burchell's sketch of a bleak-looking Longwood House with an acacia some gumwoods and a Norfolk Island pine, made on a damp Boxing Day, 1807, eight years before Napoleon would take up occupation and establish a small but luxuriant garden.

The main issue was the condition of the Longwood complex. The house began life in 1746 as a barn for barley, oats and wheat. A decade later, it was converted into a residence for Lieutenant-Governor Charles Hutchinson. The Longwood estate was more than 600 acres (242 ha), including a 94-acre (38 ha) common. It tended to be portrayed as a barren plateau buffeted by the violent trade winds, with two-thirds covered in stunted gumwood trees which all bent in one direction at an angle of 45 degrees. What few other trees existed there were old with 'decrepit trunks'. Or, as Basil Jackson put it in 1815, the island had 'a dearth of trees throughout, save at Longwood, where the monotonous gum-wood covers an area of thirty or forty acres'. By the time Napoleon was deposited here, 60 years after the estate's inception, there was still a remnant of the old Deadwood, sufficient for Napoleon's trustworthy valet Louis-Joseph Marchand to describe it as a forest.[10] But by then the makeshift Longwood farm building, in part held together by papier-mâché, was in a fairly dilapidated condition.

Matters were not assisted by Longwood's intermittent water supply. Initially it was fed from only one drain. This had been sufficient for the farm but the encampment of a large body of troops on Deadwood Plain meant that water shortages were frequent and sometimes barrels of water had to be brought in. This was alleviated in 1817 when a second spring at the base of Diana's Peak was utilised and a channel built to connect it with the old watercourse between Hutt's Gate and Longwood.

The second problem relating to Longwood House was its physical size. Much of Napoleon's establishment was squashed into a former army officer's home. While Napoleon was not a confined prisoner in a jailhouse, his movements were severely restricted within what was a kind of open prison with its own grounds. To prevent any escape, Napoleon was restricted to a specific area. At night, this area narrowed down to little more than the garden. Indeed, the British built a trench around part of the property. This was not, as pointed out by some tourist guides, to allow the diminutive Napoleon to walk along it unseen, but ostensibly to keep cattle out and, by inference, Napoleon in.

This is confirmed when Governor Lowe inspected the trench and became very animated when he observed a tree's overhanging branches. This was perhaps one of the trees planted by Porteous and Thomas Ritchie in September 1794, which appear to have replaced earlier failed plantings.[11] Lowe ordered that Porteous come up to Longwood House immediately. Once there, Porteous was ordered to see that the tree was rooted out, thus preventing a nimble emperor from vaulting out of his compound.

Napoleon was permitted to go further than the delineated area but only in the company of a British officer, something which was anathema to the emperor. Much later, when battered by the public outcry in Britain at Napoleon's treatment or alleged treatment on the island, Lowe greatly extended the area where Napoleon could move on his own. Though this led to the famous picnic on the grass in front of the eccentric Sir William Doveton's Mount Pleasant in the Sandy Bay Valley, the truth was that by then Napoleon's health was such that he enjoyed only limited benefits of his new freedom.

But there was a third major problem with Longwood and that was privacy. In 1817 Captain Barnes observed:

> Mason's Stock-House [Teutonic Hall] is situated upon an eminence, immediately opposite to Buonaparte's house at Longwood; commanding a full view of the latter place; so hence, Buonaparte and his suite could be distinctly seen, walking in Longwood grove or wood.[12]

Napoleon was a curiosity. No shortage of soldiers, sailors, locals, local administrators and visitors to the island tried to get a glimpse of the fallen emperor. The curved turf bank that Napoleon constructed against the trade winds, much of it with his own hands, also helped cut out some of the prying eyes. Needless to say, Napoleon resented these gawkers greatly. It is true that some islanders were scared by the image they had of Napoleon but that did not prevent them from wanting to peer over the garden fence at the monster. The author has a botanical tract on St Helena dated 1836 on the cover of which is written in pencil:

> Mrs C [Carrol] the Miss Legge [Legg, daughter of John Legg] of whom Mrs Abell/ Miss [Betsy] Balcom relates that Napoleon used to frighten her so greatly.[13]

⤳ Forming a garden ⤳

In his *Les derniers moments de Napoléon*, Francesco Antommarchi, Napoleon's 30-year-old Corsican physician during the closing phase of his captivity, included a letter he had written from St Helena in July 1820. In this, he took credit for turning Napoleon's mind to thoughts of gardening:

> The remedies I had adopted seemed to have produced a beneficial effect; he was recovering, took exercise, and I had advised him to superintend, or rather to conduct, the formation of a garden consisting of a few toises of ground round his house.

This should perhaps be taken with a pinch of salt. Napoleon had already well been associated with gardens in Europe so it was natural that being so confined he would turn his energies to creating a proper garden at Longwood. The emperor had for long taken walks in what there was of a garden, especially if no one was around, even during the night. This is not to say that Antommarchi did not also encourage this pursuit and his arrival in September 1819 coincides with the height of Napoleon's gardening frenzy, which had commenced in earnest a couple of months before. To Antommarchi Napoleon asserted, 'Well, Doctor are you satisfied with your patient – is he obedient enough? This [gardening] is better than your pills, Dottoraccio; you shall not physic me anymore.'[14]

During 1819 and early 1820, the Longwood garden was Napoleon's passion. Lord Rosebery in his admirable book about the emperor's time on St Helena records:

> Napoleon threw himself into the operations with his usual ardour: spent much time and money on them: bought large trees and moved them, with the aid of the artillery regiment and some hundreds of Chinese. All this distracted him for a time, and gave him exercise.[15]

It was in July 1819 that Napoleon turned his mind to gardening, with eventually all hands being called in to assist. As well as his courtiers and, in particular, the long-suffering Count Montholon, this also occasionally included the British army, or rather individual soldiers drafted in by the orderly to assist. It is said that Napoleon 'used to trace out all his [garden] plans and field-works on the ground of his little garden, with his officers and attendants around him, to whom he pointed out his ideas'. His attempts, however, to drag the wives of his courtiers into his gardening endeavours appear to have failed. St Denis's memories of this episode in the Longwood saga leave no doubt about what he thought about the emperor's new enthusiasm:

> All this work which the Emperor made us do was extremely trying to us who had never before handled a pickax, a shovel or a spade, or pushed a wheel-barrow. When we came in from work our breeches, our stockings, our shirts, our waistcoats were all wringing wet, and our faces were covered with sweat and dirt. We often said that the Emperor would kill us if he had the idea of making another garden.[16]

Napoleon's head gardener was a Swiss man called Jean-Abram Noverraz (1790–1849), who had until then been one of his three valets. The emperor instructed him to create two gardens, one parallel to his bedroom and the second adjacent to the library, each initially 30 feet by 60 feet (9.1 by 18.2 m) and bordered by a low wooden fence. These improvements, where a scorched lawn had been, had the added advantage of instantly pushing back the proximity of the night sentries. Noverraz first appears in the role of gardener in Nicholls's journal on 14 October 1819. Apart from Noverraz there were also several British gardeners. One was called Sowerby, and the under-gardener was a man called Taylor. As will be seen, these men were not all that they seemed.

By November 1819, Nicholls was recording:

> He [Napoleon] is picking holes in one part of the garden, and raising mounds in other parts.
> The General was in his dressing-grown amidst the people at work, directing them; takes a spade at times, and begins to put in seeds – messages to me for carts, shovels, and spades. God send he may always continue in his humor during my residence at Longwood! 30th. This afternoon he stood in Count Montholon's little garden looking at my servants watering some flowers at my door.[17]

As the months passed Napoleon's plans became more ambitious, until Sir Hudson Lowe began to get suspicious of Napoleon's intentions. Writing to Lord Bathurst on 1 December 1819, the governor observed:

Nothing can exceed the bustle and activity which has been recently displayed by General Bonaparte, in giving directions about his flower-garden, and superintending the workmen employed at it. He is hemming it in all round with as [many] bushy trees and shrubs as he can get transplanted, and with sod walls, so as to screen himself as far as possible from external observation.[18]

The sod walls referred to by Lowe were made of grass and earth sods. Ostensibly, they were windbreaks, something badly needed on the Longwood plateau. Of course, they also acted as screens. Sometimes Napoleon himself lifted each sod up onto the bank and then the unfortunate Montholon had to hammer it down with a large mallet. Of course, the indentured Chinese labourers assisted and were joined by Chinese domestic servants in the Longwood establishment, Napoleon ringing a large bell to summon his workforce. The use of indoor servants alongside labourers created some tension. Captain Lutyens, who replaced Captain Nicholls as orderly officer at Longwood, noted:

The four Chinese who have constantly been employed in the garden got sulky at the General having given a bottle of wine to each of the Chinese that are employed in the house, who worked at the sod wall, and did not give them the same indulgence; they therefore refused doing what the General wanted them to do, which put him in a great rage, and he ordered them off instantly.[19]

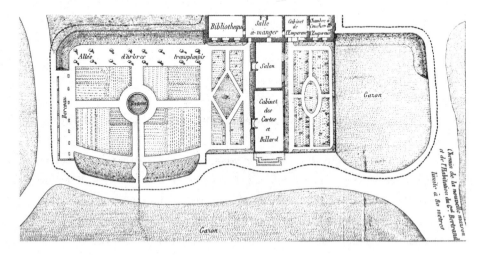

23. Plan of the Longwood garden. This detail from a plan of Longwood House and compound was included in Count Montholon's book on Napoleon on St Helena. The two formal gardens are clearly shown on either side of the old, dilapidated Longwood farmhouse.
Montholon, *Récits de la captivité de L'Empereur Napoléon à Sainte-Hélène*, 1847, opp. p. 192. Provided by Donal P. McCracken.

Nonetheless, Napoleon saw to it that each Chinese labourer had a large straw hat like his own as protection from the sun. And with an additional 30 shillings plus rations a month, their skills were duly rewarded.[20] There were those contemporaries who thought that Napoleon was unduly influenced by his labour force. An anonymous letter writer in 1822, probably J. Kerr of the 66th Regiment and the creator of some of the finest drawings ever produced of St Helena, recorded the following:

> From some time after the arrival of Napoleon, he was in the habit of taking much exercise on horseback, and making frequent visits to the farmers near his residence; but this did not continue long, and latterly he confined himself almost entirely to the grounds at Longwood. He lived very retired, saw no strangers, and was principally occupied in reading, and superintending the improvements of a small garden adjoining his apartments. But he seemed rather to have acquiesced in the taste of his Chinese gardeners, than to have displayed much of his own. However the embankments resembling fortifications, facing the road, evidently thrown up to screen him from observation, were somewhat characteristic, and might be deemed exclusively his choice.[21]

The emperor adopted gardening clothes, consisting of loose-fitting trousers, a yellowish-white nankeen flannel jacket, a hunting waistcoat, sometimes a cravat or Madras, sandals or red or green slippers and a very large broad-brimmed straw hat with a black ribbon, rather than his famous black bicorne. The straw was said to be stuffed for lining with a British newspaper dated September 1813.[22] Count Montholon summarised matters as follows:

> It was a picture worthy of being represented by the most celebrated artists, to see the conqueror of so many kingdoms, him who had dictated laws to so many sovereigns, at dawn of day, with his spade in his hand, a broad straw hat on his head, and his feet clad in red morocco slippers, directing our labours, and those, assuredly more useful, of the Chinese gardeners of the establishment. In a few days he succeeded in this manner in raising two circular walls of tufts of bad grass, about eleven or twelve feet high, on a diameter of twenty yards, on a line with his bedroom and the library.[23]

He conducted the operation with great vigour and sometime with great humour, using a rosewood billiard cue as baton, walking stick and measuring rod.[24]

By the time Napoleon died, there were two formal gardens adjacent to Longwood House. These had emerged out of two smaller gardens he had formed, both adjacent to the house. It was in either of these that Napoleon liked to take his breakfast, frequently in the company of Montholon. To the west of the house beside the emperor's bedroom, and now connected by a new French door, was the older one, the little garden or Jardin Marchand, as it was sometimes called in honour of one of his loyal valets. This had existed in part, in the form of a 'cabbage patch', when the French contingent moved into Longwood. Napoleon had it created along a formal pattern and extended the full length of the salon and the billiard room. There were several beds here including one which was triangular. In the middle of what he called his parterre was a coffee plant that the emperor had been given. It also had two large lemon trees which had been transplanted and gave shade for the emperor to sit under. There was no shortage of roses and strawberry plants.[25]

The great work of gardening, the library garden, occurred on the east side of the building, and was termed the Jardin Ali, the nickname given to Napoleon's other valet, Louis Étienne St Denis. Its creation was made possible because of Napoleon's rapid actions – as in his generalship of old – in outwitting Sir Hudson Lowe by tearing down the old palings and creating a formal garden nearly four times as wide as the little garden. Eventually, both the Marchand and Ali gardens were extended down the slope beyond the limit of the front steps of the house down to the grass at the end of the salon / billiard room annex. Lowe said that 'in depth' the garden was about 100 toises (about 600 ft or 200 m).

The library or Ali garden had two sections. One, fronted by the L shape of the library, salon and billiard room, approximately mirrored the shape of the little garden. But adjacent to this library garden was a much larger formal garden with the famous nine-foot (2.7 m) high and 26 yards (24 m) long curved turf bank and parterres. A grotto was constructed into the bank where Napoleon was meant to take meals when he wished. But with wooden floor and sides, albeit decorated by Chinese dragons, it resembled a mine shaft. It soon began to subside and was abandoned.

Early attempts at transplanting trees were not very successful, with several oaks dying soon after replanting. A major logistical enterprise was then put in motion, involving the artillery company and the labour of several hundred indentured Chinese workers. This proved more successful. A row of 24 trees was transported 'at considerable expense' and constituted an avenue in the classical style adjacent to the library windows. Each tree was planted 'with two yards square of earth round their roots'. The artillery and the Chinese workers did their job well, for by the time the military withdrew from Longwood in 1821, only one tree had died.[26]

This library garden was formally divided with a water basin in the middle, some terracing and what was called the cradle along the easternmost extremity. An interesting sketch of this eastern garden by Captain Guy Rotton exists in the Hearl collection in the Bodleian Library, Oxford.[27] Montholon's description gives some idea of the engineering work undertaken in creating this library garden:

> The library garden was shut in to the height of the steps of the topographic cabinet, or billiard cabinet as it was called, by a semi-circular construction of tufts of grass made in steps, each range of steps being planted with rose-trees. In this construction was a space six feet wide, which, being made with a double row in the centre, formed a cabinet with grassy seats. A wooden trench, on a level with the ground, crossed it, and carried off the superfluous water of a kind of basin with a jet-d'eau, formed in the centre of this garden by an enormous tub, twelve feet [4 m] in diameter and three [one metre] deep, to which the water was brought by means of leaden pipes communicating with those which supplied Longwood.[28]

As well as the pathways, there was a tent in the garden which Napoleon used a lot during his last summer for taking his lunch and working at his papers. This was donated by the ever-considerate Rear-Admiral Sir Pulteney Malcolm. Lowe proposed replacing the tent with a military wooden building 70 foot (21 m) long by 20 foot (6.4 m) wide – 'fitting it up in the style of the Knightsbridge houses' – however time was by then running out for Napoleon and nothing came of the idea. What was erected was a square pavilion, from which it was said Napoleon could see the sea.

The formal garden was limited to this because of the stringent nightly lockdown, when Longwood House was surrounded by a phalanx of sentries allegedly ten strides apart from each other, making a total of thirty-five sentinels in total, the one at the garden gate catching the most curfew defaulters. Article seven of Governor Lowe's restrictions, dated 9 October 1816, ran as follow:

> At sunset, the enclosure of the garden round Longwood will be regarded as the limits. At this hour, sentinels will be placed all round it, but in such a manner as not to incommode General Bonaparte, by overlooking his person, if he should wish to continue his walk in the garden some time longer. During the night, the sentinels will be placed close to the house, as was before done, and admission will be forbidden until after the sentinels have been withdrawn from the house and garden next morning.[29]

There was, however, also a more informal garden extending into the heath grassland down the slope in front of the basin garden and the little garden, and indeed slightly east of the latter where General Gaspard Gourgaud pitched his tent for a while and where an orchard was established. Another tent or pavilion was placed on the lawn down from the steps up to the billiard room. At the end of the turf embankment was a raised turf mound with a six-foot-square wooden platform. On this was constructed a small, elegant light-green Chinese pavilion, with sail-cloth roof and drapes which had tiny diamond-shape coloured-glass windowpanes in them, complete with Chinese bamboo furniture and a Chinese weathervane. This was used by Napoleon as a lookout to spot ships. At one time there was also a three-tiered aviary constructed by indentured Chinese carpenters, whose inhabitants had a chequered and short existence thanks to disease and local cats.[30] The arbours and fences were covered with passion flowers, which was something of a weed at Longwood.

There was also the famous sunken walkway, filled in some decades later, and a row of aloes which made a convenient natural barrier for the British for the nightly lockdown. In summary, Antommarchi asserted:

> The Emperor urged us, excited us, and everything around us soon assumed a different aspect. Here was an excavation, there a basin or a road. We made alleys, grottoes, cascades; the appearance of the ground had now some life and diversity. We planted willows, oaks, peach-trees, to give a little shade round the house. Having completed the ornamental part of our labours we turned to the useful. We divided the ground, we manured it, and sowed it with abundance of beans, peas, and every vegetable that grows in the island.[31]

We have no catalogue of plants that grew in Napoleon's garden. What has survived, apart from a few lists of plants sent from the Cape to St Helena at the time by the Company's agent at the Cape (see appendices), are two sketch maps by Montholon from his book and various illustrations which vary in accuracy. From these fragments, we know that it included a series of paths, at least one of which had trellis-work.

There was some garden furniture including wooden tables and a covered walkway. And there was a mobile pump, the hose used by the emperor to water the plants and the pump operated by his courtiers. From a few illustrations, we know that there were already a small number of trees around Longwood House. Written accounts of life at Longwood in the early part of Napoleon's captivity also note that on occasion the emperor would dine and take his coffee under the shade of a tree.

Ponds and water supply

In one part of the Longwood garden, Napoleon set to constructing three large ponds or reservoirs in different shapes. However, it was soon found that none of them retained water, so Count Montholon had to request that they be lined with lead. The cost would have been expensive, estimated to be around £300. Instead Lowe suggested that a stone reservoir be constructed, 'which would be always found useful'. In the interim, Napoleon had an 'immense vat' built of wood. This might have been the 12-foot (3.6 metre) square tub which William Gordon alias Cooper, brought up from Jamestown on 20 January 1820, and for which act Napoleon gave him a glass of wine with his own hand.[32] William Gordon was probably the plumber whom Nicholls told Lowe he had sent to sort out a lead tank 'on the right of the house'.

Napoleon was very keen on regular bathing, something which disturbed Sir Hudson Lowe greatly, partly because he found it unnatural but also because water was scarce on the Longwood plateau. It is recorded that at least once Napoleon forsook his warm interior bath and sat in the stone reservoir in the garden. The water served to soothe both his skin and his state of mind, for as 1820 progressed it was becoming obvious that the emperor was not well.

Pipes were laid to the basin and the pond filled with water. Next, Napoleon obtained some goldfish, or little red fish as St Denis has it, which it is said he placed in the pond with his own hands. Here he would stay for hours on end looking at the fish, throwing bread to them and studying their 'loves and their quarrels'. It is said that he sometimes 'sent for his attendants to communicate his remarks' to the fish. Such an innocent pastime was, however, brought to an end when the emperor's fish began to die. Why this was so is not certain. It was thought that the 'coppery cement', which plastered the bottom of the pond, or the earlier lead paint had poisoned the water. There may also not have been enough oxygen getting into the water. Whatever it was, these deaths upset Napoleon, who lugubriously asserted, 'You see very well that there is a fatality attached to me. Everything I love, everything that belongs to me, is immediately struck; heaven and mankind unite to persecute me.'[33]

The surviving fish were removed from the basin and placed in a tub, probably the large tub in the middle of one of the sod walls which had been placed halfway up the side, 'to form a sort of cascade into the long tank'. St Denis recalled how the emperor would, in instructing him to turn the water stopcocks feeding the system, jokingly cry, 'Come, let us make the fountains play!'[34] No doubt these water features were a breeding ground for the mosquitoes which, along with the rats, were such a nuisance at Longwood.

ᘐ The vegetable initiative ᘐ

Porteous had been in charge of the Longwood garden and farm before Napoleon arrived, when it was said to produce 'remarkably fine vegetables'. The farm was constituted as follows:

65½ acres [26.5 ha] of arable land growing mainly potatoes with some oats and a little barley.

1,210 acres [490 ha] of pasture for the black cattle and the sheep.

10 acres [4 ha] of garden including Napoleon's garden and some vegetable growing.

The Company's holding of animals in April 1818 was not particularly large: 156 black cattle; 121 sheep; 65 pigs; 18 donkeys; 18 saddle horses and 18 farm horses.[35]

On 3 August 1816, Dr Barry O'Meara, the emperor's controversial Irish doctor, announced that, on the orders of Major Gorrequer, in future the supply of vegetables would come from the Honourable Company's garden (botanic garden). But Napoleon developed the new idea that with a regular supply of water, Longwood could provide itself, the Deadwood military camp and passing ships with a supply of fresh vegetables.[36] A vegetable garden was established but the plateau climate and a lack of sufficient piped water led to its failure, even after a series of retaining basins were constructed both to provide an additional water feature and to supply

24. Napoleon working in the Longwood garden
Abbott, *Napoleon at St Helena*, p. 627. Provided by Donal P. McCracken.

NAPOLEON'S GARDEN ISLAND

the vegetable garden on the lower part of a slight incline. With such a large garrison on the island the military establishment looked elsewhere, such as Luffkins House, for land that might produce food. They even contemplated appropriating to the Company land such as that attached to Rose Cottage, where in late 1816 Emmanuel Las Cases had been under house arrest prior to his expulsion from the island. As mentioned elsewhere, extensive tree planting was undertaken under Lowe in 1818/1819, including oak, firs and other forest trees, much on Company ground at Alarm Cottage, near to Longwood.

Napoleon also had his own afforestation plan, and an extensive scheme was commenced to plant new trees at Longwood and to transplant to Longwood established and sometimes sizeable ones from other parts of the island, complete with retaining balls of earth around their root systems. On Boxing Day 1819, Captain Nicholls recorded:

> I saw General Bonaparte this afternoon in one of his little gardens in his dressing-gown. They are doing nothing but transplanting trees. Even this day, though Sunday [26 December], they are moving peach-trees with fruit on them. They have been moving young oaks in full leaf, and the trees probably will survive, but the leaf is falling off as in autumn.[37]

Indeed, a row of peach trees was planted in February 1820 in an attempt to block the view from the officers' quarters.[38] These trees did indeed survive, as did several oaks 'of some size' which were also transported. The following September a spat occurred when Napoleon perceived that Lowe was trying to interfere in his scheme to establish a plantation. The emperor instructed Captain Lutyens that as long at the much-hated railings remained beside the new and adjacent house being built for him, no orders would be given as to where the trees were to be planted.

ৎৼঌ Napoleon's fern ঌৼ৭

Today the Longwood garden is packed with Cape plants such as pokers, lilies and agapanthus, which is hardly surprising as they were and are a feature of the island. The modern re-established Napoleon's garden at Longwood is in such a fine state today thanks to the dedication of the honorary French consul.

Although today's garden reflects Napoleon's efforts, the garden he originally made was destroyed after his death. Under Napoleon, flower beds were dug and shrubs and flowers planted, in addition to the flower seeds sown. Along with this came an extensive system of watering using pipes and hoses.

What plants were in the flower beds makes for interesting speculation. Tradition has it, however, that one plant in particular was known to have been grown by Napoleon. This is the New South Wales yellow everlasting or everlasting daisy (*Xerochrysum bracteatum*, known until recently as *Helichrysum bracteatum*). The story goes that along with the boxes of books which Elizabeth Fox, Lady Holland, sent to Napoleon in St Helena were seeds of this metre-high flower, which Melliss referred to in 1875 as 'a thorough weed in the Island'.[39] Lady Holland was interested in plants and successfully introduced the dahlia to Britain from Spain in 1804. The tale has a certain credibility, at least to having a Napoleonic link, in that the everlasting daisy was first described for science in 1803 by Josephine's botanist Étienne Ventenat in his lavish book *Jardin de Malmaison*. Then there was the Jamaican giant granadilla (*Passiflora quadrangularis*), which grew luxuriantly over hedges and verandas on St Helena and was called Napoleon's creeper.

Ironically, the nomenclature of the only indigenous plant on St Helena named after Napoleon has a disputed history. Commonly named the small kidney fern, this is an endangered, attractive dark reddish-green fern, which has had no fewer than six scientific names: *Nephrodium napoleonis*, *Lastrea napoleonis*, *Aspidium napoleonis*, *A. petersenii*, *A. pulchrum* and currently *Dryopteris napoleonis*. It was first named *Nephrodium napoleonis* by the extraordinary French soldier-scientist Jean Baptiste Bory de Saint-Vincent. As a young man of 23, he had been briefly on St Helena. Many years later, and having fought in the principal battles with the Grande Armée and subsequently been outlawed by the returning Bourbons, this dedicated Bonapartist returned to France in the 1820s to varying fortunes. It was in 1831 that he named the small kidney fern after his hero, which was appropriate enough on several counts.

The specimen used, which has an extensive root system included, is credited to the great French colonial botanic garden curator Charles Paulus Bélanger (spelt Bélangé on the specimen sheet). On the same sheet is an earlier specimen of the fern dated 1828, collected by Captain Dumont d'Urville.[40] It was not until 60 years later that the well-travelled and controversial Dr Otto Kuntze, whom Stafleu describes as a 'polemic nomenclatural reformer', named the fern *Dryopteris napoleonis*. That was in 1891, the year Kuntze published his controversial two-volume *Revisio Genera Plantarum*. However, in 2020 the authoritative website The Plant List was still describing *Dryopteris napoleonis* as 'an unresolved name'.[41] So, as with much else relating to Napoleon on St Helena, controversy remains.

The main location of Napoleon's fern was underneath Diana's Peak along the banks of the bridle path known as Napoleon's Cabbage Tree Road. This curved its way round to Newfoundland. Further populations existed, and to a degree still do further west below Mount Actaeon, High Ridge and Cason's Wood. There was an outlying colony to the north-east at Haystack, on the eastern side of the Barn overlooking Longwood. The fern did not grow at Longwood farm as far as we know but did grow nearby. It is thought the name emanates from the colony of ferns which grew at the famous spring in the Sane Valley, where Napoleon's tomb was placed.[42]

Considering the impact Napoleon has had on the image and international reputation of St Helena, in general very few names commemorate him on the island and no statue of him is to be found. In Jamestown there is a Napoleon Street, which leads onto the Side Path road up toward the Briars and Longwood. Up into the 1870s, the name Napoleon's Cabbage Tree Road was in use, but it is now, sadly, referred to only as Cabbage Tree Road. This is under Stitch's Ridge, near to the path which leads up to Diana's Peak.

The British reaction to Napoleon's garden

The British authorities, both on St Helena and in London, greatly approved of Napoleon's island Malmaison. There were two reasons for this, one cynical and one enlightened. That the emperor was actually seen daily creating this garden greatly satisfied the nervous Sir Hudson Lowe. If gardens and gardening helped relax Napoleon himself, one suspects the sight of such also had a pacifying effect on the island's governor.

It is equally true to say that by this regency period, the educated classes in Britain had well and truly been inculcated with both an excitement about gardening but, more so, also by an enthusiasm for plants and in particular exotic plants. The whole Captain Bligh breadfruit saga had been part and parcel of this, as was the growing ascendancy of Sir Joseph Banks and of the Royal Botanic Gardens, Kew. Before and even during the Napoleonic era, scientific plant hunters were being sent from Europe to collect plants new to science. The Empress Josephine had been part of this craze, as had the Habsburg emperor and the Russian czar. Kew had sent Francis Masson to the Cape (1772–1775), and then James Bowie and Alan Cunningham to Brazil (1814–1816), before redirecting Bowie on to the Cape (1816–1823) and Cunningham to New South Wales (from 1816).

In the Napoleonic era and during Napoleon's exile on St Helena, the following British botanical magazines were flourishing:

Curtis's Botanical Magazine (1787–)

Andrews' *Botanist's Repository* (1797–1814)

The Botanical Cabinet consisting of coloured delineations of plants from all countries with a short account of each, directions for management etc. etc by Conrad Loddiges & Sons, London (1817–1833)

Botanical Register consisting of coloured figures of exotic plants (1815–1847)

Given the era's plant craze, it is perhaps not so surprising that Henry Bathurst (3rd Earl Bathurst), who as secretary of state for war and the colonies was responsible for the incarcerated emperor, became quite excited at the news that was coming in from Lowe relating to Napoleon's interest in plants and his activities in building up the Longwood garden. Writing from the Colonial and War Office in Downing Street on 2 June 1820, Bathurst was conciliatory:

> Sir – It appearing from your recent despatches that General Bonaparte has of late found much amusement in the improvement of the garden at Longwood and the cultivation of plants and shrubs, I have thought it advisable that you should take an early opportunity of expressing to him the satisfaction which His Majesty's Government would derive from contributing by every means in their power to his gratification in this particular. I have therefore to desire that you would take a fit opportunity of communicating this to General Bonaparte, and of assuring him that, if there are any plants either at the Cape or at any other British settlement, or in this country, which he may wish to add to his present collection, no effort on my part shall be wanting to procure and forward them to St Helena in the manner best calculated to insure their safe arrival.
>
> If, in consequence of this communication, General Bonaparte should express any wish to receive either seeds or plants from the Cape or the Mauritius, you will consider yourself authorised at once to address the Government of those colonies, who will, I am sure, lose no time in giving effect to any wish you may express with respect to them.[43]

As will be seen in the appendices, Lowe had in fact been utilising the Company's agent at the Cape, Joseph Luson, from as early as June 1816 to bring in plants, bulbs and seeds.[44] The listing for one consignment ran to eight hand-written pages.[45] Luson had been born in Bethnal Green, London, in 1784 and worked in the examinations' office and then in the accounting department of the East India Company offices. His break came in 1808 when he was sent out to the Cape as assistant to John Pringle, the Company's agent.[46] Here Luson married the daughter of Pieter Lourens Cloete, a local wine merchant. Luson appears to have taken over from Pringle in 1815 with his wife's brother, Daniel Jacob Cloete, as his assistant. With an annual salary of £1,600 plus five per cent of any profits from the sale of Company effects, he was a wealthy man. He died in office on 17 January 1822 and as such was the Company's agent for the entire period of Napoleon's captivity.[47]

Luson was a facilitator, be it obtaining wine through his brother-in-law's contacts or plants and seeds. So where did the Cape seeds and bulbs sent over to St Helena in the period of Napoleon's captivity originate? A faded pencil name on one plant list sheet gives a clue. This is 'Dr C. M. Villete'.[48] Charles Mathurin Villet was born in the West Indies of French extraction in about 1778 and arrived at the Cape when he was 19 years old. By 1810, he had a commercial enterprise underway, trading in products of natural history. This was based on three acres (1.2 ha) in Long Street, Cape Town. In 1819, he established a lucrative menagerie and botanic gardens in Somerset Road, Green Point, near Cape Town, which became a public attraction. Villet named it Aux Champs des Fleurs.[49]

However, two points need to be made concerning plants imported to St Helena at this time. First, there is little evidence that all these Cape specimens actually ended up in Longwood. Presumably, like the newspapers sent from overseas to the emperor, Lowe took what he wanted and passed on the rest to Montholon. Bathurst was sympathetic, as was Lord Charles Somerset, the Cape's governor, but Lowe was the key figure in ensuring that Napoleon received what plants survived the voyage from Cape Town to Jamestown, which took from three weeks to a month. Certainly, one somewhat meagre consignment did get through. On 20 November 1820, Major Gorrequer, General Lowe's aide-de-camp at Plantation House, sent the Longwood orderly officer, Captain Englebert Lutyens, a box along with the following note:

> The Governor has desired me to send you the accompanying Box of bulbs, and seeds, which he has received from the Cape of Good Hope, of which be pleased to inform Count Montholon, and shew him the List of them herewith enclosed, asking him at the same time, how he wishes to have them disposed of, that you may accordingly give the necessary directions.
>
> A Gardener will be sent to Longwood, to assist in laying them out, if so required.[50]

The second and more important point is that Lowe did not make Napoleon's love of plants and gardens a vehicle to mend the broken relationship between himself and the emperor. Had Lowe possessed the slightest imagination, he would have initiated the importation of the rarest and most exotic plants and drained the Jamestown botanic garden and the Plantation House collections for Napoleon's use, as well as constructing an orangery, stove house or the like in the Longwood gardens. But by the time Bathurst wrote to Lowe in June 1820 it was too late, in any case. Napoleon had less than a year to live and clearly his cancer was already making itself felt.

⟨⟩⟨ An alternative island property ⟨⟩⟨

It is well known that in late 1818 the British started to build a new spacious house for Napoleon and part of his entourage about 100 yards north-west from the existing Longwood farmhouse that he occupied. This new house was of yellow sandstone, but it is said that a lot of material also came from the remnant of the 'Great Wood Wall', which had been built to try and protect the old indigenous woodland at Longwood and Deadwood. The new building was completed in February 1821.

It is also frequently stated that Napoleon refused to move into this house, remaining for the closing months of his life in the cramped and damp quarters he had occupied since 1816. This is only partly true, and he did say he would prefer instead of the new house 400 or 500 books. Napoleon was not opposed in principle to the new house and indeed told Montholon that 'he would be much more comfortable there'. But there were objections. Minor irritations included the proximity of the orderly's quarters to the new house being a mere three toises (18 ft / 3.2 m), whereas in the old house it had been 15 toises (30 ft / 10 m) away. Then there was the proximity of the ornamental iron railings – 'the iron cage' – which partially enclosed a section. In the months before Napoleon's death, Montholon and Lowe discussed the new garden, including transporting trees to the site. This certainly shows an acceptance that the new house would be occupied at some stage. Lowe recorded that on 16 February 1820:

> The Count [Montholon] observed that Bonaparte would himself look about the place and see what could be done, or what he might desire to have done, in regard to making some little gardens about the new house, in compensation, as it were, for those he should lose about the old house.

One of the problems with the new house was the new garden, which was more in the St Helena style than the French. The front of the new Longwood House was rather bleak, with a field sloping away from the house to a clump of trees some way off. Montholon advised the governor that to gain shade at the front, trellis-work, such as existed in the old Longwood garden, should be constructed in front of the new Longwood House, 'to cross over the terrace down to the trees'. He also wished to extend the lawn down the slope and, of course, have the hated railings removed. None of this interest in creating a new set of gardens indicates hostility to moving into the new house, although Napoleon was frank about the matter. He 'considered the old house with the gardens adjoining it preferable to the new one, if it remained without the adoption of his suggestions'. Lowe tried to compromise, stating that he would extend the area where a garden could be established down to and including the trees.

25. Great excitement with the release of fish into the new basin at Longwood. Either because of lead or copper poisoning from the construction or a lack of oxygen, the fish died, as did the birds in the ornate Chinese aviary in the garden constructed by indentured Chinese carpenters.
Abbott, *Napoleon at St Helena*, p. 629. Provided by Donal P. McCracken.

The saga of an alternative property for Napoleon had stretched back to his arrival at the exposed and rather bleak Longwood farm. In October 1817, Lowe complained to Bathurst of Plantation House, 'I believe [it] to be the great object of his desire'. That Napoleon hankered after accommodation with established and extensive gardens and trees is clear. The famous map of St Helena dated 1817 by Lieutenant Read has Plantation House marked as:

PLANTATION HOUSE
The Residence of
BUONAPARTE.

In a later edition this was corrected but the idea of Napoleon occupying the governor's residence was certainly canvassed. Sir Hudson Lowe was convinced that that is exactly what Napoleon wanted. This was probably true.

Count Montholon wrote to Lowe on 8 July 1816:

Longwood is certainly the most unhealthy part of the island; there is no water, no vegetation, no shade; no one has ever been able to establish on this spot even a kitchen garden; the ground is scorched by the wind. This part of the island, therefore, is uninhabited and wild. Had the Emperor been settled at Plantation House, where there are trees, water and gardens, he would have been as comfortably situated as anyone can be in this miserable country. If, then, you intend to build, it would be better to do so in some part of the island already cultivated, and in some place where there are trees, water, and vegetation.[51]

Seven weeks later, on 24 August 1816, Montholon returned to the theme:

The building at Longwood was erected as a barn for the Company's farm; the Lieutenant-Governor of the island has since added some rooms to it; it served him for a country house, but is by no means fit for a constant residence.

As for Napoleon himself, he had no illusions concerning the superior qualities of Plantation House to the windswept plateau he had been assigned:

[Napoleon] It is the Oasis of the desert. But close against a chain of mountains, it is sheltered from being dried up by the south-east winds: plants, shrubs, of the most opposite natures, grow and thrive there, and present to the eye an aspect of vegetation which is seen on no other part of the island. The spot is unique of its kind, like the Calabrian who inhabits it: but one is not more a favourable specimen of the island, than the other is an unfavourable one of mankind.

[Antommarchi] There are places worse than...

[Napoleon] No! there are none like that where we are. No shade, no verdure; we have only a few gum-trees, and they are mutilated; the wind has bent them in the direction in which it blows. At the height at which we are (two thousand feet) vegetation and life cease. British magnanimity had its motives for hoisting me up here.

However, Lowe would have none of this. One may speculate on why this was so. A much underrated figure in the St Helena-Napoleon melodrama was Lady Lowe. She had a stronger personality than her husband. She had been a Delaney, a prominent Irish family, married before and with two grown-up daughters. She was certainly not willingly going to move out of the governor's house for an inferior residence. According to Henry Russell, Lady Lowe 'who has a great deal to say was little reserved in saying it'. This included her opinion that Colonel Sir Thomas Reade, the deputy adjutant-general, was the governor of St Helena. And of Reade, Russell drily observed, 'he has the credit of harshness that may occasionally appear in the treatment of Bonaparte or those around him'.

Lowe himself, leaving aside his natural stubbornness, had his own reasons for not giving way to the emperor's demands. The occupation of Plantation House became a symbol of power. Writing to Bathurst on 29 September 1816, Lowe revealed what were probably his true feelings about giving up Plantation House to Napoleon:

So far as relates to myself the objection [to moving from Plantation House] might have been soon removed and even with respect to my family, had any other house in the Country presented a convenience to us: - for the castle which is the town residence on account of the difference of the Climate as well as the Bad state of the building has been of late years rarely inhabited; - but from the view I am enabled to take of the General principle of all Bonaparte's movements, I am inclined to think it is not so much that Plantation [House] is at present the best house in the island it is so warmly desired, as that it is the residence of the Governor, & that the cession of it therefore to him, would imply a regard and distinction which might have its Consequent Influence to apply as time and Circumstance might best direct. In other respects Rosemary Hall, the place pointed out in a former letter, presents equal advantages of situation with Plantation House, and does not interfere with the Company's Establishment and improvements on the latter spot, which have been very extensive.[52]

When Dr O'Meara broached the subject of the emperor moving residence, Lowe retorted:

> The fact is that General Bonaparte wants to get Plantation House; but the East India Company will not consent to have so fine a plantation given to a set of Frenchmen to destroy the trees and ruin the gardens.

That Lowe was interested in plants and gardens is clear. An interesting example of the power of the Plantation House gardener at this time is an incident in June 1817. Major Gorrequer, who by necessity had to be close to the governor, moved into a substantial cottage previously built for the head gardener. This accommodation suited Gorrequer well, as his servant could live there also and there was room for his trunks and saddles. Besides, it gave him a break from the tensions and constant drama in nearby Plantation House. But a new Company gardener and his wife suddenly turned up and naturally wanted occupation of the gardener's residence, which he had been promised before he left England. Gorrequer protested that 'being deprived of the Cottage as a very great inconvenience'. But the gardener triumphed against the aide-de-camp and, with ingratiating promises from Lowe of a bedroom, furniture and a cupboard room, Gorrequer had to move into Plantation House.[53]

৫~৪ Rosemary Hall and its botanic garden ৫~৪

The saga of a new residence for the emperor did not end there. The French looked elsewhere. Napoleon talked about the Briars, Rosemary Hall and Captain Smith's property (Forest Lodge).[54] On 27 July 1816, Lowe wrote to Bathurst:

> Whether a new house is built for him [Napoleon] or not, the repairs at his present place of residence are indispensable; and therefore little time is lost in making a reference to your Lordship's judgement as to the constructing a new house, should he require it, in a part of the island more agreeable to him. The spot which unites the most advantage is a place called Rosemary Hall. It lies about a mile from Plantation House, in one of the most beautiful and cultivated parts of the island.[55]

The old house at Rosemary Hall is now reduced to a ruined foundation. In 1816 it was owned by William Wrangham. In 1809 Burchell lists two weeds he found in its garden, the southern Indian climber treebine (*Cissus vitiginea*) and the Roman nettle (*Urtica pilulifera*). But this gives a wrong impression of what had been a commodious and elegant double-storey gentleman's residence, laid out in the St Helena fashion with a long grass frontage lined by trees and with an arboretum at the rear.

The month after Lowe wrote to Bathurst about Rosemary Hall, on 24 August 1816, Montholon penned an extensive 'remonstrance' to the governor. This Lowe believed to have been dictated by Napoleon. Part of this effusion ran as follows:

> There are, however, in this miserable island some agreeable localities with trees, and gardens, and pretty good houses – Plantation House among the rest; but positive instructions from the ministry prohibit your granting that house, which would have saved considerable expense to your treasury – money laid out in building wooden huts [at Longwood], covered with tarred paper, and which are already unserviceable.[56]

The matter drifted into 1818 with Lowe, at least in part, persuaded that a move to Rosemary Hall was possible. Indeed, he went so far as to begin negotiations to buy the property. This, however, was brought to an abrupt halt, ironically by one of the Longwood House set, the excitable French artillery officer General Gaspard de Gourgaud. He believed that Longwood was most suited for *surveillance*, a comment Bathurst picked up and used to put paid to Napoleon moving to more salubrious quarters and surroundings.[57]

There was another Napoleon link to Rosemary Hall, however. The principal allied powers, Austria, Russia and the restored Bourbon France, each sent out to St Helena a commissioner to ensure that Napoleon was indeed well secured in his island prison. These notables were not, of course, allowed to visit Napoleon and, having nothing to do, soon became bored, gossiped, schemed and were generally troublesome for the British authorities. The Habsburg representative was Barthelemy Baron de Stürmer (1787–1853). He arrived on board the *Orontes* on 18 June 1816, along with his wife, four servants and an Austrian botanist called Philippe Welle. They all had the good fortune to be accommodated in William Wrangham's old home Rosemary Hall.

Vienna was at the time a worthy rival to the Royal Botanic Gardens, Kew, the Emperor Franz Stephan having established the Dutch Botanical Garden in the grounds of Schönbrunn Palace in 1753. Every emperor since then had built up the botanical collection, not least the enlightened Joseph II, often sending out plant collectors to remote corners of the globe. Not surprisingly, the nobility followed suit, most notably the Hungarian Nikolaus II, Prince Esterházy (1765–1833), whose magnificent palace outside Eisenstadt, in eastern Austria on the Hungarian border, was noted for its extraordinary collection of plants. It appears as if Welle was the employee of Esterházy rather than the Habsburg emperor Francis I. But permission for Welle to be part of Stürmer's entourage and specified as a botanist was granted by no less a figure than Prince Ferdinand von Trauttmansdorff (1749– 1827), one of Joseph II's and then Francis II's right-hand men. Trauttmansdorff invariably was tasked with the difficult and unpleasant matters of state and was the principal logistical architect of the Congress of Vienna, 1814/1815. His name therefore carried considerable authority.

On arrival at St Helena, Welle spent about two months scouring the island and then planting his botanical finds out in the grounds of Rosemary Hall. All would have gone well were it not for the fact that the young botanist fell foul of Governor Lowe. Napoleon's first valet on St Helena was Louis Marchand (1792–1876), son of the nurse to the baby king of Rome (1811–1814), Napoleon's son François. When Welle was leaving Europe for St Helena, Madame Marchand gave him a letter for Napoleon containing a lock of the hair of the five-year-old boy. On arrival on the island, the young Welle told a local entrepreneur and chancer called Richard Prince that he had a message for M. Marchand. Prince, who owned Red Hill Cottage (Prince's Lodge) and Farm Lodge and who had business dealings with Longwood, informed Marchand. A meeting between Marchand and Welle soon took place in Jamestown, where Welle dutifully executed his task and handed the valet the package. In turn, Marchand passed this on to Napoleon.

Needless to say, Governor Lowe heard of the matter and was suitably enraged that the letter had not been delivered into his hands to determine what should be done. The hapless Welle became the focus of suspicion and attack, and was ordered off the island. Lowe's approach seems to have been that Welle had arrived illegally without proper authorisation and approval of either Lord Castlereagh or the Earl of Bathurst, the two British secretaries of state. In a superbly crafted courteous and methodical letter to Lowe, written in French and dated 29 October 1816, Stürmer laid out the situation, pointing out that Lowe was questioning Welle's credentials only after he had been on the island for more than four months. Trauttmandorff's letter to Stürmer relating to Welle was attached for Lowe to study, reminding him that Austria's ambassador had indeed given the secretary of state a list of those accompanying Stürmer, including that of Welle. Warming to his subject, Stürmer continues, 'You know also that M. Welle has been received on board an English royal frigate and made the journey at the cost of the British government'. He also reminded Lowe of the 'long conversation that we had together on the subject of M. Welle.'

Stürmer had suggested that Welle go to the Cape to collect for four months and then return to Europe via St Helena, picking up the Rosemary Hall plants on his way through. But Lowe was adamant that once Welle left St Helena, he would not be allowed back onto the island.

It was clear that the young botanist could not remain on the island, but Stürmer stuck his heels in about when his departure should be, reminding the governor, 'you know that transporting exotic plants to Europe successfully they have to arrive in the good season'. Stürmer asserted that March 1817 would be the earliest Welle could take his plants back to Europe:

If M. Welle leaves now for Europe, he will have to abandon his plants here, and the considerable costs of his stay could become completely useless to us. On account of this, please weigh up in your wisdom if I can take upon myself sending him [Welle] back if the ministers of His Britannic Majesty were duty bound to oppose his staying in St Helena they should need to make the motives clear to Pc Esterhazy. The desire to act on this occasion like all the others, which would be agreeable to the English government here and His Majesty would be spared in this case much useless expense.

You were the master, Governor, in giving M. Welle the facility to collect plants on the island and to open all areas to him. That was a courteous act on your part that I cannot but thank you for in the name of my Court, an act on which I never would have insisted if you had not foreseen my wishes, fearful of contravening the established surveillance measures on the island; but what you will never persuade me of is that the presence of M. Welle, whose conduct is irreproachable whether living in the countryside, at my house under my protection and under my guarantee, and only rarely sets aside his duties.

Baron Stürmer had his way and Welle departed on 1 March 1817. Richard Prince, who had on a previous occasion in April 1815 been ordered off the island but had delayed and delayed his departure, now also had to depart. But Prince was back on St Helena when circumstances permitted, gaining respectability, becoming a magistrate and eventually dying on the island in 1838.[58]

Napoleon was well aware of the shenanigans surrounding Welle. Writing to Las Cases on 12 December 1816, a fortnight before the courtier's deportation, the emperor asserted:

If you should someday see my wife and my son, embrace them, from me. For two years I have had no news from them, direct or indirect. A German botanist, who saw them a few days before his departure, in the Schönbrunn, has been residing here six months, but the barbarians will not allow him to come and tell me what he knows of them.[59]

7

Grande salle d'état

Sir Hudson Lowe

As several recorded instances show, Napoleon had no quarrel with the British troops stationed on St Helena. He sent some turtle soup from the Longwood kitchen over to the officers' mess of the 55th Regiment, for example. There was the famous incident when a sentinel with musket and bayonet barred the path of the 'little corporal' when Napoleon was out for a night walk beyond the prescribed garden limits. The next day the emperor sent for the private and commended

26. Burchell's sketch dated 27 March 1809 of the Swanley Valley with willows and a pond, which may be a spring. This site is possibly that of Napoleon's future grave.

him for his diligence. But Napoleon's attempt to be fraternal by sending a copy of Coxe's *Memoirs of John, Duke of Marlborough*, 'the greatest English general', to the 20th Foot Regiment garrison 700-book library – 'to show them that I honour the brave men of every nation' – was stymied by the island's governor. This was on the grounds that the emperor's name was engraved in the book and also that it had not been sent according to protocol via himself. What Napoleon described as this piece of 'extreme insolence' was the act of Sir Hudson Lowe.

Lowe was Napoleon's chief gaoler and bête noire, an Irish army officer who arrived on the island with his wife and two stepdaughters on 14 April 1816. In 1821 Henry Russell, who visited St Helena on his way home from India, wrote of Lowe:

> He is a small man, apparently nearly 50 of a fair complexion with a hanging brow and a reserved thoughtful countenance. In address towards a stranger he is silent and awkward, evidently not from pride but embarrassment; which is remarkable as he mixed much in polished Society on the continent and is both a sensible and accomplished man.

To this can be added the comment of the Russian commissioner Count Alexandre de Balmain, who married Lowe's stepdaughter:

> If asked a question about Bonaparte his [Lowe's] forehead wrinkles with suspicion. He believes one is trying to entrap him and gives an evasive reply. He never expresses himself clearly and logically, so that listening to him one becomes confused. He is quick to anger, and if one attempts to reason with him or contradicts him in any way, he loses his head and no longer knows what he is saying. To do business with him and feel relaxed and at one's ease is an impossibility.[1]

But Lowe had a difficult brief, being pressurised from opposite directions by Napoleon's Longwood establishment and by the British authorities back in London. His response was to become a bureaucrat, following instructions too much to the letter. Lowe had seemed the ideal officer to carry out the role: he could speak Italian and French, and he had commanded a Corsican corps in the Mediterranean. But his genuine attempts to assist Napoleon – he sent books, newspapers, and the occasional pheasant over to Longwood, he invited 'General' Bonaparte to dinner at Plantation House – were too often clumsily handled and often misinterpreted by his enemies, then and since. The reference to Napoleon as general, a studied and unnecessary insult, was not Lowe's doing, but his masters', yet one to which Lowe rigidly and foolishly adhered during the captivity.

Lowe and Napoleon only ever met six times, and those meetings were within Lowe's first three months in office. Lowe's attitude and approach to Napoleon prompted the Frenchman to put Lowe down and belittle him in retaliation. Lowe was not the man to rise above this, much as he later seems to have tried. He was at once high-handed, grouchy, insecure and awkward in his dealings with the fallen emperor, at times officious and at others exasperated. He did not handle Napoleon well and for his part Napoleon disliked Lowe intensely, calling him at various times an 'embesille', 'a Sicilian grafted onto a Prussian' and someone who possessed 'refined cruelty'. Days before his death, Napoleon said that he was being killed by three things: the climate of St Helena; then, referring to Lowe, 'by pin pricks'; and 'finally thanks to lack of exercise'. Napoleon also blamed Lowe for not allowing him to move beyond certain defined limits unless accompanied by a British officer. From October 1816, Napoleon was limited to the house and the garden at Longwood at night; and during the day to the Longwood estate as far as Hutt's Gate, and to the signal gun near Alarm House. Part of the road down from Hutt's Gate towards the Briars was removed from the limits for most of 1816, before being restored.

Lowe's pettiness and paranoia about Napoleon are well chronicled. One of the most ridiculous was when Count Montholon gave the Marquis de Montchenu some haricot bean plants from the Longwood garden. These were both white and green, something which led Lowe to, in Lord Rosebery's words, detect a plot – as white was the colour of the Bourbons and green was Napoleon's colour and that of the livery of his servants at Longwood. Lowe complained to Lord Bathurst in London of the propriety of Montchenu accepting both colours and not just the haricot blanc. Rosebery drily commented that all this was not burlesque but serious.

Lowe's fellow countryman the Duke of Wellington was probably near enough the truth when he observed that Lowe 'was a very bad choice; he was a man wanting in education and judgement. He was a stupid man, he knew nothing at all of the world, and, like all men who know nothing of the world, he was suspicious and jealous.' A wiser man such as Governor Brooke might have handled Napoleon better and produced less gossip about cruelty towards the emperor. A pamphlet dated 1817 on this subject, reportedly dictated to Count Montholon by Napoleon, contained the following passage:

> The house at Longwood was built to serve as a barn for the Company's farm; the Deputy Governor of the Island had since built some chambers; it served him for a country-house, but it was not in a proper habitable state: workmen have been employed at it for a year, and the Emperor has been continually subjected

to the inconvenience and insalubrity of inhabiting a house in the progress of building. The chamber in which he sleeps is too small to contain a bed of ordinary dimensions; but every alteration at Longwood prolongs the inconvenience of having workmen there. There are, however, in this miserable territory, beautiful situations, presenting fine trees, gardens, and good houses.

There is, besides, Plantation House; but the positive instructions of Government forbad you from giving up this house, although much expence would thereby have been saved to your Government – an expence incurred in fitting up at Longwood a hut, covered with paper, which is already unserviceable.[2]

There was certainly more than an element of truth in all this. Matters were not helped by the miserly income devoted to maintaining the 51 inhabitants of the Longwood complex, initially fixed at £8,000 (compared to Lowe's salary of £12,000 a year), though later increased under pressure from Longwood and abroad.

All this said, the reality was that Napoleon was a prisoner and a very real danger to Britain and her allies. He had already escaped from one island confinement, Elba. Given the actions of the reinstated Bourbons back in Paris, Napoleon might well have been received back in France again as a saviour. Interestingly, two key historians of St Helena in the late 20th century show little sympathy with Napoleon and express support for Lowe, who was ultimately ensuring there was not a second island escape which could possibly renew a European conflict that had already lasted over 20 years, bringing with it much misery and much loss of life.

The Longwood establishment included an outdoor area that became a garden and was the scene of many a conference and meeting. The confined nature of the interior of the house made the garden a better venue when weather permitted, having a certain grandeur of setting with a wide vista. The small rooms of Longwood also made eavesdropping easy but this was more difficult outdoors. Inside, Napoleon frequently behaved like a caged lion. The freedom to pace around the garden, followed by whomever he was interviewing, was a relief to him.

It was in the Longwood garden that a famous row between Napoleon and Lowe occurred. On 18 August 1816 Napoleon was walking in the garden when Lowe and his entourage turned up. Napoleon had on several occasions avoided meeting his enemy by being indoors, but this time he felt that he had no alternative but to face the governor. Also present were Rear-Admiral Plampin, Captain Poppleton, Major Gorrequer, Sir Thomas Reade, Bertrand, Montholon, Las Cases and his son. It was the ubiquitous Dr O'Meara who recorded the event for posterity. Napoleon was walking along the garden path, 'frequently stopping and again hurried in his walk, and accompanying his words with a good deal of action'. Lowe was equally agitated and after half an hour of this circus, Lowe turned on his heel, without saluting, and left. Next day Napoleon recounted to O'Meara what he had said:

"Know you sir," I [Napoleon] said, "How could I know you? You have never commanded in battle. You have never commanded any but vagabond Corsican deserters, Piedmontese and Neapolitan brigands. I know the name of every English general who has distinguished himself, but I never heard of you except as a *scrivano* [clerk] to Blucher, or as commandant of brigands. You have never commanded, or been accustomed to men of honor."[3]

Not surprisingly, the result of a few encounters like these was that Lowe was intimidated and kept away from Longwood, ironically something which probably was to Napoleon's detriment.

It was Dr Barry Edward O'Meara (1786–1836), one of the no fewer than five Irish doctors Napoleon had at various times on the island, who destroyed Lowe's reputation.[4] We have little reason to doubt the truth of much of what O'Meara wrote in his two-volume book *Napoleon in exile, or a voice from St Helena* (1822), though that does not necessarily negate Count Bertrand's view of O'Meara as being a rascal. Matters cannot have been helped for O'Meara being the recipient of a complimentary joint of lamb sent to him by Norfolk man Thomas Breame, clerk of Longwood farm, whose slapdash accounting and possible dishonesty was denounced by Porteous and cost Breame his job.

The reality was that the British, who stood between the former emperor and execution, got what they wanted. Lowe's lack of tact merely caused embarrassment; it did not alter reality. Napoleon was put out of the way and left with a small retinue, limited facilities and provisions to see out his days. It seems evident that Napoleon realised that this was the intention. It was not so much that he turned in on himself, but rather that he drew out from his memory those things which had pleased him and given him pride. The greatest manifestation of this would have been the record of his past victories but, as matters played out, smaller things, such as his garden at Longwood, comforted him equally. Why was this?

Exile inevitably drew out from Napoleon's past the memory of his first wife, Josephine, whom he had divorced for reasons of state rather than through any lack of affection. It must not be forgotten that Napoleon was not ignorant of gardens and the enthusiasm for plants which swept the educated classes in the late 18th and early 19th centuries. Indeed, he had gone to great lengths to assist Josephine in building up and maintaining her great garden of Malmaison, on the Seine, some 15 kilometres west of Paris. Here the greatest botanists and botanical artists of the day came and worked. She had purchased exotic plants from the London nursery firm of Kennedy and Lee, and had piggy-backed on Napoleon's successes to receive plants and seeds from the great botanic gardens at Schönbrunn outside Vienna and also from the West Indies. She died in 1814 while Napoleon was on Elba so she could not facilitate the shipment of plants to Napoleon's second island of captivity.

After the battle of Waterloo, Napoleon had drifted into Paris. Here, in the face of defeat, political instability, intrigues and betrayal, he retreated to Malmaison and its gardens. He remained there between 25 and 28 June 1815, quietly awaiting his fate while reading novels. It is hard not to conjecture that later, sitting at Longwood, the memory of Malmaison and of Josephine did not encourage his consulting his dictionary of natural history and embarking on a venture to create a proper garden on St Helena. When in Cairo during his Egyptian campaign, Napoleon had been the driving force behind the establishment of the Institut d'Égypte, in whose grounds a botanic garden was established. It perhaps should also be pointed out that when in exile on the island of Elba, where, unlike on St Helena, Napoleon was sovereign ruler, he designed a flag which was dominated by the insignia of three bees.

The salon

Forced to live in a rickety prefab house, Napoleon salvaged a considerable amount of dignity by using his garden complex as his state rooms. Here he walked, read under trees, met people, fought with his jailers, ate many breakfasts and lunches, and, according to his valet Louis St Denis, would 'go into the garden, singing some old opera air that he remembered'.[5] He also held court there. His principal courtiers were Emmanuel, Comte de Las Cases, Grand Marshal Bertrand and, in particular, Count Montholon. Sometimes Napoleon was seen with the Countess Montholon and very occasionally with the less-favoured Countess Bertrand. We find the emperor using the garden to have breakfast with Dr O'Meara; to play nine pins with his courtiers; or to meander deep in discussion with this rump of his courtiers.

There was, however, one great drawback to this al fresco arrangement. Not surprisingly, the former master of continental Europe was not keen to become a circus exhibit for the gawking public. There was clearly great curiosity to see Napoleon. Army surgeon Henry Walter goes so far as to say passing ships coming up from the Cape en route to Britain created false excuses to give to the hardened Royal Navy captains of the frigates which constantly circled St Helena. This was to get permission to put into Jamestown for emergency provisions, but in reality the purpose was to allow the passengers and crew an opportunity to go up to look over the wall at Longwood.

There are accounts of Napoleon retreating from his garden when he saw people approaching and rushing into the house, followed by servants carrying tables, chairs and food. This happened when the eminent Lord Charles Somerset, governor of the Cape, turned up with his daughter on 26 January 1820. Somerset wrote of 'the large garden in the wood', a reflection of how much Napoleon had achieved by early 1820.[6]

His scuttling away to the safety of the house could take on near comic proportions on occasion. While staying at the Briars and strolling along the avenue of pomegranate trees in the company of the precocious Balcombe children, the emperor heard strangers approaching and ran down towards the gate which led into the enclosed garden. But the gate was locked and the people were coming closer. So he climbed the fence only to discover his path blocked by prickly pear plants. Rather than face the oncoming party, Napoleon plunged ahead, tearing his clothes and scratching his legs so badly that Dr O'Meara had to be called to extract the tiny and painful thorns.[7]

Napoleon was also especially irritated to learn that someone such as the despised Governor Lowe was to call, necessitating him 'to remain shut up in my room to avoid meeting him in the garden'.[8] It was not that Napoleon did not like meeting people – indeed he had a definite affinity with the ordinary person – it was just that he liked such meetings to be on his terms.

As Lowe became more nervous about security and his captive's possible escape, the net tightened around Napoleon and his access to locals became more difficult. Initially the perimeters of his permitted domain had included the cottages of locals. Napoleon had never been averse to stopping and chatting with ordinary people and, indeed, clearly enjoyed the honest and straightforward nature of such encounters in contrast to the discourse of the officials who surrounded him. This was as much the case in St Helena as it had been in Paris. A good example of this was Napoleon's relationship with the enslaved gardener Toby, mentioned in the previous chapter.

Under the Lowe dispensation, Napoleon was not banned from greeting anyone he might meet on the road, but conversations with such folks were, at least in theory, prohibited. Being friendly with Napoleon was viewed with the gravest suspicion by Sir Hudson Lowe. He even kept a list of locals whom he regarded as possibly fraternising or who were potentially ready to assist the emperor with escaping.

Some locals, and indeed some British military officers, were not only granted an audience with Napoleon with or without an appointment – and invariably in the garden – but were treated with the utmost courtesy and charm. One such was none other than the pretty 18-year-old Susanna Johnson, who was Governor Lowe's stepdaughter. She breezed in on her horse with groom following. Springing to the ground, she accosted Count Montholon, taking his arm, with a plea to see the gardens:

> We had scarcely gone a hundred paces, however, before, on making a turn in the covered walk, we found ourselves face to face with the Emperor, who, seated on a bench, appeared to be watching us. My surprise was great, but less so, I think, than the impression made on Miss Johnson. Her pretty face was lighted up with indescribable animation, and her looks expressed at once her timid embarrassment, and her joy at seeing the Emperor. His manner towards her was amiable and kind; he had a plate of sweetmeats brought to her, appeared to take pleasure in showing her his gardening labours, said not a word which might remind her that she came from Plantation House, and as she was taking her departure, plucked a rose, and offered it to her as a souvenir of what he termed her pilgrimage.[9]

As endearing a meeting with a younger woman, albeit less jolly, occurred when Betsy Balcombe came to Longwood in March 1818 to say goodbye to Napoleon:

> He walked with us in his garden, and with a sickly smile pointed to the ocean spread out before us, bounding the view, and said, 'Soon you will be sailing away towards England, leaving me to die on this miserable rock. Look at those dreadful mountains — they are my prison walls. You will soon hear that the Emperor Napoleon is dead.' I burst into tears, and sobbed as though my heart would break. He seemed much moved by the sorrow manifested.[10]

Another young woman who made it through the British lines was Charlotte Knipe. The Knipes and the Porteous families were close and, as previously mentioned, the island's botanical superintendent Henry Porteous married Mary Knipe in 1808. The Knipe family home was or had been Horse Pasture Farm, later called Woodlands.[11] The house had an inscription on it which read 'This stone was laid by Henry Porteous 1789.'

Charlotte Knipe was described as a 'tall, fair, polished, fresh, Beauty'. She was born on 22 April 1799, so was 16 when she met the emperor on 7 January 1816. She was with Henry Porteous in the garden at Longwood when she met Napoleon, who called her Le Bouton de Rose [Rosebud].[12] At one time the Countess de Montholon thought Miss Knipe might become Napoleon's mistress. For a time the countess had endured living in Porteous' boarding house in Jamestown, where Napoleon had spent his first night on the island. It was called the Old Blackhouse, though Albine de Montholon referred to it as the 'maison portions' because of its small, pokey rooms.[13] If the Knipes did not live there, they were certainly regular visitors. The colourful Rev. Richard Boys married Charlotte and Daniel Hamilton Jn on 8 June 1820, a year after Porteous' death. They seem to have lived at Sandy Bay. Sadly, Charlotte died aged only 36 in September 1835.

Porteous and Napoleon did meet again when Charlotte Knipe was present, on 21 July 1816. Porteous and the emperor discussed botany. Porteous also talked to the emperor twice in October 1816 and probably at other times as well. Porteous had been in charge of the Longwood garden before Napoleon arrived, when it was said to produce 'remarkably fine vegetables'. But during the captivity, we find Porteous reprimanded for sending up to Longwood mutton which was 'not of a tolerable quality'.[14]

Then there were visitors from passing ships, which took place until Lowe insisted all visitations had to get his approval. Sometimes these were ship's captains, such as Captain Hamilton of the *Havannah* (21 January 1816) or Captain Cook of the *Tortoise* (2 April 1817). The arrival of the great China and India fleets were occasions when notables such as Sir Stamford Raffles, on the way home to Britain and bored after months at sea, sought excitement and distraction by attempting to meet the most famous man in the world. These encounters invariably occurred in the garden rather than Napoleon's private quarters. One such was on 14 May 1816, when it was recorded of a group of distinguished ladies and gentlemen from the East India fleet:

He [Napoleon] received them in the garden. The grand marshal [Bertrand] conducted them to his presence. The Emperor met them with that grace and that captivating smile which ever exercised such irresistible power. He conversed with each individual, and, with that tact peculiar to himself, seizing upon topics in which each was interested. With the supreme judge he discoursed on legislation and the administration of justice; with the officers of the East India Company, on trade and the internal affairs of India; with the military gentlemen, on wounds and campaigns; while he complimented the ladies upon their fair appearance, remarking that the climate of India had not injured their complexions.[15]

Garden spies

One of the British gardeners at Longwood was called Sowerby, and the under-gardener was a man named Taylor. There were also labourers who were brought in to undertake heavy work. Both gardeners were said to be useful contacts to have if a visitor wished to get a view of Napoleon.[16] But matters went further than that for both were frequently used as spies by the orderly who needed to confirm that Napoleon was still on the property.

There were four orderlies in total who had the unenviable task of monitoring Napoleon at Longwood: Captain Thomas Poppleton (53rd Regiment); Captain Henry Blakeney (66th Regiment); Captain George Nicholls (66th Regiment); and Captain Englebert Lutyens (20th Regiment). There is a surviving journal recording sightings of Napoleon kept by 42-year-old Captain Nicholls (1776–1857), who was orderly officer at Longwood for just under 18 months between 5 September 1818 and 9 February 1820.[17] Nicholls has the distinction of having been in the favour of both Napoleon and Lowe for most of the time. However, Nicholls in turn was closely watched by his keeper, the meticulous and pernickety Major Gideon Gorrequer, Lowe's loyal aide-de-camp. Nicholls's dealings with Napoleon were no doubt helped by the fact that Nicholls had fought in the Peninsular War, though Nicholls's personality – openness combined with tact – was the determining factor. He died a major-general in Cheltenham, in 1857.

Nicholls's main duty appears to have been to ensure Napoleon was spotted every day, either inside the house through a window or in one of his gardens. On several occasions, Nicholls was instructed by Governor Lowe to ensure that he had sight of Napoleon twice a day. The reason, of course, was to ensure that Napoleon had not escaped and was on the high seas returning to France, where given the behaviour of the returned Bourbons he would, no doubt, have been greeted with a warm reception by the Parisian crowd.

Not surprisingly, Napoleon was not amenable to being monitored by an army captain. As Nicholls recorded in his journal:

I saw Genl Bonaparte this afternoon about 5 a clock. he was leaning against a tree in the lower walk of the garden ...

[Talking to Count Montholon] I had not seen Napoleon Bonaparte today though my instructions require that I should see him twice a day. I also mentioned to the Count that I should be greatly obliged if Napoleon Bonaparte would be pleased to point out a certain hour in the day for me to see him, that it would not be expected that I would pass the <u>whole of my time</u> in the garden looking out for him. The Count said that he knew Napoleon would never degrade himself so much as to admit any one into his room on this account – and asked me if I wished him to deliver this communication to Genl B <u>after some consideration</u> I informed the Count that he was at liberty to do so. (13 June 1819)

So Nicholls had to rely on sightings by the Longwood gardeners and by the three orderly sergeants at Longwood, David, Kitts and Lacey. As will be seen in appendix 4, Nicholls relied heavily on these five individuals. Sometimes Nicholls himself was forced to spent long hours 'skulking' about the Longwood garden or using a telescope in the hope of seeing Napoleon in his billiard room, the dining room, dressing room or undertaking his daily ablutions, and on one occasion in his bath looking 'ghostly'. Needless to say, Nicholls complained bitterly of this boring pastime.

The other source on whom Nicholls was forced to rely for a sighting was a member of Napoleon's entourage, especially the worldly, and, according to Sir Thomas Reade, sly and artful, Count Montholon, who had known Napoleon since the count was a child of ten years old. But for obvious reasons of loyalty and devotion to Napoleon, Montholon could not be relied upon. In one journal entry Nicholls records (10 July 1819):

Sowerby [gardener] told me that Napoleon walked in his little garden this a morning (about 10 a clock) with Montholon. One of the stable men (Fuller) also saw him at the same time. As I had no opportunity of seeing Nap/on myself today having been dressing when he was out I this evening mentioned to Cn Motholon that I had not seen him today. The Cn said that Napoleon had been unwell with the bowel complaint and consequently <u>had not been out of his quarters today</u>. for he had just left him (5 a clock PM) to take his (cold) dinner after which he had orders to return to Napoleon – so much for the veracity of these People.

One gets the impression that Montholon quite enjoyed this cat-and-mouse game that was being played on the hapless junior British officer. There is an element of comedy in the following entry by Nicholls (17 May 1819):

Sergt David acquainted me that he had seen Genl B at ___ between 9 and 10 a clock – Count Montholon informed me that Genl B was then walking in the little garden I immediately went round the House but he had gone in.

Napoleon, however, did not enjoy the game and for days on end would hide away in his house, sometimes using the small holes drilled in the billiard room wooden shutters to look out upon the plain. An analysis of the records in appendix 4 reveals that for a 15-month period (November 1818 to January 1820), there were 202 mentions of Napoleon's garden or Napoleon visiting the garden at Longwood. Figure 5 illustrates how significant the garden became for Napoleon.

FIGURE 5
Sightings of Napoleon in his garden

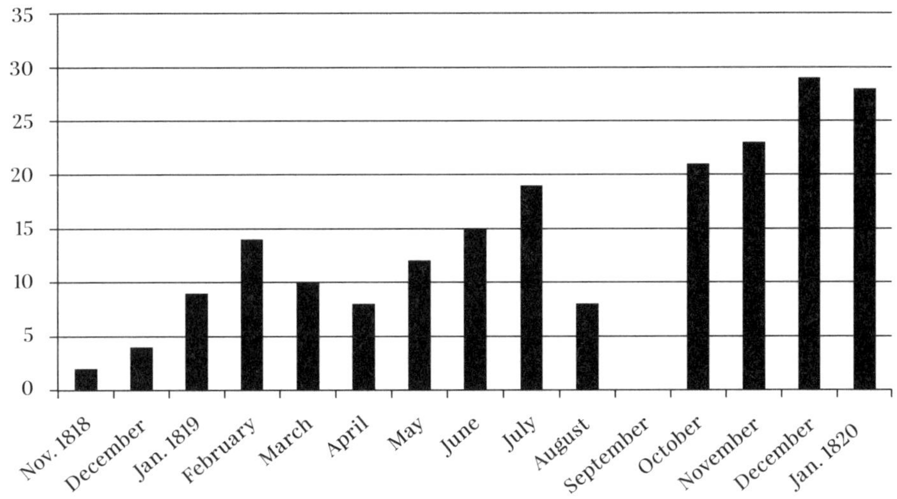

❦ Unwanted intruders ❦

It was not just Sir Hudson Lowe who was unwelcome at Longwood. Attempts by many eminent individuals failed to elicit an invitation from Napoleon, invariably because they came via Lowe, something they had no choice about. Those that did manage to penetrate the ring of steel and enter the garden were, equally invariably, shot dead. They included goats, rabbits, hens and one unfortunate bullock, all of which belonged to others. As William Forsyth observed, these animals were added to the 'menus plaisirs of the ex-Emperor'. Indeed, so keen was Napoleon on this pastime that he actually had such domestic creatures released in the garden area for him to shoot. Inevitably, this led Sir Hudson Lowe to become anxious. Instead of leaving well alone, Lowe blew the matter up out of all proportion, even consulting London on the issue. It was not that Lowe objected to Napoleon having firearms. What concerned him was what would happen if his captive accidentally shot dead a human being. What would be the legal situation, and what would happen if Napoleon was guilty? It was an unnecessary worry for Lowe, as Napoleon did not shoot anyone and ignored the warnings from Lowe that came to him second-hand. Indeed, by 1819 Napoleon ignored the governor completely, considering him beyond the pale.

⸱ Death of Napoleon ⸱

Napoleon died on Saturday, 5 May 1821. He was clearly ill for a long time before that, and the decline in his gardening activity can simply be put down to that. He still used his new garden, which now gave a degree of privacy over what had existed before. Indeed, during his final decline he saw the garden as his refuge rather than a salon. Having leapt out of bed on one occasion, he said he would go to the garden. Then he collapsed:

> We raised him up, and entreated him to get into bed again; but he did not recognize any body, and began to storm, and fell into a violent passion. His head was gone, and he continued to ask to go and walk in the garden.[18]

The British were not at first convinced that Napoleon was sick. In February, Lowe wrote to Bathurst, 'He [Napoleon] walks unassisted when in his garden.' From August 1819, Captain Nicholls had believed that General Bonaparte's sickness was part of the cat-and-mouse game that the French inhabitants at Longwood were playing with him. For example, Nicholls's journal entry on 22 August 1819 contains the following:

> This eveng at about 6½ a'clock I heard persons talking pretty loud in the little back garden of Genl Bonaparte This man had not been seen by any English person for several days. I was therefore determined to pass near to the Garden. It was rather dark I however could distinguish two persons very plain. The one appeared to be Count Bertrand the other was a short person with a big coat wrapped round him. This person I took to be Genl B ... At half after 6 a clock I believe that I saw Genl B walkg in his garden – ten minutes afterwards Count Bertrand came to my quarters to say that he [Napoleon] was ill in bed and required the assistance of Mr Stokoe – The Docr.[19]

However, such games were soon superfluous as the emperor's condition deteriorated and onto the scene came Dr Archibald Arnott (1771–1855). He was surgeon to the 20th Foot Regiment, one of the two guarding regiments camped near to Longwood. Dr Arnott held the rank of captain and was well known on the island.[20] He had to deal not only with the dying emperor but also with the difficult character of Dr Antommarchi, who was fast losing favour with the emperor. Arnott achieved this with great aplomb, though privately he admitted that he had never known such a peevish patient as Napoleon. Despite this, Napoleon trusted the easy-going Scot and the two got on as well as could be expected in difficult circumstances. This was probably due to Arnott being frank and straightforward with the emperor.

Although seriously ill and suffering considerably, Napoleon kept his wits about him. On one occasion, on 24 April 1821, less than two weeks before he died, Napoleon set out to test the doctor with a barrage of questions. These and the responses were recorded in shorthand by Count Bertrand. Part of the catechism ran:

"Have you seen the École de Médecine at Paris?"

"Yes."

"Is it better or less good than yours?"

"I attended none of the classes and heard none of the professors lecture."

"Did you see the Botanical Gardens?"

"Yes."

'Is the one in England finer?"

"No."

"Did you visit any of the Paris hospitals:"

"Yes."

'Were you pleased with the Hôtel Dieu?"

"Yes."

"Is it as well kept as the one in London? Is it finer? What did you most admire in Paris?"

"The view from the Tuileries, the gardens."[21]

Not surprisingly, as his end drew near, Napoleon ventured out less and less, though occasionally he was seen in his garden for brief periods. He did, however, like to keep the house doors onto the garden open when possible. Count Bertrand was unpopular with the Plantation House set, Sir Thomas Reade describing him as 'one of the greatest scoundrels in the world'.[22] This hostility was primarily the result of Bertrand reportedly being 'uniformly discourteous and offensive'. Bertrand's dealings with Napoleon were different, of course, and we find a rather sad reference to Bertrand going out into Napoleon's garden and cutting a rose for the emperor. Then two days later, he picked two bunches of flowers for the dying man's bedroom.[23]

Death of Napoleon's garden

The night before Napoleon died a great storm passed over the island and the Longwood plain, ripping up several of the older trees in the garden. It was a harbinger of what was to befall the emperor's St Helena garden.

The body of the emperor was laid out in the room next to his bed chamber, each room only being 12 by 15 feet [3.6 by 4.5 m]. Appropriately, the body faced the glass doors which faced out into his little garden.

The burial of Napoleon on Tuesday, 8 May 1821 was dignified and the grandest affair that St Helena had ever seen. Appropriately, it started in Napoleon's garden:

> At half-past twelve the grenadiers took the coffin, which they could not lift without difficulty, and after repeated and persevering efforts, succeeded in carrying it to and placing it on the hearse, which was waiting in the great walk in the garden; and it was then covered with a violet-coloured velvet cloth, and the cloak which Napoleon wore at Marengo.[24]

Ironically, given his treatment of the exiled emperor, Governor Lowe behaved in an exemplary manner. He and his party rode out with the funeral procession from the gardens, then down into the valley carpeted with yellow Cape everlasting flowers (*Helichrysum* sp.).

With Napoleon dead and his retinue departed for Europe, the question was now what to do with the Longwood complex of houses. The new house – all 23,000 square feet (2,137 m^2) of it – had become a white elephant.[25] Not surprisingly, the Company turned the estate back into a working farm. When Sir Hudson Lowe called off at St Helena in 1827 on his way back to Britain from Ceylon (Sri Lanka), he found the building where his captive had lived reverted to its original use 75 years earlier. It was a barn – and the emperor's bedroom, a stable.[26] Napoleon's garden was also largely gone, replaced by a potato field. Soon afterwards, in 1829, the Company rented out Longwood.

In 1851, thirty years after Napoleon's death, Joseph Lockwood visited the Hutts:

> This Hutts Gate is renowned through all the length and breadth of St. Helena. It is the *ultima Thule* of all the Yamstock's [islanders'] journeys, hopes, and wishes. Next to the Tomb and Longwood it is the grand point of attraction for strangers and idlers. It is a little roadside tavern, ensconced within a pretty garden, famous for its hospitality – for eating, drinking, and festivity; famous for a cook so dexterous, that he can make a veal cutlet out of mutton chop ...

It is too an historic place, for it was sometime the residence of Bertrand, the faithful attendant of Napoleon during his detention on the island. In this house the ex-emperor passed many pleasant hours, and whiled away the *ennui* of his heavy time, in many a frolic with the general's children. He often wandered down the gentle slopes of the garden, to the little spring in the valley below, and there under the shade of a cluster of willows, communed with himself in silence, reviewed the past, with all its glories and misfortunes, and fixed upon the little glen, at last to be his final resting place.

To a sombre piece on what had been Napoleon's last home, now a crumbling farm building, Lockwood adds:

> The gardens are all gone, a lawn of parched and stunted grass is all around, and there beneath a clump of straggling trees, is a little lank [tank] lined with stone – Napoleon's fish pond, half choked with grass and weeds, but still in preservation.[27]

The new house which was constructed for the emperor was, for a period, occupied by the governor. In 1834 it was described as 'in an excellent state of repair and surrounded by about 20 acres of pleasure ground and indifferent land', with a value of £3,000 and a possible rentable value of £150.[28] Governor Dallas lived and regularly entertained in the new 56-room house at Longwood and certainly paid some attention to its garden. The 'olden chase of Gum Wood' nearby still survived 'where the ladies had their archery ground'. But across the road at the old house, a vegetable garden was now in front of the house where Napoleon had walked, though at the side was still the aloe hedge which bordered the smaller garden that the emperor enjoyed so much. To Dallas's credit he did make an effort that it be 'kept and dressed'.[29] In 1834 there was still an attractive avenue of 'venerable lichen-covered gum trees' leading up to the Longwood complex, but the commission of that year recommended that estate be disposed of. This was easier said than done and it served a variety of purposes over the next century. The remains of the folly were finally demolished to make way for a creamery in 1949.

Between 1933 and 1936, the old house at Longwood was repaired in order to be turned into a museum. The Second World War then intervened. So it was not until the 1950s that renovation continued. The building finally, nearly a century after being acquired by the French, opened to the general public on 27 March 1955. However, the garden had at least partially been restored well before that. A Pathé News clip of the brief British royal visit to St Helena in 1947 clearly shows the extent of this renovation.[30] In 1960 the two iron gates which had originally stood at the entrance to Napoleon's tomb enclosure were returned from South Africa to the old house at Longwood.[31]

Today Napoleon's garden has been restored, at least in concept, with the French tricolour flying proudly in its centre. And the old house itself was meticulously restored from the threshing barn and stables it had been reduced to – which, in Captain Alexander's words, had heaped 'insult on the memory of the extraordinary man, whose astonishing intellect, and most singular fortunes, raised him to be dictator of the European continent'.[32]

According to Gaspard Gourgaud, not always a reliable witness, a corner of Napoleon's garden at Longwood was used to bury various manuscripts written or dictated by the emperor, 'and did not apparently, see the light of day'. Nor have they since.[33]

⤳ The sepulchre garden ⤳

A footnote can be added to St Helena's Napoleonic saga. The place of the former emperor's entombment was in the Sane Valley, some two miles from Longwood House. A later governor of the island recounted:

> Going out of Longwood gate he used to stroll along the main road, skirting the Devil's Punchbowl, to a house at Hutt's Gate, about a mile away, occupied by one of his entourage. This house had a charming garden with lawns and green banks. At the end of the garden was a valley known as Geranium Valley, whilst just at the head of the valley is a spring, the water therefrom running down the valley.[34]

Napoleon had so liked the taste of the spring water (Torbett's fountain) that he required two silver flasks containing it be brought to Longwood every day for his use. According to Dr Teale, this spring produces 60 gallons (272 l) of water an hour at 1,750 feet (533 m). It is said Napoleon expressed a wish to be buried near this spring in what was then called Geranium Valley, if his body was not permitted to be returned to France.

Of course, Lowe did not change in attitude or temperament after his captive's death. He forbade the single name of Napoleon being carved on the tomb's covering stone – so it remained, and still remains, bare of inscription. Insensitive to the symbolic impact the railings at Longwood had on Napoleon, Lowe insisted that railings be placed around the whole burial site. His motivation was the need 'for the preservation of the [two] willows, many sprigs of which have already begun to be taken by different individuals who went down to visit the place after the corpse was interred'. It was a pointless exercise and the two willows were soon dying, although long after Lowe departed the island, cuttings were taken and replacements planted. A note by Lowe's assistant, Syms Covington, concerning the garden at Napoleon's tomb is worth recording:

ON the 11th, went to Napoleon's Grave, a distance of about two and a half miles from port. This tomb is situated in a valley, WHICH has gardens, houses, etc. The grave is simple for so <u>great</u> a man, having no more than a large oblong stone with no inscription, surrounded in same form by iron railings AND also with wooden railings round the iron ditto leaving a space of about ten to fifteen feet for visitors to walk, and that beautifully green with grass, with the willows and cypresses. Outside the wooden railings is the small beautiful, clear well, where he (NAPOLEON) constantly every morning used to send for water to wash etc. Beautiful, clear water. Here is stationed a noncommissioned officer, an old soldier, to take care that no one injures the above. The willow is strictly forbidden for anyone to touch, but from the cypresses, a small twig is allowed only. At the East end or head of tomb, within railings, is a geranium, planted by Lady Warren (Admiral Warren's wife) and HER daughters; at THE West end or foot are several Cape bulbs, etc. The house IS situated from THE tomb, about a mile, along a ridge of mountains. I went to house the 13th; which is in a very decayed state, one room is a billiard room for visitors (wine sold also!). The remaining part serves as a barn and dwelling for the servants of the clergyman who inhabits the new house, which was built for Napoleon, but HE never inhabited it.[35]

With the passing of the years, the appearance of the emperor's last garden changed as foliage grew up and died. It is said that the violets, probably Cape violets, near the tomb were planted by some of Napoleon's attendants. They were certainly a feature for a number of years. In 1839 Mrs Postan paid 30 shillings (£1-10-0) to be taken up the steep, treacherous and narrow road out of Jamestown to Napoleon's tomb:

Its situation is exquisitely beautiful, and unlike, in its sequestered stillness, any other portion of this picturesque island. When the agony of perturbed feelings pressed too heavily upon the exiled Emperor's heart, he was wont to retire among the cypress shades of this quiet dell, and, with his eagle eye fixed upon the world of waters, endeavour to regain his mental equilibrium. Beneath this chosen soil does the frame now repose, once agitated by a higher and more ambitious spirit than ever ruffled the feverish world of human aspiration, and the bare and nearly leafless willows wave slowly over a monumental stone, ungraven even by a word to chronicle who rests beneath. The long grass waves in rank luxuriance around the grave, and a hedge of gay geraniums shades the cool spring, from which the emperor is said to have loved to drink, after his varying walk over the exposed and sunny paths, which separated him from Longwood...

At the head of the tomb, a small geranium still lives, originally planted by the hand of Madame Bertrand, but its leaves look withered and sapless, and the buds fall ere they gain vigour to swell into a maturity of bloom.[36]

Napoleon's body in its wood and lead coffin remained in this verdant valley from May 1821 until October 1840. The valley was damp and there were attractive willow trees scattered around, one overhanging the grave itself. The St Helena burial site was, both during the 19 years Napoleon lay there and indeed ever since, a popular visiting site for the public and, frequently, French naval personnel. Eight months before Napoleon's body was exhumed and sent to Paris, Joseph Hooker visited the tomb site. The scene he encountered was reminiscent of the 'tourist trap' encountered elsewhere at the time, such as at the Giant's Causeway in Ireland:[37]

It is situated at the head of this valley, guarded by a sentinel who duns you about the mighty dead, and gives you water that the Emperor drank; on turning your heel upon him, numerous children assail you with flowers, Geraniums, that the Emperor was fond of. On turning into a pretty cottage to get some ale at 2s. a bottle, the cork was no sooner drawn than out came the Emperor with it; it was the Emperor this, that, and the other thing; our hostess's daughter came in with the Emperor on her lips; his ubiquity certainly astonished me. As a last resort I commenced gathering Lichens; surely the hero of Marengo could have nothing to do with Lichens on a stone wall, when another disinterested stranger came to inform me that the Emperor had from it marked out the position of his tomb, and that the Emperor was fond of the wild plants I had in my hand. I fairly took to my heels ...[38]

The ground where Napoleon was buried had belonged to Richard Torbett, a trader and shopkeeper who had a ready eye for a money-making opportunity. His harassing the authorities for 'injuries sustained by the internment of Napoleon Bonaparte upon his land' went on for several years. Torbett – having given his permission for Napoleon to be buried on his land – demanded and eventually got compensation for the land: £650 plus £50 annually, eventually commuted into a single payment of £1,200.[39] But he went further, erecting a hut and demanding an entrance fee from visitors. The authorities put a stop to this. Then there was the matter of Torbett's idea of erecting a tavern at his house near Longwood, which would sell wine (probably Cape rather than French) and beer 'for the purpose of the entertainment of strangers'. Permission was reluctantly granted.[40]

In May 1858 the British, after negotiations which lasted four years, sold both the old Longwood House as well as the enclosed area of the tomb to Napoleon III. The 1858 price was a hefty £7,000, but that included both sites, with buildings and about 33 acres, three being around what remained of the old Longwood House. Julia Blackburn, in her book *The Emperor's Last Island*, wrote:

> In 1869 a group of men under the command of Captain Masselin were busy scratting at the walls of the rooms in search of a fragment of the original paint or a scrap of wallpaper that would reveal a colour or a design that they could copy. They went back to the memoirs that were written while Napoleon was in residence, trying to work out how the rooms had been divided and how they had looked when in use. They dug at what had been the garden hunting for evidence of a path or covered walkway, a channel of water, a heap of earth, and slowly they reconstructed an approximation of the past.[41]

Captain, later Brigadier-General, Eugène François Masselin of the 3rd Engineer Regiment, with two soldiers, was sent out to St Helena from Britain to try and clear up and restore as much as possible of both Napoleonic sites. He was on St Helena from March 1859 to December 1860 and achieved a great deal, creating a path that others would follow. In particular, he pieced together a picture of the physical environment surrounding Napoleon at Longwood, and on his return to France published a book about his time on the island.[42]

The British retained the new house, renting it out to the newly appointed first curator of old Longwood House and the tomb. This was the colourful character of Gauthier de Rougemont (1794–1868), a veteran of the first empire now with the imposing title of Commander of the Imperial Residences of St Helena. At French government expense, he lived in greater style in the new Longwood than his hero had in the old, though he was not beyond grumbling to Paris about the shoddy workmanship in the new house. He finally left St Helena in January 1867. He died a year later.[43] Though de Rougemont might have exerted himself with more energy on the properties under his stewardship, he nonetheless stopped and to a degree reversed the process of decay. This applied as much to the gardens of both houses as it did to the old house itself. The garden of the new Longwood House was essentially an overgrown meadow with a couple of beds containing some shrubs and, here and there, an occasional stunted tree. The front of the building did, however, have an excellent panoramic view over Deadwood Plain.

By the early 1880s, visitors were coming to the tomb in some numbers and, by appointment, to Longwood House:

> The gate leading to the Old House is now opened and passing through the visitor meets the Gardien et Conservateur Monsieur MORILLEAU [1835–1907] — who politely conducts him to the room where the bust of the Great Conqueror stands in the exact spot where he breathed his last. Neat little flower beds and a kitchen garden are to be observed in the enclosure, which is encircled with privet. At the back of the house is the Emperor's fish pond, a few yards from which is the Signal Station, from which almost every ship coming to St. Helena is descried and telegrams passed to all parts of the Island.[44]

De Rougemont was succeeded by a series of French custodians:

Jean-Claude Mareschal	1868–1880
Lucien Désiré Constans Morilleau	1880–1907
Louisa Elizabeth Thompson née Morilleau	1907–1908
Henri Roger	1908–1916
Bazett Legg (acting)	1916–1919
Georges Pierre Louis Colin	1919–1945
Georges Peugeot	1945–1954
Steven Strong	1954–1956
Gilbert Martineau	1956–1987
Michel Dancoisne-Martineau	from 1987[45]

By the end of the 19th century, the site of Napoleon's former tomb remained a place of pilgrimage, as indeed it still is today. A guard's sentry box came and went. The Lowe railings also disappeared. In the early 1880s, Benjamin Grant's description of the tomb garden ran as follows:

> We soon arrive at the gate and boundary hedge of privet (about ¾ths of a mile) almost encircling the Tomb land. A few yards after leaving the gate a bed of rushes is noticed just below the road; passing this we come in full view of the residence of the sous-Gardien, in front of which are neat flower beds; also kitchen garden, orange, peach, shaddock, apple, pear, loquat, coffee, and black olive trees; also pineasters and thorn trees. In two minutes after passing the house the Tomb,

surrounded by a neat iron railing, 5 fine Norfolk Island pines and 18 cypress trees, and a young weeping willow, an offshoot of the parent tree, which was blown down by the wind about two years ago, now meets the admiring gaze of the Tourist, who dismounts his steed, enters the gate and proceeds to view the spot where the remains of the Great Emperor lay for 20 years. On the left of the Tomb he will observe a little well in which the delicious water of NAP's favorite spring trickles, and as he will no doubt partake of this invigorating, icy-cold beverage, we would advise him to wet the tips of his fingers before drinking so as to avert ill consequences (if he is walking) after a fatiguing journey.[46]

The saga of the Briars and French ownership comes a hundred years after the acquisition of Longwood and the tomb site. The Briars Pavilion passed from private to French hands only in May 1959, having been donated by Dame Mabel Brookes, William Balcombe's great-granddaughter. The three sites are now termed by the French Des Domaines Nationaux à Sainte-Hélène.

8

The Company's twilight years

In his unpublished guide 'A handbook and gazetteer of the island of St Helena', Geoffrey Kitching, the 1930s government secretary of St Helena, observed:

> From 1836 to about 1860, St Helena was never more prosperous. Towards the end of 1860 the Crown suddenly removed all its establishments, and then came the opening of the Suez Canal. From 1873 onwards Governors were powerless. They had no money and no staff. In 1932 the poverty, distress and the housing were painful to see.[1]

27. Burchell's sketch of Sisters Walk – named after Governor Robert Patton's daughters. It looks inland with Jamestown on the right and a palm from the famous Castle Garden, 27 September 1810. By the 1840s the promenade was being used for 'nightly depredations & nuisances'.

In fact, St Helena's decline began much earlier in the 19th century, long before the Suez Canal was opened in 1869. Although the canal clearly did not help matters, the introduction of steamships, which were often much larger and faster, drastically cut sailing times and so reduced the need to revictual en route. Keen competition among shipping companies meant costs must be cut where possible, including avoiding harbour dues in some colonial ports. Matters were not helped by a tariff of a penny per ton being imposed on ships in the roadstead at Jamestown for some of the period up to the early 1880s. From then on, it was a duty-free port. More rapid passage to Britain greatly assisted many colonies, which could get their products to market more quickly. But with St Helena having no industry and practically no export products, it had the reverse impact on the island. Another often forgotten factor in the island's steady decline occurred even earlier. With the British acquisition of the Cape in 1795. Table Bay became a viable alternative for ships and fleets needing to revictual on the long haul to Europe, a fact recognised by Alexander Beatson in 1816, two years after the Dutch formally ceded the Cape to the British.[2]

There were additional, less obvious reasons for decline, too. The introduction of the Plimsoll Line and legislation to eliminate 'defective ships' from the high seas meant fewer vessels coming into Jamestown Bay for repairs. Another factor was cited by Governor Grey Wilson, who observed, in 1888, that the introduction of tinned foodstuffs 'rendered ships more or less independent of the ports of call'.[3] Water storage onboard improved. Even the whaling ships came to St Helena in fewer numbers than before.

The mail ships continued to call at St Helena: in the late 1880s, 13 times each year on their south-bound (outward) voyage and 26 times on their northern (homeward) leg. But these were subsidised calls, those outward being paid by the British government and the homeward by the St Helena government, the rate being £34-13-5 if Ascension Island was also visited, but if not then the St Helena government had to pay £100 a call.[4]

Then there was the reduction and finally the evacuation of the army garrison, the Royal Navy having long since selected Ascension Island as their 'battleship headquarters', although a squadron was at times based at Jamestown to serve West Africa. The arrival of a man-of-war was good news and more than once saved St Helena from serious want, providing enough labour for a while in a variety of manual jobs. But in 1869 the St Helena Royal Navy squadron was withdrawn. Ten years later, in 1888, the year that Jamestown had its first – rather dim – street lights erected, troop numbers on the island were reduced. Finally, in October 1906, the British garrison was withdrawn and with it went employment and a market for some of the produce from local farmers.

But accepting the above factors, there was a more fundamental reason why St Helena declined. The East India Company had regarded the island as strategically vital to their route from India, even after the Cape of Good Hope was captured. Government and military salaries were high in St Helena, salted beef was subsidised and a regular garrison was maintained, with large fleets returning from the East Indies, including China, calling regularly.

FIGURE 6
Number of ships calling at St Helena, 1834 to 1934

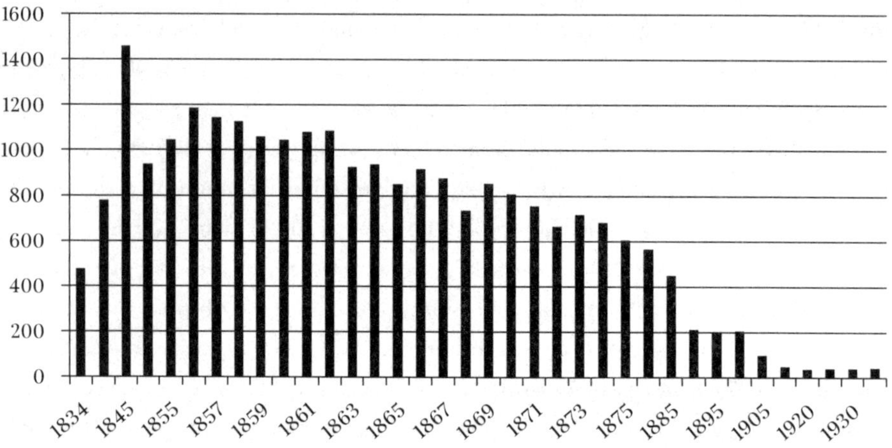

The vast grants supplied by the East India Company soon petered out in the 1830s and British government grants-in-aid disappeared in 1877. Worse, from 1872 under Governor Patey, St Helena was encumbered with two loans which had to be paid off to London. One was for £19,500, at 7 per cent interest, used to rebuild the white rat-ravaged Castle in Jamestown. Much else in Jamestown was destroyed by termites, including in the 1860s a Wardian case for transporting plants which belonged to the Royal Botanic Gardens, Kew. The second debt was for £5,158. After 20 years, the larger loan was finally paid off in 1891. While the aspirations of the reforming Company governors had not always been met, the attitude and endeavours of the small Company administration meant that a spirit of enterprise and experiment had been disseminated. Benjamin Grant, the newspaper editor and printer, denounced the quality of Crown Colony governors who were sent to run over the island as being, 'old Major-Generals, worn out Colonels, and pensioned Admirals ... They knew nothing of, or were wholly indifferent to, the requirements of the place and its inhabitants.' As will be seen, there was the occasional exception, such as Sir Charles Elliot.

NAPOLEON'S GARDEN ISLAND

The spiral of decline in the later Victorian era was not assisted by a population shift from the countryside, where the old estates had once flourished, to Jamestown and Half Tree Hollow, where former cottagers ceased to plant their own potatoes and other vegetables. The shift to pasture in the countryside compounded the problem, inevitably meaning less employment.

⁓ The old botanic garden ⁓

What is extraordinary about St Helena Botanic Garden is that again it contradicted the wider pattern. The botanic garden had flourished when Britain was in a life-and-death struggle with revolutionary and then Napoleonic France. But during the Victorian era, when botanic gardens multiplied and flourished around the expanding of empire, eventually numbering about 120 in total, the St Helena Botanic Garden was reduced to little more than a public park.

St Helena Botanic Garden issued no annual reports or catalogues, so it is difficult to track its fortunes in detail, even when it was flourishing. There were several serious rock falls in the vicinity of the botanic garden in March 1828. One woman was killed but there was no report relating to damage in the gardens. We know that in 1816 there were 135 black cattle, 109 sheep and 13 pigs on the Plantation House farm. Also known is that ten tons of potatoes, priced at £10 a ton, were shipped out of St Helena that December. Yet we know little of what was growing in the Jamestown or Plantation House gardens, save that quite a timber plantation was springing up behind the governor's residence and a tree nursery there distributed at this time over 7,000 young *Pinus pinaster* plants to various parts of the island. Writing in 1817, Captain John Barnes observed:

> Colonel Wilks, the late governor, has raised and put out many thousand pineasters
> on the side of a hill near Plantation House, which are growing exceedingly well,
> and will add to the beauty and value of that estate in an eminent degree.[5]

The Plantation House garden was under a man named Jennings, who had previously served there under the eagle eye of Governor Beatson. In front of Plantation House were allotment beds where barley, black-speckled beans, mangel-wurzels, potatoes and salsola or saltwort were grown experimentally. As less than 100 acres of the 47 square miles of the island was then under cultivation, this continued to be regarded as important work. On 30 July 1821, less than a month before Governor Lowe sailed back to Britain, he was complaining that the Plantation House lands available for the governor's use had shrunk since the time of Beatson and Wilks from 1,500 acres [609 ha] down to 200 acres [81 ha], out of which he had to 'feed his own stock and provide his own table'.[6]

Behind Plantation House was an arboretum, sometimes referred to as a botanic garden. As well as the *Pinus pinaster* forest, there was a *Pinus longifolia*, a 50-foot (15 metre) high *Gleditsia sinensis* (*Gleditsia horrida*) – the 'most stately and most beautiful' tree on the island – and a peach tree bearing very tasty fruit, as well as a couple of stunted tea plants.[7]

By this time Porteous was running the Company's farming enterprise. This was so much the case that in June 1817 the governor appointed Edward Charlton as the Company's gardener at five shillings a day (*c.*£76 a year) plus the use of a cottage in the gardens, as well as coal, candles and free vegetables, the last being converted into an allowance of £25 a year. The departure of troops who served as guards for Napoleon resulted in another economic setback for the island. With Burchell long gone and Porteous dying on 23 June 1819 at the age of 57, matters had drifted. The dual practice of paying the Company's garden staff a wage and additional sums to plant out trees on Company lands on the island was discontinued by Governor Walker in June 1825.

Charlton's basic salary had by then risen to £116, on top of which he earned £60 to £70 for selling young trees. Edward Charlton and a recently arrived gardener named James Cameron, aged about 23, received £43 and £28 respectively in lieu of lost earnings incurred by Governor Walker's decision. This brought their annual salaries up to £150 and £100. As the gardeners had previously pocketed any profits from this forest tree-planting system, attention to other aspects of the island's Company gardens had been much neglected.[8] Charlton appears to have been based at the Plantation House garden and farm, where a new employee, Mr Brookie, was also posted. Selling fruit from the gardens to the public and supplying fruit and vegetables gratis for the governor's table had also contributed to the horticultural enterprise's decline. The result of this neglect and poor staff management was that many rare and valuable plants died and the garden was 'at no very remote period entirely destroyed'.[9] Porteous' grand post of superintendent of the Company's lands passed to the 26-year-old Archibald Seale.

The grounds of what had been the demesne of Plantation House were not what they had been. A report following the death of Napoleon contained the following comment:

The Grounds formerly attached to Plantation House Demesne having by the establishment of the Company's farms reduced that Demesne to a very small portion of land, and that small portion having been subsequently diminished by the planting of Forest trees, the remainder had become wholly inadequate to render any acceptance worth noting to the raising of produce for stock – it had therefore become a matter of necessity in the present Governor to have had for the maintenance of his table.[10]

Governor Walker

Lowe's successor as governor of St Helena was a very different personality. Governor Alexander Walker (1823–1828) was a brigadier-general. He was a Scot, widely read, with much experience of the world and an educated man with an interest in natural history. In August 1824, he wrote an eight-page memorandum, with appendices, reminding the Company's directors that:

> The science of Botany is very much cultivated at present and the establishment of Botanical Gardens and Horticultural Societies in every considerable place of Great Britain shows the vast importance which is attached to the subject. A Botanical Establishment at St Helena would not only advance the improvement of the island but might be made productive of much advantage to the Mother Country.

Walker wanted for St Helena a 'Scholar and a man of real Science, capable of giving public lectures on the natural History and culture of plants'.[11] In this endeavour he was partially successful, in that he was allowed to appoint someone to be in charge of botanical matters who had been a resident on St Helena since 1819. At the time, the normal practice in the British empire was to appoint a medical man as superintendent of an important botanic garden, and more often than not a Scot. St Helena was no exception to this unwritten rule. Walker turned to Edinburgh-born Dr Archibald Arnott (1771–1855), famous for having attended Napoleon during his dying days.

Governor Walker hoped that Arnott taking up the position as superintendent of gardens was 'a measure which we trust will prove furtherance to the objects for which those gardens were formed'. Arnott was given the small house in the upper garden so he could be near to his work. His task was to lay out and replant the garden anew, and he had full control of the gardening staff. A minute dated 27 June 1825 recorded:

> This garden had been originally intended for botanical purposes and at one time contained many valuable and rare plants, but it is to be lamented that by mismanagement, neglect, and some injudicious experiments the greater part

of those plants have been lost and the Garden at no very remote period entirely destroyed. It has lately been put into better order, but I have still the mortification of seeing that the attempts which have been made to introduce into it rare and valuable plants from foreign soils have very generally failed, and in most instances from want of care and proper management in the Gardeners ... Fruit and vegetables were also grown formerly in this Garden principally for the use of the Governor's Table, after supplying which the surplus was sold ... I have further requested Dr Arnott to take charge of and superintend the exotics and other plants which may be found in any of the other public Gardens and to give to the Gardeners from time to time such instruction as he may see necessary for their management.[12]

Arnott appears to have been keen to get started on his new task and prepared a series of public lectures on botany. But not all were enthusiastic about botany. Some of the Company officials pointed out that as Arnott was also the island's medical superintendent, he had other duties. In 1827 these included being on the committee tasked with ascribing a value to each of the island's enslaved individuals. The last enslaved people had been landed on the island in 1789. Then in 1818 Governor Lowe had decreed that all chidren born of enslaved woman after Christmas of that year would be regarded as free but apprenticed at the age of 16 if female and 18 if male. By 1827 there were 1,255 enslaved people and whom 336 were described as 'free children'. The committee on which Arnott sat was part of a five-year phased emancipation plan, whereby owners of enslaved people were financially compensated for their loss by the Company, with the costs considered loans to the formerly enslaved individuals. In fact, it was not until May 1836 that the last enslaved person was 'freed' and only in 1839 was enslavement officially prohibited.[13]

Governor Walker inaugurated fairs and organised agricultural shows, with the usual prizes for best produce and for a ploughing competition. Where he could encourage enterprise and innovation he did so, praising, for instance, the quality of baskets made on the island from locally grown bamboo.[14] He also resurrected the idea of the island having a silk industry.[15] The Company's gardeners were assigned to planting land at the Briars and near Longwood with thousands of mulberry seedlings. The first silkworms arrived on the East Indiaman *Repulse* on 17 March 1825.[16] Only three survived the long journey, down from thirty-three alive a week earlier before the ship hit bad weather. However, up to 100 eggs hatched from the survivors. Captain Daniel O'Connor of the St Helena Artillery, one of the islanders behind the scheme, was optimistic that all would be well.[17] The Company formally purchased the Briars in 1827 for the princely sum of £6,000. Over £10,000 was then spent on land, machinery, buildings, and salaries. This was an extraordinarily large investment on a risky project. But it was not just Company funding which was to disappear. The Briars' garden which Napoleon had so enjoyed was obliterated. As Betsy Balcombe asserted many years later:

> On the side nearest the cottage the defences of the garden were completed by an aloe and prickly pear hedge, through which no living thing could penetrate. The garden at the Briars, like the bright dreams and hopes of my own early youth, is now withered and destroyed: it was sold to the East India Company, by whom it was dug up and planted with mulberry trees, which speedily became 'food for worms,' if I may be guilty of a conceit on — to me — a melancholy subject. I believe the intended speculation proved unsuccessful.[18]

It was more than unsuccessful. It was disastrous. Between 1826 and 1834, the venture netted 336¾ lbs (153 kg), which sold in London for £300. It is therefore little wonder that the 1834 commission recommended 'the total abolition of the silk establishment, and the sale of the land and houses and (if practicable) of the machinery, utensils, cocoons, and stock in hand'.[19] One later governor put this disaster down to 'incompetence and carelessness'.[20] But it would not be the last time the St Helena government invested over-optimistically in a cure-all scheme.

By 1834, the Briars was described disapprovingly as:

> ... 59 acres of land, one moiety rocky and barren. This estate was previously considered valuable as garden ground and was extremely productive. It is now, with the exception of a small part, planted with shrubberies.[21]

The efforts to establish a St Helena wine industry about this time – whether produced from grapes, blackberry or lemon – sank without trace. Of the three fruits, blackberry was by far the most common. Indeed, by the early 19th century it was regarded as a noxious weed, even if it did have some uses. Just before and during Napoleon's captivity dried blackberry wood was frequently used as fuel. Off-duty soldiers were allowed to seek extra work from farmers rooting it out. Tenders were called for the supply of blackberry wood and root for use in heating the garrison oven.[22]

Governor Walker's efforts to re-establish the St Helena Agricultural and Horticultural Society assisted the island's farmers. The granting of premiums on certain crops by the Company, spread over a three-year period, had already increased land under the plough by 80 acres. Walker established a public market that also assisted agriculture. As he said, it 'destroyed a kind of monopoly which diminished the profit of the grower and enhanced the price to the buyer'.

As far as tree planting was concerned, Walker continued Lowe's enthusiasm for establishing great tracts of forest both on Company and private land. As Table 16 illustrates, he resurrected the bounty on tree planting among the gentry. In June 1822, a provision was made to prevent farmers planting trees on 'good pasture land fit for garden growing or cultivation'. Saplings could be bought from the Company's nursery. Pinaster (*Pinus pinaster*) cost a farthing each; Botany Bay willows (*Acacia myrtifolia*) were twopence (2d) a dozen; 'and the prices of other Plants will be settled hereafter on the same moderate rate'.[23]

TABLE 16
Premiums for the planting of trees on private land on St Helena[24]

Date of proclamation	Trees to be planted before	Minimum acreage	Minimum number of trees in a thriving state	Space between trees	Premium to be paid/date
22 July 1818	1 Sept 1819	2 acres	5,000	4 feet	£150 1 Jan 1820
		1 acre	2,500		£70 1 Jan 1820
		½ acre	1,200		£30 1 Jan 1820
12 June 1823	31 Oct 1823	3 acres	7,500	4 feet	£50 30 April 1824
		2 acres	5,000		£25 30 April 1824

The Agricultural and Horticultural Society held its first meeting at the castle in Jamestown on Thursday 3 July 1823, with 'landholders, gentlemen and respectable inhabitants' being present. The chair was taken by Governor Walker, who pretty well dictated the aims, functions and office-bearers, be they 'permanent' vice presidents or just vice presidents. The existence of the society is a good indication that the St Helena gentry class had survived the uninvited if lucrative Napoleonic– British military occupation.

Number 15 of the 21 society aims proposed by the governor read:

As Horticulture or the art of cultivating Gardens is of great importance to this island, and yields to many, a comfortable support, I should also consider all that belongs to Garden culture to be included within the aim & encouragement of our

Society. – Under this view it will be proper to offer premiums for the best fruits and the most beautiful flowers. – Planting which is so essential to the ornamentation of the island and the comfort of its inhabitants, and which has within these few years made so much progress, will in a high degree require our attention, and be entitled to honorary premiums and Rewards.

We are fortunate that the St Helena Archives has the manuscript proceedings book of the society for the years 1823 to 1825. From this, it is clear that the emphasis was on agriculture rather than botany. There is within the volume a great deal of interest relating to horticultural and agricultural produce as well as to meteorological matters. Walker attended some of the society's meetings, giving his observations on a variety of relevant subjects both in person and by letter to the group. For instance, he suggests to the society that insects on the island are worthy of study:

The Plants and vegetables which are articles of cultivation are great objects of their depredations and they rarely attack those which are natural or indigenous.

Gardens occasionally came within the ambit of the society, albeit tangentially, such as 'Acorns, the Plantain Tree and even Peaches' being successfully used to feed cattle and pigs.[25]

Kitching comments on Walker's legacy:

In agriculture he [Walker] persevered with all the zeal of a [Governor] Beatson, but with no more success, and the great silk industry was one of his conceptions; but the lavish expenditure of £20,000 on land, mulberry, and staff, only produced a return of £300 in the seven years in which the experiment was in operation.[26]

No doubt it was Governor Walker's activities in promoting St Helena that attracted the interest of the Horticultural Society in London to the island. In this, they were supported by Sir Stamford Raffles and Major Pritchard. A letter written by Joseph Sabine, secretary of the society, dated 20 December 1824, contained the following passage:

Orders have consequently be given by the Council of the Society to prepare four Chests of living trees and three boxes of seeds to be sent to that Settlement addressed to General Walker for the use of the Farmer's Society of the Island or such other application as may appear to him desirable.

The letter's interesting conclusion harks back to an earlier use of the island during Governor Brooke's time as a resting place for rare and valuable plants from the East:

> From the experience we have had in the transmission of Plants from China and other countries in the East to Europe we are satisfied that very valuable things which will not endure the entire voyage at one time might be introduced, if the Company's Garden at St Helena could be used as a Depôt for such things as might be left there by any of the homeward bound Ships and forwarded from the Island by subsequent opportunities.
>
> I avail myself of this Communication to introduce the subject to the notice of the Court of Direction, because I am certain their sanction alone is wanting to the success of such an arrangement.
>
> The readiness with which Mr Cameron, the Company's Gardener, had assisted our Collectors on all occasions make us confident of his zeal and endeavors to be useful in every way possible.
>
> It is proposed that some of the Plants left lately by Sir Stamford Raffles at the Island shall be returned in the Chests now proposed to be sent there, they are constructed carefully for the safe conveyance of plants on Ship Board.[27]

The arrival of the London Horticultural Society's 'plentiful supply of seeds and plants' on board the East Indiaman *Farquharson* prompted Governor Walker to reassert his belief that the London society's plan to make St Helena a depot 'for such plants as it is desirable to transmit from China and India to Europe would [be] of great advantage to the island and to Botany'. He also felt that different species might be placed on the island at different altitudes depending upon their origins.

The arrival of plants sent to St Helena at this time – 'remarkable for their timber, the beauty of their flowers, and foliage, or their delicious fruits' – was not without high adventure. Both Dr Nathaniel Wallich (1786–1854), the famous director of Calcutta Botanic Garden from 1815 to 1841, and the eminent Sir Stamford Raffles (1781–1826) were involved in this enterprise to provide St Helena with plants from the east. Raffles suggested that both clove and nutmeg might succeed on the island, at least in the valleys where there was deep soil. He added, rather practically, that if they did not succeed as a cash crop, 'they will at all events be beautiful and interesting trees in a shrubbery'. Given the eclectic composition of the gentry's gardens on St Helena, this was good enough advice and, as it turned out, at least some of the plants Raffles did send were from the hottest part of China and were not expected to survive on St Helena.[28]

PLATE 20
Burchell's coloured sketch of Terrace Knoll, 16 February 1807. Bamboo and yams grow along the water course as does a castor oil plant. The hillside behind the house is covered with invasive thorny furze or gorse. A stone pine grows to the left of house, fig trees to the right and agave down the slope. On the top of the far right hill is Rosemary Hall.

PLATE 21 Burchell's coloured sketch of West Lodge. 13 March 1806. Peach trees border the field in front of the house and giant bamboo grow on the right.

PLATE 22

Oakbank House. The jewel in the garden crown of St Helena. This planter's house had a magnificent garden containing both rare endemic plants as well as unusual exotics. But, as can be seen, Oakbank also had a superb arboretum. For many years, it was the home of the Melliss family before becoming the residence of the Anglican bishop of St Helena. The house to the left is Rose Bower. Fowler, *Views of St Helena*, 1863. Provided by Donal P. McCracken.

PLATE 23 *Pleopeltis macrocarpa*, the indigenous spotted-tongue fern living on the stems of cabbage trees and tree fern, was first introduced to Britain by Governor Poirier in 1701.
Drawn by William Burchell on Diana's Peak on 24 January 1808

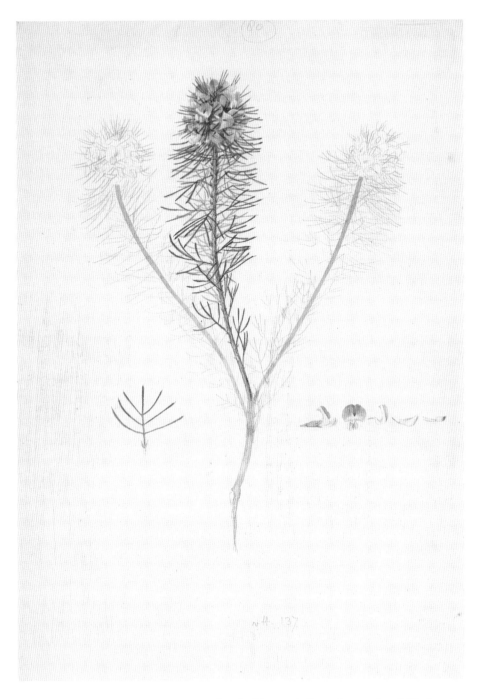

PLATE 24 This detail of *Psoralea pinnata* sketched by Burchell on 15 December 1809. Growing to about three metres, the gobblegheer or goblin's hair, is referred to as the St Helena Christmas tree. It is possibly indigenous to the island.

PLATE 25 Burchell's sketch of 'a curious species' – *Mesembryanthemum cryptanthum* [*Hydrodea cryptantha*], growing in arid soil near the sea at Prosperous Bay on 19 January 1809. Known today as babies toes.

PLATE 26 'Amused the morning in making a drawing of the Bastard Gum Tree'. *Commidendrum robustum* or gumwood is the handsome national tree of St Helena. Sketched at Longwood by Burchell, 8 March 1810.

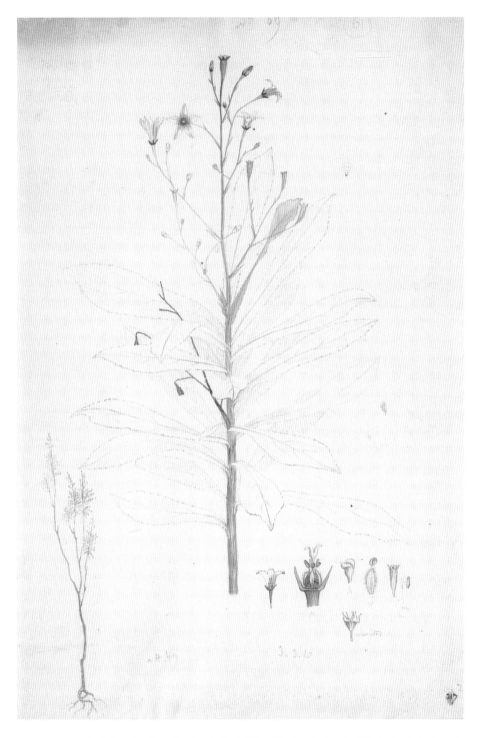

PLATE 27 Burchell sketch of *Wahlenbergia budelli* [*Wahlenbergia burchellii*], 3 March 1810. This endemic bellflower is now extinct.

PLATE 28 The Jamestown trench, 1812. This extraordinary engraving on copper by J. Clark was drawn by James Wathen. Wathen spent three days on St Helena in 1812 when he drew this exaggerated scene of the Jamestown valley. Captain James Cook described this valley in 1772 as a trench. The zigzag road to Ladder Hill still exists, but the indigenous plants, including cabbage trees, precariously and dramatically hanging off the cliffs of this valley, have largely gone.

Wathen, *A Series of Views Illustrative of the Island of St. Helena*, 1821. Provided by Donal P. McCracken.

The task of getting plants to Governor Walker on St Helena was not an easy one because of 'the protracted voyage, and the necessity of their passing through a region particularly exposed to storms' on their way from China, India and Mauritius:

> Dr Wallich of Calcutta, a zealous and celebrated Botanist, has sent to this island in the course of the season upwards of 600 seeds and fruits, the produce of India, Napaul and Himmalia; – but all the growing plants perished on the voyage, and only a small number of seeds have vegetated – Among those which we have lost, the Doctor mentions a highly interesting plant called prangos from Luddak, where it is indigenous and extensively cultivated as fodder for cattle.

Worse than this, 'a vast collection of valuable plants, flowers & seeds' sent by Wallich went down when a ship sank. Sir Stamford Raffles, however, stepped into the breach and despatched a new, if less numerous and varied, shipload of plants. This duly arrived at St Helena 'in a state of perfect preservation'.[29]

Table 17 lists the plants and seeds eventually received at Jamestown during Governor Walker's first two years in office. It is interesting to see the volume of mortality among the introduced plants which arrived. It also illustrates the tenacity shown by those administrators interested in botanical and horticultural matters when introducing species which they thought might benefit the regions they controlled. Typically for the time, they were oblivious of later scientific understanding of the environmental impact that these alien introductions could have if they became invasive.

The East India Company went to great lengths in its attempt to protect the plants it sent out to St Helena from England on board its ship the *London*. Dr Robert Briscow Owen observed that the *London* sailed from England in midwinter (February 1824) and took two months to reach St Helena. The young forest and fruit trees and strawberry canes were placed in boxes on the ship's poop deck. These were protected by strong wooden hoops and netting. During the first part of the voyage when there was frost at night, the boxes were covered with a tarpaulin. As they neared the tropics buds began to appear on the saplings. So healthy were the young trees that after five weeks out to sea, some had grown so tall that they began to emerge above the netting. Twice the netting was raised as the trees' growth continued and the air temperature reached 25° Celsius. An insect attack on the fruit trees was seen as a benefit as it retarded this rapid growth. Irrigation was irregular but, being exposed, rain watered the plants naturally. Apart from the netting, the plants were given no protection from the sun. So impressed were the Company's officials by Dr Owen's observations that it was decided to include them in the next general letter to the directors of the Company's governing Court.

Such care was the exception, however. As discussed in chapter 1, only after the invention in the 1830s of the glass-sided Wardian case was human distribution of plants across the globe transformed.[30]

There was, therefore, no shortage of plants coming into St Helena at this time.

TABLE 17
Lists of plant consignments received at St Helena from EIC ships, 1823 and 1824

Received from	Plants	Seeds	Plant names/condition
Mauritius	Box of sickly plants – all since died	Parcel of seeds	Seeds coming up well
Bengal	Box of plants containing 22 varieties	2 boxes with 118 sorts of seeds	*Pterospermum acerifolium* (dead) *Indigoferactra purpumae* (dead) *Dalbergia sisso* *Dalbergia robusta* *Marsdenia tinctoria* *Terminalia catappa* *Ficus elastica* *Wrightia tinctoria* *Pterocarpus marsupium* *Pterocarpus delbergioides* *Mimosa dalais* *Sansevieria zeytinia* *Nauclea cadumba* *Nauclea undelata* *Asclepias tenacissima* *Urtica tonnacissima* (dead) *Bignonia chelonoides* (dead) *Bignonia suberasa* *Cedrela toona* *Lagerstroemia grandifolia* (dead) *Lagerstroemia regisia* *Artocarpus integrifolia* (dead) [jack fruit]
Nepal		Box containing 178 var of seeds	Seeds appear very old. Of Nepal and Himalaya seeds only 9 var came up
Huimalhia		172 var of seeds and 323 cultivated. Bag of Teak seeds. Bag of Lisso seeds	Seeds appear very old Teak seeds very good in coming up. Lisso seeds seem in a bad state
China	Some boxes of plants		All in good order and appear to be doing well

Received from	Plants	Seeds	Plant names/condition
England from General Harris	2 casks of garden seeds		In very good order
EIC ship *London*	4 cases of forest trees; 1 of fruit trees; 1 of strawberries		The greater part in a healthy state and likely to do well Spruce fir (good) Larch (dead) Ash (good) Beech (good) Birch (good) Silver fir (dead) Horse chestnut (good) Elm (good) Elm grafted 25 (good) Poplar (favourable) Apple (very good) Pear (very good) Plum (very good) Nectarine (delicate) Cherry (delicate) Apricot (good) Strawberry (good)
EIC ship *London*		3 casks of forest tree seeds; Small box of flower seeds	Horse chestnut (decayed) Birch (decayed) Beech (decayed) Silver fir Spruce fir Flower seeds good
Bombay	60 boxes containing 120 plants	5 boxes of seed grain	Plants mostly dead because of protracted voyage, being kept too confined and without a sufficient quantity of water. All that arrived alive: 1 mango plant grafted 1 small mango plant grafted 20 pomponaes sweet lime 1 mamma apples 1 flower plant 11 pine apples 35 alive Grain: Gram (nearly all destroyed by insects) Mutt Moony uzid Badjirie
Batavia	1 box of 12 plants		5 dead on receipt and 4 died since. Others doing well.
America	5 casks of fruit and forest trees and ornamental shrubs		All doing well

From mid-1821, with Lowe gone, the St Helena fortress was rapidly being dismantled by General Coffin. The civic responsibility reverted to the Company with Thomas Henry Brooke, the colonial secretary on the island, in charge. It is significant that no sooner was the Company back in charge again than they decided to send out a new gardener to the island, a young Kew gardener called Thomas Fraser, with a mandate 'to grow vegetables' to supply the Company's homeward-bound ships. Fraser's period on the island fitted well with Governor Walker's drive to improve horticulture and agriculture.

In March 1825, Kew received probably the greatest variety of endemic plants yet despatched in one consignment from St Helena. This was from Governor Walker and was no doubt collected by Fraser. It included a large covered tub which contained: one tree fern; three white he cabbage trees; three red she cabbage trees; and one specimen each of a black cabbage tree, a stringwood tree, a St Helena dogwood tree, a whitewood, a St Helena redwood, and a specimen of lobelia, probably the endemic *Trimeris scaevolifolia*. In addition, a large, covered box contained: two tree ferns; five gumwoods; six red cabbage trees; five white cabbage trees; two black cabbage trees; and one specimen each of an unnamed palm, a St Helena ebony named as *Melhania erythroxylon* and a variety of the alien *Sansevieria*.

Unfortunately, such a treasure-trove of St Helena plants at Kew was not to be. John Smith, Kew's curator, scrawled in pencil on the list of specimens, 'All Dead'.[31] Shipping plants from St Helena to Britain could be as risky as shipping them from China to St Helena.

Thomas Fraser remained on St Helena from 1821 until 1825 when he returned to Britain, taking with him a small collection of plants including *Dimocarpus* (longan), *Solanum madagascariensis* and *Buddleia*.[32] Along with these was a branch from the willow tree which overhung Napoleon's grave. The lower part was decaying, but the top two inches (5 cm) showed signs of life. At Kew, John Smith placed it under a glass bell where it soon rooted. Nurturing it along, in 1827 Smith planted it beside the main path near the public entrance of the gardens. At first, this was thought to be a St Helena species but later it was identified as *Salix babylonica*. The tree flourished and was soon called 'Napoleon's willow'. Indeed, the young tree had a following, especially after 1853 when Kew was opened to the general public on Sundays. Great crowds flocked to see Napoleon's tree.[33]

In 1840, when the body of Napoleon was exhumed and moved from St Helena's Sane Valley to Paris, Prince de Joinville, who was in charge of the French party, got Captain Alexander, the commissioner in charge of the enterprise on the British side, to request George Bennett to 'press and mount upon paper, sprigs of the willow'. These were for distribution by the prince, presumably on his return to France. Others in the French party sought out other relics, be they rocks, 'handfuls of earth, water from Napoleon's spring, leaves, flowers, bulbs – nothing came amiss to them'.[34]

By the late 1860s when Napoleon's willow at Kew died, it had three stems and had reached 40 feet (12 m) high with a 44 foot (13.4 m) wide canopy and a girth of eight and a half feet (2.6 m) at five feet (1.5 m).[35] It was said that nurserymen cashed in on the popularity of the tree by selling willows with the fictitious Latin name of *Salix napoleonis*. Certainly, in the post-exhumation period, having a Napoleon willow growing on one's estate was something to boast of. Joseph Harrison of Downham Nursey in Norfolk published an account of the Ealing Park estate of the society horticulturist Louisa Lawrence in Middlesex in his *Floricultural Cabinet and Florists' Magazine* in 1845:

> A noble Cedar of some two hundred years' growth sheds a sacred halo over these
> representations of antiquity; contiguous to this also is a lovely dell with fountains,
> and other appropriate objects of a similar kind, overshadowed with Willows from
> the tomb of Napoleon, at St. Helena.[36]

❦ The end of an era ❦

Too much reforming zeal did not always go down well with the gentlemen farmers. It was noticed disapprovingly that with all his dedication to agriculture, Walker had attended the theatre in Jamestown only twice in three years.[37] The departure of this enlightened governor proved the end of an era in more than one way. The new – and last – East India Company governor was Charles Dallas (1828–1836), 'an elderly Indian Officer', famous for being in charge when the celebrated Jacob's Ladder was constructed.

The last years of Walker's rule had not been particularly easy. The expenses of running the island were high. The 300,000 trees planted only a few years earlier had not yet grown up and Walker had to spend £2,500 a year importing fuel.[38] Worse was a drought which badly affected farmers, with cattle dying in some numbers. As Walker simply put it, 'when stock become weak, if the grass be not abundant, they must perish'. This knocked the enthusiasm out of the agricultural society which had had such a promising start but which with Walker's departure rapidly went into decline. Strangely enough, Walker noted that the island's gardens were still abundant, and wondered if the drought affected crops more than trees. As an example, he noted 'the beautiful Acacia at Plantation House' which had produced flowers and seeds, which it had never done before, and that 'the young trees which were planted in the two last years bear a promising appearance'.[39] Of course, those trees from the Cape, such as Walker's acacia, might well have preferred the drier weather experienced on the island.

With the agricultural society moribund, the botanic garden was exposed to attack. Barely a year after Walker's departure, in 1829 it was proposed to abolish the garden which, it was said, 'had been replaced by 'Sisters Walk' above the water 'Run' and the Castle Garden'. This walk was named after the two daughters of Governor Robert Patton. Fortunately, inertia triumphed and the botanic garden survived for the time being, though the cottage in the gardens was rented out for £10 a year. By 1840, the Sisters Walk was being used as a back door for 'nightly depredations & nuisances' in the Castle Garden – what in Belfast Botanic Gardens was referred to as 'scandalous goings-on among the bushes'. An iron gate was erected in the vain and forlorn hope of stopping such practices.[40]

James Alexander left a rather evocative description of the apartments in the Castle during Dallas's tenure:

> There is a delightful baradaree, or air chamber, open on all sides, with seats round it, and looking towards the sea: here in the evening the caleoon, or pipe of Persia, could be enjoyed, the grateful infusion of Mocha sipped, the sail from distant lands observed entering or leaving the port, and the agreeable conversation of intelligent friends enjoyed; while from the garden below, with its serpentine walks, would come the perfume of roses and orange trees.[41]

At Plantation House, by contrast, Governor Dallas considered the 'overgrowth of trees' to be unhealthy – the 'rank vegetation tainting the atmosphere'.[42] Writing in 1835, Captain Alexander asserted of the Plantation House estate:

> A grass field and terraced gardens are before it; and most beautiful and strange flowers and shrubs from foreign climes are round the walls. Behind the house is a bank, which ought to be cut away; the drains also should be cleared; and a dell to the left, damp and choked with trees, should be exposed to the sun. Then would Plantation House be perfectly healthy.[43]

Governor Dallas soon decamped for Napoleon's new house at Longwood. But worse was soon to befall St Helena than a perhaps somewhat crusty governor.

28. Little Stone Top lies in the south-east of St Helena, its vegetation much decimated formerly by goats and people collecting firewood and building material, though in 1807 a 'small thin wood of Gum shrubs' still survived. Ironically, it is from these remote and craggy areas that some endemic plants survived and have been rediscovered growing precariously on the side of cliffs. Sketched by William Burchell, 8 December 1807, who climbed the steep rock with the aid of a 'little cold punch'.

Section III

CROWN COLONY

9

The new order

In July 1823 Governor Walker had said of the Company's rule in St Helena, 'in the hands of any other Government, it is more than probable that St Helena would have been merely a fortified rock, without any other inhabitants than its soldiers, and destined only for selfish purpose of excluding others'.[1] Nine years later a great blow befell the whole island when its status changed with the transfer of the island from the East India Company's control to that of the British government.[2] The act carrying this out was passed in August 1833, with the transfer dating from 22 April 1834, though the Company continued to administer the island until the arrival of the island's first Crown Colony governor in February 1836. In 1938 Philip Gosse asserted that the colony 'has never recovered' from this event.[3] This blow to the island was greatly exacerbated by the arrival on the island of two commissioners.

29. After the death of Napoleon, the old Longwood estate returned to being a working farm, and the house inhabited by the emperor was used as a threshing barn and stable. Not surprisingly, it went to rack and ruin, not helped by visitors who stripped much that was removable as souvenirs. Apart from a few trees, Napoleon's original garden was destroyed.
Le Monde Illustré, 11 October 1862, taken from Masselin's *Sainte-Hélène*, Paris, 1862, p. 84. Provided by Donal P. McCracken.

Even before the transfer, all was not well. Writing in May 1832, W. D. Bennett commented:

> The Island at present is in a wretched state. There are a great number of ships in, but they stay so short a time that they do no great good. Some vessels come in merely for water & don't spend a farthing; others again have a number of things for sale & want nothing but a few vegetables. Some there are who lay out a good deal of money but they are few nowadays. In wartime money is so plentiful that they think about as much of Pounds as they do now of halfcrowns.[4]

On 15 October 1833, two grim reapers arrived on St Helena: one a technocrat, a Royal Engineer attached for lengthy periods to the Admiralty, and the other an unobtrusive treasury official. The mandate of Captain Henry Brandreth (1794–1848) and Edward Walpole (d.1857) was clear enough. They were to study the East India Company's on-the-ground operations and recommend drastic cuts to the cost of running the island. In the end, they recommended in some detail expenditure reductions for both the civil and the military administrations from about £90,000 a year down to £33,000. For an island which had served Britain so well, this was a devastating reduction of nearly two-thirds of budget.

The commission report and the appendices and correspondence surrounding it give an interesting view of certain key elements in the island's administration, though the report is strangely devoid of much concerning life on the island at the time. When discussing areas of possible cost savings incidental references are made to matters concerning parks and gardens, and what little comment there is on agriculture and forestry is mostly negative. The following extract relating to the governor's civil establishment illustrates both the tone and approach to anything which was not deemed essential:

> The experimental system of farming, of arboriculture, and of botanical gardening, which has been adopted under the East India Company at Plantation House and elsewhere, we recommend should be discontinued; but as Plantation House and gardens have, since the settlement of the island, being granted as an indulgence to the Governor, we recommend that this indulgence should be continued, inasmuch as the Government House [Castle] in town is partly occupied as public offices, will continue to be so, and is, as a family residence, inconvenient …
>
> The advantage of the gardens at the Castle in James Town, as the only resort to the inhabitants, and the extent of the grounds at Plantation House induce us to recommend that a sum, not exceeding £200, should be placed at the Governor's

disposal for the purpose of keeping them up, that sum to cover every expense. The present useless establishment of head gardener, under gardener and labourers at Plantation House, Longwood, the castle, and the botanical gardens, will of course cease; and the produce of the plantations will be carried to the public account.[5]

The appendices to the report are as interesting as the lugubrious report itself, and the historian is grateful to Colin Fox and Edward Baldwin for the published transcription of fifteen of these, including a table of the Chinese establishment. This names 12 Chinese gardeners, two of whom were free settlers and the other indentured under contract to work for a specific period of time.

TABLE 18
Chinese gardeners on St Helena, February 1835[6]

Name	Age (d.o.b.)	No. year on island	How came to St Helena	Health	Future wishes	English speaking	Remarks
As–sam	50 (1783)	14 (1820)	Came on the *Establishment*	Good	To remain	A little	In the service of Dr Lorimer 7 years & of good character
At–chee	44 (1789)	13 (1821)	*Establishment*	Good	To remain	A little	
As–suo	44 (1789)	15 (1819)	*Establishment*	Good	To remain	A little	
At–chook	38 (1795)	14 (1820)	*Establishment*	Good	To remain	Very well	
At–lum	42 (1791)	20 (1814)	*Establishment*	Good	Wishes to go to China	A little	
Ah–lam	59 (1774)	19 (1815)	*Establishment*	Good	To remain	A little	
Am–moi	54 (1779)	19 (1815)	*Establishment*	Very infirm	To remain	Very imperfectly	Pension 1833 @ 8/– a month
At–chick	45 (1788)	15 (1819)	*Establishment*	Good	To remain	A little	
Ah–yung	44 (1790)	17 (1817)	Came from England and engaged in HC [Hon. Company] service	Good	Wishes to go to China	A little	

Name	Age (d.o.b.)	No. year on island	How came to St Helena	Health	Future wishes	English speaking	Remarks
At–tim	50 (1784)	19 (1815)	*Establishment*	Good	To remain	Tolerably well	Faithful, honest and industrious in the employ of Mr Young
At–chun Free settler	57 (1777)	25 (1809)	*Establishment* Free settler: 28 Feb 1831 to follow agricultural pursuits		To remain		
Ah–fun	50 (1784)	22 (1812)	*Establishment* Free settler: 9 Dec 1834 to follow agricultural pursuits		Wishes to remain a year or two		

From the dates of arrival, it is possible that several of these Chinese gardeners had worked for Napoleon on the Longwood garden. Captain James Alexander in the 1830s, commenting upon the generous allowances permitted the old East India Company governors on the island, mentioned that the perks included a number of Chinese gardeners:

> I saw, as we rode along, some of the Chinese gardeners who are employed on the island, in their broad straw hats, loose blue dungaree jackets and trousers, and long pigtails. They are now reduced to one hundred in number, and set an excellent example of industry; being almost the only people who use the nightsoil of the town for their cultivation.

Alexander also commented upon the 'joss-houses' of these Chinese labourers in the lower part of the Plantation House gardens, 'with their grotesque dragons and griffins on the roofs, their paper lanterns and flags inside, and their sacred vessels and altars before the portly figure of the god Fo [Fo tuo/Buddha]'.[7] Forty years later, Benjamin Grant would comment of the Chinese, 'As gardeners they were unsurpassed, and it is to their labor and perseverance that we are indebted for so many of the fine fruit trees now flourishing on the Island.'[8]

The decline in the status and fortunes of St Helena was greatly assisted by the new governor, the first for the Crown Colony of St Helena. This was 'the bad mannered and discourteous' Major-General Middlemore, and arrived at St Helena in February 1836. A hundred years later George Kitching stated that Middlemore, 'approached Jamestown as if he was invading some hostile shore'.[9] It was not just the civil establishment which was decimated, the military presence was also drastically reduced in number, the salaries of officials from the governor down were slashed and the glory days of large fleets calling and the crews spending lavishly in the settlement were gone. Figure 7 illustrates the level of the garrison between St Helena becoming a Crown Colony and the removal of that garrison 70 years later.

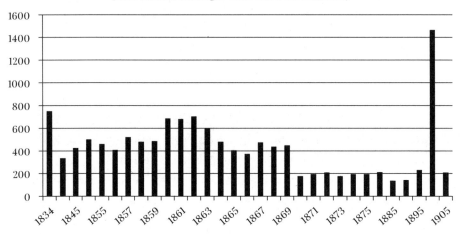

FIGURE 7
Strength of the St Helena garrison, 1834 to 1905
(1900 reflects the Anglo-Boer War POW situation)

It is interesting to note that in the late 1890s Governor Sterndale believed that as long as a proportion of about one soldier for every ten inhabitants existed on the island 'no external pressure was felt'.

The draconian attitude of the 1830s commissioners and the subsequent implementation of many of their recommendations meant that botanical enterprise on the island went into rapid decline and with it the government gardens in Jamestown and at Plantation House. As gardening was no longer considered a necessity, James Cameron, at 37 years old and now the company's head gardener, faced dismissal. He earned a salary of £150 a year as well as a full ration and allowance for a horse and houses in Jamestown and in the country.[10]

As for the old botanic garden in Jamestown, it was grudgingly spared by the two commissioners:

NAPOLEON'S GARDEN ISLAND

As the Botanical Garden is a place of recreation to the inhabitants and visitors, we do not feel inclined to propose that it should be disposed of at present. It is the centre of a densely populated part of the town, and tends to the health of the inhabitants. The future Governor will probably suggest some mode, by which the public will not incur any expense on this account.[11]

From a map of Jamestown dated 1837 in the National Archives in London, it is clear that by then the St Helena Botanic Garden was formally laid out and quite separate from the lower Castle Garden. Also in that year there appeared an extraordinary, and, in the annals of Victorian British imperial botanic gardens, unique, advertisement dated 1 March 1837. This announced the 'St Helena Botanical Garden' was to be let. The benefit appears to have been the cottage on the site, probably the old house where the gardener had lived and which had a decade earlier been placed at the disposal of Dr Arnott, whose tenure as superintendent remains largely a closed book. The lessee in 1837 was to permit 'respectable persons' entry during the day and was not to cut or remove any tree. They were also to maintain all walls, piers and gates – in other words, to act as a kind of caretaker. Three years later the St Helena government again advertised the property for the remaining two years of the lease, as Mrs Bayes, the tenant, had given it up as part of an agreement to pay off her late husband's debts. The next occupant was Mr Janisch, at a reduced rent of £12 a year. This seems to suggest that the botanic garden's cottage is what became known as Palm Villa, which still exists in somewhat altered form.[12]

In 1839 a Mrs Postan visited St Helena on her way home to Britain from India and commented:

The botanical gardens of James Town are well laid out, and contain some very fine specimens of cactus, euphorbia, and aloes, with particularly choice lilacs and lilies, for which St. Helena is justly famed. Wherever soil is to be found, vegetation is abundant, and the gardens of the island produce fine vegetables of various descriptions, with tolerably good fruit, pears, peaches, figs, grapes, the Chinese loquat, plantains, apples, &c.[13]

By 1840 there was a large tank or reservoir at the top of the botanic garden which was fed by four sets of lead pipes from the four Chubb's springs. This was to become the basis of a permanent piped water supply to the town below.

But beyond the botanic garden's wall there were 'miserable looking mud hovels ... a picture of filth and wretchedness', from which, as the writer W. H. Leigh put it, 'we gladly turned to the town houses of the rich with their pretty villas, ornamental gardens, cocoanut trees, palms and plantations flourishing in all the beauty and luxuriance of summer'. It is likely that these were occupied by indentured Chinese who lived in that upper part of Jamestown.[14]

❧ The *Waterwitch* memorial ❧

Down the valley in the Castle Garden, a monument was erected a few years later to the dead crew members of H. M. Brig *Waterwitch*. The British outlawed first the trade in enslaved people and subsequently the institution of enslavement, Governor Middlemore prohibiting enslavement on St Helena in May 1839. Though many European powers followed suit, in particular Portugal in 1839, the practice of trading in enslaved people continued along the West African coast and also across the Atlantic. Britain led the assault against this inhuman practice, utilising a squadron of Royal Navy crusiers along the West African coast with their headquarters on St Helena, where a Vice Admiralty Court was established to try those crew members who had been captured along with their ship and who were suspected of being involved in the trade. Between 1840 and 1867 some 425 such ships were captured and brought to St Helena. Along with these ships were upwards of 25,000 people who had been liberated, though for a period they were not paid for work undertaken. Because of the horrifying conditions and the treatment they endured, an estimated 8,000 enslaved people either were dead from starvation or disease on arrival in the ships at St Helena or subsequently died. They were buried in several burial grounds in Rupert's Bay Valley and in Jameson Valley.

Many of these 'Liberated Africans' were kept in primative conditions in Rupert's Bay Valley. Most subsequently left the island, mainly crossing the Atlantic to the British West Indies or to Guyana (British Guiana), and a few went back to Africa. Some, perhaps about 1,000, remained on St Helena. Whether any of these liberated people were gardeners is not known, not least bcause gardening was frequently temporary employment, but it is likely.[15]

The *Waterwitch* was one of the British brigs which patrolled the West African coast in the 1840s and which, on 9 June 1840, landed four enslaved people who were freed on the island, the first of a number brought from captured slaving vessels. In 1844 the officers of the *Waterwitch* sent the memorial out to St Helena to commemorate the deaths of fellow crew members and to express thanks for hospitality received on the island. One inscription reads:

This Column was erected by the Commander, Officers and Crew of her Majesty's Brig Waterwitch to the memory of their shipmates who died while serving on the coast of Africa A.D. 1839–1843. The greater number died while absent in captured slave vessels. Their remains were either left in different parts of Africa or given to the sea their graves alike undistinguished. This Island is selected for the record because three lie buried here and because the deceased as well as their surviving comrades, ever met the warmest welcome from its inhabitants.[16]

There were still some under Colonel Hamelin Trelawny's governorship (1842–1846) who retained an interest in botany. Kew Gardens received two consignments of plants in 1843. One full of ferns 'nearly all dead' arrived on 18 May 1843 and the second, a 'glazed box' containing *Dicksonia arborescens* and other St Helena ferns, arrived on 26 July.[17] The Castle Garden remained a place of promenade and a spot where one should be seen. As William Bennett noted of one aspiring socialite:

She dresses finer than her mistress & walks about the Castle Garden & looks like a lady. I should not think she is likely to remain here long by her fine airs.[18]

᠅ Coffee in the Victorian era ᠅

Coffee had been introduced to St Helena about 1729. Like so many such plants there is no continuous record of its being grown and it was probably reintroduced several times. In 1805 Francis Duncan had observed that 'Some good coffee has been raised'.[19] Forty years later coffee growing received a boost. On 22 December 1845, yet again, another St Helena Agricultural and Horticultural Society was established. This is interesting given the revival of Kew Gardens about then – but there are no signs that the St Helena Agricultural and Horticultural Society sought to revive the island's botanic garden.

On 5 June 1851 a correspondent identified as B. W. J. in the island's newspaper, *The Advocate*, lobbied for growing cotton and especially coffee on St Helena and criticised the Agricultural Society for giving prizes for cabbages and flowers instead of for the best coffee plantation or for the most coffee trees planted in a certain period of time. It should be remembered that when Napoleon first tasted St Helena coffee at Longwood, he thought it so bad that he refused to drink it, stating he had been poisoned. In 1808 the best coffee plants seem to have been in the Plantation House garden, where there was a primitive irrigation system, and at Rock Rose farm. According to Governor Beatson, at the turn of the century the

Rock Rose farm had produced 650 lbs [295 kg] of coffee beans, or '5 Gallons or 25b' from each tree. Beatson, who knew about coffee growing on Mauritius[20] and the Reunion islands, was of the view that if properly managed like the Plantation House trees were, 'the cultivation of coffee at St Helena might be very advantageous to the Honorable company'.[21]

In 1851 the famous Crystal Palace exhibition was held in London. The St Helena Agricultural Society sent a bag of local coffee which won a prize. This had been grown at Bamboo Grove, then the property of the 61-year-old George William Alexander. At the time, his was the only coffee plantation on St Helena. Bamboo Grove was in the Sandy Bay area, and had been in the Alexander family since the house was built by John Alexander in 1808.

By the 1870s, coffee plants were found growing wild in 'some of the sheltered parts of the south side of the island, also in ravines on the eastern and western parts at Mulberry Gut and Terrace Knoll'.[22] It was established at this time that St Helena could grow good coffee, 'quite as good as the best Mocha'. Then, in the 1890s, Father Daine tried again. Coffee plant seed was introduced, with Sterndale reporting, not without reason, that he was 'not sanguine' of success. The governor stated that St Helena coffee 'of an excellent quality is produced but the culturable area is limited'. In the mid-1890s at Plantation House, 286 coffee bushes in one very dry year had produced 428 lbs (194 kg) of dried beans, and the crop at Sandy Bay was said to be even better.[23] Writing in 1900, Governor Sterndale, who had extensive experience of India, observed:

> Providence has been kind to the coffee-tree [on St Helena], which still flourishes and bears abundant crops of excellent coffee of the old Mocha stock, but for all the care that man takes, it might have gone the way of the grape and the peach. I, who have seen the care, the pruning, manuring and hoeing of coffee plantations in India, have never ceased to wonder at the generosity of the St. Helena tree, which often bears its white starry blossoms whilst the pickers are gathering the ripe fruit. There is much land now devoted to pasturage which would yield a better return under coffee cultivation, but there is the drawback of scarce and dear labour; however, this might be overcome.[24]

The Agricultural Society also sent a box of Alkali (from the salsola or saltwort plant) and some rock salt to the 1851 Great Exhibition in London. The other St Helena exhibits at this famous exhibition in Hyde Park included a sample of what was probably the island's dwarf ebony (named as *Dombeya melanoxylon*) and specimens of St Helena raw cotton.[25] Cotton had been grown on St Helena since

1720, though never as a viable commercial crop, and, according to Brooke in 1806, was 'regarded as little better than a weed'. Some of the exhibits are still housed in Kew's Economic Botany Collection.

It was also in 1851 that Joseph Lockwood commented of the main route out of Jamestown:

> The road is rough and stony, up hill, and tiresome; but proceed, and leave the church yard all behind us, naked and desolate places as they are, sans tree or shrub to hide their ghastly trophies from the public gaze. Pass by the barracks and its row of trees, and plod along by the wall of what has been facetiously called the Botanic Garden, till we reach: 'China Town,' the second city in the island.[26]

Further along the road which led towards Longwood, Lockwood comments:

> On clearing the town we find ourselves in a position to look over all the houses, yards, and gardens, and pry into the back slums of the place if we think fit; but as there is nothing to reward us for our trouble we will pass on, taking a bird's-eye view of the Barracks, the Botanic Garden, and all the naked grave yards that disfigure the place, and disgust both eye and heart to look upon.[27]

Botanist visitors

Occasional visitors, officials and local St Helena residents had been interested in the island's native plants. Herbarium specimens had been sent back to London by Governor Stephen Poirier and then by his clerk Antipas Tovey between 1698 and 1714. Then, in the early 1770s, Daniel Solander had undertaken what appears to be the first plant species list for St Helena.[28] Sir Joseph Banks, on Captain Cook's *Endeavour*, was on St Helena for four days in May 1771.[29] The first comprehensive investigation into the island's flora was undertaken by William Burchell when superintendent of the St Helena Botanic Garden. As discussed, other early 19th-century botanist visitors included William Roxburgh and James Bowie. As the century progressed some of the notable botanists of the age spent short periods on St Helena.

Charles Darwin was on the island in July 1836. In this period the 27-year-old scrambled around much of the island greatly enjoying himself and visiting:

Friday 8 July:	High Knoll
Saturday 9 July:	Finding lodgings in Sane Valley

Sunday 10 July:	Longwood, Flagstaff and The Barn
Monday 11 July:	Prosperous Bay (experiencing the extraordinary updrafts from the cliffs)
Tuesday 12 July:	Ridges and Sandy Bay area
Wednesday 13 July:	Ridges and Sandy Bay area
Thursday 14 July:	Returned to Jamestown and the *Beagle* sailed

In his endeavour, Darwin was assisted by two very different men. One of these is mentioned in his diary entry for Sunday 10 July 1836:

Things improved. — hired guide 55 years old — feet like iron — mulatto.

So many times crossed, that has not disagreeable look — quiet very civil old man, was slave, has 40£ to pay for freedom. How is this?

Walked to Flagstaff along same course, elevated plain — Passed long wood, cultivated fields — rather but no very bleak — gentlemans houses — hovel where he really lived & died very poor — I took shelter during heavy rain, shutter rattling about Walls scored with names of Seamen & Merchant captains. It appeared degradation, like profaning old castle — Green plain short thin grass — few Syngenesia trees = great red & white Hills called Flagstaff & great Black barn: Lime Uninteresting view: every Govt. path blockaded — such wild little spots, old picket houses. — Wild arid villages — Even near sea Cactus & 2 or 3 plants in very small quantities[30]

Darwin's second guide on the island, Robert Francis Seale, came from the ranks of the St Helena gentry, and was St Helena's eccentric colonial secretary and a recently retired major in the St Helena Regiment. Seale was an enthusiast and had an extraordinary home at Deadwood House full of cabinets displaying natural history specimens. He is also remembered in particular for constructing a large wooden model of the island which was proportioned 540 feet to 1 inch. This sat in Addiscombe College in England for many years before, as previously mentioned, it was given to a London museum, where it was neglected, attacked by woodworm and eventually destroyed. Two years before Darwin arrived on the island, the East India Company published Seale's 25-page pamphlet entitled, *The Geognosy of the Island St. Helena, Illustrated in a Series of Views, Plans and Sections; Accompanied with Explanatory Remarks and Observations*.

Darwin made no comment on the botanic garden, though it is difficult to believe that he missed it. He did, however, remark on the number of alien plants on the island, but no doubt because of Seale's guidance, his interest was concentrated on the geology of what he termed the 'St Helena model'.[31] There are a few comments in Darwin's diary relating to the flora he saw during his few days on the island, such as these dated 13 July 1836:

> In latitude 16° & at the trifling elevation of 1500 ft, it is surprising to behold a vegetation possessing a decided English character. But such is the case; the hills are crowned with irregular plantations of scotch firs; the sloping banks are thickly scattered over with thickets of gorze, covered with its bright yellow flowers; along the course of the rivulets weeping willows are common, & the hedges are formed of the blackberry, producing its well known fruit. When we consider the proportional numbers of indigenous plants being 52, to 424 imported species, of which latter so many come from England, we see the cause of this resemblance in character.
>
> [Opposite diary page] These numerous species, which have been so recently introduced, can hardly have failed to have destroyed some of the native kinds. I believe there is not any account extant of the vegetation at the period when the island was covered with trees; such would have formed a most curious comparison with its present sterile condition and limited Flora. It is not improbable that even at the present day similar changes may be in progress.

30. The homes of enslaved people and, after the 1830s, of the freed but still poor labourers, are well illustrated in this sketch by James Charles Melliss. There are, however, references to the pretty gardens which grew around some of these cabins. High Knoll Fort is in the background. Melliss, *St Helena*, plate 16. Provided by Donal P. McCracken.

Many English plants appear to flourish here better than in their native country, some also from the opposite quarter of Australia succeed remarkably well, & it is only on the highest & steep mountain crests where the native Flora is predominant. The English, or rather the Welsh character of the scenery, is kept up by the numerous cottages & small white houses, some buried at the bottom of the deepest valleys & others stuck up on the lofty ridges – Certainly some of the views are very striking; I may instance that of Sir W. Doverton's house, where the bold peak called Lott is seen over a dark wood of firs, the whole being backed by the red, waterworn mountains of the Southern shore. — But a glowing tropical style of landscape would have afforded a finer contrast than the homely English scenery, with the wild arid rocks of the coast.[32]

The botanical Indian summer

The 23-year-old botanist Joseph Hooker, the son of Sir William Hooker who was soon to be director of Kew Gardens, had previously spent nine days in January/ February 1840 on the island with Captain James Ross's expedition. Here Joseph Hooker made the acquaintance of George Bennett, son of the late James Bennett of Maldivia House. Another useful link for Kew on the *Erebus* was Lieutenant John Lefroy, with whom George had been at school in England and who was to remain on the island to take terrestrial magnetic readings. Hooker found Jamestown deserted and unexciting, but of the interior he recorded in his journal:

> A ride of 4 miles opened to us a totally different scene, a country here shut out from the sea, and at 1700 ft elevation, was intersected by numerous broad deep valleys filled with rocky places and covered with fir trees; among which the white houses of the inhabitants, chiefly retired officers, scattered here and there in most romantic situations, with gardens, pastures etc. Furze and blackberries were as common as in Scotland, mixed with Pelargoniums, Gelsemiums, Hibiscuses, Sidas [Sidalcea] , Buddleias in abundance; the scenery was perfectly Scotch, and heightened by numerous mists and fogs that soon wetted us to the skin.

Hooker was greatly taken by the monkey puzzle tree (*Araucaria* sp.) in Mr Wilde's Rose Cottage garden in Sandy Bay. It was then a rare tree in Britain and Hooker climbed it to collect cones, which he subsequently hung up in his cabin onboard the *Erebus*. He also visited the Gideon home at Fairyland House. He ventured inland, climbing Diana's Peak and commenting upon the remnants of indigenous flora such as the cabbage trees and ebony, adding of these, 'Large masses of the wood are still found in some valleys, though I was unable to procure any specimens.'[33]

Joseph Hooker was again briefly on St Helena on the return voyage home of the *Erebus*, in early 1843. By then Lieutenant Lefroy was back in England after his St Helena sojourn and was in contact with William Hooker, now director at Kew, to whom he recommended his friend George Bennett. So George was drawn into that web of colonial soldiers, administrators and settler-botanists upon whom the Hookers so much depended. For years, both when on St Helena and later when the army transferred him to the Cape after 1851, he corresponded with Kew. One of his early letters contained the following:

The botany of this island, I have been often told, bears a very peculiar character. I can't exactly tell you when to expect the first parcel of dried plants from me, but I will comply with your wish as soon as I conveniently can. My office duties keep me much in town and the ferns and other more curious plants grow principally about Diana's Peak, some miles from where I reside. I propose paying the peak a visit early in the dry weather, now setting in, and will devote my time to the collection of plants — I know the plants you mention — the cabbage tree, as they are called here. They are generally small trees affording excellent and almost imperishable timber for building purposes. They do not attain any great size but have all the habit of trees. They, as well as the gumwood Aster gummiferum, bear syngenerious flowers [flowering at night] and are, I believe, on this account deemed curious.

I will attend to the directions given in the printed paper you have favoured me with — with regard to the collection of seeds of our native plants, I sometime since forwarded, through Mr Lefroy, a collection of those of the Arborescent compositae for the botanical secretary of the R.S. [Royal Horticultural Society] I had them closely soldered up in a small tin box but never heard whether they vegetated — would you recommend this plan in the future? They are very small light seeds covered with a papus and I should think their vitality would be severely tested by the voyage thence to England unless secured in some such manner as before adopted. I have engaged to forward from this March next, a gentleman in London who has sent out a glass case for the purpose, plants of Dicksonia arborescens and the other ferns Lycopodium etc. — we exchange productions with each other and as the request emanated from him he bears all the expense of freight etc. to and fro. Indeed, army pay as a humble scribe in the Commissariat is so very small that I could not afford to carry on this arrangement unless he bore the expense of it — the gentleman I mention is John Allcaid of the firm of Overend, Gurney & Co. Lombard St. I sent him one batch and he succeeded in growing two Dicksonia safe out of about a dozen. The others were killed off by seawater getting in. In consequence of this he has sent me a proper case, glazed and made airtight as nearly as can be. This he filled with plants which he deemed would be desirable here, and most acceptable would they have been, but, by an accident on board, nearly all killed off so this case is now to be filled and returned to him. Now, as he bears the expenses, I cannot put into the case any plants for other parties without his sanction. If you deem it worthwhile to ask that gentleman for the use of a corner of his case for the Royal Gardens, I might get you an answer in time, as I do not intend to send it away till March next or would the gardens bear the expense of a case should send direct to you? The construction of a box and the freight would not be more than 40s I imagine.[34]

George Bennett showed Joseph Hooker a letter he had received from William Hooker, which Joseph 'perused with great pleasure and emotion'. Joseph Hooker described George Bennett as 'a very gentlemanly person indeed'. He also observed that 'their garden [Maldivia] is the best on the island'.[35] Though Bennett and Joseph Hooker ventured up Diana's Peak, this collecting trip on St Helena in May 1843 was not a great success. As Huxley points out, Sir William Hooker admitted that Hugh Cuming, who visited the island a week or two after Joseph, had 'in one strenuous day made a much more brilliant collection'. Nonetheless, Joseph Hooker did collect 22 species of fern, and scattered in the Wardian case seeds of his much-prized land cabbage plant (*Pringlea antiscorbutica*), which had been collected on the Kerguelen islands of the deep south Atlantic.[36]

Joseph Hooker never forgot his visits to St Helena and in 1867 published a series of articles on island vegetation in the *Gardeners' Chronicle*. In this, he told the world for the first time about the Burchell herbarium, which Kew had recently acquired. Of St Helena, Hooker commented:

From such fragmentary data it is difficult to form any exact conclusions as to the affinities of this Flora, but I think it may be safely regarded as an African one, and characteristic of Southern extra-tropical Africa. The genera Phylica, Pelargonium, Mesembryanthemum, Osteospermum, and Wahlenbergia are eminently characteristic of Southern extra-tropical Africa, and I find amongst the others scarce any indication of an American parentage, except a plant referred to Physalis. The Ferns tell the same tale; of 26 species, 10 are absolutely peculiar, all the rest are African, though some are also Indian and American.

The botany of St. Helena is thus most interesting; it resembles none other in the peculiarity of its indigenous vegetation, in the great variety of the plants of other countries, or in the number of species that have actually disappeared within the memory of living men. In 1839 and 1843 I in vain searched for forest trees and shrubs that flourished in tens of thousands not a century before my visit, and still existed as individuals 20 years before that date. Of these I saw in some cases no vestige, in others only blasted and lifeless trunks cresting the cliffs in inaccessible places. Probably 100 St. Helena plants have thus disappeared from the Systema Naturæ; since the first introduction of goats on the island. Every one of these was a link in the chain of created beings, which contained within itself evidence of the affinities of other species, both living and extinct, but which evidence is now irrecoverably lost. If such be the fate of organisms that lived in our day, what folly it must be to found theories on the assumed perfection of a geological record which has witnessed revolutions in the vegetation of the globe, to which that of the Flora of St. Helena is as nothing.[37]

By 1867 Joseph Hooker was himself director of Kew and St Helena had no gardener or botanist employed by the St Helena government. Eminent botanists had come and gone in the past without much effect. But in this instance there was to be a combination of like-thinking influential persons who, at least for a while, made a difference. This was a troika consisting of Joseph Hooker at Kew Gardens, the island-born Charles Melliss (1835–1910) – whose government jobs as surveyor and colonial engineer took him out into the countryside – and the island's governor, Admiral Charles Elliot.

Elliot had been on St Helena as a midshipman during the period of Napoleon's captivity 50 years before.[38] Indeed, Elliot had led an adventurous life as a naval officer and as an administrator. Some of his tasks had included being chief superintendent of trade with China; administrator of Hong Kong when it was being established as a British possession; serving as 'protector of slaves' in British Guiana; and successively governor of Bermuda, Trinidad and his last posting, St Helena.

As will be seen, John Charles Melliss made a significant contribution to the study of botany on the island. He became commissioner of crown property on St Helena as well as, from July 1860, being the island's surveyor and colonial engineer. It is hard to exaggerate not only what Melliss did by way of botanical exploration but also the importance of his bringing to wider attention the island's native species in his impressive book on St Helena.

Both Melliss and Elliot represented in good measure that enthusiasm for the amateur study of nature so prevalent among educated Victorians. In September 1867, Melliss commented to Hooker, 'I cannot help thinking that S. Helena is one of the most interesting spots in the world to the naturalist, it seems to claim so little relationship with any other land, that, where did its Vegetation and insect Kingdoms come from, is a puzzling but important question.'[39]

It is clear that Melliss had his own small botanic garden at Oakbank House. And in return for his natural history endeavours, in 1867 Hooker named the endemic boxwood *Mellissia begonifolia* after Melliss. This very rare plant disappeared from the botanists' gaze until it was rediscovered at Lot's Wife by Stedson Stroud in 1998. Melliss had commented to Hooker in the year of its naming:

> I take a very special interest in the 'Mellissia Begonifolia' and am glad to be able to tell you that it is by no means extinct; it is still to be found on the low barren rocky parts of the island on the S.E. side & you will be pleased to know that by this Mail I send you some of the seed together with a dry specimen of the leaf & flower. I have also 15 or 16 young plants in a box doing well & these with some of the dry stems I hope to send you early next spring. I found a snail (Succinea) feeding upon the leaves of the plant and I have ventured to send you some of the shells as possibly it may be a new one.[40]

Melliss sent various snail shells to Hooker, some intended for his son. These included the indigenous blushing snail (*Succinea sanctae-helenae*), 'amber color'd', four shells of which he had collected upon cabbage trees at 2,700 feet; four *Succinea picta*, which, as mentioned above, fed upon his beloved *Mellissia*; and four 'very small ... adhering to the rocks' *Succinea solidula*, upon which the St Helena wire bird liked to feed.[41]

If the *Mellissia* was Melliss's great find, he was less successful with the stringwood shrub (*Acalypha rubrinervis*, *A. reticulata* or *A. rubra*), which Burchell had seen, as indeed had Melliss himself in the 1850s when a specimen was at Oaklands House. In 1867 Melliss wrote:

> I am sorry that I can yet give you no tidings of the Stringwood, <u>possibly</u> it may be in some of the thickets near Diana's Peak but it will, if so, take long & hard searching to bring it to light. – you can almost imagine my delight when a few weeks ago a man (fisherman) came and told me he knew where 'Green Ebony' (as he called it) was to be found. He said it was only accessible by water; & after I had planned an expedition in search of it, you can still more readily understand my great disappointment at finding his information incorrect.[42]

After this unsuccessful quest, Melliss noted in his 1875 book on St Helena, 'This beautiful little plant I believe now to be extinct.' For posterity, he added to the book a drawing of the plant by his wife.[43]

He did, however, report to Kew that he had seen some trees of the St Helena olive, *Nesiota elliptica*:

> which is now very scarce, it is now in flower [October 1867] & when the seeds are ripe I shall endeavour to get & send you some, I have taken a quantity of cuttings which I hope may take.

In his book, Melliss stated that very few trees of this species, only 12 or 15 at most, remained on Diana's Peak. Rediscovered by the redoubtable George Benjamin in 1977, sadly it is now believed to be extinct.[44] Others were still on the wanted list:

> I have been long looking for 'Plantago robusta' [*Petrobium arboretum*, whitewood] as well as 'Spilanthus titranda' [St Helena plantain] of Roxb's list, I fancy it but I have found the former, at a place called 'wild rams spring' on the extreme S.W. Coast of the Island it grows somewhat like a carnation or pink.[45]

Cinchona

It was Melliss who first started growing cinchona on the island at Oakbank. This was from seed given to him by Hooker. In 1867 Melliss raised 19 seedlings, commenting, 'I suppose I would not treat them better than by transferring them to the high land amongst the tree ferns and the cabbage trees'.[46] Of course, by that time, even before the environmental disaster of the New Zealand flax, the slopes of Diana's Peak had become a reservoir of increasingly dominant species of alien plants. Thirty years earlier Captain Armstrong had spoken of the 'umbelliferous shrub, called here the cabbage tree' and the 'black stems of the tree-ferns' along with the Cape gooseberry, furze and blackberries as well as 'a few stone pines and masses of Botany Bay willow'.

It is possible that Melliss's gardener was Henry Augustus Samuel, who died on 5 October 1867 and merited a mention in the 1868 *St Helena Almanac*.[47] While the idea of St Helena again having an official gardener came from Sir Joseph Hooker, Melliss emphasised the need get the Colonial Office to fund the project, as the colony was 'so poor'. Elliot was 'much pleased' with the proposal. In March 1868, Kew proposed that George Chalmers be appointed as 'superintendent of cinchona plantation and government gardener' in St Helena, the plan being that he would go to St Helena and propagate various plantation crops, especially cinchona. His salary would be £150 a year.[48] The funding was granted and Chalmers arrived on the island in May 1868. He was placed in Melliss's department and the two men clearly worked well together – 'he seems a nice young man', Melliss observed to Hooker back at Kew. Within days, Melliss and Chalmers were climbing the slopes of Diana's Peak staking out the site of the new cinchona plantation.

Chalmers established a nursery, probably on the site of the botanic garden, by then invariably referred to as the Maldivia Garden. This was in effect a precursor of the botanic stations of the late 1880s and 1890s which would be established in the West Indies and in some of the West African British colonies under the overall direction of Kew's Dr Daniel Morris, who would also feature later in the St Helena saga.[49] At Kew's bidding cinchona was also tried in botanic gardens in Burma, Fiji, Jamaica, Mauritius, Natal, Tobago and Trinidad.[50]

The Jamestown cinchona nursery was to supply young plants to be established on land allocated in the upper region of the island along the south face of Mount Actaeon near Diana's Ridge between 2,500 and 2,700 feet.[51] Newfoundland Cottage was the centre of the operation. Elliot's extensive experience in the tropics and subtropics made him very keen on the St Helena cinchona project, as indeed he was in introducing other plantation crops. Chalmers had a small propagating house built and grew seedlings of *Cinchona succirubra*, *C. officinalis*, *C. pahudiana* and *C. calisaya*. The first cinchona seedlings were planted out at Northumberland Cottage under Diana's Peak on 14 October 1868. By 9 December 1868, 545 (5 per cent) of the cinchona seedlings were planted out, 1,940 (19 per cent) were in the nursery, and 7,735 (76 per cent) were growing in boxes under glass.[52] Chalmers was also involved in growing other plants, mainly trees including conifers, in the warmer climate of the government gardens in Jamestown. He also established a small experimental tobacco plantation and introduced four hives of bees into the Maldivia Garden in Jamestown.[53] Cocoa was also sent from Kew, but proved not to be the saviour of the sagging St Helena economy.[54]

St Helena's cinchona experiment stimulated debate on the island about growing other (hopefully) lucrative crops. The *St Helena Guardian* lamented the 'now commonly expressed opinion that "St Helena is going to the bad"' and asserted:

> We know, that our Pine Timber is of better quality than that we import, and, by employing wind or water power for cutting it, need not cost more; also that our Coffee has been classed with the best, the trees, producing abundantly, even when left to grow wild and neglected; our Tobacco also need not be second to any other so far as we can see.[55]

Tobacco seed was distributed at a nominal charge to planters by Chalmers. Much was made again of the possibility of a successful silk industry, but it was cinchona which remained the main hope of the financially beleaguered island. It was on this that Melliss, as surveyor of Crown lands, the acting colonial secretary H. R. Janisch and Governor Elliot pinned their hopes.

It is interesting to note in Table 19 the nature of the consignments received at Kew Gardens from St Helena in the period after Kew's revival in the mid-1840s. Governor Elliot's enthusiasm is clear to see for the period of his governorship (1863–1869), and he himself sent five Wardian cases and one consignment of seeds to Kew. Between June 1865 and May 1870, his friend Melliss sent Kew no fewer than twenty-seven consignments, three Wardian cases, twenty-three consignments of seeds and one tree fern stem.[56] This included a replacement Wardian case which Melliss had made after one had been devoured by the voracious St Helena termites, which had eaten the greater part of the public buildings in Jamestown.

TABLE 19

Details of consignments of St Helena plants and seeds sent to Kew Gardens, 1852–1878

Date arrived at Kew Gardens	Nature of consignment	By whom despatched to Kew	Governor of St Helena
1852 (1 July)	Seeds of redwood		Col. Sir Thomas Gore Browne
1853 (1 June)	Bottle of stag horn moss	Capt Robert C. Tylter	Gore Browne
1854 (*c.* May)	Small Wardian case of ferns	Mr Mason	Gore Browne
1856 (10 July)	Wardian case of plants from St Helena	Capt Knife	Drummond Hay?
1858	Seed of *Rhizozum* sp.[?]		Sir Edward Hay Drummond Hay
1864 (1 March)	Wardian case: Stems of *Dicksonia arborescens* two x7 feet high and one x3 feet high	Governor Elliot	Admiral Sir Charles Elliot
1864 (4 June)	Wardian case	Governor Elliot	Elliot
1864 (*c.* Oct)	Wardian case in bad condition	Governor Elliot	Elliot

Date arrived at Kew Gardens	Nature of consignment	By whom despatched to Kew	Governor of St Helena
1865 (4 Jan.)	*Pandarus* seeds and 11 roots of ferns in bad order in single closed box		Elliot
1865 (18 May)	Wardian case	Captain Haughton	Elliot
1865 (21 June)	Stem of *Dicksonia arborens* one x 5 feet high brought home by Captain Strutt	J. C. Melliss	Elliot
1865 (26 June)	*Dicksonia arborescens*	Melliss	Elliot
1865 (*c.* Aug)	Spores of *Dicksonia arborescens*		Elliot
1866 (26 Sept)	Seed of *Dombeya erythroxylon* [redwood: *Trochetiopsis erythroxylon*]	Governor Elliot, who also sent 2 Wardian cases of plants including ferns (in bad condition) collected on Ascension Island	Elliot
1866 (27 Oct.)	Two Wardian cases of ferns	Governor Elliot	Elliot
1867 (Nov)	Seeds of *Angelica bracteata*	Melliss	Elliot
1867 (29 Nov.)	Seeds of *Araucaria excelsa* [Norfolk Island pine] A box full of these seeds were sent by Melliss	Melliss	Elliot
1867 (3 Dec.)	Seed of *Araucaria* and Wardian case with earth taken from the ridge below Diana's Peak	Melliss	Elliot
1867 (20 Dec.)	Seeds of *Dombeya erythroxylon*	Melliss	Elliot
1867 (Dec.)	Seeds 3 spp.	Melliss	Elliot
1867 (26 Dec.)	Wardian case containing seeds and seedlings *Araucaria excelsa*. This was probably brought from St Helena by Mr Solomon.	Melliss	Elliot
1868 (16 Jan.)	Seeds	Melliss	Elliot
1868 (24 Jan.)	Seeds	Melliss	Elliot

Date arrived at Kew Gardens	Nature of consignment	By whom despatched to Kew	Governor of St Helena
1868 (21 Feb.)	Seeds	Melliss	Elliot
1868 (12 Mar.)	Seeds	Melliss	Elliot
1868 (21 Mar.)	Seeds	Melliss	Elliot
1868 (11 April)	Seeds *erythroxylon*	Melliss	Elliot
1868 (6 May)	Seeds	Melliss	Elliot
1868 (26 June)	Seeds	Melliss	Elliot
1868 (7 July)	Seeds	Melliss	Elliot
1868 (27 July)	Seeds	Melliss	Elliot
1868 (30 July)	Wardian case all but *Pelargonium cotyledavi* [*P. cotyledonis*] dead	John Chalmers	Elliot
1868 (18 Aug.)	Wardian case *Balantitum calata* and other ferns (to Edwards)	Chalmers	Elliot
1868 (31 Aug.)	Seeds	Melliss	Elliot
1868 (8 Sept.)	Seeds	Melliss	Elliot
1868 (27 Oct.)	Seeds	Chalmers	Elliot
1868 (27 Oct.)	Seeds	Melliss	Elliot
1868 (29 Oct.)	Wardian case	Chalmers	Elliot
1868 (11 Nov.)	Seeds	Melliss	Elliot
1868 (19 Dec.)	Seeds	Melliss	Elliot
1869 (13 Feb)	Wardian case 4 ferns	Melliss	Elliot
1869 (2 Mar.)	Seeds of *Wahlenbergia angustifolia*; scrubwood; wild rosemary	Melliss	Elliot

Date arrived at Kew Gardens	Nature of consignment	By whom despatched to Kew	Governor of St Helena
1870 (8 April)	Seeds of *Psoralea pinnata*, *Dombeya erythrinoxylon* to Mr Dick	Melliss	Elliot
1870 (25 May)	Seeds of *Desmodermum argenteum*; *Chrissa natal* [Natal plum, *Carissa macrocarpa*]; Leguminosae	Melliss	Elliot
1877	9 herbarium specimens	T. V. Wollaston	Janisch
1878	Fine collection of St Helena ferns including: *Acrostichum dimorphum*, *Asplenium platybasis*, *Dicksonia arborescens*, *Nephrodium napoleonis*, and *Polypodium molle*	Captain Oliver	Hudson Ralph Janisch
1878	6 herbarium specimens	Rev. H. Whitehead	Janisch

As the St Helena plants were valuable to Kew at the time, so is Melliss's correspondence with Joseph Hooker today, not least for estimating historic location. For example, of the dwarf jellico or St Helena Angelica (*Berula burchellii* syn. *Sium burchellii*), Melliss told Hooker that it grew 'on the windward side of the central ridge near a place called 'Taylor's flat' about three-quarters or one mile to the west of Diana's Peak'.[57] The jellico was a tall plant with a stem which was cut and collected 'like bits of bamboo' and was eaten raw by the locals. It was sold in the Jamestown market, which cannot have assisted its survival. Melliss drew Joseph Hooker an interesting sketch of where it and the cabbage trees grew in relation to Diana's Peak.[58]

Unfortunately, Governor Elliot left the island in 1870. His replacement, Admiral Charles Patey (1811–1881), governor from 1869 to 1873, was not interested in the cinchona project, which had in its initial stages all the hallmarks of being expensive. With the garrison now cut by 60 per cent, more economies were likely. 'The multitude of rats' and 'exceedingly numerous' caterpillars also proved a great enemy to Chalmers and his endeavours.

The arrival of Patey also put an end to what might have become an interesting cooperation between the West African island of Fernando Po (Bioko) and the much smaller island of St Helena. Between 1827 and 1858, Fernando Po had been under British suzerainty before reverting back to the Spanish. This meant in reality that it was run by the Royal Navy, which used it as a base in its drive against the trade in enslaved people. As a younger man, Charles Elliot had been in the British West African squadron and had visited Fernando Po. Nearly 50 years later in 1869, he looked back and wrote to the commander-in-chief of the newly created joint Cape and West Africa Royal Navy station, Commodore William Dowell, pressing the crusty naval officer to visit the Spanish governor at Fernando Po. He encouraged Dowell to emphasise to the governor the health benefits for the region of his planting cinchona, and offered the St Helena cinchona gardener to provide advice:

> Unless my memory has cheated me, the aspect of the vegetation up the mountain [on Fernando Po] is not unlike that of our own under Diana's Peak. In point of temperature it is certain that the same conditions may be secured at Fernando Po as those of the regions of Guayaquil [Ecuador] & that part of Central & South America where the Chinchona formerly flourished. At Madrid there must of course exist full and exact information as to the conditions of temperature, soil, etc etc in which the various descriptions of Chinchona thrive best.[59]

Chalmers's last report to Elliot on the cinchona experiment was received in December 1869 and was warmly praised by the governor, who instructed it be sent to the colonial secretary in London with the expression of hope that he would in turn forward it to Dr Joseph Hooker at Kew Gardens.[60] But it was all to no avail. What had started with such vigour and enthusiasm was now destroyed. By December 1870, the cinchona experiment had been abandoned. Chalmers was moved from Melliss's section to Plantation House, where he spent his days planting trees, in particular Bermuda cedars (*Juniperus bermudiana*), which reportedly did very well on St Helena and which had been introduced and reared in some numbers by former Governor Elliot.[61] Needless to say, Chalmers's 'ardour has been much dampened'. This is hardly surprising as Governor Patey regarded Chalmers to be 'an idiot!!' Melliss, who felt that Chalmers knew his work well, wisely told the young gardener to 'show no opposition, but simply do as he was told' by Patey, advice Chalmers followed, planting a fine path flanked with South African yellowwoods (*Podocarpus* spp.).

Not surprisingly, in early 1871, when the young cinchona trees were up to nine feet (2.7 m) in height, the young Kew gardener left the island. For a few years, a man was employed to clear around the cinchona trees but soon even this labouring position was cut. The trees were left to fend for themselves.[62]

But cinchona was not the only victim of the new austerity regime, John Melliss himself was by necessity forced from St Helena in 1871, a terrible loss to the island. Writing to Hooker, he lamented:

My assistance [sic] in office is being gradually taken away & I am told to do the work myself – I scarcely think the <u>Colonial Office</u> would treat me in this way, but I shall not appeal so long as I can possibly avoid it. The policy towards me appears to be <u>force</u> him out of office, upon a small pension or if possible none at all.[63]

He was correct, and in May 1871 Melliss reported to Sir Joseph Hooker at Kew Gardens,

We are in the adjourn of packing up in a hurray. Int Mail brought us news from the Colonial Office that my office here is abolished & a similar one in Grenada W.I. offered. It has been so handsomely offered that of course I accept it, though I heartily wish it were <u>not </u>the <u>West Indies</u>.[64]

Although Melliss did not settle in the West Indies, St Helena's loss on the cinchona project was Jamaica's gain and it was there Kew devoted its attention to forwarding the planation crop. A decade after the departure of Governor Elliot and John Melliss, William Thiselton-Dyer, the assistant director of the Kew Gardens, would complain that in St Helena 'which by this time [1880] cinchona planting might have restored to prosperity', the cinchona plants sent out from Kew have merely grown into trees, unseen and uncared for, and choked with vegetation: 'they have obstinately persisted in living, notwithstanding the determined protestations to the contrary of the colonists, who prefer to occupy themselves with New Zealand flax'. In St Helena in the 1890s, it was said that the cinchona plantation which Governor Elliot, Melliss and Chalmers had started below Diana's Peak could still be seen, 'the trees having run wild and thrive'.

Elliot died in 1875 and, perhaps appropriately given his adventurous, peripatetic life, was buried in St John-in-the-Wilderness, Exmouth. Today some surviving cinchona plants from the great experiment can still be seen on Diana's Peak, a kind of memorial to this intrepid man, though it is possible that these were actually planted on the instruction of Governor Janisch during the late 1870s or early 1880s.[65]

When Melliss departed St Helena, he left behind on the island the blackbirds, thrushes and sparrows he had introduced there 18 months before. Though seemingly en route to the West Indies, John Melliss made his way to London, where he seems to have remained. Here he survived, on a St Helena government pension of £186 a year. With his usual tenacity, in 1878 he founded the successful engineering firm of J. C. Melliss and Company.[66] But Melliss was not quite finished with his beloved island, which he campaigned for well into the new century, serving in the Edwardian period as treasurer to the St Helena Committee headed by the eminent conservative politician 'Black Michael', M. H. Hicks Beach. By then Melliss's name was irrevocably associated with St Helena for, in 1875, there appeared his 400-page *St Helena.* It is probably the finest book ever published on St Helena.

10

The long decline

There was no shortage of scientists either stopping off or residing briefly on St Helena in the second half of the 19th century. A small but steady flow of their scientific articles covered everything from beetles to birds and geology to meteorology. Botany also featured and there is a scattering of collectors' names attached to St Helena herbaria specimens in Paris and London. As with the very early collectors in the late 17th and early 18th century, however, it is questionable whether a great deal was achieved. Certainly no great flora emerged and Melliss remained the standard botanical reference text for 125 years.

31. View from the market house in Jamestown onto the wooded cemetery, complete with former governor's tomb. This photo dates from the 1878 flood, when part of the cemetery wall was destroyed. A remnant of street planting can be seen on the right.
© Donal P. McCracken

᠙᠍᠍ᡂ The Melliss legacy ᠙᠍ᡂ

Hudson Ralph Janisch (1824–1884) was the only British Crown governor of St Helena to date who was an islander, born in Teutonic Hall, the house where Captain James Cook spent his second day on the island.[1] Janisch was governor from 1873 until his death in 1884. During that time, he lived at his small but architecturally rather interesting home Palm Villa, complete with a small observatory, in upper Jamestown, next to the Jamestown botanic garden. Plantation House was leased out to the island's military commander and was no longer the official residence of the Crown's representative between 1873 and 1889. This was a very difficult time economically for the island. In July 1874 Janisch presided over a St Helena industrial exhibition in an attempt to stimulate local craft business, including the use of wood for cabinet work, fishing rods, walking sticks, wood carving and the like to sell to visitors.[2]

The following year Janisch lamented, 'unfortunately there are no skilled gardeners in the island and little attention paid to either agriculture or horticulture beyond the growth of potatoes for home consumption and the use of passing ships'. This was the same year that Melliss's book on St Helena appeared. In this Melliss commented, 'there are three gardens, two of which are public, and the other, well known to visitors as 'The Maldivia Fruit Gardens,' is situated at the head of the town and valley in which it lies, and where grow the only mango trees in the Island'.[3]

Janisch was friendly and accommodating to scientists David and Isobel Gill when they visited St Helena briefly in 1877 on their way to conduct astronomical research on Ascension Island. Isobel wrote of her trip to Diana's Peak:

> In one or two places we noticed the curious grass-like *Polypodium marginellum* growing parasitically on the tree-fern, and here, too, alas! and laid waste, are still to be seen some plants of *cinchona*, which our Government began to cultivate on St. Helena by the advice of Sir Joseph Hooker. The plants flourished well while care was given to them; but this is no longer done – a neglect much to be deplored.[4]

Occasionally a passing traveller or a soldier stationed at St Helena who was interested in plants and gardens would relay gloomy news back to Kew Gardens. One such garrison member was Captain Samuel Pasfield Oliver (1838–1907) of the Royal Artillery who, like the naturalist Thomas Vernon Wollaston, worked with Rev. Whitehead. In November 1876, Oliver wrote an interesting letter to Kew from Ladder Hill. Part of it ran:

In the present depressed state of the little colony there is little or no chance of establishing any plantations or introducing any economical plants even on the smallest scale.

There is no capital in the island and the properties are with few exceptions uncultivated.

The last sentence is particularly significant given that the old Georgian residences once had supported gardens, albeit of an eccentric character.

The publication of Melliss's book by L. Reeve of London, the great publisher of mid-Victorian scientific tracts, was a seminal event for science in and of St Helena. The full title of the 426-page book was *St Helena: A physical, historical, and topographical description of the island including the geology, fauna, flora and meteorology*. It had sixty-three illustrations: forty-six coloured plates, two coloured maps, one coloured plan and fourteen plain plates. Many of the botanical plates were from drawings made by Alice Elizabeth Louisa Melliss (née Stace) who was described in the book as 'Mrs J. C. Melliss'. Her drawings were suitably amended where necessary by John Nugent Fitch, the nephew of Kew Gardens' more famous artist Walter Hood Fitch. Both Fitches each drew some of the plates for *Curtis's Botanical Magazine*.

Melliss's *St Helena*, along with Brooke's *History of the island of St Helena* and Jackson's *St Helena: The historic island from its discovery to the present date* and Gosse's *St. Helena 1502–1938* are the classic books about St Helena in the period before the Second World War. For the scientist, Melliss's is the most useful, being divided into five sections: historical (45 pages); geology and mineralogy (33); zoology (142); botany (163 pages); and meteorology (12). The botanical section is the most detailed, reflecting not only the volume of known plants species but also Melliss's interests. Where possible, Melliss gives a note about the plant's location, which one can take as referring to the late 1860s before he left the island. These details are particularly useful to the botanist and the garden historian. As mentioned in the preface, the breakdown of plant localities mentioned is in the region of 498 (47 per cent) plants found in the wild; 334 (32 per cent) in particular named gardens; and 226 (21 per cent) listed as being found generally in gardens without locality being provided. This gives a total of 1,058 species of plant. The 334 plants found in 46 named gardens are listed in Table 20. The figures must be taken to be approximations as some, though not a great number, were found in more than one garden by Melliss. The table compares Melliss's estimates with those from gardens mentioned by Benjamin Grant probably a dozen years later.[5]

TABLE 20

Numbers of plant species noted by Melliss in specific gardens in 1875 and by Grant in 1883

Farm or garden	1875	1883	Farm or garden	1875	1883
Plantation House	85	55	Luffkins	2	0
Oakbank	42	24	Hutt's Gate	2	0
Maldivia Gardens	25	17	Rose Cottage	2	2
The Hermitage	18	1	Woodlands	2	2
Terrace Knoll	13	52	Sam Alexander's	1	0
St Paul's churchyard	12	1	Bevin's	1	0
Rock Cottage	11	0	East Lodge	1	0
Oaklands	10	0	Elder Cottage	1	0
Rosemary Hall	9	0	Harpers	1	0
The Briars	8	6	Longrange	1	0
Castle Garden	8	0	Longwood Rectory	1	0
Longwood	8	2	Napoleon's tomb garden	1	0
Mount Pleasant	8	1	Picquet House	1	0
Scotland	7	2	Rose Bower	1	2
Fairyland	6	2	Rupert's old jail garden	1	0
West Lodge	6	5	Stonetop	1	0
Prospect	5	1	Sydenham	1	0
Rock Rose	5	1	Wells	1	0
Botanic Gardens	4	19	Willow Cottage	1	0
Southens	4	0	Woodcot	1	0
Arnos Vale	3	0	Chubb's Spring Cottage	0	1
Lowe's garden	3	0	Francis Plain	0	1
Myrtle Grove	3	0	Retreat	0	1
Walbro Cottage	3	0	Rupert's Bay [old jail garden?]	0	2
Bamboo Grove	2	0	St John's Villa	0	1
Farm Lodge	2	1		334	202

This table can be read only as an indication rather than an actual reflection of decline, as Grant did not list ferns, grasses or 'ordinary garden flowers'. His was also, one suspects, a less rigorous surveyor of the island's plant life. In an interesting example of familial plant distribution, a relative of Benjamin Grant, Frederick E. Grant, had left St Helena and settled in Boston, Massachusetts, in the United States. Here he had become acquainted with the legendary plant propagator at the Arnold Arboretum, Jackson Thornton Dawson (1841–1916).[6] As a consequence, in an 18-month period in the 1880s, nearly 2,000 trees and slips were shipped out from the Arnold Arboretum to St Helena, some of the recipients being Longwood, Plantation House, Scotland and Terrace Knoll.

The Melliss list makes an interesting comparison with Burchell's lists, mentioned in a previous chapter. Plantation House remained pre-eminent as the botanical treasure house and the sad decline of the botanic garden in Jamestown is clear. The rise of Oaklands as a botanical reservoir can be attributed to the Melliss family living there.

Captain Oliver praised Melliss's book but commented that since Melliss's time, 'the whole place has become worse'. However, Oliver does make an observation which sends a hint of things to come and which, to a degree, contradicts his earlier statement:

> I forgot to add that everyone here is now planting New Zealand flax. Phormium for a fibre company. I believe the first cargo home & at Philadelphia fully realized the expectations of the quality of fibre etc. The great difficulty in this island is want of transport facility & expense of labour.[7]

Three months later, in November 1876, we find Oliver writing again to Kew, this time from Hutt's Gate instead of Ladder Hill:

> I will let the few planters here know that you will send out some seed of the Bermuda Cedar, if they will take the trouble to raise it but they are all very apathetic.

In fact, this tree, not a true cedar, succeeded very well on St Helena being termite-resistant to the extent of becoming a problem, an irony given the scarcity of the tree in its native Bermuda. Indeed, it succeeded so well that today's St Helena gin is flavoured with its berries.[8]

In more recent times, botanists have been more circumspect about Melliss the citizen botanist. Q. C. B. Cronk, while recognising the fact that Melliss's work 'remains the most recent and most interesting published complete account of the flora', states that it should be treated with caution, as Melliss:

> omitted certain species, and subsequent introductions have occurred, together with extinctions and changes of distribution and status; also he tended to conflate those plants found in gardens with those found wild (of the 907 vascular plants he included, about 500 were confined to gardens).

Cronk also highlights the scarcity of Melliss's own plant collecting and indeed the failure of Kew Gardens to retain all that he did send them in the way of herbarium specimens.[9] Melliss wrote about the situation he found in the late 1860s and early 1870s, when so many of the old St Helena gardens had declined badly and contained only what had been planted earlier and what had blown in. By the 1880s, the houses and cottages scattered about the countryside had seen grander days and were generally dilapidated, such as Canterbury, Chubb's Spring (roofless), Willow Cottage (untenanted) and the 'romantically situated' cottage called Shipway's, which was 'out of repair, though tenantable'.

32. Castle Garden, c.1910. With the departure of the garrison in 1906, Jamestown fell on hard times, as these deserted streets show. The old 17th-century Castle Garden, with its anti-enslavement memorial pillar to HMS *Waterwitch* (1839-1843), survived but no longer witnessed officers and their wives promenading under the now-maturing Bengal fig trees.
© Donal P. McCracken

It was also during Janisch's time as governor that the celebrated entomologists Thomas Vernon and Edith Wollaston stayed for six months on the island collecting insects. Thanks to the intervention of Joseph Hooker at Kew, Janisch allowed the Wollastons the use of Plantation House. But there was a price to pay for Hooker's assistance, and soon Hooker was enquiring about possibly being sent indigenous plants from the island. In October 1875 Thomas Wollaston wrote a long letter to Kew not saying a great deal and blaming his lack of botanical productivity on the cold and wet weather. In one section, however, he talked about Diana's Peak:

> Of introduced things there are swarms everywhere, seeding (more or less) at all times; but the genuine St Helenans are not only few in number & difficult of access, but chiefly in a semi torpid state just now, – hardly preparing even to flower. There are of course a few exceptions. The whitewood Cabbage Tree (Petrobium arboretum) is just out of blossom, & indeed magnificent). Blackwood Cabb. Tree (Melanodendron intrifolium) is just coming into a blaze of flower, – & a superb sight it is, on the almost inaccessible slopes of Diana's Peak. Indeed anything more interesting than these dense groves of Cabbage Trees (interspersed with a few Tree Ferns) I have never seen; & the whole fauna of Coleoptrous parasites to dance attendance upon them is enough to plunge an ordinary beetle-collector like myself, who has a special interest in the islands, into the seventh heaven.

A month later, Wollaston was able to despatch a parcel of eight species to Kew, still complaining that it was a bad time of year to collect seeds:

> ... in addition to being extremely few in number, nearly all grow in places very difficult to access at a time the upper ridges are mainly always covered with cloud, & only a certain proportion of them are showing any symptoms of active life (in the shape of flowers & seeds); but I have been able to collect 3 out of 4 species of cabbage trees, a lobelia, two or three Wahlenbergias, & (best of all) the extremely rare <u>Aster</u> (or <u>Commidendron</u>) <u>Burchellii</u> [*Commidendrum gummiferum*]. The last is, I think, as nearly extinct as anything still living can be. Mr Mellis says that there is only one plant of it in the is<u>ld</u>, but in that he is wrong, for we counted 2 or 3, in full blossom, in the same grove of the Aster gummiferum in w<u>h</u> he records the existence of his single individual. We have, however, seen it no where else, & it is decidedly on its last legs. Even the <u>S. gummiferum</u> is excessively rare, & I shall hope to get you seeds of it before we leave the island; as well as of the

<u>Commidendron robustum</u> (the <u>true</u> 'gumwood'). But, you know, I am no botanist, & have a little difficulty at first in recognising the genuine (& <u>few</u>) natives; added to w<u>h</u>, some of them are in parts barely accessible even in the finest weather.[10]

The specimen of the now-extinct *Commidendrum gummiferum* referred to by Melliss was found 'near the old Picquet House above West Lodge'.[11]

The Wollastons were greatly assisted by Rev. Canon Henry Whitehead (1817–1884), who in 1861 had been transferred to St Helena from the Cape, where he had botanised in the north of the colony.[12] Whitehead remained on St Helena until his death in 1884. He lived at Woodcot, the old home of the Leech family and later a Thorpe residence. Wollaston was especially helped by Whitehead's son Philip, who clambered over the Barn mountain in search of what proved to be an assortment of nine insects new to science.[13] Rev. Whitehead was a very different personality from the opinionated Rev. Richard Boys, who had dominated ecclesiastical affairs on the island a generation earlier. Whitehead had served in parishes in Namaqualand and Tulbagh at the Cape, and had developed a great love of ferns. Arriving on St Helena he spent the rest of his career quietly serving the island and studying its flora. In April 1878, Captain Oliver frankly asserted to Kew that Whitehead was 'the only person on this island who knows about, or cares at all for, the native flora'. This was somewhat confirmed when, writing separately on the same day to Kew, Whitehead diplomatically raised the issue of paying locals to collect:

> I could furnish you with a complete representation of our flora if you would return the Ward's cases and provide for the expenses of gathering, particularly such plants, as the Erodium of Roxburgh [*Pelargonium cotyledonis*] growing on the cliffs and for proteceps.[14]

໑ั๛๏ The re-emergence of Kew Gardens ໑ั๛๏

Apart from these occasional contacts, Kew did not completely give up on St Helena after the cinchona experiment ended. William Botting Hemsley (1843–1924), who came from the Sussex village of Uckfield and was self-educated, joined Kew in 1860 as a teenager and, with one break of seven years, worked his way up to become keeper of the Kew herbarium in 1899.[15] He was a prodigious worker who, sadly, is largely forgotten today. One of the herculean tasks he took on was to write up most of the botanical section in the lengthy report on the famous HMS *Challenger* scientific expedition (1873–1876). Hemsley was responsible for 767 pages on 'insular floras', covering various islands in the north and south Atlantic, the Indian

ST. HELENA GUARDIAN.

No 132 (SECOND SERIES.)   WEDNESDAY, MAY 13, 1868   PRICE 4D

Commissariat Notice.

SEALED TENDERS in Duplicate will be received at this Office till noon on Thursday 2nd July (next), from persons who may be willing to supply such quantities of ,

FRESH MEAT

as may be required for Army, Navy, and other Public Service for Three Years, from 1st November 1868, under certain terms and conditions which may be ascertained at this Office.

The rate per lb. to be expressed in the Tender in *Pence* and *decimal parts of a Penny.*

Commissariat, St. Helena,
10th April, 1868.

       C. SWAIN,
Assistant Commissary General
Controller of Army Expenditure.

SHERIFF'S NOTICE.

FURNITURE, &C.

The undersigned has been instructed

TO SELL
BY PUBLIC AUCTION
AT " ROSEMARY "
on Saturday the 16th instant,
At 10 o'Clock,

A QUANTITY OF

Household Furniture, &c,

COMPRISING :—

Dining, Loo, Sofa and other Tables
Chairs
Chests of Drawers
Wardrobe, plate glass front
Marble and other Washstands
Sofas
Pier Glasses
Carpeting
Window Curtains
Iron Bedsteads
Bedding
Breakfast, Dinner and Tea Services
Plated Side Dishes
  Do.   Candle Sticks
Knives
Cooking Utensils
China, Crockery, and Glassware
Saddlery

" ROCK ROSE."

The undersigned has been instructed by G. V. SEALE, Esq.,

TO SELL
BY PUBLIC AUCTION
Under the Trees
on Monday next the 18th Inst,
At 12 o'Clock,

The whole of the above

ESTATE,

comprising the following LANDS,

VIZ :—

Tinsley's, Home Pasture, Long Pasture, Upper Robinson's, Lower Robinson's, Upper and Lower Long Ground, Alice's Cottage, Garden and Lands, Simouses, Bull's Chamber, High Hollow, and Deep Valley, in all 480 acres land thoroughly watered throughout.

ALSO,

That valuable well constructed House

" ROCK ROSE,"

replete with every convenience, having an ENCLOSURE containing

---

33. By the mid-to-late 19th century, the old St Helena country houses were in rapid decline, often saved only by occupation by military officers or civil servants.
St Helena Guardian, 13 May 1868. © St Helena Archives

Ocean and the Pacific Ocean. This included 74 pages, with a detailed enumeration of plants, on St Helena. However, Hemsley never visited St Helena. One of the naturalists on the *Challenger*, Henry Nottidge Moseley (1844–1891), sent botanical specimens direct to Kew from the various ports where the *Challenger* called on its 120,000-kilometre voyage. These were then worked upon by Hemsley. Hemsley also utilised Kew's own collections as well as that in the British Museum. By the time he was working on the St Helena section of the report, the Burchell collection was housed at Kew. So Hemsley had access to Roxburgh's report, Burchell's papers and Melliss's book on St Helena, which was published while the *Challenger* was at sea. The flora lists by Beatson in 1825 and by Stephen F. Pritchard and James Bowie in 1836, Hemsley dismissed summarily as based on Roxburgh and 'utterly devoid of botanical interest'.[16]

Hemsley pronounced Melliss's work an 'interesting book', whose author carried out 'diligent search', but also criticised some aspects of the volume. He asserted rather unfairly that the 'botany [section of the book] is perhaps the least satisfactory part in some respects'. Hemsley then went on to say:

> Unfortunately, Melliss followed Roxburgh's example, and included native and introduced plants in one general list, which is extended to 1058 species, so that the native element is as it were overpowered by the exotic. Then there is no attempt to elaborate the synonymy and exhaust the literature of each species, and a few species are omitted altogether. The *Cyperaceæ* and the *Gramineæ* had not been critically examined, and several of the indigenous ones had not been described; hence the enumeration is imperfect for these orders. Apart from these defects, the work is most valuable and useful, and we are greatly indebted to the author for particulars respecting the distribution and relative rarity of a large number of the species up to the date of his work.[17]

Hemsley then goes on to make extensive use of Melliss's work in his own enumeration of the plants on St Helena.

Printers and plants

An official government printer had existed on St Helena since the Company days, Arthur Hill holding the position in 1806. Later occupying this pensionable position came George Gibb, John Elliott, Edward Watson and Charles Bruce. In 1851 a 'free press' had been regulated on the island beginning with the short-lived *St Helena Advocate* printed by James Bennett. In ten years the *Advocate* came and went, as did the *St Helena Chronicle*, the *St Helena Herald* and the *St Helena Record*. The colonial government was never slow to take away advertisements when it disagreed with what was being printed, not least when the editor was a government official. This would effectively close the newspaper. Only in 1861 was some stability found with the publication of the *St Helena Guardian*, which became the standard St Helena newspaper.

The government printers supplemented their incomes with private work. James Elliott owned and printed the *St Helena Herald* and after its demise in 1860, in 1861 became the founding proprietor/editor of the *St Helena Guardian*. Needless to say, such a conflict of interest did not go unnoticed. But the official printers were not without competition in the guise of Benjamin Grant, whose printing works was in Napoleon Street, Jamestown. From the 1870s onward, Grant printed the *St Helena Guardian*, the *Church News*, the *Monthly Critic*, the *St Helena Times*, *The St Helenian* and finally, in 1901, he was quick to make some profit from the Boers by printing their POW newspaper, *De Krijgsgevangene*.[18]

In 1883, Benjamin Grant teamed up with a Captain R. A. Oliver of the Royal Artillery to produce a 70-page guide to the island. This Captain Oliver should not be confused with the amateur botanist Captain S. P. Oliver. The Grant / R. A Oliver publication had the cumbersome title, *A few notes on St. Helena, and descriptive guide by Benjamin Grant. To which is added some remarks on the island as a health resort; Captain J. R. Oliver's geology of the island and a numerous appendices (places of worship, societies, trees, fish, heights, etc.) illustrated.*

This guidebook is a treasure-trove of information concerning St Helena in the period after Company rule had passed. It includes details on some of the island's gardens. There are 271 plant species listed, including 26 indigenous trees. Grant left out ferns, grasses and 'garden flowers', so while this is not a complete list, it is an interesting indicator, coming about a dozen years after Melliss did his work. Figure 8 indicates the number of plants listed as growing in various gardens and areas. There are overlaps, with the same species growing in more than one area.

FIGURE 8
Plants listed on St Helena properties by Grant's guidebook, 1883

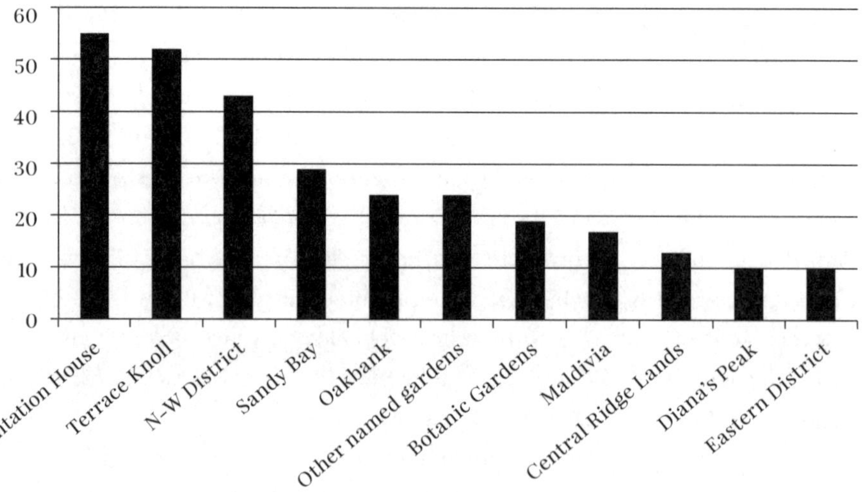

A list of 25 indigenous plants is given in full in Table 21. Some of these still grow in the old gardens such as Longwood, Mount Pleasant, Oakbank, Plantation House, Terrace Knoll and West lodge.

TABLE 21

Plants listed in Grant's guidebook, 1883, as indigenous

Scientific name	Common name	Notes
Frankenia portulacifolia	St Helena tea	Rare
Pharnaceum acidium		Rare
Melhania erythroxylon	Redwood	Rare
Pelargonium cotyledonis	Live for ever	Very common
Nesiota elliptica	Wild olive	On Central Ridge Lands and Diana's Peak etc.
Phylica polifolia syn. *P. ramosissima*	Rosemary	Rare Plantation House, Terrace Knoll, Sand Bay, North-Western district and Oakbank
Fuchsia coccinea	Fuchsia	Central Ridge Lands
Lichtensteinia	Angelica	
Hedyotis arborea	Dogwood	Rare Plantation House, Terrace Knoll, North-Western District and on Central Ridge Lands.
Aster burchellii		Rare West Lodge
Aster glutinosus	Scrubwood	Sandy Bay and Eastern District
Aster gummiferus	Bastard gumwood	Rare West Lodge
Commidendron robustum	Gumwood	North-Western District and Eastern District
Melanodendron integrifolia	Cabbage tree	Central Ridge Lands
Psiadia rotundifolia	Cabbage tree	Longwood
Petrobrium arboreum	White wood	Rare Central Ridge Lands and Diana's Peak
Lachanodes prenanthifolia	She-cabbage	Central Ridge Lands and Diana's Peak
Pladaroxylon leucadendron	He-cabbage	Sandy Bay, North-Western District, Central Ridge Lands and Diana's Peak
Tripterus burchellii		Rare Sandy Bay and Eastern District
Wahlenbergia augustifolia		Rare Central Ridge Lands and Diana's Peak
Wahlenbergia linifolia		Central Ridge Lands, Diana's Peak and North-western District

Scientific name	Common name	Notes
Wahlenbergia burchellii		Central Ridge Lands and Diana's Peak
Plantago robusta	St Helena plantain	General
Boerhaavia helenae	Hogweed	Rare Sea shore
Acalypha reticula [*A. rubrinervis*]	Stringwood	Very rare Diana's Peak

Also of note were the scattered entries for the now fast-deteriorating smaller old gardens on the island.

TABLE 22

Plants of interest in the smaller gardens, Grant's guidebook, 1883

Garden	Scientific name	Common name
The Briars	*Averrhoa carambola*	Chinese gooseberry [star fruit]
The Briars	*Acacia spectabilis*	Thorn [Shittim Wood]
The Briars	*Olea europea*	Olive
The Briars	*Persea gratissima*	Avocado
The Briars	*Pandanus utilis*	Screw pine
[The Briars village]	*Ailanthus glandulosa* [*Ailanthus altissima*]	Tree of heaven
Chubb's Spring [cottage]	*Anethum foeniculum*	Fennel
Fairy Land	*Hoya carnosa*	Wax plant
Fairy Land	*Ulmus parvifolia*	Chinese elm
Farm Lodge [Only]	*Lodoicea seychellarum* [*Jubea spectabilis* of Mellis]	Double Cocoa Nut/coco de mer, only example on St Helena. Also had fine oak avenue
Francis Plain [garden?]	*Schotia afra* syn. *Schotia tamarindifolia*	Karoo boer-bean
Hermitage	*Quercus suber*	Cork oak
Longwood	*Ficus elastica*	India rubber
Longwood	**Psiadia rotundifolia** [*Commidendrum rotundifolium*]	Cabbage tree [bastard gumwood]
Mount Pleasant	*Cheirostemon plantanioildes* [*Chiranthodendron pentadactylon*]	[Devil's] Hand tree
Prospect	*Synara*	Artichoke
Retreat	*Gardenia florida*	Cape jasmine
Rock Rose	*Leptospermum*	Tea tree
Rose Bower	*Hibiscus mutabilis*	White rose
Rose Bower	*Juniperus mediterranea*	Spreading cedar

Garden	Scientific name	Common name
Rose Cottage	*Hydrangea hortensia*	Brazilian pine
Rose Cottage	*Araucaria brasiliensis*	
Rupert's Bay [Jail garden?]	*Citrus limonum*	Lemon
Ruperts	*Citrus decumana*	Shaddock
St John's Villa [near Maldivia]	*Cereus purpurea*	
St Paul's [graveyard/glebe]	*Cupressus sempervirens*	Cypress
Scotland	*Ehretia pyrifolia*	
Scotland	*Banksia speciosa*	Bottle brush
West Lodge	*Eugenia pimenta*	Spice tree
West Lodge	***Aster burchellii*** [*Commidendrum gummiferum*]	
West Lodge	***Aster gummiferus***	Bastard gumwood
West Lodge	*Ilex aquifolium*	Holly
West Lodge	*Leucadendron argenteum*	Silver tree
Woodlands	*Cedrela toona*	Toon tree
Woodlands	*Calodendron*	Wild chestnut

ᒡᘓ Kew reappears again ᘐᒥ

Dr Daniel Morris visited St Helena in July/August 1883. He had been assistant director of Peradeniya Royal Botanic Gardens on Ceylon (Sri Lanka) before becoming director of Public Gardens and Plantations in Jamaica. He was held in high esteem at Kew and later, in May 1886, was appointed assistant director of Kew Gardens itself. His coming to St Helena predated a much more extensive enquiry relating to botanical enterprise that he would undertake in the West Indies. Both ventures were strongly backed by Kew.

From St Helena, Morris sent Kew two Wardian cases and two hampers of specimens, samples and seeds which he had collected. On his ship home, reaching Plymouth, Morris wrote to Joseph Hooker:

> I finished up work at St Helena very satisfactorily. I had a large meeting of people
> at the Castle and discussed with them fully numerous ways & means whereby they
> might improve the cultivation of plants and improve their present position. From
> what the governor [Janisch] said & from my own impressions I believe my visit
> will not be lost; but tend to give fresh impulse to many small industries and place
> the cultivations in the way of making them profitable.[19]

Morris duly compiled a report on St Helena for the Colonial Office. This did not recommend that cinchona growing be recommenced on the island. By then only 156 trees had survived in what was considered to be unsuitable soil for their growth.[20] Anyway, St Helena cinchona could not then have competed with the large cinchona plantations in the Dutch and British possessions in the East, though it might have assisted west and southern Africa.

Morris did, however, go into some detail about what plants might thrive on the island. Of the island's middle zone, which he defined as being between 400 and 1,800 feet (122 and 549 m), he commented:

The English brooms, brambles, willows, and poplars, Scotch pines and gorse bushes, Cape of Good Hope bushes, Australian trees, and American weeds have driven out most of the indigenous plants from this belt. The tendency of these introduced plants is to encroach more and more upon the higher lands where the indigenous flora remains. As regards the larger trees, such as pines and willows (acacias), they appear to be spreading downwards in the direction of the valleys; following no doubt, the distribution of their seeds by the action of the trade winds.[21]

His only reference to the botanic garden was the following:

At present there is a small sum expended in the maintenance of a small garden in Jamestown which might be added to the above [Plantation House] for working them under one officer.[22]

Only 23 years later, in November 1906 when things were desperate, was the report of the by now Sir Daniel Morris published under the title *Reprint of a report (written in 1884) upon the present position and prospects of the agricultural resources of the island of St Helena.*

The year after Morris visited the island, William Hudson Janisch, the island's only native-born governor, died on 19 March 1884 aged 59. Morris was rather uneasy about Janisch's 'tentative dealings' with the Colonial Office, but given the state of fiscal starvation imposed on Janisch, his cautious dealings with London are unsurprising.[23]

Perhaps appropriately, given his interest in plants, in 1884, the year that Janisch died, the *St Helena Almanac* carried a list of 27 'indigenous Trees and Plants', commenting that they were to be found 'in the more inaccessible parts, notably, the high ridge lands about Diana's Peak and secluded ravines on the Westwards and Southward sides of the island'. The list is included in Table 23. As will be seen, 24 are endemics – only to be found on St Helena; two are alien imports; and one was a long-term naturalised plant of the island but also found elsewhere on the globe. Twelve of these 27 species are marked as 'least common'. Using Lambdon and Cronk's modern categorising, this included one plant species which today is locally common, one which is endangered, one vulnerable, five critical, one extinct in the wild and two which are totally extinct. Then there are the alien species, one was the well-known fuchsia, but the other was the extraordinary devil's hand tree, the only specimens of which in the 1870s and 1880s were at Mount Pleasant, Oakbank and Plantation House. Why the last of these plants was listed as indigenous is not known, but the list does give an interesting picture of what was considered at the time to represent the indigenous flora, albeit constituting only about 50 per cent of the island's endemic flora and excluding plants such as the spectacular giant tree ferns, *Dicksonia arborescens*.

34. 'Under the trees': Until the early 19th century, enslaved people were auctioned under the peepul trees that have stood outside the Canister building at the top of Jamestown's Main Street. Photograph, *c.*1910/1920.
© Donal P. McCracken

TABLE 23
St Helena Almanac list of 'indigenous' St Helena plants, 1884

Botanical name [1884] Those marked * are the least common	Local Name [1884]	Notes L&C = Lambdon and Cronk 2016 category rating
Frankenia portulacæfolia [*Frankenia portulacifolia*]	St Helena tea[24]	Endemic L&C critical
Pharnaceum acidum [synonym of *Hypertelis acida*]	No local name given	Endemic Salad plant L&C critical
Melhania erythroxylon [synonym of *Trochetiopsis erythroxylon*]	Redwood	Endemic L&C extinct in wild
Cheirostemon plantanioides [*Cheirostemon platanoides*] [synonym of *Chiranthodendron pentadactylon*]	Handtree [devil's hand tree]	Alien No longer grows on island. In 1875 two specimens 'of the celebrated "hand-trees" were growing at Oakbank. In 1787 only one tree was supposed to exist in the world, but in 1801 forests of the species were seen in Guatemala'.
Pelargonium cotyledonis	Live for ever	Endemic Old father live forever[25] L&C critical
Nesiota elliptica	Wild olive	Endemic St Helena olive L&C extinct
Phylica ramosissima [*Phylica ramosissima*] [synonym of *Phylica polifolia*]	Rosemary	Endemic L&C critical
Fuchsia coccinea	Fuchsia	Alien/Naturalised
Lichtensteinia [?*Lichtensteiniana burchellii*] [synonym of *Berula burchellii*]	Angelica	Endemic Dwarf jellico St Helena name was angelica L&C endangered
Sium Helenianum [synonym of *Berula bracteata*]	Jellico	Endemic Jellico L&C vulnerable
Hedyotis arborea [synonym of *Nesohedyotis arborea*]	Dogwood	Endemic L&C critical
Aster Burchelli [synonym of *Commidendrum robustum gummiferum*]	No local name given	Endemic Cluster-leaved gumwood Extinct
Aster glutinosus [synonym of *Commidendrum rugosum*]	Scrubwood	Endemic L&C critical

Botanical name [1884] Those marked * are the least common	Local Name [1884]	Notes L&C = Lambdon and Cronk 2016 category rating
Aster gummifera	Bustard gumwood	Endemic [Same as *Aster Burchellii/ Commidendrum gummiferum*. If bastard gumwood then it is *Commidendrum rotundifolium*.] L&C critical
Commidendron robustum [*Commidendrum robustum*]	Gumwood	Endemic L&C critical
Melanodendron integrifolium	Cabbage tree	Endemic Black cabbage tree L&C vulnerable
Psiadia rotundifolia [synonym of *Commidendrum rotundifolium*]	No local name given	Endemic Bastard gumwood L&C critical
Petrobrium arboretum [*Petrobium arboretum*]	White wood	Endemic L&C endangered
Lachanodes prenanthifolia [Synonym of *Lachanodes arborea*]	She cabbage	Endemic L&C extinct in wild
Pladaroxylon leucadendron [*Pladaroxylon leucadendron*]	He cabbage	Endemic L&C critical
Tripterus Burchellii [synonym of *Osteospermum sanctae-helenae*]	No local name given	Endemic Boneseed L&C locally common
Wahlenbergia angustifolia	No local name given	Endemic Small bellflower L&C vulnerable
Wahlenbergia linifolia	No local name given	Endemic Large bellflower L&C critical
Wahlenbergia Burchellii	No local name given	Endemic Burchell's bellflower L&C extinct
Plantago robusta	No local name given	Endemic St Helena plantain L&C critical
Boerhaavia Helenæ [synonym of *Commicarpus helenae*]	Hogweed	Native to St Helena and elsewhere L&C critical
Acalypha reticulata [synonym of *Acalypha rubrinervis* var. *rubra*]	Stringwood	Endemic L&C extinct

The decline of the private rural garden

The most succinct account of the decline of St Helena in the late 19th century can be found in Geoffrey Kitching's typescript guide of the island history, now available online. Kitching had been government secretary in St Helena in the 1930s and writes in a precise and perceptive manner.[26] The island's decline was the result of a number of factors, including the advent of steamships; the severing of the link with the East India Company; the opening of the Suez Canal; the withdrawal of a substantial part of the garrison; and the failure of the Royal Navy to take control of the island. Economic woes were matched with a decline in what can only be described as island morale. Migration links with the Cape had existed for a great many years. In the 1870s these were formalised, with a St Helena community also established in the colony of Natal. But migration schemes were infrequent and a passage to the Cape in the late 1880s cost £10 for the five-day voyage, so there was a poverty trap with little hope of escape. The island's economic decline also affected those further up the social scale. This is reflected in the decline and ruination of the island's country house phenomenon. As pointed out earlier, these had not been landed estates but respectable Georgian farmhouses.

In 1884 Daniel Morris had written:

> The country houses which in the East India Company's time were inhabited by prosperous merchants and officials, and surrounded by well kept gardens and orchards, are now fast falling into decay and becoming ruinous. The cultivated areas around them are simply converted into grazing lands, and a few cattle and sheep are the only indications of life for miles around.[27]

In 1890 Acting-Governor Reginald Antrobus wrote of St Helena and 'the ruins of well-built country houses, and the deserted cottages, which are to be seen in every direction'.[28] Some of these ruins such as Bradleys, Rock Rose Cottage, Salt Spring and Sane Valley House are marked in the 1922 Admiralty map of St Helena. Thanks to the attention given to St Helena during the period of Napoleon's captivity, we know perhaps more about the island at that time than at any other prior to the 20th century. In 1806, just a decade before the arrival of 'General' Napoleon, Thomas Henry Brooke, a member of the island's governing council, observed:

> Without reckoning Government houses, and exclusive of huts inhabited by slaves, herdsmen, or poor people, there are eighty dwellings in the country, of which thirty-seven are of a respectable description, and twenty particularly so.

Brooke also noted the old practice of plantation owners living in the country and coming to their town houses in Jamestown only when ships arrived. This afforded an opportunity to sell produce, buy goods from ships and be part of the social circuit.[29]

Full abolition of enslavement on the island was enshrined in the Ordinance for the Abolition of Slavery in the Island of St Helena, enacted on 27 May 1839. The costs of payments made by the authorities to the gentry owning enslaved people. During the years of phased emancipation from 1827 to 1836 had been passed on to formerly enslaved individuals as loans. These were written off in December 1839. Unable to prosper from enslaved labour and now no longer benefiting from the affluence the East India Company had brought to the island, the gentry – and their rural houses and gardens – went into decline. Several generations later, Governor Grey Wilson asserted:

> It must be remembered that, when that change took place [end of company aid], very near the whole of the landed proprietors and upper classes, who were famed for their lavish hospitality, found themselves either involved in, or on the verge of, bankruptcy.[30]

Both late-Victorian governors Grey Wilson and Sterndale believed that the old St Helena gentry had been kept going by the Company's 'fictitious inflation' and that once this evaporated they had neither the energy nor resources to adapt. Moreover, they became a brake on 'the natural growth of enterprise which elsewhere characterises British colonists'. In short, St Helena was trapped in the 18th century.

It was not just that the garrison and with it the officer corps declined in number, or that 'Indians' – white Company employees and soldiers from India – who could not afford or did not wish to return to Britain for furlough increasingly sojourned at the Cape. The decline of the great fleets, as well as the new imperialism which opened up vast tracts of the world to British colonial exploitation, contributed to St Helena no longer being fashionable even among the genteel poor.

There was still some money to be made out of the island but the businessmen who succeeded in this tended to be of a different breed. Although there was still a handful of administrators, such as Melliss in Oakbank, who maintained country residences, the new money had little interest in creating great parks on their land like small-time gentry. Ironically, this meant that those country houses which have survived are often unspoilt, at least in their facades, by later renovations. The only major exterior alteration was the replacement of the old slate roofs, which originally had been straw, with corrugated iron, pressed tin or zinc sheets on iron rafters, examples being Oaklands, Rose Bower and Plantation House. This was a result of the white ant having destroyed so many roofing timbers.[31] This dangerous beetle had been said to have been imported in the rotten timbers of an old slave ship in the 1840s, though it was at least a decade before the infestation became fully apparent.[32] The beetle, *Cryptotermes brevis*, is well known to anyone who has lived in the tropics or subtropics for any time. What it did to St Helena was repeated in many other such regions. The use of teak and cedar in building as well as iron rafters had by the 1890s alleviated the problem in St Helena. As a result, the old, attractive St Helena Georgian farmhouses with their elegant garden settings were not usually destroyed by the white ant but by the changing order on the island. In 1891, a country residence on St Helena complete with a 'comfortable garden' could be rented for about half the price of such in a London suburb. Ironically, the price of land was still relatively high, averaging in 1900 at between £10 and £15 an acre. There was a shift away from cultivation towards pasture, and similarly the 'big house' was now largely surplus to requirements. It was a sign of the times that Oakbank, once the property jewel in St Helena's crown but now decimated by white ant, was sold in 1918, complete with 40 acres, for a token £12-10-0.[33]

৬৲৯ Plantation House ৬৲৯

The one garden which survived relatively intact throughout the 19th century and early 20th century was that at Plantation House. This is hardly surprising given the occupants and the Victorian fascination with the plant world. But it is also to be remembered that with the new dispensation in the 1830s the governor's salary dropped by about 20 per cent and he lost his discretionary £200 annual allowance. The 1834 commission report stated that the grounds and gardens comprised about 176 acres, with 'the garden part consisting of fir plantations and ornamental timber'. The commissioners recommended that 46 acres be let out for £45 a year, including part of the garden grounds as well as the laundry and a cottage. In the report's appendices this area was broken down into one acre of laundry and lawn (£15 proposed rent), eight acres of garden ground (£12), and 37 acres of wood and pasture (£18).[34]

The only area established by Governor Brooke around the old house to remain largely unaltered was the nursery. As the century drew to a close and a new one began, the Plantation House gardener grew and distributed, frequently free of charge to the public, about a thousand seedlings annually. These were primarily

35. The dog has gone but Governor Sterndale's cast-iron fountain survives. The Castle Garden under military occupation, complete with bell tents when St Helena was home to Boer POWs, *c.*1901.

Jackson, *St Helena*, 1903, opp. p. 248. Provided by Donal P. McCracken.

eucalyptus species, Cape yew (yellowwood), cedar, Indian fig species, Norfolk Island pine, olive and Port Jackson willow. For a number of years, the gardener at Plantation House gave classes in horticulture at one of Jamestown's schools.

This situation was not to last and by the 1870s the grounds were in a sorry state. Captain S. P. Oliver of the Royal Artillery looked askance at what had happened:

> In Plantation Grounds the Colony has been ~~very~~ up till now very wanting in forethought. The pine woods have been allowed to be deforested too liberally. Full-size pines (Pinaster) are or have been sold to any-one for 2/6[d] a tree, and none are planted to replace those cut down – Col. Warren R.E. as Colonial Engineer is supposed to look after the woods but altho a good officer as to roads etc. He knows nothing of forestry.[35]

A decade later, however, as illustrated in Table 24, the list of shrubs and trees at Plantation House was impressive enough at 55 species.

TABLE 24
Species listed as growing at Plantation House in Grant's guidebook, 1883

Scientific name (endemic in bold)	Common name
Lirlodendron tulipifera	Tulip tree
Magnolia fuscuta	Magnolia/banana shrub
Mimosa australis	Mimosa
Caesalpina pulcherrima syn. *Poinciana pulcherrima*	{Barbados) flame tree
Althea rosea	Hollyhock
Trochetiopsis erythroxylon syn. Melhania erythroxylon	St Helena redwood
Cheirostemon plantanioides [Note: Marked as a rare indigenous St Helena plant, but originates from South America.]	Hand tree
Camellia japonica variegata	Variegated camellia
Citrus limonum	Lemon
Citrus nobilis	Mandarin orange
Citrus vulgaris	Seville orange
Pistacia terebinthus	Cyprus turpentine [Terebinth]
Phylica polifolia syn. P. ramosissima	St Helena rosemary
Nephelium lappaceum	Litchi (rambutan of China)
Erythrina corallodendron	Coral tree
Spartium junceum	Broom
Virgilia capensis	Sophora/Keurboom
Acacia verticillata	
Fragaria elatior	Strawberry
Pyrus malus	Apple
Eucalyptus globulus	Blue gum
Aralia papyrifera	Paper plant
Curtisia faginea	Assegai tree
Nesohedyotis arborea syn. **Hedyotis arborea**	St Helena dogwood
Serissa foetida	Stinkwood
Cotula australis	Pagoda tree?
Plumbago capensis	Plumbago
Bignonia (?)	

Scientific name (endemic in bold)	Common name
Bignonia tecoma	Yellow bignonia/Trumpet flower
Thunbergia alata	Black-eyed susan
Ehretia pyrifolia	
Solanum esculentum (white, red striped)	Tomato?
Olea laurifolia	Purple olive/Ironwood
Olea fragrans	Sweet olive
Lazarus nobilis	Sweet bay
Persea gratissima	Avocado
Banksia speciosa	Bottle brush
Poinsettia pulcherrima	
Morus nigra	Mulberry
Pinus pinea	Stone pine
Pinus densiflora	Dwarf pine
Coryphya umbraculifera	Fan palm
Strelitzia capensis	*Streltzia reginae/S.alba?*
Ixia monadelpha	
Ixia patens	
Trichononema ochroleucum	
Watsonia rosea	
Amaryllis formosissima	Aztec lily
Agave variegata	
Crinum amabile	Spider lily
Haemanthus toxicaris	Book lily
Narcissus biflorus	
Pancratium littorale	Steamer lily
Celastrus euonymus	Spindle tree
Arundinaria nana	Dwarf bamboo

Between 1873 and 1889, Plantation House was leased out, only to be occupied again in 1890 by Governor Grey Wilson. Of the house he wrote, 'Plantation is a far finer Government house than any I have yet seen except Madras, but it is really too large without a big income.'[36] Grey Wilson was one of the late Victorian governors who occasionally contacted Kew Gardens, in his case to investigate the possibilities of the fibre industry in St Helena. On request, Grey Wilson sent Kew a section of *Trochetiopsis* and offered Dr Morris to supply 'any of his naturalist friends' who would like specimens of the endemic wirebird's eggs.[37] But despite such distractions, the misfortunes of the governor's residence continued, and from 1898 it was attacked by white ants. Only in the late 1920s was a serious attempt made to rehabilitate the building.[38] As for the grounds, by the early 20th century, after a century's growth, the trees were in their full majesty:

> The grounds are very extensive, embracing a broad, undulating space between two ranges of pine-covered hills. The extraordinary adaptability of soil and climate I have before alluded to is here very apparent, for in the woods round the house may be noticed trees from every part of the world—huge Norfolk Island pines, one of them 110 feet high; the Araucaria excelsa we buy in pots at home, and value for house decoration, here a timber tree ; the Australian blue eucalyptus, of which a giant near the house measures 16½ feet in circumference at a man's height from its base; the English oak and the Indian bamboo grow side by side. The Pandanus of the South Seas, stone pines from Italy, Scotch firs, Bermuda cedars, trees from Ceylon and China, and flowers from all lands. The arum lily, which in English winters we buy at a shilling a flower, is a weed here, filling swampy places with its broad green leaves and snow-white blossoms, and pigs are fed on its roots.[39]

ೋ⁀ঃ The destruction of the St Helena Botanic Garden ೋ⁀ঃ

By the 1870s, the St Helena Botanic Garden had become in effect an annex to the Governor Janisch's small but attractive Palm Villa residence. The public entrance to the gardens at the lower end was through an imposing and high iron gate which, one suspects, was opened only on request. Grant's guide to St Helena gives the following description:

> The Barrack Square is about 100 yards [91 m] long by 30 [27 m] wide. Leaving the Barrack Gate, we soon reach the Botanical Garden, just below which are staff quarters. In front of these are two fine margossa trees, whose handsome flowers, when in bloom, perfume the air with sweet odours. It is said the flowers of the margossa closely resemble the lilac. Looking through the gate of the Botanical Garden the handsome foliage of the numerous graceful trees and the pretty flowers meet the admiring gaze of the Visitor, who would be highly gratified by promenading through the shaded, well-laid-out walks. This garden contains a hedge of pomegranate (along the walk leading to the Governor's private residence), peach, guava, Kaffir date, Bussorah date, orange, chirimoya, rose apple, loquat, Kei apple, papau apple, Indian almond (1), Rambutan of China (2, called litchi here), cocoa nut palm, India-rubber (1), acacia, margossa, mahogany (5), Indian

fig (Ficus Indica) (This tree is a trlpod, two of its branches having thrown down stems which have taken root and now rival the parent stem in size.), tamarind, and cotton trees; American hemp, vegetable and flowers. The upper part of this garden is about 100 yards [91 m] long by 20 [18 m] wide, and the lower (which was partly destroyed by the flood of 1878) about 100 yards [91 m] by 15 [14 m]. It adjoins the Governor's residence called 'Palm Cottage,' deriving its name from a fan palm which grows in front of the building. Here may be observed a neat iron railing enclosing a small, tastily-laid-out garden, containing excellent and choice flowers, oleanders, grape vine (from cuttings sent by Mr. F. E. GRANT, of BOSTON U.S.A.), guava, orange, shaddock, mango, avocado pear, mulberry, robal, and other trees.[40]

In 1890 a letter to the *St Helena Guardian* advocated the planting of fig trees at the base of the steep St James' Valley as a protection against occasional rock falls.[41] The anonymous writer recalled that in the 1850s the banyan trees in the botanic garden 'proved their usefulness' against such occurrences. The same newspaper recorded the bazaars and the band concerts that were held in the garden, which by then was clearly a public pleasure garden like the old Castle Garden.[42]

But the reality was that the botanic garden was no competition to the lower Castle Garden with its proximity to government offices and the harbour. When the 20-gun American frigate USS *Delaware* arrived off Jamestown in October 1870 on its way home from its posting in East Asia, there was a carnival in the town. It was not at the botanic garden where the American naval band played 'select music', but the Castle Garden.[43]

36. The lower part of the St Helena Botanic Gardens *c.*1880, showing the elaborate entrance, water tank, pathways, split level of the gardens, high surrounding wall and the military parade ground below.
© Donal P. McCracken

There were still some interesting plants in the garden, as indicated in Benjamin Grant's 1883 list, which exceeded the plant list for Maldivia.

TABLE 25
Some of the plants in St Helena Botanic Garden, Grant's guidebook, 1883

Scientific name	Common name
Magnolia fuscata	Magnolia/Banana bush
Tamarindus indica	Tamarind
Paritium tiliaceum	Gamboge
Citrus aurantium	Bitter orange
Nephelium lappaceum	Litchi (Rambutan of China)
Erythrina corallodendron	Coral tree
Bauhinia kunthiana syn. *Bauhinia rosea*	
Carica papaya	Pawpaw
Cordyline australis syn. *Dracaena australis*	New Zealand cabbage tree (Dragon tree)
Alcurites moluccana	Candlenut/Indian walnut (Only in botanic gardens)
Ficus indica	Banyan
Cocus nucifera	Coco nut
Corypha umbraculifera	Fan palm
Phoenix dactylifera	Date palm
Vanilla planifolia	Vanilla orchid (Only in botanic gardens)
Syzygium malaccense syn. *Eugenia malaccensis*	Malay apple
Bougainvillea	
Cedrela	Mahogany
Arundinaria nana	Dwarf bamboo

While the established trees in the botanic garden flourished and continued to grow into maturity, with some 20 banyan trees being a noted feature of the upper part of Jamestown, the surrounding area was becoming down at heel and derelict again.

This decline to oblivion was not an uncommon fate of botanic gardens in the late Victorian British empire. During this period, all 14 botanic gardens in the Cape colony deteriorated into public parks, even that in the centre of Cape Town, the old Dutch East India Garden, under its able director Peter MacOwan. After the First World War, austerity, a general decline in public interest in botany and the harsher new world order meant that a great many once fine botanic gardens vanished or were relegated to public parks.

The death of the St Helena Botanic Garden, 'worn out from neglect', was long and drawn out. By the late Victorian period, its botanical use had long gone. Even its function as a public park slowly evaporated as the land turned into a waste area that was used as a dumping ground and where rats multiplied. When Rev. John Walker visited St Helena in 1886 he recorded:

> There are also Botanical Gardens at the south end of the town, which are about as ill-kept as I have seen and consist merely of a fair collection of fruit and other trees, which seem to grow or otherwise without much interference. To me the most noticeable and interesting plants in the Gardens are two or three lofty date and cocoa nut palms, the former crowned with bunches of yellow fruit. Round the stem of the date palm, about a yard from the ground, a strip of tin has been fixed, such as may be often seen in Australian orchards where opossums are numerous. The object here, I was surprised to learn, is to thwart the rats of the island, which run up the perpendicular stems with great agility, making short work of the succulent dates unless thus prevented.[44]

A decade later the following letter signed 'Ratepayer' appeared in the *St Helenian*:

> A few months ago you published two very able articles on the subject of Town Sanitation. If you or anyone else expected the reforms which you advocated to be carried out, you or they are certainly to be congratulated on the possession of a singularly Sanguine disposition, but at the same time there are sanitary measures of lesser magnitude to which you would do well to draw public attention. Amongst these would be the prevention of the Botanical Gardens being in large part used as a receptacle for the filth of a considerable section of the community. The present state of affairs is simply disgusting, and the foul emanations which now proceed from the Gardens are sufficient to cause a serious epidemic of some kind. We have a Sanitary Board with a doctor as Chairman, and another doctor as a member, but up to the present we have not seen any Sanitary improvement as a result of their deliberations. The only object of the existence of the Board seems to be to give them something to do. We have the influenza, and we now have got the measles, and if we have luck we shall have diphtheria and that before long.[45]

An editorial in the newspaper's next edition commented upon this letter, stating that it was not the Sanitary Board where the fault lay, 'but with the citizens themselves, who seem to lack either the initiative or spirit necessary to bring out

37. The Jamestown wharf, 1890s. From 1903, this photograph was used as one of St Helena's first definitive sets of pictorial postage stamps. It also appeared for many years on a St Helena postcard. However, an interesting feature was cropped from the image on the stamp and is barely visible on the postcard. On the lower left of the photograph is a young peepul tree, which has been planted on the dockside and carefully staked and protected, an indication of the importance with which Governor Sterndale regarded public tree planting. Provided by Donal P. McCracken

a better state of things'.[46] This was again illustrated when yet another attempt was made to establish an Agricultural and Horticultural Society, which soon disappeared.

In 1902, the Mount Pelée volcano erupted on the Caribbean island of Martinique and destroyed the city of Saint Pierre, along with its attractive botanic garden. The *coup de grâce* for the St Helena Botanic Garden less than three years earlier had been less dramatic but no less complete. In October 1898, the War Office in London proposed that it should take over the botanic garden's site, which the Colonial Office eventually accepted in July 1899. The site was to be used to expand the military garrison, including the construction of additional military barrack accommodation for married couples as well as a school. The War Office tried to get the land free of any payment on the grounds that St Helena made no financial contribution to its own defence. The governor Robert Armitage Sterndale (1897–1902)[47] was, however, not to be bullied. He responded:

ASTER BURCHILLII.

L. Reeve & Cᵒ London.

A.Melliss del. J.N.Fitch, lith.

Vincent Brooks,Day & Son,Imp.

PLATE 29 *Commidendrum robustum* subsp. *robustum* syn. *Aster burchellii*, the cluster-leaved gumwood. Drawn by Alice Melliss, lithograph by J.N. Fitch. This was from the last-known surviving plant which grew near the old Piquet House above West Lodge. A small-to-medium sized tree, it is now extinct.

Melliss, *St Helena*, 1875, plate 36. Provided by Donal P. McCracken.

Plate 40.

A Melliss del. J.N.Fitch, lith.

Vincent. Brooks Day & Son, Imp.

MELANODENDRON INTEGRIFOLIUM

L Reeve & Cᵒ London

PLATE 30 *Melanodendron integrifolium*, the black cabbage tree. Drawn by Alice Melliss, lithograph by J.N. Fitch. This medium-sized endemic St Helena tree, with a broad trunk was heavily exploited for its timber in the early days of settlement. It survives today on the slopes of the central ridge.

Melliss, *St Helena*, 1875, plate 40. Provided by Donal P. McCracken.

Plate 43

A Melliss del. J N Fitch lith

Vincent Brooks Day & Son Imp

LACHANODES PRENANTHIFLORA

PLATE 31 *Lachanodes arborea* syn. *L. prenanthiflora*, the she cabbage tree. Drawn by Alice Melliss, lithograph by J.N. Fitch. Once thought extinct, small numbers of this interesting, tall and slender St Helena endemic tree with distinctive reddish–purple leaves still exist on the island.

Melliss, *St Helena*, 1875, plate 43. Provided by Donal P. McCracken.

Plate 50

PLANTAGO ROBUSTA

PLATE 32 *Plantago robusta*, St Helena plantain. Drawn by Alice Melliss, lithograph by J.N. Fitch. A curious small shrubby St Helena endemic found in drier areas such as cliff faces and crevices. One of the earliest St Helena plants to be sent to Britain.

Melliss, *St Helena*, 1875, plate 50. Provided by Donal P. McCracken.

Plate 54

DICKSONIA ARBORESCENS

L. Reeve & Co. London

PLATE 33 *Dicksonia arborescens*, the St Helena tree fern. Drawing and lithograph by J.N. Fitch. This plant was first collected and taken to Britain after Captain Cook's 1770s expeditions and was much sought after by collectors and botanic gardens in the 19th century. This impressive St Helena endemic tree-fern grows up to about four metres high and is found on the slopes of the island's central ridge.

Melliss, *St Helena*, 1875, plate 54. Provided by Donal P. McCracken.

PLATE 34 Burchell's sketch of Plantation House on 19 September 1815, not greatly changed today. The garden has migrated to the right of the building, having previously been to the left and then in front of the governor's residence. On the hill is behind the trees is St Pauls, 'the country church.

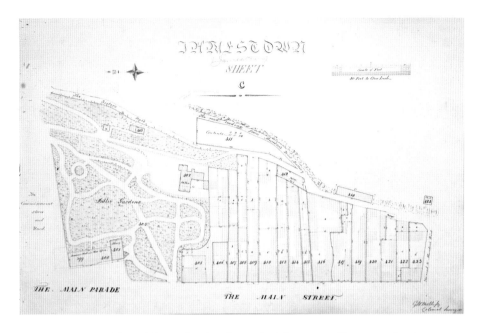

PLATE 35 Layout of the public Garden (Castle Garden), by G.W. Melliss, 1839. The Sisters Walk is immediately to the east. TNA, CO700/St Helena8, sheet C.
© The National Archives, London

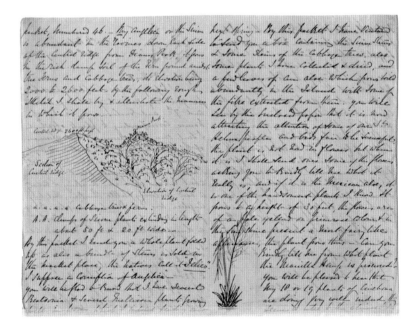

PLATE 36 John Charles Melliss's letter to Kew Gardens complete with sketch of the locations on Diana's Peak of endemic tree ferns and cabbage trees (marked a) as well as the endemic sium or jellico (*Berula burchellii*) (marked A).
Kew Archives, DC vol.181, Melliss to Hooker, 20 January 1868, f.217.

PLATE 37 Jamestown, 1872. Photograph by J. Hazward (8 March 1872) showing the Maldivia gardens in the foreground, the botanic gardens in middle ground, with the military parade ground and barracks below.
Provided by Donal P. McCracken

PLATE 38 All that remains of the St Helena Botanic Gardens today is an old banyan fig, remnants of the walling and the steps dividing the upper and lower sectors of the gardens.
© Donal P. McCracken

A new garden will have to be put in order, certain valuable trees in the old garden will have, if possible, to be transplanted, and lastly a large iron reservoir, holding about 40 tons, connected with the water supply of the town, will, with the pipes leading thereto, have to be removed from the centre of the garden to a place outside.

The governor, supported by the Colonial Office, initially requested £500 as compensation partially on the grounds of establishing a new botanic garden. A subsequent offer of £350 was accepted by the colonial secretary, Joseph Chamberlain. This sum was to be utilised to remove the iron reservoir and replace it with a concrete one; to move valuable and rare trees from the old garden; and to set the nearby Maldivia Garden in 'thorough order, making roads, laying on water, and building three concrete reservoirs'. In fact, three iron tanks, still in use today, were erected just outside the upper section of the old botanic garden. When the destruction was complete most of the 18th century botanic garden was obliterated except for a section in the upper part where a few trees remained.[48] It is ironic that less than a decade later the military would evacuate St Helena.

Governor Sterndale tried to keep his word about a new botanic garden. Maldivia was purchased for the sum of £391 and renamed the Maldivia Botanical Garden. In his 1899 annual report he commented:

The old Botanical Garden in Jamestown has also been sold to the Imperial Government, as they adjoin the new barracks. There are some fine trees (which will be preserved as far as possible), but as a botanical garden it was useless, as the soil is thoroughly worn out, and the new gardens at Maldivia are in every way more suitable for the purpose.[49]

That same year, at both Maldivia Garden and Plantation House, 225 American vine grafts imported from the Cape were planted, many vines on the island having being killed off some decades before by the fungal disease oidium. From the early 1880s fruit had been attacked and 'more or less been destroyed' by the ravages of the Mediterranean fruit fly, so attempts to introduce new species of fruit trees in the Edwardian era were very important for local gardeners.

Following the ravages of a peach fly on the island, for example, a new selection of fruit trees was planted at Maldivia, including what was believed to be the island's first cherry tree. For a number of years there was, as can be seen in Figure 9, a modest income obtained from sales of fruit.

FIGURE 9

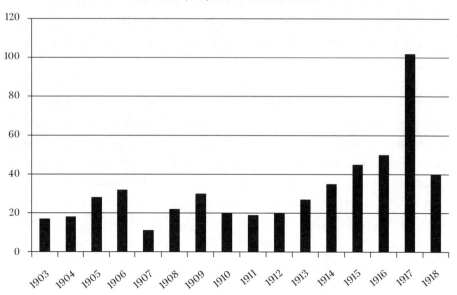

It should be noted that several of the old mahogany trees (*Swietenia mahogani*) from the old botanic garden still survive, one in particular being a very fine specimen worthy of protection. Seeds from these survivors were collected and planted out, presumably in Maldivia and the Plantation House nurseries.

An account of the Castle Garden in the early 1880s is worth quoting:

> The Garden is a favorite resort of the cream of the Island for promenading, and in former years it used to be thronged with persons who assembled there to listen to the sweet music discoursed by the fine band of the late St. Helena Regiment (styled the 'Old Saints') twice a week in fine weather, and that of the St. Helena Volunteers on moonlight nights. Bazaars are generally held in the Garden, it being the only place in Town adapted for such. It contains a few nice walks which are shaded by graceful trees, such as evergreens, oleanders, gamboge, India rubber, margossa, Cape yew, cotton, Barbadoes' pride, tamarind, almond and banyans, and flowers.[50]

Fifteen years of decline later, the picture was rather different. The Castle Garden had a bad name and had for some time been 'the haunt of noisy rough lads and persons of doubtful character'. The garden was also without a 'competent gardener'. Sterndale tried to take matters in hand with some success, despite the natural problems of a poor soil and scarcity of rainfall in the lower valley. Manure from the commissariat cattle yard was brought in to assist new plantings. Several orchids were also introduced. The governor also had the three gates into the garden locked at 9 o'clock every evening, which helped matters. A cast-iron fountain was procured that still stands in the garden, though in bad need of restoration. It was erected to commemorate Queen Victoria's diamond jubilee in 1897, being donated to St Helena by Governor Sterndale.[51] Three goldfish were subsequently added by local entrepreneur W. A. Thorpe (1845–1918) and the Union Castle shipping line promised to bring out from Britain anything that was needed for the garden and museum. Sterndale would have liked to grow the spectacular *Victoria amazonica* giant lily in St Helena. This was much prized by Victorian curators and Sterndale must have seen it growing outdoors during his varied career.[52] He had spent a life working in the Indian civil service and was also a distinguished artist and a keen naturalist, having edited the *Journal of the Bombay Natural History Society*. Mention needs also to be made of a small but picturesque iron drinking fountain in the main street of Jamestown, erected in September 1891 to commemorate the 9 people who were killed and the 12 injured when a serious rock fall destroyed 14 houses in the town on 17 April 1890.[53] Such acts were appreciated, as were the monthly receptions Sterndale held for government officials at Plantation House.

Within the grounds of the Castle Garden, Sterndale established a small but interesting museum where he gave classes on taxidermy for those interested. There were stuffed animals, some of which were donated by Rowland Ward Limited, the famous taxidermy firm in Piccadilly, London. Also there were shells and mineralogical specimens, as well as a glass case with indigenous St Helena ferns collected by Captain D. B. Thomson. Sterndale was clearly greatly upset when the old endemic bastard gumwood tree (*Psiadia rotundifolia*) growing in its own enclosure in the middle of a field at Longwood died in 1897, so adding to the extinct St Helena ebony tree (*Trochetiopsis melanoxylon*).[54]

Sterndale considered introducing various kinds of rubber-producing trees to the island and consulted Kew about this. His attitude was a simple one:

> In a small and poor island like St Helena it is of importance to encourage everything which may bring in some return, however small.

In this instance, the climate was not tropical enough for a successful rubber industry.[55]

ᛒᚱᚾᚷ War again ᛒᚱᚾᚷ

Then the military returned in numbers as war clouds were quickly appearing far to the south-east in the South African sky. The streets of Jamestown witnessed scenes of noisy activity and reckless driving as four-in-hand mule wagons dashed along them disturbing the tranquillity. St Helena had been closely connected with the Cape for at least a century. Now, during the Anglo-Boer War (October 1899 to May 1902), St Helena was used as one of the colonial islands to confine Boer prisoners of war. Large camps were established on the island at Deadwood and Broadbottom, with Boer POWs arriving from February 1900. Most of the POWs departed in October 1902. Needless to say the economic situation changed, with imports doubling between 1899 and 1900. There were also jobs for islanders – which in turn meant that many could save enough to emigrate. Against this, the cost of living rose sharply during the war.

Another negative impact of so many POWs living on the island was the large-scale destruction of trees for firewood for the prison camps. Writing to Sir William Thiselton-Dyer, then director of Kew Gardens, Governor Sterndale observed:

> I was about to write to you for help, for St Helena has been cruelly deforested since the arrival of the Boers. I could of course control the Government forests but the high prices paid for fuel by the Army Service Corps induced many private owners to cut down every tree they could lay hands on and the hillsides near Napoleon's Tomb, once covered with pine trees, are now bare.[56]

Some Boer POWs were employed in tree planting both at Plantation House and Half Tree Hollow. In the post-war period, much energy would go into forestry on St Helena, the island eventually having its own timber mill. But some dangers never disappeared. In the Edwardian period we still find governors denouncing goats – 'that unpleasant and voracious quadruped' – for destroying young saplings which were being planted out in great numbers in government woods. Attempts at planting up the sides of Jamestown's steep valley and in Lemon Valley failed. But roadside planting was more successful, so along with the apple, pear and plum trees from the Cape also came the coral trees (*Erythrina caffra*) which had been present on the island since at least the early 19th century and which now became a more common and lasting attractive feature of many rural roads in the centre of St Helena.[57]

On 10 November 1900, an 'International Exhibition' was held in Jamestown, which while modest caused great excitement on the island. Botanically sourced exhibits included wood carvings and crystallised fruits. Emily Jackson, the pioneer of the local lace cottage industry, displayed her students' work and 'a beautiful and original' exquisitely designed piece of lace by herself 'composed of arum lilies and leaves with the words "St Helena".[58] The arum lily is still very much a feature of damp parts of the island and was for many years the floral emblem of the island.

During the Anglo-Boer war the British military occupied the Castle Garden in Jamestown, which became an encampment of bell tents for 40 prisoners who were working on improving the nearby landing wharf. This was an interesting example of a public garden being occupied by the military in wartime, another instance being Hong Kong Botanical Gardens during the Second World War. A poignant photograph from this period appears in Emily Jackson's book on St Helena. showing a dog drinking out of the iron Jubilee Fountain in the Castle Garden, with the museum and the military tents in the background (page 251, illustration 32). Apart from the Longwood saga, old St Helena houses used to accommodate prisoners in the 1890s included Francis Plain House, Maldivia House and Rosemary Hall, where King Dinuzulu and his entourage were accommodated at one time or another. Boer general Piet Cronje was lodged in Kent Cottage in Half Tree Hollow. The availability of these homes suggest that the age of the St Helena gentry and their gardens had passed.

With Sterndale's departure on leave and his subsequent death in Britain in October 1902, St Helena lost for many years any hope of re-establishing a botanic garden on the island. Governor Gallwey's 1902 report bluntly stated, 'There is no Botanical Station in the island. There are Government Gardens in Jamestown in charge of an ordinary labourer.'[59]

The following year Gallwey noted:

> The Government Gardens in Jamestown are the nearest approach to a Botanical Station in the Colony. The soil is very poor, which, added to the fact that the annual rainfall in Jamestown is only seven inches, makes it impossible, with the unskilled labour and small funds available, to attempt more than a careful supervision of the fruit trees in the gardens.[60]

The end of an era

In 1905 Henry Gallwey made the astute comment that 'although the majority of the people of St Helena are certainly poor, there is very little real poverty'.[61] The events of the following year would result in matters changing for the worse for those inhabitants of the island. For 1906 was probably the darkest year in St Helena's history. It was the year that, for the first time in its history as a British colony, the island was denuded of its garrison. As the governor succinctly put it, 'without the garrison the Island became a derelict'. The island fortress was now surplus to requirements. And with the departure of the military went the islanders' only consistent employer of labour. The situation could have been saved had an earlier plan for the island to become a Royal Navy base been implemented. But the navy had Ascension Island for itself, with a small civilian population under its control. One of the Edwardian governors had advocated the construction of docks in Jamestown Bay, which would certainly have altered the picture. But now St Helena was left without a means of self-support and with mail ships being paid to call. Talk of expanding the growing of vegetables which were produced in the government gardens and of establishing a vegetable-canning plant came to nothing. A hare-brained scheme to bring out a trained horticulturist for a mere two months to train islanders how to grow vegetables also did not materialise.[62]

Salaries of officials on St Helena were reduced, including a 10 per cent cut for Governor Gallwey, who had worked tirelessly in the island's cause, and who also now had his £200 table allowance abolished. Things got so desperate that scrap metal was collected, including old lead pipes and a discarded ship's cable, all shipped off to Britain where it was sold and brought the beleaguered island government £367. A further £285 was raised by selling off timber stocks and some government stores. It was out of this transaction that funding was raised for material to construct a government flax mill in 1907. A government grant also helped restart the island's lace-making endeavour.

This dire situation proved the kickstart for the plantation crop which would keep the St Helenian economy ticking over for half a century and provide some labour for an increasingly impoverished island community. Known as flax, this was in fact New Zealand flax (*Phormium tenax*), used for producing a rough twine, rather than the ordinary flax (*Linum usitatissimum*) from which linen is produced. Suggestions that the latter be tried in St Helena were quickly quashed by Kew on the grounds that it would not do well in the tropics. New Zealand flax was another matter, and its potential was pushed by the island's government, particularly in the light of yet another failed attempt to establish cotton as a cash crop as well as the failure of the fish-curing business. On top of this a serious deluge in April 1904 resulted in much damage across the island, including to market gardens which were swept away down steep hillsides.

While in New Zealand on the *Endeavour* voyage (1768–1771) Joseph Banks had collected seed from a useful plant known as harakeke to the Māori, who used its fibrous leaves for many purposes, including to make *pākē* (capes or cloaks). He was greatly excited by the plant's economic potential, writing in his journal that it would 'doub[t]less be a great acquisition to England'.[63] It was said to have been introduced to St Helena about 1853, though, as seen in an earlier chapter, we now know that Burchell recorded it growing at West Lodge in 1809. In 1868, Charles Melliss wrote to Sir Joseph Hooker at Kew Gardens:

By this packet I have ventured to send you a box containing the Suim stems (Jellico or St Helena Angelica – *Berula burchellii*) & some stems of the cabbage trees, also some plants I have collected & dried, and a few leaves of an aloe which grows wild abundantly in the island with some of the fibre extracted from them. You will see by the enclosed papers that it is now attracting the attention of some of our St Helena people and bids fair to be successful.

He made a small sketch of the plant at the bottom corner of the letter.[64] In 1873 Rev. Henry Whitehead also sent Kew specimens of the flax leaf along with an offer to send Kew specimens of the island's flora. One suspects that when he did this, Kew was rather irritated by his requests to forward on some of the plants in the cases he sent to various friends in England.[65]

Joseph Hooker never lost his curiosity about St Helena. Writing to Charles Darwin in 1879, he returned to the theme he had expounded in the *Gardeners' Chronicle* 12 years earlier:

I have come to the conclusion that the Flora of St. Helena is very S. African and not in the least North Atlantic, and as the plants must have got to St. Helena before the insects, these must, if they came from the North, indicate that the Flora has survived the Glacial epoch, i.e. had come from the Cape before it.[66]

Despite much talk earlier, it was not until 1875 that the first steam-driven flax mill was opened on St Helena. An attractive print illustrating the long driveway to Longwood House and dated about 1852/1853 shows New Zealand flax serving as an established, flowering hedge on the west side of the road, with Signal Hill and the Barn looming in the distance. The Jamestown flax mill was owned by the Colonial and Foreign Fibre Company and had 16 machines driven by two engines. In its best year the mill produced just over 100 tons or 615 bales of fibre. This was worth only £1,867, however, so the earliest experiment at flax growing and fibre production failed and in 1881 the mill closed. Subsequently, so did the mill of Messrs W. Erridge and Company. A quarter of a century later, the crisis of the Edwardian era led to the revival of the enterprise. It was no coincidence that Sir Daniel Morris's report on St Helena was finally published in 1906 and that the new government-owned mill at Longwood commenced work on 2 December 1907, with Mr A. W. Hall as manager.[67]

Largesse from the Union Castle shipping line had been promised in 1905 thanks to the intervention of Governor Gallwey, with the shipping line agreeing to carry to Britain six shipments of 10 tons each of flax free of freight charge, a target which was only reached in 1907.

The First World War saw St Helena under martial law. 'I cannot speak too highly of the loyal and patriotic spirit shown by the whole population,' wrote the governor. A wartime garrison appeared but it would depart when the conflict concluded and did not employ great numbers of local inhabitants. There was, however, some growth in the flax industry. Not surprisingly, as is clearly seen from Figure 10, given the demands of war, fibre exports increased in monetary value from £7,439 in 1914 to £61,136 in 1918.

38. Hutt's Gate. This clachan of houses with its old tavern, once famous for a dextrous cook who could make 'a veal cutlet out of mutton chop', was at the junction where the road turned up to Longwood. The house is where General Bertrand stayed for a while. It was frequently visited by Napoleon, being at the limit of the area that he might roam in daylight without a British officer in attendance. The emperor liked to walk down the slope of the then pretty garden to the valley below where he was eventually to be buried. This photograph, dating from the first half of the 20th century, shows only a few stunted trees surviving in an otherwise bleak landscape.
Provided by Donal P. McCracken

FIGURE 10

Exports (£) of processed fibre from St Helena during the First World War

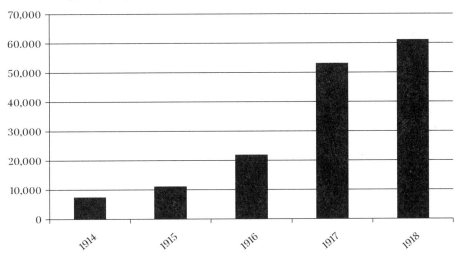

Impressive as this seems, the reality was that even with a phenomenal eightfold growth in export value due to war demand and high prices, by 1918 the St Helena government flax mill employed only 25 men. By this time there were also three privately owned mills, one at Broadbottom and another at Sandy Bay, both owned by Messrs Solomon and Company, and one at Hutt's Gate owned by Messrs Deason Brothers. The labour force of all the mills in 1918 amounted to 183 men and 59 women. By 1923, six mills were employing 300 workers. To these figures must be added the low-waged labourers who worked the flax plantations, which by the end of the war covered about 1,000 acres. With a population of some 3,700, the percentage of the population employed remained very low. Besides, flax growing was not without problems and thanks to economic depression in the early 1930s, all the island's mills closed for a period, resulting in serious economic distress for many islanders.[68] By then Deason's had about 2,200 acres under flax, Solomon's 2,000 acres and Thorpe's 940 acres.[69]

The flax industry eventually restarted again after the Second World War and in 1946 177 islanders were employed in the flax mills. In 1949 the mills were re-equipped, with the eight surviving mills employing 237 workers by 1956. This was a brief revival and by 1966 there were only 42 workers. The last flax mill on St Helena closed in 1970.[70]

The significance of these mills to the saga of St Helena's old gardens was twofold. Firstly, they came to dominate the agricultural sector and thereby destroyed the already dying larger farms which had flourished in the Company days. This is well illustrated by the fact that by 1931 three companies – Deason's, Solomon's and Thorpe's – owned three-quarters of the land in private hands. William Alexander Thorpe, owner of the Mount Pleasant, Woodlands and Woodcot estates, had, perhaps not surprisingly, the largest cattle herd on the island.[71] The death of the mills, of course, altered this, but not with the resurgence of a new gentry class. In 1966, the following land use situation existed on St Helena:

728 acres described as bush (41 per cent)
512 acres for grazing (28 per cent)
355 acres still under flax (20 per cent)
206 acres cultivated (11 per cent)

Of this last category, only one farmer was stated to have more than ten acres.[72] The second impact was even starker. The flax mills were invariably close to an old planter's house and built on ground formerly occupied by the garden or arboretum, which inevitably perished, save for the occasional surviving tree. Flax replaced the goats of old as the destroyer of the indigenous pastures, and it now also decimated what was left of the old plantation gardens.

The First World War led to a drive to create allotments to try and make St Helena self-sufficient in food. It was reported in 1917 that 'the inhabitants again suffered during the year from temporary shortages of foodstuffs of one sort or another'. To alleviate this situation, gardens and park land were put under the plough, including those at Plantation House. This had actually started in the early 1900s, before the war, after the garrison had withdrawn, and the 'Government garden' was in part put to vegetable growing. The 1903 annual report recorded that this was done with the intention of growing feed for government transport animals. Also at Plantation House, four acres of woodland damaged by white ant was cleared for flax growing.

Plantation House itself was now in a sorry state. Between May 1928 and February 1931, it had to undergo extensive restoration, with the governor, Sir Charles Harper, having to live in Prince's Lodge.[73] The Plantation House tree nursery continued to exist during these interwar years and distributed hundreds of trees annually to the public and for planting on wastelands. In 1917, Acting-Governor Lieutenant-Colonel W. Dixon began growing saplings of the very rare endemic St Helena redwood (*Trochetiopsis erythroxylon*), which he reported were doing well.[74]

As the decades after the First World War passed with New Zealand flax as the staple crop, the island was condemned to become a peasant economy with low wages and few opportunities. By the 1960s, St Helena was producing 17.5 per cent of the world supply of flax, much of it used by the Royal Mail for mailbags. Mauritian hemp (*Furcraea foetida*) was also tried and was grown on a small scale for a number of years.

This minor success came at a terrible price, exacerbating the incalculable ecological harm already caused and destroying indigenous colonies of surviving plants, especially on the slopes of Diana's Peak. Acting-Governor Dixon recorded in 1918:

> It is much to be regretted that two or three owners of land on the ridges commenced considerable clearing of the indigenous ferns and vegetation growing there in order to plant flax. Setting aside the interest from a botanical point of view of this vegetation, its great importance due to its effect on the rainfall and water supply of the Island should never be overlooked, and great stress was laid on it by Sir D. Morris in a Report made by him in 1884. The condition which the Island, its crops, and its population would be in with a much reduced rainfall needs no explanation, and it is to be hoped that no more clearing on the ridge lands will be carried out.[75]

St Helena was certainly now not a place for either elegant or indeed wild places to flourish, though the memory of fine gardens lingered on. In November 1919, Governor Sir Harry Cordeaux pressed the colonial secretary in London on the issue:

> I am strongly of [the] opinion that any grant which it may be possible to obtain for the purpose of developing the resources of this Colony should be devoted towards the establishment of a botanical garden for the promotion of improved methods of agriculture and the development of the numerous industrial plants already in the island, on the lines suggested by Sir David [Daniel] Morris.

Cordeaux had been born in India and like many colonial officers he had a keen interest in natural history. He was especially active when deputy commissioner of British Somaliland, where he identified a subspecies of dik-dik antelope that was later named after him.

Although Cordeaux was supported by Kew, which advocated the expenditure annually of £1,000 to resurrect the gardens at St Helena or establish a plant experimental base, nothing came of this. Governor Cordeaux also encouraged Captain Mainwaring's rope-making project at Longwood, another St Helena endeavour which was to fail, as had several previous attempts at whaling and commercial fishing.[76]

39. This interwar postcard shows the old planters' houses scattered along the valley with, on the right, flax laid out to dry. St Paul's Cathedral is in the background.
Provided by Donal P. McCracken

It was only in 1928 that the fortunes of the Castle Garden revived, when the South African Harry Bruins-Lich (1904–1977) was appointed horticulturist at Plantation House. Despite drought and flood, for many decades the tree nursery had been producing saplings for distribution, frequently free of charge, many to replace plantation woodland decimated by white ant. Under Bruins-Lich's stewardship, £800 was spent renovating the Castle Garden, turning what had become 'a waste and derelict open [space] into a most attractive garden'.[77] Unfortunately, in 1932, as a cost-saving measure, Bruins-Lich was retrenched. Back in South Africa, he eventually became a renowned director of public parks in Pretoria (1942–1967).

St Helena's interwar export of arum lilies from 1935 was yet another plant experiment which failed, though this time owing to war, insect infestation and later Japanese competition. More focused destruction occurred during the Second World War when as a wartime propaganda exercise the old Castle Garden was sectioned into allotments – a 'futile gesture of digging up the lawns to grow a few heat-bitten cabbages and withered beans'.[78] Other continued attempts at improvement in the mid-20th century included the work undertaken by the island's agriculture and forestry sector, with its headquarters inland at Scotland. Despite its name, this old house and farm dating from 1834 was named after a local called John Scott, not the country.[79]

As for the old botanic garden, much of the area above that remained open ground for many decades after the military vacated in 1906. At times it was little more than a refuse dump; at one point it was allotments. When the Duke of Connaught visited St Helena in 1910 a triumphal arch was erected over the road beside the old botanic garden site with the Gaelic greeting 'cead mille failte'.[80] In the early 1950s, the final blow came – two blocks of flats were erected, called to this day Botanical Garden. All that remains of the real botanic garden are the old fig tree and a portion of the old walling from Mr Burchell's first and only curatorship. As for Maldivia up the hill, in the 1930s three large bee hives arrived there, with Philip Gosse reporting:

> At Maldivia by Jamestown there still grow a few banana trees which produce short, thick, yellow fruit, delicious and scented, unrecognizable as belonging to the same family as the tasteless and enormous plantains which pass for bananas in England.[81]

40. The lost world, Sandy Bay. A ruined cottage in the lower Sandy Bay Valley, where once the area bustled with British troops and workers from a nearby lime works. Today it is a remote and wild part of the island.
© Patricia McCracken

Postscript

The way through the woods

St Helena lies within the tropics but is blessed with a year-round fairly temperate climate coupled with plenty of bright, sunny days. The fairly limited fluctuation in climate has been well recorded, which usually neither prevents the establishment of gardens nor indeed, if properly managed, entails their destruction, though occasional drought and downpour have taken their toll over the centuries. For a third of a millennium, the island has developed a rich heritage of garden history. That it has been shaky at times was not so much the fault of the plants or the gardeners who attended them, but of the economic vicissitudes of an economy which was based on military foundations.

It is difficult to assess the significance of the St Helena Botanic Garden in its heyday. Printed reports or visitor guides do not exist for the period. Even what was grown there remains largely a mystery, with one or two occasional references as well as the lists attached in the appendices of this book. As a resting station for plants en route for Britain or the West Indies, it certainly assisted greatly. The botanic garden also acted as a base for Porteous and Burchell and, to a lesser extent, Roxburgh. It provided the first two men with a salary, enabling them to experiment with plants of possible economic value to the island and to investigate and collect the flora of the island, indigenous and exotic. Indigenous plants at one time or another did grow in the garden, but there was no continuity and the garden did not act as a nursery for indigenous flora.

What is more extraordinary about St Helena Botanic Garden was that its heyday – when it prospered and when botanists and an able horticulturist were associated with the garden – coincided approximately with a prolonged period of Anglo-French warfare. This is very unusual, for warfare tends to militate against the study of scientific botany and the prosperity of botanic gardens.

Today the original St Helena Botanic Garden is gone; only a few of its trees survive among the buildings of the 19th century and two blocks of flats. The Castle Garden is attractively laid out. Alongside the giant figs a few of the island's indigenous plants grow. In the rest of the island, there are several designated areas on the high ground as well as near to the new airport millennium forest where indigenous flora has been re-established. However, St Helena does not have a botanic garden to showcase its endemic flora and the history of introduced exotics, an omission which needs to be rectified.

The trend today is for conservation areas where indigenous plants may be seen in their natural environment. But there is still something to be said for a confined area within an urban setting devoted to specific species of interesting or rare indigenous plants, readily accessible to the general public and discerning tourists. This is particularly the case where otherwise access to such plants is dependent upon stout shoes, able limbs and no qualms about heights. In the case of St Helena, the delicacy of many of the endemic plants also necessitates a close inspection to appreciate each species. This cannot be achieved from a car window or staring up a steep hill or down a precipitous cliff. Besides, reclaiming the ridges of the island's central highlands is proving a tedious and lengthy process and will

41. The end of the old era. This poignant photograph shows one of the old planter's houses, Bamboo Hedge at Sandy Bay, beside a New Zealand flax mill. The gardens had gone with the old order. In more modern times this land would house Solomon's piggery.
Provided by Donal P. McCracken

remain so until the decision is taken to completely clear the massive sweeps of New Zealand flax and convert the land into indigenous woodland. Equally important is the need to then maintain those areas cleared. While the work initiated by George Benjamin heralded a pioneering start, subsequent progress has been steady but not dramatic.

There is also a disappointing lack of planting in private gardens of at least some endemic plants, though many retain the lushness of an Indian hill station or a well-watered South African Karoo or Eastern Cape garden. While babies toes or some such might delight the eye in Sandy Bay, might they not do so equally in some other areas where soil and microclimate permit?

In 1868 Charles Melliss wrote to Sir Joseph Hooker at Kew Gardens, 'we should also Establish a Garden of native plants and try to preserve them from disappearing'.[1] The Castle Garden has a small plot of endemic plants. It also has a handful of older centenary trees. The rest of the growth might as well have come from Bournemouth's main municipal esplanade park – unusual to local eyes, perhaps, but not a draw for the new generation of cosmopolitan tourists.

The garden landscaping is more memorable. Part of the charm of the Castle Garden is that the serpentine paths follow those which existed 180 years ago. They must be retained intact. The charming Victorian cast-iron water fountain where the dog was photographed drinking when the garden was a POW camp needs to be restored to its former glory. But the rest of this 320-year-old garden requires a complete master plan as a modern botanic garden. In the centre of Jamestown, opposite an hotel and just down the street from Jamestown's grand old Consulate Hotel, now restored, the Castle Garden has the potential to be a key, easy-to-reach tourist site.

Today the purpose of a botanic garden is twofold: to be a resource which can be used for scientific research purposes and a venue which is informative and educational for the plant specialist and the general public alike. The Castle Garden certainly has the potential to fulfil these two important functions. It can provide an accessible showcase for St Helena's surviving endemic plants, or at least for those which will grow there. Secondly, it can act as a botanical and agronomic archive, growing those plants introduced in numerous attempts to provide the island with a staple crop which would generate substantial income and provide widespread employment. As we have seen, such plants ranged from the *Pinus pinaster* to the mulberry tree for silkworms, and from the cinchona tree for quinine to the ubiquitous flax. Equally important in establishing such a garden is the vital necessity to have full, clear explanatory modern signage. Without that, a botanic garden soon deteriorates into a public park.

The island's two adjacent arboreta, the Clifford Arboretum and the George Benjamin Arboretum near Carson's Gate, also offer great potential if well curated and marketed. The grandeur of the old trees – in some instances breathtaking – and the more recently planted indigenous trees offer curious gardeners, professional botanists and environmentalists much to ponder.

As for the old plantation estate gardens, in a way they pose the least challenge as what is required here is initiative and drive from modern owners. The advent of modern air tourists, restricted in numbers but generally fairly affluent and well educated, means that showy 18th-century plantation gardens, coupled with representations of the rare indigenous flora of the island, offer potential revenue generation for the owners, especially with the backdrop of what were in effect fairly modest Georgian farmhouses frequently perched in romantic and dramatic settings. Government of St Helena restoration grants both for properties and gardens would create a lasting legacy for the much-discussed but elusive economic stimulus. An 1881 pamphlet talking of Prince's Lodge, then owned by the legendary Saul Solomon, commented upon the trees which existed on the property: Bermuda cedars, eucalypti, white olives and willows, as well as the Australian grass tree (*Xanthorrhoea australis*).[2] Today across the island there still remains a scattering of old trees, ghosts of a previous age, both indigenous and exotic. These need to be recorded and named where appropriate as heritage trees.

Last but certainly not least, there are the homely yet striking gardens of the Saints themselves. In the 1966 St Helena census, it was recorded that there were 1,016 gardens on the island: 283 kitchen gardens, 101 food gardens and 632 ordinary gardens.[3] Today, domestic kitchen gardens, with their splashes of coloured favourites, have an appealing feel about them. This could mean, however, that there is a danger of the island's indigenous flora becoming the preserve of professional botanists and visiting scientists, with the island's endemic flora relegated to the school excursion for its remaining inhabitants.

The cross-cutting strands of St Helena's flora reflect the island's history as few other places in the world do. St Helena was for many centuries a hub for exploration, trade, warfare and travellers. The island's flora reflects the extraordinary diversity of those who visited and their journeys, not least with plants from southern Africa and Asia. It is clear that the indigenous flora should take precedence but, equally, there is no prospect of the island being returned to its natural stage of vegetation. Over the years, various schemes have been initiated both to protect and expand the areas where indigenous flora survives. In part, the Darwin Plus project has opened a new chapter in this endeavour. Darwin Plus is a British government initiative to provide environmental funding for the United Kingdom's Overseas

Territories. In January 2019, Andrew Turner reported the following in *The Sentinel*, St Helena's only newspaper:

A project valued at nearly £300,000, aimed at restoring endemic habitats in St Helena's Peaks National Forest, has been approved by the Darwin Plus Initiative.

Invasive [alien] plants make up 99% of all the plant life on St Helena. In the Peaks, invasives are blocking the growth of severely endangered endemic plants such as the He Cabbage and Whitewood, both of which have a worldwide population – all located in the Peaks – of less than 50.

And in terms of invertebrates, St Helena has an astounding 470 endemic species – more than the rest of the UK and its Overseas Territories put together. The survival of these endemic invertebrates relies heavily on the survival of the endemic plants at the Peaks National Forest.

Only seven people are currently employed on-island to take care of the endemic invertebrate habitat that is the Peaks.

But this month, it was announced that the resources dedicated to restoring the Peaks' environment will increase. The Terrestrial Conservation Section (TCS) of the Environmental Management Division (EMD) on St Helena has been granted £294,309 for a three-year project named 'Fragmented cloud forest habitat rehabilitation through innovative invasive plant management.'

The project is due to start in April 2019. It is funded by Darwin Plus, and will focus on managing invasive plants in order to restore habitats for endemic plants and invertebrates.

'As soon as a plant flowers, insects will come to it and then they will take the pollen to the next flower, but the next flower is likely a weed,' said Terrestrial Conservation Officer Lourens Malan. 'With this new project, we're going to take these important remaining [endemic] trees and slowly expand the habitats outwards.'

The project will also focus on ensuring other non-endemic insects can effectively pollinate endemic plants.

According to Lourens, the project team will make corridors of endemic ferns between endemic trees, so that insects can move more freely and carry pollen more effectively.

Planting ferns will also have the advantage of increasing water capture in the Peaks, as ferns collect moisture from the air very effectively and then soak it into the soil. This means the Peaks will store more water, even in dry seasons.

In preparation for the work to commence, the TCS hired additional help, including a dedicated Project Manager. All new employees will, according to Lourens, be putting 'boots on the ground' to see the project through.

This project could also be highly beneficial to the more isolated endemic plants that grow on inaccessible cliff faces. These plants are extremely difficult for conservationists to work on because of their location, but by creating these corridors for insects would mean they can survive there more naturally.[4]

The slow and stop-start progress of propagating indigenous plants on the ridge of Diana's Peak over the years well illustrates the problems of calling back the past. While the removal of vast tracts of New Zealand flax is essential, careful consideration needs to be made as to how that land can be re-indigenised – and to what purpose. The Royal Botanic Gardens, Kew has been actively involved in this endeavour. One of Kew's current primary research and conservation thrusts involves St Helena, Dr Colin P. Clubbe overseeing Kew's endeavours relating to the island.

Apart from its 250-year historic link with the island, Kew Gardens has in more recent years contributed extensively to the island's indigenous conservation programmes. Kew's collection of the island's living plant specimens and herbaria specimens continues to grow. A significant seed-collecting programme has been undertaken both on the island and for repatriation from Kew's living collections. The latter has included thousands of seeds of the St Helena boxwood, *Mellissia begonifolia*. This rarely seeds on the island, so plants were hand pollinated at Kew. Kew has been at the forefront in assisting with work of the environmental rehabilitation programme based at the island's endemic nursery at Scotland.[5]

The gardens of St Helena, which once fell under the guardianship of the East India Company, such as the two in Jamestown, and Plantation House and Longwood gardens, are worthy of remembrance and, where possible, resurrection. The efforts put into revitalising and restoring Napoleon's garden of the 1810s deserve sound praise. But there are also the gardens which once adjoined the old settler farmhouses. Many of these are now, sadly, gone. These include Horseridge House, Old Luffkins and Rosemary Hall. The 1966 St Helena census records that, excluding Crown properties and those of the two companies W. A. Thorpe and Sons and Solomon, only 5 landholders owned more than 50 acres. A further 129 owners had between 2 and 49 acres, and 406 possessed under 2 acres. Of cultivated land, only one held ten acres or more.[6] The old St Helena Company system had long since gone.

One healthy development in recent years has been a recognition of the tourist value of these singular homesteads in the middle of the Atlantic Ocean. W. A. Thorpe pioneered this with his restoration of the old Sandy Bay home of the Dovetons. But in more recent years Teutonic Hall, Rock Rose Cottage and Wranghams have also been saved from imminent destruction, as has the old and historic Hutt's Gate inn and store building.[7] What is now required is some landscaping to set off these old properties of St Helena to best effect. As long as the land is available this is not too difficult, as the layout pattern was fairly universal: an open lawn and/or pasturage in front of the house, with possibly an avenue of trees to each side of the grassland. Then shrubs around the house and an arboretum to the rear. This process would run parallel with the admirable drive to promote and expand the growth of indigenous plants. In this endeavour, the systematic removal of the acres of redundant flax plants is necessary. This is, however, not a simple task, with cleared land exposed to the aggressive expansionist tendencies of invasive species, which are prone to smother the more reticent native plants. Similarly, the problem of cross-variety breeding in some instances poses a real challenge to botanists and horticulturists alike.

St Helena is special because its heritage is generally clear and visible to all. The redoubtable Lady Ross, once first lady of St Helena and a long-time, resident observed, 'Our island is an emerald set in bronze.'[8] One truth about that emerald remains deceptively hidden. Beneath the fortress island story and the Napoleonic saga lies another factor adding to St Helena's glories: its status as the world's garden island.

Appendices

Appendix I

'A Catalogue of Trees and Shrubs growing in the Honble East India Companys New Botanic Garden in Jamses Vally, St Helena, 1789'

Notes:

1 Source: British Library, India Office Records (IOR), G/32/163, St Helena: Miscellaneous Papers.
2 The list was compiled by Henry Porteous some two years after the botanic gardens had been established.
3 The list was made for submission to the council of the East India Company in London.
4 'Those marked X have been lately introduced' is noted on the list.
5 Where possible, modern spellings have been used but nomenclature has not been updated.

Latin names		English names	Observations	
Guaiacum officinale	X	Official lignum vitae	3 plants healthy	
Camellia japonica	X	Single white flowering camellia		
___ flo pline alba	X	Double white flowering D°	These two varieties are the most beautiful shrubs when in flower that nature or art can produce. We have 4 plants in the garden which grow vigorously.	
___ flor pline rubro	X	Double scarlet camellia		
Citrus aurantium	X	Seville orange	2 plants	
___ limon	X	Lemon fron China	3 plants	
___orientale	X	Willow leaved orange	2 plants	
___ humilis	X	Dwarf nutmeg orange	4 plants	Healthy
___ decumanum	X	Shaddock	2 plants	
___ medica	X	Citron	2 plants	
Dracaena erecta	X	Chinese dragon		
Croton sebiferum	X	Chinese tallow		
Musa sapientum	X	Common plantain		
___ var. fruit. flavo	X	Bassine plantain	We have sent several plants of this variety to the different plantation[s] which grows vigorously	

Latin names		English names	Observations
___ var. *fruit purpurio*	X	Bassine plantain ? fruit	This variety Mr Brooke had from Capt Burrows it is said to be much preferable to all 6 plants in the garden the vegetation of which seems more rapid than the common plantain.
Annona muricata		Custard apple/ soursop	Healthy
___ *asiatica*		Asiatic D°	
___ *glabra*		Smooth D°	
Amygdalus persica		Common peach	
___ var.		Flat peach	This fruit is peculiar to China and is said to be one of the most delicious fruits of the East. We have 2 plants both of which are healthy.
Prunus species		Plum tree	Received from China and planted out of which there were 2 varieties one of which is said to resemble our green gage the other having fruit of a deep crimson.
Pistacia terebinthus		Turpentine tree	2 plants both grow well.
Salsola prostrata		Samphire	From which Barilla for soap Glass An may be obtained equally good as from the salsola native or soda all the plants of that genus possessing that quality See Mr Brooke's experiments on the subject.
Hypericum monogymum		Chinese St John's wort	2 plants both in flower
Myrtus zeylanica		Zeylon myrtle	1 plant Healthy
Achras sapotar		Sapola apple [sapodilla]	This is a most beautiful evergreen. We have one plant which grows vigorously.
Laurus Indica		Broad leaved bay	1 plant Healthy
Saccharum officinarum		Sugar cane	
Gardenia florida		Umky of the Chinese [jasmine]	Used in dyeing scarlet pulp that surrounds the seeds being immersed in warm water gives a more excellent yellow colour inclining to orange.
Jasminum aroricium		Arorian tasmimi	2 plants Healthy
Tamarindus Indica		Tamarind tree	2 plants
Rosa Indica		Chinese rose	2 plants
Daphne Indica		Indian spurge [laurel]	1 plant

For the last three rows, the "Healthy" observation spans: Tamarind tree (2 plants), Chinese rose (2 plants), Indian spurge [laurel] (1 plant) — Healthy

Latin names		English names	Observations	
Mimosa nilotica	X	Gum Arabic tree	From this species of Mimosa the gum Arabicifis produced. We have 2 plants both of which are Healthy.	
Mangifera indica	X	East India mango	There are four plants in the Garden of this valuable tree which begin to grow vigorously.	
[*Clausena lanium*]	X	Wompy [wampee]	A fruit tree peculiar to the Southern provinces of China and has every promise of becoming naturalised to this island.	
Bubon regedeus	X		1 plant Healthy	
Garcinea mangastona		Mangosteen tree	1 plant begins to vegetate	
Hymenea courbaril	X	Gum copal tree	This tree is known to yield the true gum copal of which we have 1 plant Healthy.	
Phyllanthus species	X			
Barringtonia speciosa		Tulip tree	3 plants	
Pyrus cydonia		Quince	6 plants	
Cafora legustrina		Horse acacia	2 plants	Healthy
Melia azederach		Selack tree [syringa]	6 plants	
Vinea rofaca		Madagascar poruinela	4 plants	
Thea vividis		Green thea	1 plant in flower	
Cocos nucifera		Coconut		
Chamaerops humilis		Dwarf [fan] palm		
Palma species				
Capsicum frutescens		Shrubby Capsicum [chilli pepper]		
Coffea Arabica		Coffee tree		
Carica papza [papaya]		Oapa tree [papaya]		
Salix babylonica		Weeping Willow		
Ficus carica		Cape fig		
___ *nitida* [*microcarpa*]		[Chinese banyan/ Indian laurel]	Of these two species there are several young plants growing amongst the rocks on each side of the hills.	
___ *religiosa*		[peepul tree]		
___ *benghalensis*		[Listed as] Jack tree [banyan?]	1 plant Healthy	

Latin names		English names	Observations
Agave Americana		American aloe	
___ *virginica*		Virginian aloe	
Punica granatum		Pomegranate	
Erythrina corallodendron		Coral tree	These plants grow vigorously
Phoenix dactalyphera		Date bearing palm	
Hibiscus rosa sinensis		Chinese rose	
Mimosa species			
Hydesarum ginens		Moving plant	
Arbor fol. pinnatis		[mahogany]	
Arundo bamboo		Bamboo	
			21 Different trees and shrubs the names of which I have not been able to ascertain as they are but added to the collection and just left to vegetate. Henry Porteous

Appendix II

Catalogue of trees and shrubs growing at Plantation House [1789]

Notes:

1   Source: British Library, India Office Records (IOR), G/32/163, St Helena: Miscellaneous Papers.
2   The list was compiled by Henry Porteous.
3   The list was made for submission to the council of the East India Company in London.
4   Where possible, modern spellings have been used but nomenclature has not been updated.

Latin names		English names	Observations
Siya orientalis		Chinese arbour vita	
Myrtus communis		Narrow-leaved myrtle	
Rosa provincialis		Province rose	
___ musufera	X	Moss rose	
___ eglanteria		Sweet briar	
Camellia japonica fl. Plino		Double white camellia	2 plants flowering
Protea argentea	X	Silver tree	Grows luxuriantly of which we have several plants.
Ficus benghalensis		Jack tree	
___ religiosa		Red banyan tree [peepul]	
Lea erispa	X		
Manehausea speciosa			
Ficus carica		Cape fig	
Milia azedrach		Lilack	
Syringa vulgaris		Common liac	
Ligustrum vulgare		Privet	
Mespilius germanica		Heather	
Chamerops humilis		Dwarf palm	
Commlina africana		Creeping commelina	

NAPOLEON'S GARDEN ISLAND

Latin names		English names	Observations	
Psorala pinnata		Goble gier	The vegetation of this plant is very rapid and affords quick shelter against the bleak dry winds. The wood when dry makes good fuel. It is not an indigenous plant but perfectly naturalised.	
Vitie indica		Velvet thoren		
Arundo bamboo				
Solanum sodomeum		Apples of Sodom	Grows about the commons but [is] not indigent plant.	
Quercus robur		English oak	The vegetation of this tree is much more rapid than in Europe. We have several large trees which bear acorns in great abundance the cultivation of this tree has been but little attended to I have planted between 2 and 3000 acorns most of them begin to vegetate.	
___ *gramuntia*	X	Holly leaved oak	2 plants	
___ *phellos*	X	Willow leaved oak	2 plants	
___ *rubra*		Scarlet oak	2 plants	Healthy
___ *urris*		Luccomb oak	1 plant	
___ *exonensis*		Turkey oak	1 plant	
___ *suber*		Cork oak	1 plant	
___ *ilex*		Evergreen oak	Of this species we have several large trees one of which is between 40 and 50 feet high This species bares acorns but not in such abundance as the former of which we have several large trees and bear [sic] Chestnuts in abundance it grows equally well as in Europe it will generally live in	
Fragus castanea		Spanish chestnut	most of the valley that are sheltered from the bleak winds and forms a very handsome tree.	
Asculus hippocastarum		Horse chestnut	Of this tree Mr Brooke received 2 plants from Capt Cummings which began to vegetate.	
Eugenia malaoncis		China rose apple	This is a beautiful evergreen	
Ilex europaus		Common Surz	This plant is completely naturalised and is used by the inhabitants for fuel.	
Pyrus mallus		Common crab apple		
___ *var*	X	___ Siberian crab		
___ *lativa*		Pear		

Latin names		English names	Observations
Hernandia species		Jack in a box	This species is not described by Linnaeus 2 plants healthy.
		Fob.palmatin integorimus	
Gleitsia horrida		Chinese accasia	1 large tree healthy
Musa sapientum		Plantain tree	
___ var		Bassine plantain tree	
Thea vividis		Green thea	2 plants healthy
Pruniea granatum		Pomegranate	
Pinus pinea	X	Stone pine	Several plants healthy
___ *sylvestris*	X	Scotch pine	Several plants healthy
Inacana erecta		Chinese dragon tree	
Fraximus excelsior	X	Common ash	This plant grows vigorously
Philadelphus coronarus		White syringa	Healthy
Poldums pomiferum		Guava	
Salix babylonica		Weeping willow	
Theobroma cacao	X	Chocolat nut	This plant grows luxuriantly
Croton sebiferum		Chinese tallow tree	Several healthy the seeds are lodged in a white matter from which they extract a vegetable tallow.
Saiurus cinamonia		Cinnamon tree	1 plant very healthy
Hedysarum zinium	X	Moving plant	2 plants healthy
Cedrela oderata	X		
Croxutarce chinensis	X		
Guilandina bondere		Prickly nectar	
Platanus orientalis		Eastern Plane tree	
Rosmaninus officinalis		Rose Mary	
Rhamnus species			
Sonicera caprifolium		Honeysuckle	
Daphne indica		Indian spurge	
Hibiscus mutabilis		Syrian rose	
Diospyros lotus		Indian date plum	
Coffea arabica		Mocco coffee	This plant grows luxuriantly under cover from S. wind.

42. Redwood (*Trochetiopsis erythroxylon*) detail, probably from the garden at Brooke's farm. It is an endemic hardwood decimated for tanning purposes in the 17th century. By 1875 there were only 17 or 18 known survivors, most in gardens: two at Arnos Vale; one at Oakbank; three or four at Bower's at Sandy Bay; two at Samuel Alexander's; one at Southens; six or seven young trees at The Hermitage; one on Diana's Peak; and one at High Peak. Today redwood is part of a major attempt to regenerate and save St Helena's rare endemic flora. Sketch by William Burchell, 31 August 1809.

Appendix III

Catalogue of trees and shrubs growing at High Ridge [1789]

Notes:

1 Source: British Library, India Office Records (IOR), G/32/163, St Helena: Miscellaneous Papers.
2 The list was compiled by Henry Porteous.
3 The list was made for submission to the council of the East India Company in London.
4 Where possible, modern spellings have been used but nomenclature has not been updated.

Latin name	English name	Observation
Juniperus suecica	Swedish juniper	2 plants healthy
Fraxinus excelsior	Common ash	4 plants healthy
Ulmus sativa	Common elm	1 plant d°
Juglans regia	Common walnut	2 plants d°
Pyrus malus	Common apple	12 plants d°
___ *lativa*	Pear	6 plants d°
___ var.		4 plants d°
___ *cydonia*	Quince	9 plants d°
Punica granatum	Pomegranate	2 plants d°
Rosa provincialis	Province rose	Several plants
___ *eglanteria*	Sweet briar	Several plants
Tilia americana	American lime	6 plants grow well
Prunus armeniaca	Apricot	6 plants healthy
___ var		2 plants d°
___ *carasus*	Kentish cherry	4 plants d°
___ *domestica*	Common plum	4 plants d°
___ var		2 plants d°
Psoralia pinnita	Goble gier	
Thiya orientalis	Chinese arbour vita	Several healthy
Salix babylonica	Weeping willow	
___ *alba*	Huntington willow	
Sambucus nigra	Black elder	

Latin name		English name	Observation
Protea argentea		Silver tree	1 plant healthy
Queus robur		English oak	
___ ilex		Evergreen oak	
___ rubra		Scarlet oak	
Platanus orentalis		Castren plane tree	1 plant healthy
Diospyrus lotus		Indian date plum	
Morus nigra		Black mulberry	
Acer pseudoplatanus		Sycamore tree	
Aesculus hippocastanum		Horse chestnut	
Fagus castanea		Spanish chestnut	
		White wood	These are indigenous plants and do not appear to be described by Linnaeus
		Black wood	
		Red wood	
		Cabbage tree	
		Fern tree	Henry Porteous
		Gum wood	

Appendix IV

Burchell: Catalogus plantarum quæ Sta Helena variis hortis inveniuntur [*c*.1809]

Source: Kew Archive, William Burchell papers, WJB/1/4.

Note:

This is a list of the plants Burchell lists as growing in gardens on the island of St Helena in the period of 1809/1810. This is an untidy set of seven pages, each with two columns written in ink and giving the scientific names known to him of the plant, occasionally a very brief description such as colour of flower and sometimes the name of the garden.

Garden	Owner	Plant
Botanic Gardens [Jamestown]	East India Company	*Canna glauca*
		Amomum Zanzibar
		Jasminum undulatum
		Olea europæa
		Justicia monanthera
		Justicia betonica
		Commelina bengalensis
		Panicium [guinea grass]
		Verbena bonariensis
		Valeriana nodiflora
		Tamarindus indica
		Xia Sparaxis crocata
		Aristata
		Melasphærula graminea
		Hliliotropium indicum
		Borago zeylanica
		Pittosporum tobira
		Convolvutus pes capra [Ipomoea]
		Impomæa quamocht
		Impomæa coccinea
		Impomæa grandiflora
		Impomæa leucantha
		Impomæa folius hastatis
		Datura stramonium
		Datura arbosea
		Datura arbosea purple stramonium
		Cordia latifol
		Achyranthus

Garden	Owner	Plant
Botanic Gardens [Jamestown]	East India Company	*Celosia cristata* *Asclepias curassavica* *Asclepias fruticosa* *Asclepias fruticosa salicifolia* *Stapelia variegata* *Stapelia hirsuta* *Compluent globosa* *Ziziphus* *Sambucus nigra* *Linum usitatifrum* *Crassula coccinæ* *Peliosanthes teta* *Hermanthus cocemius* *Agapanthus umbellatus* *Hibiscus cannabinus* *Hibiscus surattensis* *Hibiscus esculeutro* *Hibiscus vitifolius* *Hibiscus tomentosus pilosus* *Hibiscus* _____ from China *Hibiscus pruriens* *Hibiscus radiatus* *Hibiscus bifasciatus* *Robinia pseudoacacia* *Aeschynomene carabina* _____ _____ *grandifil. R* *Aeschynomene sagminto* *Gabæ* *Trigonella timmugracum* *Crotalaria bractea* *Crotalaria laburnifolia* *Crotalaria junscea* *Crotalaria do.* *Crotalaria terragona* *Arachis hypogaea* [peanuts] *Dolichos purpureus* *Phaserlais* *Cylista villosa* *Clitorea ternatea* *Lathyrus* *Erivium disperimum* *Spilanthes obracius* *Bidens ~~importila~~ bipinnata* *Cacalia* *Artemisia chinensis* *Xeranthernum lucidmum* *Zinnia violacea* *Chrysanthemum tricolor* *Rudbeckia turbinata*

Garden	Owner	Plant
Botanic Gardens [Jamestown]	East India Company	*Passiflora lauriafola*
		Xanthium orientale
		Amaranthus caudatus spinosus
		Amaranthus tricolor oleraceus
		Amaranthus cruentus angustifol
		Pinea longifolia
		Thuja orientalis
		Ceus bicolor
		Mimosa glauca
		Mimosa milotica?
		Minosa mineriva
		Mimosa farnesiana
		Acalypha ~~indica~~
		Ricinus com fanticosa rubra
		Aleurites triloba
		Momordica charantia 'Kurryla'
		~~Inchosanthis~~ Silffa foetida
		Bryonia
		Inga ~~unquislati~~ manilla
		Panax fruticosum
		Phoenix reclinata dwarf
		Orinithogalum aureum
		Pracæira australis
		Aloe
		Aloe
		Aloe
		Aloe
		Aloe
		Aloe
		Guilandina bonducella
		Triumfetta
		Euphorbia hirta
		Cactus nopal
		Mesembryanthemeum
		Mesembryanthemeum
		Rosa indica
		Corchorus olitorius [jute]
		Corchorus capsularis
		Delphinium ajacis
		Sajureia hortensis
		Origanum onites
		Ocimum gratissimum
		Ocimum ____ from India
		Gmelina asiatica
		Browallia elata
		Ruellia sp
		Volkameria inermis
		Thunbergia fragans
		Cheiranthus incanus

Garden	Owner	Plant
Botanic Gardens [Jamestown]	East India Company	*Pelargonium inquinans* *Pelargonium lobatum* *Penapetes phoenicia* *Sida rhombifolia* *Sida alnifolia* *Sida asiatica* *Sida cristata* *Alcea rosea hollyhock* *Urena lobata* *Gossypium barbadense* south sea cotton *Hibiscus tiliaceus* *Hibiscus sabdariffa*
Bramin's house	Inchosanthis	*Quercus ilex*
The Briars		~~*Mercurialis arenas*~~
Castle Garden (Jamestown)	East India Company	*Panicium* [guinea grass] (Cathis' Garden?) *Mangifera indica* *Mangifera prossagong* *Codia sebest* *Erythrina corallodendron* (Caffra R) *Ficus elastica*
Chubb's Spring		*Phaserlais*
Mr Dunn		*Delphinium ajacis*
Horse Pasture Farm [100 acres]	Mr Knipe [later James Seale]	*Lathyrus tringitanus* *Chochlearia arumoracia* *Pelagonium capitatum*
Longrange [Near Rock Rose? Long Ground? 31 acres: Henry Alexander/W. Henry Seale]		*Prunus* China small yellow plum *Pyrus cydonia* *Rosa indica* *Hibiscus mutabilis*
Longwood [Estate 633 acres]		*Cissus vitiginea* *Psoralae aphylla* *Hypericum (monogynum)* *Crotalaria incana* *Lathyrus odoratus* *Clutia pulchella* *Thuja* sp. *Mimosa odorata* *Mimosa farnesiana* *Cufnessus horizontalis* *Stillingia sebifera* *Cucurius sativus* *Furcæa* Spanish aloe *Cotyledon orbiculata pig's ear* *Mesembryanthemum edule* *Hibiscus rosa sinensis*
Maldivia [Jamestown]	Lt-Gov House	*Pistatia* *Spondias mombin* hog plum

Garden	Owner	Plant
Plantation House Estate [176 acres New garden 20 acres Mulberries 5 acres]	East India Company	*Canna glauca*
		Ligustrum vulgare
		Olea europæa
		Olea adornitissima
		Protæa argentea
		Protæa conocarpadendron
		Protæa speciosa
		? X
		Curtisia faginea
		Banksia
		X
		Hakea gibbosa
		Embothrium sericeum
		Babiana plicatus
		Iris xiphium
		Pittosporum tobira
		Gardenia florida
		Gardenia 'Klip essen'
		Impomæa grandiflora
		Celastrus
		Prectonia ventosa
		Strelitzia regina
		Plumerioides
		Serissa foetida
		Rhamnus
		Bulon macedon
		Cassine
		Sambucus nigra
		Bromelia ananas
		Haermanthus coccineus
		Agapanthus umnbellatus
		Psoralæa aphylla
		Critus nobilis (mandarin)
		Logershænnia speciosa
		Lathyrus tingitanus
		Aster fruticosus
		Aster obtusatus
		Buptithaluum frutiscens
		Arum esculentum
		Casuarina stricta
		Coix lachrymal
		Quercus ilex
		Carppinus betulus
		Pinus pinaster
		Dwarf pine
		Pinea longifolia
		Thuja orientalis
		Podocarpus elongata
		Podocarpus chinensis

Garden	Owner	Plant
Plantation House Estate [176 acres New garden 20 acres Mulberries 5 acres]	East India Company	*Clutia pulchella* *Mimosa sinifolia* *Cupressus sempervirens* *Acalypha indica* *Stillingia sebifera* *Aleurites triloba* *Inga unquislati manila* *Gleditsia horrida* *Brabejum stellatfolium* *Diospyros kaki* *Rhapis flabelliformis* *Zinnia huvida* *Gloriosa superba* *Asparagus fruticosus.* *Pracæira australis* *Polianthus tuber* *Aletris invaria Tritoma uvaria* *Yucca gloriosa* *Aloe* *Aloe socotrina* *Furcæa Spanish* *Alstroemeria lighter* *Arbutus unedo strawberry tree* *Royena lucida* *Cunonia capensis* *Averrhoa bilimbi cucumber tree* *Oxalis purpurea* [purple woodsorrel] *Cactus nopal* *Philadelphus coronarium* *Mesembryanthemum edulis* *Rosa muscosa* *Rosa indica* *Rosa triphylla* *Rubus fruticosus* *Calycanthus præcox* *Magnolia fuscata* *Michelia champaca* *Crescentia cujete* *Pelargonium betulinum* *Urena lobata* *Hibiscus rosa sinensis*
Prospect House	Secretary Brooke	*Pittosporum tobira* *Pinea sylvestris* *Cyprus sempervirens* *Inga unquislati manilla* *Arbutus unedo* [strawberry tree] *Philadelphus coronarium* *Myrtus communis* *Pyrus cydonia* *Pelargonium glutinosum*

Garden	Owner	Plant
Rock Rose		*Hibiscus* (*arintus R*)
Rosin or Rosem [Rosemary?] Hall	William Wrangham [1830s; Ann Haynes. Estate 41 acres]	*Cissus vitiginea* *Urtica pilulifera*
Sandybay [Mount Pleasant]/Sand	Sir William Webber Doveton	*Curcuma longa* [Turmeric] *Briza media* *Convolvulus braziliensis* *Convolvulus pes capra* *Impomœa hederæa* *Luprinus luteus* *Mimosa sebbek* *Cupressus horizontalis* *Rhapis flabelliformis* *Amygdalus Flat peach* *Amygdalus Foliis densis* *Prunus armeniaca* *Pyrus chinensis* *Rosa muscosa* *Fragaria vesca* *Cheiranthus cheiri* *Adonias antumnalis* *Pelargonium cucullatum*
Shadrock		
Forest Lodge	Col. Smith [Later Richard Price. 60 acres]	*Rosmarious officinalis* *Salvia officinalis* *Ficus* sp. *Asparagus office* *Amygdalus communis* [Cape almond] *Fragaria grandiflora* *Origarnum majorana*
West Lodge	[1830: Charles Sampson 119 acres]	*Curcuma longa* [Tereric] *Olea adornitissmund* *Antholyza æthiopica* *Ilex aquifolium* *Pittosporum tobira* *Gardenia florida* *Gardenia* 'Klip essen' *Plumerioides* *Lonicera pæriclymenum* [honeysuckle] *Serissa foetida* *Agapanthus dinbellatus* *Amaryllis forumosiprima* *Hibiscus* _____ *arboratius* *Camellia japonica* single red *Spartium scoparium* *Othonna abrotanifolia*

Garden	Owner	Plant
West Lodge	[1830: Charles Sampson 119 acres]	*Mercurialis arenas* *Podocarpus longata* *Clutia pulchella* *Aletris invaria Taitoma invaria* *Hemerocallis fulva* [orange day-lily] *Phormium tenax* [New Zealand flax] *Hydrangea mutal* *Oxalis purpurea* [purple woodsorrel] *Eugenia caryophyllata clove* *Myrtus communis* *Prunus cerasus* [morello cherry] *Spiræa chaemadryfolia* *Rosa rubinginosa* Swanley valley *Thea vividis* *Caryophyllus aromaticus* *Magnolia purpurea* *Magnolia fuscata* *Pelargonium betulinum*
Major Wright	Major Wright	*Curcuma longa* [Turmeric] *Podocarpus longata* *Diospyros kaki* *Fragaria grandiflora*
	Miss Mrumny Garden	*Rhus*
Ribstone pits		*Pyrus malus*
Rufset (Ruffkins?) (Fulkins?)		*Pyrus* _ _ _ _ _
Wintersavory?		*Saturia hortensis*
Clough's Plain	[Craig 20 acres]	Malva tree mallow

$$\mathcal{Appendix}\ V$$

Garden sightings of Napoleon and garden references recorded by Captain Nicholls, 15 October 1818 to 9 February 1820

Source: Extracted entries from British library, Lowe papers Ms 20,210, Journal of Capt. George Nicholls 66th Regt. Orderly Officer Longwood.

Date	Comment
15 Oct 1818	Napoleon was walking in his garden about 5 o'clock. He had a handkerchief tied about his head and was in his Dressingown. I saw him from Deadwood Barracks thro' a Telescope.
19 Oct 1818	Napoleon was view[ed] at his dressingroom Window this mg & Walking in his small garden this afternoon.
19 Nov. 1818	I saw Napoleon walking in his little Garden.
20 Nov. 1818	Napoleon was seen walking in his garden and also in his dressing room window.
10 Dec. 1818	Napoleon was seen today sitting outside his dinning room door in the back Garden.
23 Dec. 1818	Napoleon was seen this afternoon sitting astride the door in his back Garden with a Tablet & papers before him.
30 Dec. 1818	I saw Genl Bonaparte today. He was in company with Montholon & in his little Garden – he was in his dressingown with a telescope in his hand. I was only 20 or 40 yds from him.
31 Dec. 1818	Monothon was talking with him in the little garden before the library
1 Jan. 1819	He was seen in his little garden by a servant.
5 Jan. 1819	Althorp of the Dragoons told me that he saw Genl B later in the evg in the small garden in front of the library.
6 Jan. 1819	One of my Dragoons told me he saw Genl B last evg in the garden dressed & with a Cocked hat on
7 Jan. 1819	My servant here and two others in the Garden told me they saw NB out for a very short time in the little back garden about 3 o'clock
8 Jan. 1819	I saw Napoleon this evg in the little garden in front of his library. He took one turn around in pretty quick time in a few minutes after appeared again and was looking towards the new house. He wore his dressingown & had a handkerchief about his head. Sergt David was near him and saw him also.
9 Jan. 1819	I saw genl B walking this evening in his garden.
10 Jan. 1819	Napoleon was seen walking for a very short time this evg in his little garden with Madame Montholon.

Date	Comment
13 Jan. 1819	Napoleon was seen to day walking in his little garden a good deal more than usual.
14 Jan. 1819	Napoleon was seen in his little garden by one of the gardeners.
2 Feb 1819	I heard a person reading in Napoleon's garden between PM
3 Feb 1819	Sergt David told me that he saw Napoleon in his Flower garden a little after 6 AM he was in his dressing Gown and had a red handkerchief on his head
5 Feb 1819	Sergt David told me that he saw Napoleon this mg walking with Montholon in the Count's Flower garden
9 Feb 1819	I saw Napoleon walking in company with Monthlon in his back flower garden.
11 Feb 1819	My Groom Lee saw Napoleon this evg in his flower garden in his dressingown
15 Feb 1819	The Gardener Sowerby told me that he saw Genl B between 5 & 7 PM. He was in his dressingown
16 Feb 1819	I saw Genl B walking in his flower garden. David & Sowerby also saw him
18 Feb 1819	The Gardener told me that he had seen him [Napoleon] at his bedroom window
20 Feb 1819	Sergt Kitts told me he saw the shadow of two persons walking this Eg in the garden. He believed one of them to be Napoleon but it was so dark that he cd not distinguish
21 Feb 1819 Sunday	I saw Genl Bonaparte to day in his Flower Garden he was in his dressingown ¼ to 5 PM
22 Feb 1819	Sergt David told me he was Genl B this mg in his flower garden ... One of the gardeners saw Genl B this afternoon
23 Feb 1819	I saw Genl B at 6 PM in his flower garden with one of the counts. Seg David saw him this mg
24 Feb 1819	My Groom Lee saw Genl B this mg Taylor the gardener also saw him in his verandah at 11 AM
28 Feb 1819 Sunday	Orderly Sergt told me that he had seen Genl B walking in his little garden
1 March 1819	Napoleon was seen walking in his little garden with Montholon by Sergt David
2 March 1819	Napoleon was seen walking with Montholon in his garden by Sergt David
4 March 1819	Sergt David told me that he saw N this mg in his flower garden. I believe that he walked on the lower walk after dusk. I saw him with my telescope
5 March 1819	I believe that I saw NB this evg in the lower garden walk
7 March 1819 Sunday	Sergt Kitts saw NB in his little garden this evg
12 March 1819	I saw NB between 3 & 4 PM in his little garden
13 March 1819	I saw NB this morning walking in his little flower garden
15 March 1819	Genl B was seen in his flower garden this mg

Date	Comment
20 March 1819	Bonaparte keeps himself very close. Sergt Kitts thinks he saw him for a moment out at the little garden door
26 March 1819	Sergt Kitts told me that he saw Genl B about 4 PM in his little garden dressed in green in a round hat and a star on his side
16 April 1819	One of the Gardeners told me that he [Napoleon] was walking in the vegetable garden this morning
17 April 1819	Sergt Kitts told me that he saw NB walking with Bertrand in the lower walk in the garden at 7 PM the dinning hour and that they were there a considerable time
18 April 1819	She [Madame Montholon] told me that NB was walking in the lower walk in the garden the evening before
19 April 1819	A few min p 6 PM Genl Bonaparte appeared in his back flower garden dressed in green with his Cocked hat. I believe it was Bertrand that met with him. I was nearly 12 hours on my legs this day endeavouring to see NB before I succeeded & I have experienced many malidays since I have been stationed at Longwood. While at dinner this evg Sergt Kitts told me that Napoleon was walking in Longwood gardens 7 & 8 PM Montholon told me this day Genl Bonaparte cd not appear out of his quarters. he was too chilly and cold
20 April 1819	This day about 5 PM NB walked in the lower Garden for 2 or 3 hours
	Taylor the gardener told me that he had seen Napoleon in his front verandah about 5 PM Kitts told me that he saw him in the Garden this Eg & that he went in before 8 PM
24 April 1819	Between 1 & 2 PM Count Montholon called on me to request me to apply for john Huisham to be allowed to remain at Longwood as private servt to Napoleon He told me that Napoleon had been in the little back garden at 8 AM playing with his children.
29 April 1819	Dr Verling told me that he saw Napoleon Bonaparte this afternoon and several others also saw him out to day he was walking in the lower walk of the Garden last eveng
30 April 1819	Napoleon was walking in his little garden with Ct Bertrand, this afternoon & I had a slight view & Seregt David saw him plain
5 May 1819	I saw Genl Bonaparte in his little garden – Montholon and his son were with the Genl
6 May 1819	The Gardener Sowerby told me he saw the General Bonaparte in his little back flower garden
8 May 1819	This morning Genl Bonaparte was seen walking in Longwood Garden between 7 & 8
13 May 1819	Sergt David reported to me that that he saw Napoleon in his Garden to day at 12 a clock
15 May 1819	Sergt David told me that he saw genl B
17 May 1819	Sergt David aquainted me that he had seen Genl B at between 9 and 10 a clock – Count Montholon informed me that Genl B was then walking in the little garden I immediately went round the House but he had gone in

Date	Comment
18 May 1819	I this morning saw Napoleon Bonaparte walking in his little garden in his dressing Gown
21 May 1819	This morning at the park & orchard I saw Genl B He was in the corner of the Longwood Garden looking into Tuker's Valley near the Stable yard
24 May 1819	Sergt David informed me that he saw Genl B walking outside the paling of his little garden with Bertrand this morning.
25 May 1819	The Gardener told me he had seen Genl B in the morning in the small garden
26 May 1819	Count Montholon told me that Napoleon had walked out this morning in the small garden
31 May 1819	I saw Napoleon this morning. He was sitting in his dressing room reading – Taylor the Gardener also saw him
1 June 1819	I saw Genl B this morning at about 11 a clock in the little garden in the rear of his quarters
6 June 1819 Sunday	I saw Genl B this afternoon walking in the little garden
7 June 1819	I saw a table and chair under the tree [?] in Napoleon's little garden so I fancy he had been sitting there though I did not see him nor the gardener
9 June 1819	I saw Genl B at about quarter past 9 this morning. he was standing in the verandah in his dressing gown, The Gardener Sowerby saw him & others. Genl B walked in front of his verandah for an hour this morning by moonlight
10 June 1819	I saw Genl B this morning in his little garden sitting under the trees. David also saw him.
11 June 1819	I saw Genl B this morning. plain in his little garden talking to ct Montholon.
13 June 1819 Sunday	I saw Genl Bonaparte this afternoon about 5 a clock. he was leaning against a tree in the lower in the lower walk of the garden … [Talking to Count Montholon] I had not seen Napoleon Bonaparte today though my instructions require that I should see him twice a day. I also mentioned to the Count that I should be greatly obliged if Napoleon Bonaparte would be pleased to point out a certain hour in the day for me to see him, that it would not be expected that I would pass the whole of my time in the garden looking out for him. The Count said that he knew Napoleon would never degrade himself so much as to admit any one into his room on this account – and asked me if I wished him to deliver this communication to Genl B after some consideration I informed the Count that he was at liberty to do so.
17 June 1819	I saw Genl B walking in his little garden today at ½ past 2 a clock
19 June 1819	The two Gardeners told me that they had seen Genl B this morning walking in his small garden I have been round the House several times this morning since ½ past 6 a clock. but he would not let me see him – he has it in his power to pop out for a second into the Garden and unless I were to station myself constantly in the garden looking out for him it is rally [really] impossible for me to get a sight of him.

Date	Comment
22 June 1819	The Gardeners and Sergt David told me they had seen Napoleon out in the front of his quarters
25 June 1819	I saw genl B this morning in his little garden … my Orderly Sergt told me that Genl B was walking in front of his house after dark
26 June 1819	I saw Genl B this afternoon walking with the Bertrands in the lower walk of Longwood garden. He was walking in front of his quarters between 7 and 9 a clock this evening as reported to me by the Adj Sergt NB walk very [?].
28 June 1819	I saw Genl Bunaparte this morning in his little garden
29 June 1819	Do Do. I believe he was singing or humming a tune
30 June 1819	Sowerby saw Genl B this day in his little garden
1 July 1819	… that he [Montholon] had sent for Marchand who had told him that Napoleon soon after the Party with the Countess [Montholon] had departed [to return to Europe], had appeared out for a short time in his little back Garden
2 July 1819	Dr Verling saw Genl Bonaparte this afternoon walkg in the lower part of the Garden full dressed and in company with him Dr V thought Nap/on walked quite strong
3 July 1819	One of the Gardeners (Taylor) told me that he saw him [Napoleon] out this morning in his little garden
4 July 1819	I saw Nap/on this morning walkg in his little Garden between 9 & 10 a clock – Sunday
8 July 1819	I saw Genl B walkg about Longwd Garden this afternoon in his Cocked hat
9 July 1819	Sowerby told me that the Genl was walking for an hour this afternoon (with Cn Montholon) in his little Garden
10 July 1819	Sowerby told me that Napoleon walked in his little garden this a morning (about 10 a clock) with Montholon. One of the stable men (Fuller) also saw him at the same time. As I had no opportunity of seeing Nap/on myself today having been dressing when he was out. I this evening mentioned to Cn Motholon that I had not seen him today. The Cn said that Napoleon had been unwell with the bowel complaint and consequently <u>had not been out of his quarters today.</u> for he had just left him (5 a clock PM) to take his (cold) dinner after which he had orders to return to Napoleon – so much for the veracity of these People.
14 July 1819	Genl B was in his dressing gown in the little garden a considerable time this morning
15 July 1819	I saw Genl B this morning between 10 & 11 a clock – walking in the little garden in the rear of the House. Sowerly saw Napoleon in his usual full dress walking about Longwood Garden this afternoon
17 July 1819	I saw Genl B this morning walking in his little garden accompanied by Cn Bertrand – this morning Ct Montholon told me that Napoleon wishes a sod wall erected to keep the wind off from the angle of his library
18 July 1819	My groom acquainted me that he saw Genl B this afternoon at about 5 a clock walking with Ct Montholon outside the little garden. I went to the Castle respecting the sod wall and obtained leave to have it commenced tomorrow

Date	Comment
19 July 1819	I and Col. Mynyard saw Genl B this afternoon at about ½ past 4 a clock he was walking in his full dress outside his little garden – some sods were collected to day for the sod wall
20 July 1819	I this day passed nearly the whole of my time in the Garden supervising the building of the sod wall from – <u>after six a clock in the morning until the same hour in the evening</u>, the Labourers went away at 4 a clock owing to the badness of the weather I remained however skulking about the Longwood Garden till 6 a clock in order to procure a view of Genl B but I could not see him to day I however believe I heard him & Montholon walking & talking in the Billard Room & most probably laughing at me.
21 July 1819	General Bonaparte appeared out this afternoon in his full dress about 5 a clock he viewed the new sod wall then went to Bertrands accompanied by Montholon
22 July 1819	Sowerby & 2 or 3 workmen at the new sod wall Genl B hwe came to view the new sod wall and did not seem to ____
24 July 1819	Sergt David told me that he saw Napoleon walking outside his little garden in his dressing gown accompanied by Motholon.
26 July 1819	Napoleon was seen by several of the workmen at the new sod wall and whilst his Groom was exercising the Grey pony on the back lawn
27 July 1819	Sowerby told me that he saw Napoleon out to day Ct Montholon busily engaged this day drawing out a plan for enlarging of Napoleon's favourite garden
30 July 1819	I saw Genl B this morning in his little garden was within <u>eight paces</u> of him I however walked away not wishing to intrude on his privacy I was directing the men working at the sod wall which they were covering with green sod in the inside
1 August 1819	I believe that I saw Genl B this afternoon in his little garden
3 Aug 1819	This afternoon a rather ridiculous affair took place in Longwood Gardens. I had reported to Sir Hudson Lowe that Napoleon had not been out – Now improvements were going on in the garden and the Governor wishes to see them. I took him with the chief engineer along the lower walk of the garden little expecting that Napoleon was out at the time when we came upon him very unexpectedly – it appears that he had been appraised of our approach for he was making play up a path towards the House with little Nap Bertrand with a long stick in his hand – he however got on very slowly – The Governor waited until Napoleon had entered his quarters then inspected the improvements – After the Governor went away – Napoleon came out again.
7 Aug 1819	<u>I spent the greater part of the day in the Garden endeavouring to procure sight of Genl B but to no affect</u>
	Genl B still keeps himself concealed I cannot properly get satisfactory information respecting him I have employed <u>myself very frequently during the day walking</u> in Longwood Garden in order to obtain a view of Napoleon but to no affect. The Gardener has not seen him since 4th inst though employd constantly round the House

Date	Comment
22 Aug 1819 Sunday	This eveng at about 6½ a'clock I heard persons talking pretty loud in the little back garden of Genl Bonaparte This man had not been seen by any English person for several days. I was therefore determined to pass near to the Garden It was rather dark I however could distinguish two persons very plain. The one appeared to be Count Bertrand the other was a short person with a big coat wrapped round him. This person I took to be Genl B ... <u>At half after 6 a clock I believe that I saw Genl B walkg in his garden – ten minutes afterwards</u> Count Bertrand came to my quarters to say that he [Napoleon] was ill in bed and required the assistance of Mr Stokoe – The Docr.
3 Oct 1819	Genl B walked out this evening
5 Oct 1819	Genl B appeared out today. Sowerby saw him
6 Oct 1819	Genl B appeared today. The Gardener saw him. The Genl had confined himself to his apartments for 2 months.
7 Oct 1819	I saw Genl B today. He appeared out. in his little garden with Matholon & his valets
8 Oct 1819	I saw genl B twice today He walked about his favourite garden for a considerable time even stood viewing the officer of the Guard posting the Lantern at Sun Set
9 Oct 1819	Several persons saw General B out today
10 Oct 1819 Sunday	I saw Genl Bonaparte this morning walkg with C. Montholon in the Garden beside the sod wall
11 Oct 1819	Genl B was out to day
13 Oct 1819	Genl B walked about Longwood Garden today He was seen by several persons – Sowerby & Capt Ford
14 Oct 1819	Genl B walked out today for a considerable time I saw him as well as several others – For several days past the Genl had amused himself superintending the improvement for his little favourite Garden – his valet Noveraz is the Genl's Gardener
15 Oct 1819	I saw Genl B out to day he was amusing himself by assisting his valet Noveraz to put up some lime in his favourite garden
16 Oct 1819	Genl B was out today a good deal of his time. I saw him – he was also walking after Dark in the Lower walk of Longwood garden
22 Oct 1819	I saw Genl B sitting beside his sod wall in his favourite Garden
23 Oct 1819	I saw Genl N this morning in his dressing gown in his garden. Sowerby told me that Genl B visited Madame Bertrand ...
25 Oct 1819	I saw Genl B walking in his little Garden to day He walked there a good deal to day
26 Oct 1819	Genl B walked out to day seen by Sowerby and Capt Ford He was in the Lower path in the evening at 7 a clock sitting on one of the seats
27 Oct 1819	Saw Genl Bonaparte today between 12 & 1 a clock walking in his favourite garden accompanied by Ct Bertrand
28 Oct 1819	Genl B was seen today in his Little Garden by Capt Ford and the Gardener

Date	Comment
29 Oct 1819	I saw Genl B to day walking in his favour Garden with Ct Mantholon he looked at me thro' a small spy glass
30 Oct 1819	I saw Genl B to day he pottered about his garden most of the afternoon
31 Oct 1819 Sunday	I saw Genl B to day in his little back garden He walked with Madame Bertrand as far as her house
2 Nov 1819	Genl B was out to day in his favourite garden The young Bertrands were playing round him I believe Major Emmett[1] and Sowerby saw the General
3 Nov 1819	Genl B appeared out today. I was within 10 paces but his back being turned towards me he did not see me – He walked very stoutly
4 Nov 1819	I saw Genl B to day in his favourite Garden a few minutes before 4 PM
5 Nov 1819	I believe that I saw Genl B to day in his little garden It was from camp with my spy glass he was accompanied by Noverraz. Sowerby saw the Genl in the afternoon
6 Nov 1819	I saw Genl B this afternoon in his little garden
8 Nov 1819	I saw Genl B in his favourite Garden in his dressing gown – C Bertrand standing behind him hat in hand
9 Nov 1819	I saw Genl B in his garden with C Montholon
10 Nov 1819	Do Do Do in the afternoon
11 Nov 1819	I saw Genl B this morning in nhis favourite Garden in his morning gown – I also saw him there again 2 or 3 times
13 Nov 1819	Saw Genl B in his favourite garden to day he had two of his Valets with him. Mr Mudd the Chief Carpenter and some others were employed to day putting up a door Genl B's bed room and a small garden Mr M told me the Genl came to look at them at work
17 Nov 1819	I saw Genl B in his favourite garden this [morning] he was out also part of the afternoon
18 Nov 1819	I saw Genl B in his favourite garden this morning he was out a good deal to day
19 Nov 1819	Genl B passed some hours today in his favourite garden – at times he had a <u>spade in his hand</u> at work he desired Sowerby to go to the Office for two more pickaxes holding up two of his fingers for the numbers. He had 5 or 6 Chinese at work besides C Motholon stripped and hard at work and some of his valets – the Governor came to Longwood and saw Genl B at work
20 Nov 1819	Genl B was at work in his little garden this morning by seven at least with a spade & 5 or 6 Chinese & valets The two Priests and Surgeon were likewise employed The Genl & his 9 gentleman assistants breakfasted together in the garden I believe C. Montholon is unwell to day – most probably he caught a cold so hard working. The Genl was out till late this morning
22 Nov 1819	Genl B passed a great deal of his time today in his favourite garden & had several people employed including Chinese, stablemen
23 Nov 1819	I saw Genl B this morning in the little garden opposite his bed & dressing rooms

Date	Comment
24 Nov 1819	I saw Genl B in his favourite garden today
25 Nov 1819	Do Do Do
26 Nov 1819	Capt Ford saw Genl B today in his Little Garden
27 Nov 1819	I saw Genl B today in his little Garden in front of his Dressing Room in his dressing gown with a red handkerchief over his head his usual morning dress. Genl B went to the Stable Yard this afternoon
28 Nov 1819 Sunday	Saw Genl B walking with C. Montholon in the Little Garden. The latter with his Hat off.
29 Nov 1819	Genl B was out early this morning employed in his favourite garden with a number of assistants C Montholon, valets, Chinese Gardeners Stable men see he is picking holes in one part of the Garden & creating mounds in another and conveying horse dung to other plants. <u>Poor Uncle Toby exemplified</u> The Genl was in his morning gown amidst the People at work directing them, takes a spade at times & begins to further – sends messages to me for Carts, Shovels & Spades – God send me away always continence in this humour during this residence at Longwood.
30 Nov 1819	Saw Genl B in his favourite garden today – This afternoon he stood in C. Montholon's little garden looking at my servant watering some flowers at my door
1 Dec 1819	I saw Genl B today he walked as far as the Pond of water by the Guard House afterwards paid a visit to the Comte Bertrand. Sowerby informed me that Genl B dined under the trees in his favourite Garden – I had some communication to day with C. Montholon to day he informed me that Genl B had observed men employed making enclosures in the wood – The Genl hoped they would [not?] destroy his rides particularly the one round the Farm and back by the Company's Garden – I told Count Montholon that every attention would be observed as regard to the rides this I was certain – the Count observed that it was probable when the old carriage was repaired the General Napoleon would ride out
2 Dec 1819	Genl B appeared today in his favourite garden
3 Dec 1819	I saw Genl B this morning he was turning the cock of a cistern to allow the water to run over the flowers in one of his little gardens
4 Dec 1819	Genl B had his <u>valets</u> stablemen Chinese hard at work in his favourite garden – from 5 a clock this morning the General is filling his little Gardens with trees I fancy not only to decrease heat from the sun but also from General view. The sun is now very hot now at Longwood at last – I have been here fifteen months and never found it so – I saw the General when in the Garden
5 Dec 1819 Sunday	I saw Genl B this morning in his little Garden and some of his valets were at work
6 Dec 1819	I saw Genl B this afternoon he was in full dress with a star on his side walking with C Montholon I presume he does not seem to mind any body looking at seeing him provided they don't stand looking at him He also appears completely occupied in Gardening & planting & writing & studying seem quite out of the question

Date	Comment
7 Dec 1819	The Gardener informed me that he saw Genl B in his favourite garden this morning as early as <u>sun rise</u> (day light) The Governor came to Longwood to day to look at the Reservoirs in Genl Bonaparte's garden. He gave orders that they should be cased with red stone immediately I saw Genl B this several times this afternoon. He was dressed in Green and had a cocked hat on. He was superintending the transplanting of young oaks seed in his Garden
8 Dec 1819	I saw Genl B this morning frequently he was supervising the works in his favourite garden I informed C Montholon that the reservoirs were to be cased with red stone agreeable to the recommendation of the Chief Engineer. This afternoon Major Emmett and I were looking at the improvements going on in Genl B's Favourite Garden when the Genl suddenly made his appearance. As I made it a rule never to intrude on the General's privacy Major Emmett and I consequently made our retreat in quick time.
9 Dec 1819	I saw Genl b this afternoon. He turned out very late this day very little gardening in consequence
10 Dec 1819	I saw Genl B very frequently today. Mr [William] Gordon the Cooper came to the General to receive instructions to make a tub for a reservoir in the Genl's favourite Garden
11 Dec 1819	I saw Genl B in his Garden this morning and frequently in the course of the day
12 Dec 1819	I saw Genl <u>B frequently</u> today safe.
13 Dec 1819	I saw Genl B in his Garden this morning walking with C Montholon
14 Dec 1819	I saw Genl B this morning walking in his Garden ~~with Montholon~~. The Genl was out a good deal today the Governor was at longwood and went to see the improvements going on in Napoleon's Gardens The latter remained out at the same time but they were never near enough to speak – from the Governor's conversation with me it appeared that he thought it was rather too scruplous in regard to the delivery on which I acted by keeping so much out of Genl B's way. This conversation was brought on by the Governor asking me whether I have ever taken off [?] to Genl B I told him that I <u>had never been near enough</u> which in fact was nothing but the truth. The Genl does not often walk beyond the two little gardens close to his quarters – Genl B dined in his Garden this evening at ½ past 5 a clock with C Montholon
15 Dec 1819	I saw General B this evening in his Little Garden
16 Dec 1819	Genl B was out this morning as early as six a clock amusing himself in his favourite garden
18 Dec 1819	General B was out two or three times to day and seen by the Gardeners. He also paid a short visit to the Bertrand between 7 and 8 a clock PM but he didn't assist in the gardening. I fear he is getting rather cooler in regard to this accomplishment.
19 Dec 1819 Sunday	I saw Genl B in his garden to day – He was out very little

Date	Comment
20 Dec 1819	I saw Genl B out to day in his favourite garden
21 Dec 1819	I saw Genl B today in the Garden
22 Dec 1819	I saw Genl B today after he had walked about Longwood Garden in the afternoon The General walked a good deal about this evening in the Garden after dark.
23 Dec 1819	I saw Genl B this morning in his garden. The Governor and his two daughters in law came to Longwood this afternoon. The young ladies wishes to see Genl B but he did not appear inclined to give them an opportunity after they left Longwood he had dinner under the trees in his favourite garden with some of his family between 6 & 7 a clock he saw the Miss Johnsons.[2]
24 Dec 1819	Genl B was out early this morning. I went to Plantation House … Genl B was seen out this afternoon by Sowerby.
25 Dec 1819	The gardener Sowerby told me that he saw genl B out by 9 am this morning
26 Dec 1819	I saw Genl B this afternoon in one of his little gardens in his dressing gown Sunday These People are doing nothing but transplanting Trees even this day (though Sunday) they are moving Peach trees <u>with fruit on them</u>. They have been moving young <u>oaks</u> in <u>full leaf</u> & the tree probably will survive but the leaf is falling off as in Autumn.
27 Dec 1819	I saw Genl B this morning in his little garden
28 Dec 1819	I saw Genl B frequently today
29 Dec 1819	I saw Genl B this evening. He walked about Longwood gardens a good deal to day. he took his coffee in his favourite garden this evening Montholon with him
30 Dec 1819	Genl B took his coffee this evening in his little Garden
1 Jan 1820	Sowerby saw Genl B in his favourite garden today
2 Jan 1820	About the middle of the day I saw Genl B amuse himself with the pipe of the Fire Engine spouting water on the trees Flowers in his favourite Garden
3 Jan 1820	I saw Genl B walking in Longwood Gardens
4 Jan 1820	I saw genl B several times today walking about the large garden he still amuses himself by gardening – Hortis superintending however he at times takes to watering pot in his hands and Major Emmett was with me in the General's favourite garden look at the ~~favourite garden~~ reservoir when the General came out full dressed He turned about saw us but did not go in again. I saw him again in the afternoon crossing the Garden and proceeding towards Bertrands in company with the Count [Montholon]. Count Balmain[3] came as far as the Garden gate between the House and the Guard He did not attempt to pass the Garden gate I went to him and offered to show him the New Building but he declined saying it was too late this was about 5 a clock. He wished to see Genl B very much but didn't succeed.
5 January 1820	Genl B was out in his little garden this morning very busily employed watering his flower bed. The Genl dined with C Mantholon under the trees in his favourite garden this afternoon.

Date	Comment
6 Jan 1820	I saw Genl B this afternoon in his little garden
7 Jan 1820	I saw Genl B this morning in his Flower Garden he was in his morning gown Genl B walked about his garden a good deal this afternoon & visited the Bertrands in the evening
8 Jan 1820	Genl B was out today in his favourite garden
9 Jan 1820 Sunday	I saw Genl B this morning busily employ'd amid his valets gardening, he had on his head a large Straw Hat – he did not seem to regard a little rain which was falling.
10 Jan 1820	I saw Genl B this morning in one of his favourite gardens – I also saw him again this afternoon he was sitting on the side of a reservoir of his favourite garden doing something in the water – He was in full dress cocked hat, breeches & silk stockings
11 Jan 1820	I saw Genl B this morning in his favourite garden in his Straw Hat & morning gown. He was out in full dress in the afternoon
12 Jan 1820	I saw Genl B this morning in one of his favourite Gardens – this day the one-eyed Cooper [William Gordon] came up from James Town with a very large Tub (12 feet wide) for Genl Bonapartes favourite garden – to serve as a reservoir. The Cooper told me that the Genl was very much pleased with the Tub and gave him a glass of wine in consequence with his own hand The old cooper seemed highly delighted.
13 Jan 1820	I saw Genl B two or three times to day walking about Longwood Gardens
14 Jan 1820	I saw General B this morning walking in his favourite garden in a Straw Hat & morning gown This afternoon C Montholon directed the gardeners to make a sod wall round a flower garden – The General is going to garden on a more extensive scale seemingly
18 Jan 1820	I saw Genl B in his little garden this morning Counts Bertrand and Montholon busily employed measuring out more ground for the extension of garden for the General – The General was out a good deal to day – the day uncommonly fine.
19 Jan 1820	Genl B was out all this morning dressed in his new Jacket, waistcoat & trousers & straw hat. he was superintending the building of a sod wall (I could see him while sitting at breakfast in my own room) he and C Montholon and all his own valets hard at work – The young Bertrands carrying water to wet the sod as they were laid – The Genl's appearance was rather grotesque
20 Jan 1820	I saw General B this morning C Montholon meanwhile busy building a sod wall and putting up railings round the newly enclosed garden for the General This evening General B shot a Goat belonging to the Countess Bertrand her goats were intruding the garden the Genl was up at 5 a clock this morning.
21 Jan 1820	I SAW Genl B this morning busily employed superintending the building of the sod wall Madame Bertrand sent me one of her servants to know if she might give the remaining two goats to Mrs Kingsmile 66th Reg I said there was no objection.

Date	Comment
22 Jan 1820	I saw Genl B this morning and at his favourite amusement He rises very early This afternoon he walked on the Terrace near to the new building he walked about Longwood gardens a good deal this afternoon with the two Counts
23 Jan 1820	General Bonaparte had had excellent sport with his fowling piece this morning – he shot 8 Hens belonging to the servants about Longwood House. They scratched up the flowers in his favourite garden and there was high treason with him. Sowerby told me the Genl was up this morning watering his flowers, before the Sentinel men taken off
24 Jan 1820	He had all his valets & family employed at a sod wall
25 Jan 1820	Genl Bonaparte was not at his favourite amusement Gardening this morning
26 Jan 1820	The Gardeners saw Genl Bonaparte out this morning early at his favourite amusement gardening Lord Charles Somerset[4] [governor at the Cape] and his two daughters to see the new building & grounds at this time General b sat down to dinner in his favourite garden under the oak trees with C Montholon – the Gov Lord Charles Somerset & the two ladies passed round the garden in the wood – however as soon as they were perceived from the House the General rose from his dinner & b came into the House the Dinner was carried after him into the House Lord Charles did not know Genl B was out having only walked round the large garden and did not intrude near to the House out of delicacy to Genl Bonaparte After lord Charles party had left Longwood Genl B immediate by walking out. Major [Gideon] Gorrequer waited on Count Monoloth to state that Lord Charles wished to wait on Genl B. Count Monoloth told me to say that he had mentioned this to General B twice but had had no answer.
27 Jan 1820	I saw Genl B out this morning at his favourite amusement Four horses arrived at Longwood this evening in addition to Genl B's stud They were from the Cape of Good Hope and appeared very Handsome one a beautiful Chestnut Pony which the General desired the groom to keep for him & permit no one else to ride him. Lord Charles Somerset sailed for England in the 'Tappler' this afternoon.
28 Jan 1820	I saw Genl B this afternoon in a green coat & a straw hat He was walking in his garden – with some part of his family
29 Jan 1820	I saw Genl Bonaparte this afternoon in his favourite garden
30 Jan 1820	Sowerby saw Genl B out this morning soon after 5 a clock – I saw Genl B this afternoon he was walking about Longwood Gardens with a small part of his family and the young Bertrands – the Senteries were posted at the time
31 Jan 1820	I saw General B this morning in his garden early I have been informed that the Genl shot some Fowls yesterday morng (by Tailor the gardener) The <u>Groom</u> informed me that the General shot one of his Young kids this morning he has sent his groom to day to Sandy Bay to purchase young goats as a kind of game for his amusement in shooting probably he will have them afterwards

Date	Comment
1 February 1820	I saw Genl B today often at his favourite amusement Gardening he was himself employed placing sods on a bank in short his sole amusement at present seems to be building sod walls making reservoirs to hold water in and pulling down to day that which he had raised the day before
2 Feb 1820	I saw Genl B to day – Gardening
3 Feb 1820	I saw Genl B this morning he appeared early at his favourite amusement
4 Feb 1820	I saw Genl B this morning busily employed and all his valets seen gardening
5 Feb 1820	I saw Genl B often to day at his favourite amusement gardening
6 Feb 1820 Sunday	The Gardener (Sowerby) saw Genl B often to day and at seven a clock this Evening The Gardener told me the General shot 9 Fowls this morning 2 of which belonged to Novarrez the valet
7 Feb 1820	The Gardener saw General B often today
9 Feb 1820	I saw Genl b this morning in his little garden I saw him again this afternoon. Capt Luytens[5] of the 20th Regt came to Longwood to day to relieve me I introduced him to C Montholon The Count expressed surprise at my leaving Longwood so soon.

Plants shipped from the Cape to St Helena during the Captivity, June 1816[1]

List 1: Seeds (Dr C. M. Villet)

lbs weight in seed	Type	Value
2	Cabbage seeds (best sorts)	£16
1	Cauliflowers (best sorts)	£70
1	Littice [lettuce] of sorts	£3
4	Oranges Carrots	£16
2	Radishs	£8
1	Pearsness [parsnips]	£3
4	Turnips	£16
1	Kop Kool [cabbage] (best sorts)	£12
2 parcels	Wild and Cultivated flower seeds	£37
1 parcel	Fruit tree kernels	£10
1 assortment	Wild and cultivated flower bulbs	£10
¼ lb	*Sophora capensis* seed	£1
1 once	Tomato, or love apple seeds	2/-
		£202-2-0

List 2: Fruit trees/kernels of Cape of Good Hope sold by C. M. Villet Long Street No. 71 (in the baskets)

List no.	Fruit tree
1	Winter saffron pear
2	Green plum
3	Damson plum
4	Small blue plum
5	Apples of sorts
6	Apricots
7	Sweet pear, or sugar pear
8	Saffron pear
9	Canel pear

List no.	Fruit tree
10	Charmont pear
11	Blanket pear
12	Bergamotte pear
13	Small red pear
14	Large species of street orange
15	Small species of street orange (or nartjie)
16	Citron
17	Pack of sorts
18	Bugnons peach
19	Artichoke
20	Water lemon
21	Pinus _ _ _ _
22	Walnut
23	Almond
24	Quince

List 3: List of cultivated flower seeds of the Cape of Good Hope, sold by C. M. Villet, Long Street No. 71 (in the buckets)

Mignonette
Geranium
Sweet William
Apple bearing rose
Sweet myrtle
Ranunculus
Sweet sembiasen
Convolvulus major (creeper)
Variegated hollyhock
Yellow sapiens
Larkspur
Doub balsam of sorts
Anemonus of sorts
China asters
Indian shot [Canna indica]
Poppy of sorts
Large white hollyhock
Dark red hollyhock
White rose
Nasturtium
Doub red queen stock [Amaryllis]
Rose colour hollyhock
2 species of chrysanthemum
Asclepias
Lychnis

Marigold
Small species of poppy
Mallow
Large red poppy
Asters of sorts
Purple globe amaranth
Sweet pea
Doub _ _ _ marigold
Red and blue lupins
Marnel of Persia
Sunflowers of sorts
White amaranthus
Crotalaria
Cape syringa (tree)
Amaranthus prince's feather
Pinks
Small French marigold
Hollyhock of sorts
Nigella
Wild cumin
Tobacco
White lupins
Cassia corymbosa
Borage

List 4: Wild and cultivated flower bulbs of the Cape of Good Hope sold by C. M. Villet, Long street No. 71 (in the bag)

Amaryllis orientalis
_____ *Paleatus* (sweet smelling flowers)
_____ revoluta
_____ *purpurea*
_____ capensis
Haemanthus coccineus

Anthericum aloides
White lily
Ranunculus of sorts
Jonquil of sorts [daffodils?]
Narcissus
Gethyllis ciliaris

List 5: 108 different species of wild seeds collected from the interior of the promontory of the Cape of Good Hope by C. M. Villet Long Street No. 71, packed in baskets[2]

Erica zeyermiran [*Coilostigma zeyherianum?*]
_____ gilsa
_____ *multumbellifera*
_____ *pyrolæflora* [*E. halicacaba*]
_____ baccans
_____ *pubescens*
_____ arborea
_____ *viscaria*
_____ verticillata
_____ *margaritacea*
_____ coccinea
_____ *imbricata*
_____ hispidula
_____ *albens*
_____ multiflora
_____ *tenuifloria*
_____ *triflora*
_____ calycina
_____ *phylicoides* [*E. pulchella*]
_____ unknown (beautiful)
_____ *capitata*
Protea argentea
_____ *syeciacae*
_____ *strobibimae*
_____ *conscarpae*
_____ *syeciacae nigra*
_____ *sallens*
_____ *glabra*
_____ *gratulae*
_____ *melliztina* (Sugar tree)
_____ *cucullata*
_____ *conofera*
_____ *sinifolia*
_____ *glomcratae*

Geranthenmum fulgidum Everlasting flowers
_____ *syeciasis finum* Everlasting flowers
_____ *stæhelinachronia frutescens*
Everlasting flowers
_____ *linoides*
Echium fricticosum
Phlomis leonurus
Cheiranthus strietus
Podalyria styraxifoliæ (The flower smelling very sweet)
_____ *capensis*
Taxus elongatus (the yellow wood tree)
Polygælæ myrtifolia
Othonna sectinata
Coluteæ fructescens
Mesembryæthmum aurantium
_____ *somesidianum*
_____ *edule*
2 difft species of Clusia
Pelargonium cucullatum
_____ *cæpitatum*
Euphorbia genistoides
_____ *caput medusa*
Heliophila araboides
Eoyena glabra
Malianthus? (The Hottentots wild plum)
Blæria ericoides
Indigofera aphylla
_____ *coriaceæ*
Lobelia pinifolia
Selago spuria
Lachenalia alba
Myrica gordifolia The Candle berry myrtle
_____ *quercifolia* The Candle berry myrtle

Celastrus cernusis

_____ *octogonus*

Plectronia (a large tree)

2 different species of Caysressus [cupressus?]

Cotyledon orbientater

Passerine

Anthrotyza aethiopsicæ (bulbs)

_____ *frangrans* (bulbs)

Boralea aphylla

_____ *poinnata*

Ascleysius arborescens

Plectronia ventosa (tree)

Cacalia

Aristea major

Montiniæ acris

Eæciliata

Gimassey (a tree, non-descript)

Solanum giganteum

Mimosa glaucos

Curtisia fagineæ (the assagay tree)

Senecio

Grotalaria laburnifolia

Stapelia guttatæ

great varieties of *Ixias* (bulbs)

Euclea racemosa

Melianthus major

Gethyllis spiralis (bulbs)

Gleditsatria (originaire of N. America)

Ostespermum pisiferum

Monsonia speciosæ

Diosma virgata

Gladiolus merianus (bulb)

Malva capensis

Saarda ris (a tree non-descript.)

Rhus sæviajaætum

Appendix VII

Old country houses of St Helena

North
(Half Tree Hollow/Greater Jamestown/Sane Valley)

Alarm Gun Cottage
Alarm House
Bleak House
Blundens
Brook Hill
Cambrian House
Chubbs Spring
East Lodge
Enfield House

Escourt Cottage
Friars Lodge
Halfway House
Hutt's Gate
Kent Cottage
Maldivia
Mosquito Cottage
New Ground House
Palm Villa

Prospect Cottage
Prospect House
Sane Valley House
Seaview
The Briars
Varneys
Villa Le Breton
Willow Cottage
Willowdene

East

Apple Cottage
Arno's Vale
Bates
Bertrands
Bradleys

Deadwood House
Guinea Grass
Longwood
Mulberry Cottage
New Longwood

Pink Grove
Teutonic Hall
Warbro House
Willow Bank
Winegrove

Central
Governor's Plantation House orbit

Bevins
Cathole Cottage
Cleugh's Plain
Farm Lodge
Francis Plain House
Glencot
Harpers
Hermitage
Knollcombes
Longbank
Luffkins Tower
Mackintosh's

Oakbank
Oaklands
Olive Cottage
Osbornes
Pear Tree Farm
Plantation House
Powell's Spring
Prince's Lodge
Red Hill House
Rock Cottage
Rose Bower
Rosemary Hall

Rural Retreat
Scotland
Southens/Southin/Saltons
St Paul's Villa
Sydenham
Terrace Knoll
Trapp Cottage
Vaughans
White Gate
Willow Cottage
Woodcot
Woodlands (Blenkin's)

South/High Peak/Sandy Bay

Bagleys
Bamboo Grove
Bamboo Hedge (Purlings)
Bay Cottage
Blarney House
Chestnut
Coffee Grove
Fairfield Cottage
Fairyland

High Peak Cottage
Hyams
Jenkins Cottage
Kennedys
Lemon Grove
Maria's
Mount Pleasant
Mount Rock
Peak Dale Farm

Rock Farm
Rock Rose
Rose Cottage
Unity Cottage
Virgin Hall
Windy Point
Wranghams

West

Botleys
Broadbottom
Bushes Hollow
Cowgrass Flat
Distant Cottage
Half Moon Cottage
High Hill House
Honeysuckle Cottage

Horse Pasture Farm
  (Woodlands)
Horse Ridge Hill House
Horse Ridge House
Masons Cottage
Myrtle Gove
Nettle Flat
Old Luffkins

Peak Farm
Picquet House
Poplars
Prospect
Saddle Cottage
The Firs
West Lodge
Whites

Notes

ABBREVIATIONS

BL   British Library, London
IOR   India Office Records
Kew   Royal Botanic Gardens Archive, Kew, London
SHA   St Helena Archives, Jamestown
TNA   The National Archives, London

PREFACE

1   Abel, *Napoleon*, p. 116.

2   Fox, 'Henry Russell', p. 53.

3   'Kerr's views in the island of St. Helena', https://bweaver.nom.sh/Kerr/kerr.htm, accessed 24 March 2020.

4   Kitching, *A Handbook and Gazetteer of the Island of St Helena*, p. 81.

5   Melliss, *St Helena*, pp. 281, 309 and 327.

6   Kew Archives, Director's correspondence, Melliss to Hooker, 26 March 1868, f. 220.

7   See Teale, Thesis, 2.125–126 and 2.122; and Grove, 'St Helena as a microcosm of the East India Company world', pp. 256–265.

8   Lambdon and Cronk, 'Extinction dynamics under extreme conservation threat: The flora of St Helena', in *Frontiers in Ecology and Evolution*, pp. 1 and 6.

9   Lambdon and Cronk, 'Extinction dynamics', p. 3; and Lambdon, *Flowering Plants and Ferns of St Helena*, pp. 156, 231, 294, 296, 330, 405, 436 and 582.

10   Lambdon and Cronk, 'Extinction dynamics', p. 4; and Lambdon and Ellick, 'A rare plant census of St Helena', Darwin Plus: Overseas Territories Environment and Climate Fund Final Report (DPLUS008), 2014.

11   Fennah, 'Discussion', p. 575.

12   *Flora Sta Helenica*, p. 18.

13   Gill and Teale, *St. Helena 500*, pp. 198–199; and Lambdon, *Flowering Plants and Ferns of St Helena*, p. 294.

CHAPTER 1 ~ St Helena within the global botanical network

1   McCracken, *Gardens of Empire*, pp. 211–213

2   KA, [Plant] Record Book, 1793–1809, f. 11.

3   Hemsley, *The Gallery of Marianne North's Paintings*, pp. v–vi.

4   Brooke, *History of the Island of St Helena*, pp. 115 and 155.

5   Brooke, *History of the Island of St Helena*, p. 6.

6   Brooke, *History of the Island of St Helena*, p. 234.

7   Brooke, *History of the Island of St Helena*, p. 237.

8   Grove, 'St Helena as a microcosm of the East India Company world', pp. 257–265; and Smallman, *Quincentenary*, p. 35.

9   Anonymous (Beatson), *Flora Sta Helenica*, p. ii; and Desmond, *Sir Joseph Dalton Hooker*, p. 31.

10   KA, [Plant] Record Book, 1804–1826, f. 162.

11   See McCracken, *The Palm House and Botanic Garden, Belfast*, p. 18.

12   Allen, *The Victorian Fern Craze*; Lemmon, *The Covered Garden*, pp. 175–176; Keogh, *The Wardian Case*. See also https://www.plantexplorers.com/explorers/biographies/ward/nathaniel-bagshaw-ward.htm [Accessed 13 March 2020].

13   Quoted in Fox, *The Bennett Letters*, p. 120; and KA, Director's correspondence, 58/9, 22 May 1843.

14   Anonymous (Beatson), *Flora Sta Helenica*, pp. iii–iv.

15   Huxley, *Life and Letters of Sir Joseph Dalton Hook*er, Vol. 1, p. 64.

16   Figures from Loudon contained in Lemmon, *The Covered Garden*, p. 173.

17   BL, IOR/G/32/84, 2 July 1818, f. 77.

18   SHA, Proceedings of the Agricultural and Horticultural Society, 1823–1825, ff. 221–222.

19   SHA, St Helena Record, Public Department, 126, 11 April 1825.

20   McCracken, 'Fraternity in the age of jingoism: The British imperial botanic and forestry network', pp. 49–62.

21   *The Royal Indian Engineering College, Coopers Hill*, pp. 6, 17, 53–55, 119–143 and 215–269.

22   See, for example, McCracken, 'Dependence, destruction and development', pp. 295–299 and McCracken, 'The indigenous forests of colonial Natal and Zululand', pp. 28–35.

23   Williamson, *History of the State of Maine*, Vol. 2, pp. 165–178.

24   Brooke, *History of the Island of St Helena*, p. 274. If Scots pine, it no longer grows on the island. The spruce cannot be sitka spruce as it was introduced into Europe from North America only in 1831.

25   Lambdon, *Flowering Plants and Ferns of St Helena*, p. 195.

26   Quoted in Teale, Thesis, 1.242.

27   Brooke, *History of the Island of St Helena*, p. 371.

28   Brooke, *History of the Island of St Helena*, p. 373.

29   Brooke, *History of the Island of St Helena*, pp. 414 and 418–419.

CHAPTER 2 ~ East India Company gardens

1   By the early 1800s the castor oil plant was considered a noxious weed on the island. See Beatson, *Tracts*, p. 4.

2   Pessina, 'Labour, environment and empire in the South Atlantic', p. 79.

3   Brooke, *History of the Island of St Helena*, pp. 115, 129 and 133; and Smallman, *Quincentenery*, pp. 33–35.

4   Duncan, *St Helena,* pp. 158, 201, 204 and 213.

5   Grove, 'St Helena as a microcosm of the East India Company world', p. 257.

6   For a discussion of St Helena land tenure, see Teale, Thesis, 3.1–5.

7   Extrapolated from George W. Melliss's property ownership map entitled 'Trigonometrical survey of the island of St Helena ... surveyed between the years 1825 & 1836'. A copy of this invaluable map which was housed in the castle at St Helena is contained in Teale, Thesis, Vol. 3.

8   *St Helena. Report on the Blue Book for 1903*, London: HMSO, 1904, p. 8.

9   Janisch, *St Helena Records*, p. 183.

10   Cronk, *The Endemic Flora of St Helena*, pp. 19–24.

11   Brooke, *History of the Island of St Helena*, p. 135.

12   Brooke, *History of the Island of St Helena*, pp. 174 and 195.

13   Gill and Teale, *St Helena 500*, p. 152.

14   Gill and Teale, *St Helena 500*, p. 177.

15   Brooke, *History of the Island of St Helena*, p. 236; and Lambdon, *Flowering Plants and Flowers of St Helena*, p. 195.

16   https://sainthelenaisland.info/greatwoodwall.htm

17   British Library, IOR, G/32/118, letter to the EIC directors from the island's Council, 15 July 1725, no. 42.

18   Teale, *Saint Helena 1502 to 1659*, p. 45; and Brooke, *History of the Island of St Helena*, p. 53.

19   Gill and Teale, *St Helena 500*, pp. 102 and 106.

20   J-N. Bellin, *Le Petit Atlas Maritime*, Vol. 3, l'Afrique, Paris 1764, plate 124.

21   J-N. Bellin, *Le Petit Atlas Maritime*, Vol. 3, l'Afrique, Paris 1764, plate 114.

22   Karsten, *The Old Company Garden at the Cape*, part 2; and McCracken and McCracken, *The Way to Kirstenbosch*, pp. 11–36.

23   BL, IOR, EIC, General Correspondence, letter book 12, 31 December 1703, f. 242 (pencil 121b).

24   Brooke, *History of the Island of St Helena*, p. 213; Gosse, *St Helena, 1502–1938*, p. 132.

25   Gill and Teale, *St Helena 500*, p. 169.

26   BL. EIC, Factory Records, G/32/5, 19 May 1716, included in Gerber, *East India Company and Southern Africa*, p. 331.

27   Gill and Teale, *St Helena 500*, p. 178; and 'Letters to London', 5 August 1718, quoted in Teale, Thesis, 1.149.

28   Teale, 'Saint Helaena', 1.121.

29   Gosse, *St Helena, 1502–1938*, pp. 187 and 189.

30   BL, IOR, Madras Despatches (1774), Vol. 6, E/4/866, f. 99, 23 December 1774.

31   Cambridge University Library, http://cudl.lib.cam.ac.uk/view/MS-JOD-00020/528, 10 March 2016. Journal of Captain Cook's voyage round the world on HMS *Resolution*. Copyright National Maritime Museum.

32   Desmond, *Sir Joseph Dalton Hooker*, p. 31.

33   Forster, *A Voyage around the World*, p. 299.

34   Beatson, *Tracts*, p. 280.

35   Lockwood, *A Guide to St Helena*, p. 53.

36   BL, IOR, G/32/118, letter to the EIC directors from the island's Council, 15 July 1725, f. 30.

37   BL, IOR, G/32/132, Account of St Helena, f. 4.

38   BL, Robert Brooke, 'Account of St Helena', 1792, IOR/G/32/165, f. 31.

39   'C'est au jardin de la compagnie, situé sur la place et vis-à-vis l'église, qu'on familiarise les végétaux, nouvellement arrivés, avec l'aridité du sol: ils trouvent là une assez bonne terre de rapport'. Quoted in Pessina, 'Labour, environment and empire in the South Atlantic', pp. 81–82.

40   Teale, Thesis, 2.33.

41   Brooke, *History of the Island of St Helena*, p. 213.

42   Brooke, *History of the Island of St Helena*, pp. 235–236; Gill and Teale, *St Helena 500*, p. 127; and *St Helena Almanac, 1858*, npn.

43   J. N. Bellin, *Le Petit Atlas Maritime*, Vol. 3, l'Afrique, Paris 1764, plate 123.

44   Kolben, *The Present State of the Cape of Good Hope*, Vol. 1, p. 351 and Vol. 2, pp. 4–5.

45   George, *Names of Places of the Island of St. Helena*, p. 48.

46   BL, India Office Records, St Helena, 1698–1724, G/32/118. See also Fox, *A Bitter Draught*, p. 200.

47   BL, India Office Records, St Helena, 1698–1724, G/32/118. See also Fox, *A Bitter Draught*, p. 204.

48   Irish Architecture Archive, Guinness Collection, J. Corneille, Plantation House, St. Helena, Topographical view showing the rear of the house. *c.*1780.

49   Irish Architecture Archive, Guinness Collection, drawing signed J. Corneille, Plantation House, St. Helena, Topographical view showing the rear of the house. *c.*1780.

50   British Library, IOR G/32/163, Account of St Helena, ff. 13–14.

51   Duncan, *St Helena*, p. 161.

52   Walter, *Events in a Military Life*, Vol. 2, p. 9.

53   Kitching, *A Handbook and Gazetteer of the Island of St Helena*, p. 15.

54   Thomas H. Brooke arrived on St Helena aged 18 on 11 May 1792 during his uncle's governorship. He lived at Prospect, with an official residence in Jamestown. He was twice acting governor of the island. As first member of council, he earned a salary of £1,400 a year along with two servants, candles and oil.

55   Brooke, *History of the Island of St Helena*, p. 11.

56   McCracken, *Gardens of Empire*, p. 92.

57   Akin, 'John Company at the Cape', p. 254.

58   Kitching, *A Handbook and Gazetteer of the Island of St Helena*, p. 65.

59   Gill, *Six Months in Ascension*, p. 41.

CHAPTER 3 ~ St Helena's old private gardens

1   *St Helena. Report on the Blue Book for 1891*, London: HMSO, 1892, p. 17.

2   Royle, 'Island history, not the story of islands: The case of St Helena', pp. 49–51.

3   Fox, *The Bennett Letters*, pp. 35 and 70.

4   Fox, *The Bennett Letters*, p. 138.

5   Frost, *Sir Joseph Banks*, p. 58, quoted in Loring, 'Voyages of improvement', p. 181.

6   An excellent study of slavery on St Helena in the later period is Colin Fox's *A Bitter Draught: St Helena and the abolition of slavery, 1792–1840*, Elveden, Society of Friends of St Helena, 2017.

7   These 18th-century houses of the St Helena gentry tended to be double-storey, though some were single. They had high ceilings. Some had quarters for enslaved people in a basement. At least one, Rock Rose House, had a handsome ebony staircase. Fireplaces were not common. See Kitching, *A Handbook and Gazetteer of the Island of St Helena*, np (68); and Teale, Thesis, 5.17–21.

8   Quoted in Teale, Thesis, 1.240.

9   [Duncan], *A Description of the Island of St Helena*, p. 204.

10   Brooke, *History of St. Helena*, p. 132 and [Duncan] *A Description of the Island of St. Helena*, pp. 212–213.

11   Captain Barnes (1817) quoted in Robson, *St. Helena Memoirs*, pp. 38–39.

12   Beatson, *Tracts*, p. xxxvii; and Chaplin, *A St Helena Who's Who*, p. 87.

13   Kew Archives, Mss Burchell Flora Heleniana, ff. 121 and 126.

14   Crallan, 'Listed buildings', appendix, p. 12.

15   St Helena Council Records, 1678–1681, f. 25, https://www.friendsofsthelena.com/upload/files/1678-1683_St_Helena_Records.pdf [Accessed 3 December 2021].

16   Brooke, *History of the Island of St Helena*, p. 257.

17   Fox, *The Bennett Letters*, p. 28.

18   Another damaging flood had occurred on 20 February 1873.

19   SHA, Proceedings of the Agricultural and Horticultural Society, 1823–1825, ff. 239–240.

20   Fox, *The Bennett Letters*, p. 128.

21   Grant, *A Few Notes on St Helena*; and Melliss, *St Helena*, p. 324.

22   Francis, *St Helena*, pp. 164–165.

23   The map is entitled: 'Trigonometrical survey of the island of St Helena situated latitude 15:55 south longitude 5.11 west Distinguishing the whole of the landed estates Public and Private Property, their boundaries, divisions, fences, lines of free or lease lands also the original grants of lease recently converted into permanent tenure, Roads, Telegraphs, Springs, Fortifications and Remarkable Places inland. Surveyed between the years 1825 & 1836 by George W. Melliss'.

24   Grant, *A Few Notes on St Helena*, p. 66.

25   Beatson, *Tracts*, p. lxviii.

26   Beatson, *Tracts*, pp. lxiii and lxvi.

27   Mellis, *St Helena*, p. 230.

28   Jackson, *Notes and Reminiscences*, p. 136.

29   Henry Thorpe, 'The history and re-development of Rock Rose', *The St Helena Connection*, no.26, June 2019, p. 18.

30   Teale, Thesis, 2.86.

31   Teale, Thesis, 2.80.

32   Arno's Vale was an 18th-century gentleman's house which had been owned by the Doveton family. A lovely illustration of it and its surrounds is to be found as the frontispiece of Brooke's *History of St Helena*, 1806.

33   Fox, *The Bennett Letters*, p. 122.

34   BL, IOR, G/32/136, Robert Brooke, Account of St Helena, f. 17.

35   George, *The History of the Chinese Indentured Labourers on St Helena 1810-1836 and beyond*, pp. 85-86.

36   Du Preez and Dronfield, *Dr James Barry*, pp. 274–275; and Hourican and Clarke, 'James Barry', *Dictionary of Irish Biography*, Vol. 1, pp. 331-332.

37   Lockwood, *A Guide to St. Helena*, p. 19.

38   Fox, *A Bitter Draught*, p. 45; and Fox, *The Bennett Letters*, p. 35, and Appendix 4.

39   Fox, *A Bitter Draught*, p. 91; and George, *The History of the Chinese Indentured Labourers on St Helena*, p. 56.

40   Melliss, *St Helena*, p. 256 and plate 32; and Lambdon, *Flowering Plants and Ferns of St Helena*, p. 232.

41   Teale, Thesis, 3.47.

42   Crallan, 'Listed buildings', p. 14; and Teale, Thesis, 2.72–73.

43   Fox, *The Bennett Letters*, pp. 35 and 199.

44   Fox, *The Bennett Letters*, pp. 38–41.

45   Fox, *The Bennett Letters*, pp. 199–207.

46   Fox, *The Bennett Letters*, p. 132.

47   Fox, *The Bennett Letters*, p. 222; Gumede, 'Maldivia House once belonged to the Natal government of South Africa', *Wirebird*, no. 48, 2019, pp. 21–25; *St Helena. Report for 1898. Colonial Reports – Annual. No. 265*, London, HMSO, 1899, p. 5; and Maldivia House http://sainthelenaisland.info/maldivia.htm?african [Accessed 22 April 2018].

48   Letter from George Bennett to William Hooker, quoted in Fox, *The Bennett Letters*, p. 120. KA, Director's correspondence, DC/58/9, 22 May 1843.

49   Gill, *Six Months in Ascension*, p. 25.

50   Gill, *Six Months in Ascension*, p. 42. See also Teale, Thesis, 2.31.

51   Chaplin, *A St Helena Who's Who*, p. 74; and George, *Names of Places on St Helena*, p. 45.

52   Grant, *A Few Notes on St Helena*.

53   Kitching, A Handbook and Gazetteer of the Island of St Helena, p. 41.

54   George, *Names of Places on St Helena*, p. 45. The Leech family also occupied Woodcot House (erected *c*.1770) from 1803 to 1864. See Teale, Thesis, 2.29 and 2.81.

55   Grant, *A Few Notes on St Helena*, pp. 55 and 61.

56   Fox (ed.), 'Henry Russell', pp. 38 and 53.

57   Gill, *Six Months in Ascension*, p. 40.

58   Grant, *A Note from St Helena*, p. 46.

59   Kitching, *A Handbook and Gazetteer of the Island of St Helena*, p. 35.

CHAPTER 4 ~ The St Helena Botanic Garden

1   See for example, McCracken and McCracken, *Natal the Garden Colony: Victorian Natal and the Royal Botanic Gardens*.

2   Brockway, *Science and Colonial Expansion* (1979); Drayton, *Nature's Government* (2000); Grove, *Green Imperialism* (1997); McCracken, *Gardens of Empire* (1979); and Mackay, *In the Wake of Cook* (2018).

3   Beatson, *Tracts*, pp. lxxviii and 214.

4   Fox, *A Bitter Draught*, p. xv.

5   Dawson, *The Banks Letters*, p. 154.

6   Friends of St Helena website: https://www.friendsofsthelena.com/, St Helena Ancestors section.

7   See David Mackay's comments in *In the Wake of Cook*; and Ian Boreham, 'Captain Cook and St Helena', https://www.captaincooksociety.com/home/detail/captain-cook-and-st-helena

8   McAleer, 'A young slip of botany', p. 36.

9   Dawson, *The Banks Letters*, pp. 154 and 231.

10   BL, Robert Brooke, 'Account of St Helena', 1792, IOR/G/32/165, f. 4.

11   Kelly, 'Robert Brooke', p. 877.

12   Caird, 'Charlotte Brook', pp. 869–870.

13   Fox, 'Two governors', pp. 41–42.

14   Smyth, 'A governor with a 'good heart'', p. 43; Jennings, 'Killybeggs'; and 'Memoir of Governor Brooke', p. 181.

15   *A Letter from Mr. Brooke to an Honorable Member of the House of Commons*, Dublin, printed by B. Dugdale, 1786, p. 15; and Kelly, 'Brooke', *Dictionary of Irish Biography*, Vol. 1, p. 877.

16   Brooke's period as governor officially ran from 12 May 1787 until 10 March 1802, but between March 1801 and the arrival of Governor Robert Patton in March 1802 Francis Robson acted on Brooke's behalf.

17   Kelly, 'Robert Brooke', *Dictionary of Irish Biography*, Vol. 1, p. 877. Colin Fox gives the figures of five sons and two daughters, but some of these may have died in infancy.

18   *Proceedings of the Dublin Society, from November 2d 1780, to August 23d 1781*, Vol. 17, pp. 27, 35, 55 and 70.

19   Nelson and McCracken, *The Brightest Jewel*, p. 19.

20   McCracken, 'The botanic garden, Trinity College, Dublin', *Garden History*, Vol. vii, no. 1, spring 1979, p. 86.

21   The Canister was pulled down in 1958 and the present building which replaced it was designed by St Helena's local historian, architect Percy Teale.

22   BL, Robert Brooke, 'Account of St Helena', 1792, IOR/G/32/165, f. 13.

23   Gill and Teale, *St Helena 500*, p. 243.

24   Grove, *Green Imperialism*, p. 340.

25   Thomas, 'Calcutta Botanic Garden', Phd thesis, King's College London, 2016; and Dawson, *The Banks Letters*, p. 512.

26   Desmond, *Sir Joseph Dalton Hooker*, p. 31.

27   George, *Names of Places on St Helena*, p. 7.

28   Brooke, *History of the Island of St Helena*. p. 293.

29   National Library of Australia, Journal of Arthur Bowes Smyth: https://nla.gov.au/nla.obj-233672863/view

30   Brooke, *History of the island of St Helena*, p. 4.

31   Photograph dated 1880 in possession of D.P. McCracken; and The National Archives, London, CO 700/St Helena8, Plans of properties, St Helena, July 1839.

32   Kumar, 'Botanical explorations and the East India Company: Revisiting', p. 23.

33   Kew, James and Alexander Anderson: Letters relating to the botanical gardens St Helena and St Vincent, 1790, 43/2/3.

34   British Library, IOR/G/32/163 'Account of St Helena', f. 3.

35   Beatson, *Tracts*, p. 42.

36   Dawson, *The Banks Letters*, pp. 294 and 615.

37   Dawson, *The Banks Letters*, pp. 275, 292, 486 and 615.

38   Dawson, *The Banks Letters*, pp. 294, 681, 705 and 887.

39   SHA, Register of proclamations, 1809–1823, September 1821, f. 354.

40   SHA, St Helena Records, Vol. 80, 31 December 1792.

41   SHA, St Helena Records, Vols 77, 78 and 79, 1791–1792.

42   Dawson, *The Banks Letters,* p. 246.

43   SHA, Records Vol. 70, 1786, 30 September and 31 December 1786 and 31 March 1787; and Records Vol. 71, 30 June, 30 July and 31 December 1787.

44   Dawson, *The Banks Letters*, 8 January 1791, p. 291; SHA, Letter-book, 19 January and 28 May 1787; and Desmond, *Sir Joseph Dalton Hooker*, p. 31.

45   SHA, St Helena Records, Vol. 72, 1 April 1788.

46   Dawson, *The Banks Letters*, p. 681.

47   BL, Robert Brooke, 'Account of St Helena', 1792, IOR/G/32/165, f. 14.

48   SHA, Secretary's out-letters, 1808–1814, 12 September 1808, f. 50.

49   SHA, Letters to England, 1785–1789, 28 May 1787, item 10.

50   Chaplin, *A St Helena Who's Who*, p. 249.

51   Bradlow, *Baron Ludwig's-burg Garden*, pp. 24, 26–27, 45 and 71; Porteous, *The Porteous Story*, p. 278; and SHA, letters to England, 1785–1789, letter 28 May 1787, item 11.

52   SHA, Burials, 24 June 1819, f. 6497.

53   Chaplin, *A St Helena Who's Who*, p. 11. A.A. Seale is probably Archibald Alexander
      Seale, born in December 1793.

54   Dawson, *The Banks Letters*, p. 681.

55   SHA, St Helena Record, Vol. 77, 25 July 1791.

56   Janisch, *St Helena Records*, p. 231.

57   *Indian and Pacific Correspondence of Sir Joseph Banks*, Vol. 2, p. 385. Also quoted in
      Loring, 'Voyages of improvement', p. 169.

58   Lee, Captain Bligh's Second Voyage to the South Sea: http://gutenberg.net.au/
      ebooks12/1204361h.html

59   BL, IOR, G/32/55, St Helena consultations (Factory Records), 1792, ff. 263–269.

60   Gosse, *St Helena, 1502–1938*, p. 216.

61   SHA, St Helena Records, Vol. 80, 1792–1793 and Letter-book, 1791–1793; BL,
      Consultations, IOR/G/32/55, 24 December 1792; and Dawson short title,
      pp. 106–7.

62   KA, [Plant] Record Book, 1793–1809, f. 11.

63   Teale, Thesis, 1.237.

64   SHA, Records Vol. 81, 1793–1794.

65   Cronk, *Endemic Flora of St Helena*, p. 36.

66   Fox, *A Bitter Draught*, pp. 18-19.

67   Hurburgh, *The Royal Tasmanian Botanical Gardens, 1818–1986*, p. 9.

68   See, for example, SHA, Bagley letter dated 13 September 1791.

69   SHA, Letter-book, 1793–1795, 30 June 1794.

70   SHA, St Helena Record, Vol. 82, 1794, accounts 31 March 1794.

71   'Cursory remarks on board the Friendship', in *The Asiatic Journal and Monthly
      Register*, November 1819 , Vol. 8, pp. 452–453. See also: https://joan-druett.blogspot.
      com/2014/02/mary-ann-reid-visits-island-of-st-helena.html [Accessed 27 December
      2020].

72   Gosse, *St Helena, 1502–1938*, p. 214.

73   Kelly, 'Robert Brooke', p. 877.

74   Neil Chambers (ed.), *Scientific Correspondence of Sir Joseph Banks, 1765–1820*, Vol. 4,
      London, Pickering and Chatto, 2007, p. 390.

75   Smyth, 'A governor with a 'good heart'', p. 43; and Fox, 'Two governors', p. 47.

76   See Fox, 'Two governors', p. 48; and Friends of St Helena Society website https://
      www.friendsofsthelena.com/ancestors [Accessed 7 January 2021].

77   Teale, Thesis, 1.246.

78   Dawson, *The Banks Letters*, pp. 20–21, 656 and 682.

79   Gosse, *St Helena, 1502–1938*, p. 233.

80   Dawson, *The Banks Letters*, pp. 486–487.

81   [Duncan], *A Description of the Island of St. Helena*, p. 161.

82   *St Helena Gazette*, 17 December 1806.

83   *St Helena Gazette*, 10 October 1806.

CHAPTER 5 ~ The big three: Burchell, Beatson and Roxburgh

1   Ashmole and Ashmole, *St Helena and Ascension Island*, pp. 66–67; Cronk, *The Endemic
      Plants of St Helena*, p. 46; and Dawson, *The Banks Letters*, p. 444.

2   SHA, Secretary's out-letters, 1805–1814, 4 August 1806, f. 15.

3   Susan Buchanan, *Burchell's Travels: The life, art and journeys of William John Burchell, 1781–1863*, Cape Town, 2015, p. 29; Castell, *William John Burchell*, pp. 15–21.

4   SHA. Secretary's out-letters, 1805–1814, 21 November 1808, f. 55.

5   Castell, *William John Burchell*, pp. 39–41, 109–110, 112, 144, 150 and 154.

6   Dawson, *The Banks Letters*, pp. 444–445.

7   Castell, *William John Burchell*, pp. 114–115, 147.

8   Castell, *William John Burchell*, p. 135.

9   Fox, *A Bitter Draught*, p. 133.

10   Castell, *William John Burchell*, p. 36.

11   Brooke, *History of the island of St Helena*, p. 322.

12   Castell, *William John Burchell*, pp. 29, 31 and 42–43; Desmond *Dictionary of British and Irish Botanists*, p. 634; Fox, 'Two governors', p. 50; and 'Anna Maria Walker', https://en.wikipedia.org/wiki/Anna_Maria_Walker [Accessed 8 January 2021].

13   Castell, *William John Burchell*, p. 50.

14   Castell, *William John Burchell*, pp. 52 and 109–110.

15   Lockwood, *A Guide to St Helena*, appendix, p. 41.

16   Castell, *William John Burchell*, pp. 122 and 146.

17   Castell, *William John Burchell*, pp. 146–147.

18   *St Helena Almanac 1855*, npn.

19   SHA. Secretary's out-letters, 1805–1814, 21 January 1814.

20   KA, Director's correspondence, T. V. Wollaston to Joseph Hooker, 22 November 1875, f. 279.

21   SHA, Letters to England, 1785–1789, July 1789, f. 81.

22   Kew Gardens Archive, Mss Burchell Flora St Heleniana, 18 May 1807, ff. 418–491.

23   Castell, *William John Burchell*, pp. 7 and 96.

24   KA, Mss Burchell Flora Heleniana, ff. 150–151.

25   Lambdon, *Flowering Plants and Ferns of St Helena*, p. 336.

26   Gill and Teale, *St Helena 500*.

27   KA, [Plant] Inwards Book, 1805–1809, ff. 348 and 352.

28   Castell, *William John Burchell*, pp. 166–167.

29   Castell, *William John Burchell*, p. 181.

30   Botanique livre d'Entré 1864–1900, Bibliothèque du Phanérogame, Jardin des Plantes, Paris, Nr 328/27, 28 July 1864.

31   KA, Director's correspondence, Melliss to Hooker, 26 November 1867, ff. 214–214b.

32   Thomas Coke, 1st Earl of Leicester (1754–1842), legendary agricultural reformer and owner of Holkham Hall.

33   Beatson, *Tracts*, p. 173.

34   Hearl, 'Charles Darwin on St Helena'.

35   Beatson, *Tracts*, p. 10.

36   Beatson, *Tracts*, pp. 52, 62, 83 and 104.

37   Robinson, *William Roxburgh*, pp. 52–53.

38   Robinson, *William Roxburgh*, p. 106. Original source: Roxburgh to Ricketts, 11 January 1813, BL, IOR, P/8/13, 15 January 1813.

39   Robinson, *William Roxburgh*, p. 74.

40   Ashmole and Ashmole, *St Helena and Ascension Island*, p. 67.

41   Beatson, *Tracts*, pp. 295–326.

42 Anonymous, *Flora Sta Helenica*, printed by J. Boyd, St Helena, 1825, 20pp.

43 Tavolacci, 'Vegetable gardens versus cash crops: Science and political economy in the Agricultural and Horticultural Society of India, 1820–40', in *History Workshop Journal*, Vol. 88, 2019, pp. 24–46,

44 Melliss, *St Helena*, pp. 233–383.

45 Cronk, *The Endemic Flora of St Helena*, p. 37.

46 Beatson, *Tracts*, pp. 295–326; Desmond, *Sir Joseph Dalton Hooker*, p. 32; and Jackson, *St Helena*, pp. 323–343.

47 Gosse, *St Helena*, p. 237; Morris, *Reprint of a report*, p. 11; and *St Helena Almanac*, 1884, p. 41.

48 Beatson, *Tracts*, pp. 170 and 182.

49 Beatson, *Tracts*, pp. 169–170 and 182.

50 Desmond, *Dictionary of British and Irish Botanists*, p. 96.

51 Robinson, *William Roxburgh*, p. 106.

52 Eleven of which have no species name beside them.

53 Chaplin, *A St Helena Who's Who*, p. 105; Fox, *A Bitter Draught*, pp. 254 and 303; Gosse, *St Helena*, pp. 306–309; and Kitching, *A Handbook and Gazetteer of the Island of St Helena* [p. 89].

54 Cronk, *The Endemic Flora of St Helena*, pp. 22–23.

55 Gosse, *St Helena*, p. 220.

56 SHA, Register of proclamations, 1809–1823, ff. 190–191.

57 BL, IOR/G/32/83, 13 December 1817, ff. 523–524.

58 McCracken and McCracken, 'A register of trees, Co. Cork, 1793 1860', *The Journal of the Cork Historical Society*, Vol. 81, 1976, pp. 39–60.

59 KA, WJB/1/3, memorandum from Captain Leroy 1846, f. 8.

60 Fox (ed.), 'Henry Russell', p. 53.

61 BL, IOR/G/32/85, Account of trees planted, 4 December 1820, ff. 473–473.

62 BL, IOR/G/32/85, 19 June 1820, ff. 205–210; and 12 July 1821, ff. 816–819.

63 McCracken, 'Plant hunting and the provenance of South African plants in British botanical magazines, 1787–1910', pp. 75–89.

64 *Paxton's Botanical Dictionary*, p. 189.

65 Williams, 'Select ferns and lycopods: British and exotic', pp. 113–114.

66 *The Botanical Cabinet*, Vol. 17, 1830, no.1693 *Canna patens*.

67 Lambdon, *Flowering Plants and Ferns of St Helena*, p. 604.

68 *Botanical Repository* (c. 1803–1807), Vol. 6, plate ccclxxxix, *Dombeya erythroxylon*.

69 Bretschneider, *History of European Botanical Discoveries in China*, p. 216.

70 Reginald Whitley obituary in *Gardener's Magazine*, Vol. 11, 1835, p. 160.

71 Cronk, *The Endemic Flora of St Helena*, pp. 59–61; Lambdon, *Flowering Plants and Ferns of St* Helena, pp. 292–297; Lambdon and Cronk, 'Extinction dynamics under extreme conservation threat', pp. 3–4; and Melliss, *St Helena*, pp. 228–229 and 245.

CHAPTER 6 ~ Napoleon's gardens

1 Latimer, *Talks of Napoleon at St. Helena*, p. 252.

2 Barry Porteous, *The Porteous Story: A Scottish border family from 1439 A.D.*, Canada, 1980, p. 277.

3 Abell, *Recollections of the Emperor Napoleon on the Island of St Helena*, pp. 17–18.

4 Abell, *Recollections of the Emperor Napoleon on the Island of St Helena*, pp. 66–67.

5   Abbott, *Napoleon at St. Helena*, pp. 48–50.

6   Abell, *Recollections of the Emperor Napoleon on the Island of St Helena*, p. 185.

7   KA, Mss Burchell Flora St Heleniana, 19 February 1808, f. 159.

8   O'Meara, *Napoleon in Exile*, Vol. 1, p. 79.

9   Gosse, *St Helena*, pp. 228–229.

10   Marchand, *In Napoleon's Shadow*, p. 367.

11   Dawson, *The Banks Letters*, p. 708.

12   Quoted in Robson, *St Helena Memoirs*, p. 38.

13   Abell, *Recollections of the Emperor Napoleon on the Island of St Helena*, pp. 31 and 42–42. As well as the famous incident at the Briars when Napoleon frightened Eleanor Legg, he also visited the Leggs at The Hutts on 5 January 1816. Eleanor Jane Legg married John William Carrol on 18 August 1845. See FSTS website: https://www.friendsofsthelena.com/ancestors/view_database/33/1673

14   De Bourrienne, *Memoirs of Napoleon Bonaparte*, Vol. 4, p. 290.

15   Rosebery, *Napoleon: The last phase*, p. 174.

16   St Denis, *Napoleon*, p. 207.

17   Forsyth, *History of the Captivity of Napoleon at St Helena*, Vol. 2, p. 87.

18   Forsyth, *History of the Captivity of Napoleon at St Helena*, Vol. 2, p. 89.

19   Knowles, *Letters of Captain Lutyens*, p. 63.

20   Scurr, *Napoleon*, p. 286.

21   'Kerr's views in the island of St. Helena', https://bweaver.nom.sh/Kerr/kerr.htm, accessed 24 March 2020.

22   Scurr, *Napoleon*, p. 286.

23   Montholon, *Captivity of Napoleon*, Vol. 2, p. 59.

24   St. Denis, *Napoleon*, p. 174.

25   St Denis, *Napoleon*, p. 202; and Scurr, *Napoleon*, pp. 280–281.

26   Montholon, *Captivity of Napoleon*, Vol. 2, p. 59: Marchant, *In Napoleon's Shadow*, pp. 507–508; and Scurr, *Napoleon*, pp. 285 and 288.

27   Bodleian Library, Oxford, Hearl papers, Mss Atlan.t.1.

28   Montholon, *Captivity of Napoleon*, Vol. 2, p. 59.

29   Montholon, *Captivity of Napoleon*, Vol. 2, p. 267.

30   Scurr, *Napoleon*, pp. 286 and 290.

31   De Bourrienne *Memoirs of Napoleon Bonaparte*, chapter 13.

32   Chaplin, *A St Helena Who's Who*, p. 59.

33   Abbott, *Napoleon at St Helena*, p. 632.

34   De Bourrienne, *Memoirs of Napoleon Bonaparte*, chapter 13.

35   BL, IOR/G/32/83, 13 April 1818.

36   O'Meara, *Napoleon in Exile*, p. 86.

37   Forsyth, *History of the Captivity of Napoleon at St Helena*, Vol. 2, p. 90.

38   Lees, *Letters of Captain Lutyens*, pp. 42, 44, 46 and 49.

39   Mellis, *St. Helena*, p. 288, specimen reference 377.

40   https://science.mnhn.fr/institution/mnhn/collection/p/item/p00301433?listIndex=1&listCount=1719

41   http://www.theplantlist.org/tpl1.1/record/ifn-21862 [accessed 14 May 2020]. Bélanger was the founding curator of the French colonial botanic gardens at Pontichéry in south-east India and later, as curator, he transformed along scientific lines the botanic gardens on the island of Martinique in the West Indies.

42   Cronk, *The Endemic Flora of St Helena*, p. 90; and Lambdon, *St Helena*, p. 48.

43   Forsyth, *History of the Captivity of Napoleon at St Helena*, Vol. 2, pp. 121–122.

44   Source shared by Michel Dancoisne-Martineau to Donal McCracken, per. corr., 12 January 2020.

45   BL, Lowe papers, Add Mss 20,227, ff. 1–8b.

46   Pringle (1769–1815) was the East India Company's able Cape agent from 1794–1804 and again from 1808 until his death at Rondebosch on 24 June 1816. See entry on John Pringle by Dr Arkin in the *Dictionary of South African Biography*, Vol. 1, Pretoria, NCSR, 1968, pp. 655–656.

47   See entry on Luson by M. Arkin, *Dictionary of South African Biography*, Vol. 2, Pretoria, HSRC, p. 415.

48   See Gunn and Codd, *Botanical Exploration of Southern Africa*, p. 363 as well as entry on Villet by C. Plug in the S2A3 Biographical Data of South African Science, http://www.s2a3.org.za/bio/Biograph_final.php?serial=2989 [Accessed 8 March 2020].

49   See entry on Villet by F. C.L. Bodman in the *Dictionary of South African Biography*, Vol. 3, Pretoria, HSRC, 1977, p. 822.

50   BL, Lowe papers, Ms 20,131, Gorrequer to [Lutyens], 20 November 1820. Reference supplied by Michel Dancoisne-Martineau, 21 August 2020.

51   Montholon, *History of the Captivity of Napoleon*, p. 229.

52   Forsyth, *History of the Captivity of Napoleon at St Helena*, Vol. 1, p. 293.

53   Kemble, *St Helena During Napoleon's Exile: Gorrequer's diary*, pp. 12–13.

54   Marchand, *In Napoleon's Shadow*, p. 419.

55   Forsyth, *History of the Captivity of Napoleon at St Helena*, Vol. 1, p. 198.

56   Forsyth, *History of the Captivity of Napoleon at St Helena*, Vol. 1, p. 229.

57   Forsyth, *History of the Captivity of Napoleon at St Helena*, Vol. 2, pp. 554–555.

58   BL, Lowe papers, Add Mss 20227, Sturmer to Lowe, 29 October 1816, ff. 298–300. Chaplin, *A St. Helena Who's Who*, p. 112; and Castell, *Prince's Lodge*, p. 1.

59   Montholon, *History of the Captivity of Napoleon*, Vol. 1, p. 285.

CHAPTER 7 ~ Grande salle d'état

1   Quoted in Fox, *The Bennett Letters*, p. 26.

2   [Montholon] *Napoleon's appeal to the British nation*, p. 7.

3   O'Meara, *Napoleon in Exile*, pp. 92–93.

4   Murphy, 'Barry Edward O'Meara', pp. 691–692.

5   St Denis, *Napoleon*, p. 178.

6   Forsyth, *History of the Captivity of Napoleon at St Helena*, p. 98.

7   Abel, *Napoleon*, pp. 167–168.

8   Montholon, *Captivity of Napoleon*, Vol. 2, p. 424.

9   Montholon, *Napoleon*, Vol. 2, p. 62.

10   Abel, *Napoleon*, p. 262.

11   Chaplin, *A St Helena Who's Who*, pp. 80, 117 and 120; and Kitching, *A Handbook and Gazetteer of the Island of St Helena* [p. 76].

12   SHA, Secretary's out-letters, 1805–1814, 1807, f. 27

13   The Porteous house in Jamestown was gutted by fire in 1865 and remained a grim, boarded-up ruin. It was eventually demolished in 1937.

14 Chaplin, *A St Helena Who's Who*, London, 1919, pp. 143 and 147; William Forsyth, *History of Captivity of Napoleon at St Helena*, Vol. 2, London, 1853, pp. 95 and 228; O'Meara, *Napoleon in Exile, or a voice from St Helena*, London, 1922, pp. 21 and 95; and http://www.lautresaintehelene.com/autre-sainte-helene-articles-rosebud.html

15 Abbott, *Napoleon at St Helena*, p. 200.

16 Chaplin, *A St Helena Who's Who*, pp. 106 and 107.

17 Chaplin, *A St Helena Who's Who*, p. 91.

18 Antommarchi, *The Last Days of Napoleon*, Vol. 2, pp. 141–142.

19 John Stokoe (1775–1852) was a naval surgeon who had attended Napoleon in January and met with the displeasure of Governor Lowe. Returning to Britain, Stokoe was ordered back to St Helena, where he arrived on 21 August 1819, the day before this incident. Clearly Lowe viewed the matter in a suspicious light and on 30 August Stokoe was court-martialled and dismissed the service after 25 years. See Chaplin, *A St Helena Who's Who*, pp. 106–107.

20 Chaplin, *St Helena Who's Who*, pp. 44–45.

21 Bertrand, *Napoleon at St Helena*, p. 205.

22 Fox (ed.), 'Henry Russell', p. 47.

23 Bertrand, *Napoleon at St Helena*, p. 159.

24 Antommarchi, *The Last Days of Napoleon*, Vol. 2, pp. 180–181.

25 Teale, Thesis, 2.23.

26 Rosebery, *Napoleon*, p. 91.

27 Lockwood, *A Guide to St Helena*, pp. 95 and 103.

28 Fox and Baldwin, *A Precarious Livelihood*, p. 65.

29 Alexander, *Narrative*, p. 264.

30 http://sainthelenaisland.info/famousvisitors.htm#q_ f. 17 [Assessed 26 December 2019].

31 Teale, Thesis, 1.383.

32 Steiner, *St Helena*, p. 27; and Alexander, *Narrative*, p. 266.

33 Rosebery, *Napoleon: The last phase*, pp. 175–176.

34 Galway, 'A sojourn in St Helena', pp. 229–230.

35 http://friendsofdarwin.com/articles/darwin-visits-napoleon/ [Accessed 12 March 2020]. [John van Wyhe, editor. 2002-. The Complete Work of Charles Darwin Online. (http://darwin-online.org.uk/)]

36 Postans, 'The emperor's grave', pp. 213-218.

37 McCracken, 'Beyond the Glynns'.

38 Huxley, *Life and Letters of Sir Joseph Dalton Hooker*, Vol. 1, p. 99.

39 Chaplin, *A St Helena Who's Who*, p. 107.

40 BL, IOR/F//4/767 correspondence between Richard Torbett and Governor Lowe, 26 July 1821, 8 May 1822. See also https://torbettsthelena.wordpress.com/ [Accessed 20 April 2019].

41 Julia Blackburn, *The Emperor's Last Island: A journey to St Helena*, 1991.

42 Masselin, *Sainte-Hélène*, Paris, 1862.

43 http://sainthelenaisland.info/lostbuildings.htm; and https://www.worldstatesmen.org/Saint_Helena.htm [both accessed 8 January 2020].

44 Grant, *A Few Notes on St Helena*, section 1.

45 https://www.worldstatesmen.org/Saint_Helena.htm [Accessed 16 June 2021].

46 Grant, *A Few Notes on St Helena*, p. 34.

CHAPTER 8 ~ The Company's twilight years

1   Kitching, A Handbook and Gazetteer of the Island of St Helena, p. 2.

2   Beatson, *Tracts*, p. lxx.

3   *St Helena. Report on the Blue Book for 1887*, London: HMSO, 1888, p. 7.

4   *St Helena. Report on the Blue Book for 1889*, London: HMSO, 1890, p. 9.

5   Barnes, *A Tour Through the Island of St Helena*, p. 56.

6   BL, IOR, G/32/85, 30 June 1821. f. 812.

7   Beatson, *Tracts*, pp. 13–14, 52, 61–63, 191–193, 309, 317 and 325.

8   SHA, St Helena Records, 126, 27 June 1825.

9   BL, India Office Records, St Helena, Board minutes by A. Walker, 27 June 1825 and 7 July 1825, IOR/F/4/804/21610.

10   BL, IOR/G/32/85, Consultations, 12 July 1821, f. 817.

11   BL, India Office Records, St Helena Board's Collections, F/4/766/20737, Letter, memorandum and appendices, 21 June 1824 and 5 August 1824.

12   SHA, St Helena Records, 126, minute dated 27 June 1825.

13   BL, India Office Records, St Helena, Vol. 156 (1825–1827), IOR/G/32/156, ff. 209–11; Fox, *A Bitter Draught*, pp. 85–91 and 103; and Gosse, *St Helena*, p. 279.

14   Probably what was called she bamboo (*Bambusa vulgaris*). SHA, Proceedings of the Agricultural and Horticultural Society, 1823–1825, f. 343.

15   SHA, Proceedings of the Agricultural and Horticultural Society, 1823–1825, f. 229; and Gosse, *St Helena*, pp. 292–294

16   The date given is sometimes 25 April 1825.

17   SHA, St Helena Records, 126, O'Connor, 17 March 1825.

18   Abel, *Napoleon*, p. 18.

19   Fox and Baldwin, *A Precarious Livelihood*, p. 15; *St Helena Calendar and Directory for 1832*, p. 37; and SHA, St Helena Records, 126, minute dated 4 July 1825.

20   *St Helena. Report on the Blue Book for 1891*, London: HMSO, 1892, p. 12.

21   Fox and Baldwin, *A Precarious Livelihood*, p. 66.

22   SHA, Register of proclamations, 1809–1823, ff. 122–123, 127 and 145.

23   SHA, Register of proclamations, 1809–1823, 12 June 1823, f. 288.

24   SHA, Register of proclamations, 1809–1823, ff. 209, 271 and 387–388.

25   SHA, Proceedings of the Agricultural and Horticultural Society, 1823–1825, ff. 145 and 218–219.

26   Kitching, A Handbook and Gazetteer of the Island of St Helena, p. 84.

27   BL, IOR/F/4/767/20773, Board's Collection, 20 December 1824.

28   SHA, Proceedings of the Agricultural and Horticultural Society, 1823–1825, f. 222; and SHA, St Helena Records, 126, 5 May 1825.

29   SHA, Proceeedings of the Agricultural and Horticultural Society, 1823–1825, ff. 220–222; and *Asiatic Journal*, Vol. 17, 1824, p. 649.

30   Keogh, *The Wardian Case*, chapter 3.

31   KA, [Plant] Record Book, 1804–1826, f. 192.

32   KA, [Plant] Record Book, 1804–1826, f. 232.

33   Bean, *The Royal Botanic Gardens, Kew*, p. 44.

34   Fox, *The Bennett Letters*, p. 108; and Lefroy, 'The removal of Napoleon's remains from St. Helena to France, October 1840', pp. 66–73.

35   *Gardeners' Chronicle*, 2 February 1867, p. 105.

36   *The Floricultural Cabinet*, Vol. 13, 1845, pp. 143–144.

37   Fox, *The Bennett Letters*, p. 36.

38   SHA, Proceeedings of the Agricultural and Horticultural Society, 1823–1825, ff. 250–251.

39   SHA, Proceeedings of the Agricultural and Horticultural Society, 1823–1825, ff. 337–338.

40   SHA, Out-letters, colonial secretary, 1839–1840, Seale to Connaly, 20 November 1839, f. 161.

41   Alexander, *Narrative of a Voyage of Observation Among the Colonies of West Africa*, Vol. 1, p. 253. Part of the two interesting chapters on St Helena are quoted in Teale, Thesis.

42   Consultations at the Castle, 24 January 1832, quoted in Teale, Thesis. 1.288; and Alexander, *Narrative*, p. 279.

43   Alexander, *Narrative*, p. 279.

CHAPTER 9 ~ The new order

1   Brooke, *History of the Island of St Helena*, p. 413.

2   Ashmole, *St Helena and Ascension Island*, p. 43.

3   Gosse, *St Helena*, p. 301.

4   Fox, *The Bennett Letters*, p. 79.

5   Fox and Baldwin, *A Precarious Livelihood*, pp. iii–iv, 8.

6   Extrapolated from Fox and Baldwin, *A Precarious Livelihood*, pp. 203–211.

7   Alexander, *Narrative*, pp. 258 and 280.

8   Grant, *A Few Notes on St Helena*, p. 38.

9   Kitching, A Handbook and Gazetteer of the Island of St Helena, p. 89.

10   Fox and Baldwin, *A Precarious Livelihood*, p. 200; and *St Helena Calendar and Directory for 1832*, p. 23.

11   Fox and Baldwin, *A Precarious Livelihood*, p. 67.

12   SHA, government notices dated 1 March 1837 and 4 March 1840; and SHA, Out-letters, colonial secretary, 1839–1840, Seale to Pennell, 7 April 1840, f. 253.

13   Mrs Postan, 'The emperor's grave; a sketch of St Helena'.

14   Quoted in Teale, Thesis. 1.319.

15   Van de Velde, 'Chasing the slavers', pp. 1–14; and 'Attacking the slave trade', http://sainthelenaisland.info/slavetrade.htm

16   Government notice 5 December 1844; and 'Saint Helena 15.55 South 5.43 West' at: http://jcgrimshaw.blogspot.co.za/. See also, Pearson, 'Waterwitch', pp. 99–124.

17   KA, [Plant] Record Book, 1828–1847, ff. 120 and 143.

18   Fox, *The Bennett Letters*, p. 80.

19   Duncan, *Description of the Island of St Helena*, p. 218.

20   BL, IOR/G/32/163, Beatson to directors, nd [1808].

21   BL, IOR/G/32/163, Beatson to directors, nd [1808].

22   George, *Names of Places on St Helena*, p. 4; and Melliss, *St Helena*, p. 280.

23   *St Helena. Report on the Blue Book for 1895*, London: HMSO, 1896, p. 8; and for 1898, p. 17.

24   Sterndale, 'St Helena in the present time', pp. 99–100.

25   *First Report of the Commissioners for the Exhibition of 1851*, pp. 885 and 995; and Gosse, *St Helena*, p. 375.

26   Lockwood, *A Guide to St Helena*, p. 58.

27   Lockwood, *A Guide to St Helena*, p. 76.

28   Lambdon, *Flowering Plants and Ferns of St Helena*, p. 9.

29   Desmond, *Sir Joseph Dalton Hooker*, p. 31.

30   Chancellor and van Wyhe (eds]) Despoblado notebook. EH1.6 [English Heritage
        88202326] (6-8.1835, 5-8.1836) . (Darwin Online, http://darwin-online.
        org.uk/) [Accessed 2 December 2021].

31   Gordon Chancellor, 'Charles Darwin's St Helena Model Notebook', *Bulletin of the
        British Museum (Natural History) Historical Series*, 18(2), 1990, 203–228; and John van
        Wyhe (ed.), *The Complete Work of Charles Darwin Online*, 2002: (http://darwin-online.
        org.uk/). 25 March 2017 [Accessed 25 March 2017].

32   Keynes (ed.), *Charles Darwin's Beagle Diary*, p. 428: Keynes, R. D. ed. 2001. Charles
        Darwin's Beagle diary. Cambridge: Cambridge University Press. (darwin-online.
        org.uk) [Accessed 29 April 2021]; and Kees Rookmaaker (ed.) [Darwin's Beagle diary
        (1831–1836)]. [English Heritage 88202366] (Darwin Online, http://darwin-online.
        org.uk/) (darwin-online.org.uk) [Accessed 19 January 2021]. Diary 13 July 1936, ff.
        743–744. The original manuscript is now kept in Down House, Kent, the property of
        English Heritage.

33   Fox, *The Bennett Letters*, pp. 100–103; Huxley, *Life and Letters of Sir Joseph Dalton
        Hooker*, Vol. 1, p. 98; and KA, Joseph Hooker journal, JDH/1/9/3.

34   Quoted in full in Fox, *The Bennett Letters*, pp. 116–117; and KA, Director's
        correspondence, DC/58/11, 21 October 1842.

35   Letter dated 18 May 1843 quoted in Fox, *The Bennett Letters*, p. 118.

36   Desmond, *Sir Joseph Dalton Hooker*, p. 84; and Huxley, *Life and Letters of Sir Joseph
        Dalton Hooker*, Vol. 1, pp. 64 and 77.

37   *Gardeners' Chronicle*, 12 January 1867, p. 27.

38   George, *Names of Places on St Helena*, p. 12.

39   KA, Director's correspondence, Melliss to Hooker, 23 September 1867, f. 211b.

40   KA, Director's correspondence, Melliss to Hooker, 26 November 1867, ff. 214–214b;
        and Lambdon, *Flowering Plants and Ferns of St Helena*, p. 372.

41   KA, Director's correspondence, Melliss to Hooker, 2 November 1867, f. 21.

42   KA, Director's correspondence, Melliss to Hooker, 26 November 1867, ff. 215–215b.

43   Melliss, *St Helena*, p. 318 and plate 52.

44   KA, Director's correspondence, Melliss to Hooker, 25 October 1867, f. 213b; Melliss,
        St Helena, p. 256 and plate 31; and Lambdon, *Flowering Plants and Ferns of St
        Helena*, p. 231.

45   KA, Director's correspondence, Melliss to Hooker, 11 June 1868, f. 224.

46   KA, Director's correspondence, Melliss to Hooker, 26 November 1867, f. 215b.

47   *St Helena Almanac*, 1868, p. 133. Sixteen years later the *Almanac* [1884, p. 107] would
        give honourable mention to another local gardener, George Swain, who died on 4
        December 1882, aged 64.

48   KA, Director's correspondence, Elliot to Kew, 9 March 1868.

49   McCracken, *Gardens of Empire*, chapter 2.

50   *Kew Bulletin*, 1931: 117.

51   Gill and Teale, *St Helena 500*, p. 300.

52   Jackson, *St Helena*, pp. 84–88.

53 Huxley, *Life and Letters of Sir Joseph Dalton Hooker*, Vol. 2, p. 4; KA, Director's correspondence, Melliss to Hooker, 11 June 1868, f. 224; Gill and Teale, *St Helena 500*, p. 300; and Morris, *Reprint of a report (written in 1884) upon the present position and prospects of the agricultural resources of the island of St Helena*, pp. 11–14.

54 Desmond, *Sir Joseph Dalton Hooker*, p. 221.

55 *St Helena Guardian*, 13 May 1868. See also: 3 June, 17 September and 11 January 1870.

56 KA, Accession books: Inwards: 1848–1858; 1859–1867; and 1868–1872.

57 KA, Director's correspondence, Melliss to Hooker, 20 January 1868, f. 217.

58 KA, Director's correspondence, Melliss to Hooker, 20 January 1868, ff. 217–218; and Melliss, *St Helena*, p. 279 and plate 34.

59 SHA, Entry book, out-letters, colonial secretary, 1869–1870, Elliot to Dawson, 24 December 1869, ff. 131–134.

60 SHA, Entry book, out-letters, colonial secretary, 1869–1870, Janisch to Chalmers, 18 December 1869, f. 128.

61 Devastated by disease in its native home of Bermuda, by being termite-resistant the Bermuda cedar was a boon to St Helena at one time but is now regarded on the island as 'a rampant nuisance'. Lambdon, *Flowering Plants and Ferns of St Helena*, p. 70.

62 Gill and Teale, *St Helena 500*, p. 301.

63 KA, Director's correspondence, Melliss to Hooker, 20 January 1871, f. 242.

64 KA, Director's correspondence, Melliss to Hooker, 11 May 1871, ff. 244–245.

65 Grant, *A Few Notes on St Helena*, p. 67.

66 There is a note on Melliss at http://sainthelenaisland.info/importantpeople. htm#drwjjarnold [Accessed 19 October 2019]. See also the 'Ancestor' section of the Friends of St Helena website.

CHAPTER 10 ~ The long decline

1 An important contribution which Janisch made was to compile a chronology relating to the island. This was published under the title *Extracts from the St Helena records* by the printer Benjamin Grant at the island's Guardian printing works in Jamestown in 1885. A second edition later appeared in 1908. Teutonic Hall has recently been restored. At one time or another, it has been known as Hayes's, Orange Grove and Masons. See Teale, Thesis, 2.56.

2 *Report of the St. Helena Industrial Exhibition, for 1874*, p. 2.

3 Melliss, *St Helena*, p. 38.

4 Gill, *Six Months in Ascension*, p. 32.

5 Grant, *A Few Notes on St Helena*, [pp. 69–75]. Melliss's information probably dates from the late 1860s and Grant's from 1881/1882.

6 Connor Geary and Hutchinson, 'Mr. Dawson, Plantsman'.

7 KA, Director's correspondence, Morris to Kew (Uncertain to whom), November 1876, no folio ref.

8 Lambdon, *Flowering Plants and Ferns of St Helena*, p. 70. See also https:// sthelenaisland.info/st-helena-distillery/ [Accessed 19 October 2019].

9 Cronk, *The Endemic Flora of St Helena*, pp. 37–38.

10 KA, Director's letters, T. V. Wollaston to Joseph Hooker, 22 November 1875, ff. 277–278.

11 Lambdon, *Flowering Plants and Ferns of St Helena*, p. 419.

12 Gunn and Codd, *Botanical Exploration of Southern Africa*, p. 459.

13 Wollaston, *Coleoptera Sanctæ-Helenæ*, pp. v and vi; and Gunn and Codd, *Botanical Exploration*, pp. 375–376.

14 KA, Director's correspondence, Oliver, 29 April 1878; and Whitehead, 29 April 1878. Oliver resigned his commission in 1878 and left St Helena to become a writer.

15 Desmond, *Dictionary of British and Irish Botanists*, pp. 299–300; Desmond, *Kew*, p. 427; and *Kew Guild*, 1925, pp. 331–337.

16 Hemsley, 'Report on the botany of the Bermudas and various islands of the Atlantic and Southern oceans', p. 52.

17 Hemsley, 'Report on the botany of the Bermudas and various islands of the Atlantic and Southern oceans', pp. 52–53.

18 Files of many of these titles are housed in the St Helena Archives, from which this information is extracted.

19 KA, Director's correspondence, Morris to Hooker, no date [1883], ff. 248–249.

20 Morris, *Report*, p. 13. For the saga of cinchona in St Helena, see Kew, St Helena, Cinchona, 1868–1898.

21 Morris, *Agricultural Resources of the Island of St Helena*, p. 4.

22 Morris, *Agricultural Resources of the Island of St Helena*, p. 9n.

23 KA, Director's correspondence, C/211/828, Morris to Thiselton-Dyer, 23 May 1884.

24 Lambdon and Cronk, 'Extinction dynamics under extreme conservation threat: The flora of St Helena', p. 4.

25 Melliss, *St Helena*, p. 246; and *Curtis's Botanical Magazine*, plate 5135.

26 Kitching, http://sainthelenaisland.info/kitching1947.pdf [Accessed 22 April 2018].

27 Morris, *Agricultural Resources of the Island of St Helena*, p. 5.

28 *St Helena. Report on the Blue Book for 1889*, London: HMSO, 1890, p. 17.

29 Brooke, *A History of St Helena*, pp. 33 and 132.

30 *St Helena. Report on the Blue Book for 1894*, London: HMSO, 1895, p. 4.

31 Castell, *Prince's Lodge*, p. 5; and Crallan, 'Listed buildings', p. 18. There seems to have been a practice of piling old slates removed from roofs behind the old houses and then covering them with soil.

32 'White ants at St. Helena', *Scientific American*, Vol. 32, no.24, 1875, p. 373.

33 Teale, Thesis, 1.375; and [anonymous] *St Helena, Nature's Neglected Citadel*, pp. 2 and 7.

34 Fox and Baldwin, *A Precarious Livelihood*, pp. 64, 70 and 74.

35 KA, DC/181/253, Director's correspondence, S. P. Oliver to Kew, November 1876.

36 Fox and Mabbett, 'Governor Grey-Wilson', pp. 32–33.

37 KA, Director's correspondence, Grey-Wilson, 7 December 1889, 3 February 1892 and n.d. (*c.* September 1892).

38 Teale, Thesis, 2.42.

39 Sterndale, 'St Helena in the present time', pp. 105–106.

40 Grant, *A Few Notes on St Helena* [pp. 37–38].

41 *St Helena Guardian*, 27 November 1890.

42 *St Helena Guardian*, 27 November 1890.

43 *St Helena Guardian*, 20 October 1870.

44 Walker, 'St Helena as I saw it: 1886', p. 89.

45 *St Helenian*, 7 December 1895.

46 *St Helenian*, 21 December 1895.

47   The remarkable naturalist, artist and colonial administrator Robert Armitage Sterndale (1839–1902) CMG and FZS had in fact been acting governor of St Helena as early as 1895 in the absence of Governor William Grey-Wilson.

48   TNA, WO 33/3234, Confidential. Barrack accommodation, St Helena: Correspondence respecting the transfer of the site of Botanic Gardens in Jamestown, St Helena, for erection of additional barrack accommodation. A642.

49   *St Helena. Report on the Blue Book for 1899*, London: HMSO, 1900, p. 11; and KA, Director's correspondence, 15 June 1898, f. 264.

50   Grant, *A Few Notes on St Helena* [p. 31].

51   http://www.sthelenaisland.info/castle-gardens/; and *St Helena. Report on the Blue Book for 1897*, London: HMSO, 1898, p. 9.

52   KA, Director's correspondence, Sterndale, 29 October 1897.

53   *St Helena. Report on the Blue Book for 1890*, London: HMSO, 1891. As mentioned in chapter 9, in the 1830s an eclectic museum had existed at Deadwood House, then the home of the enthusiast and government official, Robert F. Seale. Sadly, the drinking fountain in the Jamestown main street disappeared in the 1940s. A replacement has recently been imported onto the island. Baldwin, 'Replica rock fall fountain', *St Helena Connection*, no. 28 June 2020, pp. 14–15.

54   *St Helena. Report on the Blue Book for 1897*, London: HMSO, 1898, pp. 9–10. In the 1980s, the gumwood was rediscovered, though its existence is greatly in peril.

55   KA, Director's correspondence, Sterndale to Thiselton-Dyer, 8 March 1897.

56   KA, Director's correspondence, Sterndale to Thiselton-Dyer, 22 June 1901, ff. 407a–407b.

57   *St Helena. Report on the Blue Book for 1905*, London: HMSO, 1906, p. 10.

58   *St Helena. Report on the Blue Book for 1900*, London: HMSO, 1901, pp. 9–10.

59   *St Helena. Report on the Blue Book for 1902*, London: HMSO, 1903, p. 7.

60   *St Helena. Report on the Blue Book for 1903*, London: HMSO, 1904, p. 7.

61   *St Helena. Report on the Blue Book for 1904*, London: HMSO, 1905, pp. 32–33.

62   KA, Director's correspondence, Arthur Sutton to Colonel David Prain, 9 December 1908, f. 412.

63   Bank's *Endeavour* journal: https://collections.tepapa.govt.nz/topic/3642 https://www.joseph-banks.org.uk/garden-plants/ http://nzetc.victoria.ac.nz/tm/scholarly/tei-Bea02Bank-t1-body-d2.html [Accessed 2 December 2021.]

64   KA, Director's correspondence, Melliss to Hooker, 20 January 1868, f. 217b.

65   KA, Director's correspondence, Whitehead, 12 September 1873 and 17 August 1878.

66   Huxley, *Life and Letters of Sir Joseph Dalton Hooker*, Vol. 2, p. 233.

67   *St Helena. Report on the Blue Book for 1907*, pp. 13–14.

68   Teale, Thesis, 1.378.

69   St Helena Census, 1931. W. A. Thorpe owned several historic properties on St Helena and lived in Mount Pleasant.

70   St Helena Census reports for 1956 and 1966; and Teale, Thesis, 2.155.

71   Bruce and Thorpe, 'William A. Thorpe', pp. 4–20.

72   St Helena Census, 1966.

73   Teale, Thesis, 1.377; and Castell, *Prince's Lodge*, p. 3.

74   *St Helena. Report on the Blue Book for 1917*, London: HMSO, 1918, pp. 3–4.

75   *St Helena. Report on the Blue Book for 1918*, London: HMSO, 1919, p. 4.

76   There had been proposals regarding whaling in 1833 and 1875. Commercial fishing schemes, which first started in 1684, dragged on into the 20th century when schemes in 1903 and 1909 failed.

77   Cardize Jansen, 'Gardens & I' - Harry Bruins-Lich http://www.carolizejansen.com/Harry-Bruinslich-2.html [Accessed 16 March 2017].

78   *St Helena Magazine*, April 1947, no. 535, p. 175

79   Teale, Thesis, 2.55.

80   *St Helena Guardian*, 29 October 1910. The phrase means, A hundred thousand welcomes.

81   Gosse, *St Helena*, p. 375

POSTSCRIPT ~ The way through the woods

1   Charles Melliss to Joseph Hooker, Director's correspondence, 222b, 11 April 1868.

2   Castell, *Prince's Lodge*, pp. 2–3 and 98.

3   St Helena Census, 1966, table XVI (f).

4   *The Sentinel*, 31 January 2019, p. 5.

5   Clubbe, Hamilton and Corcoran, 'The role of native species nurseries in mitigating threats from invasive species: case studies from UK Overseas Territories', pp. 1–13.

6   St Helena Census, 1966, table XVII, (e) and (f).

7   See http://sainthelenaisland.info/savedbuildings.htm [Accessed 8 January 2020].

8   *St Helena Guardian*, 28 August 1890.

APPENDIX V

1   Major Anthony Emmett (1789–1872) was then commanding the engineers on St Helena. It was Emmett who designed and built the tomb in which Napoleon was buried from 1821 until 1840.

2   Charlotte and Susanna Johnson were Sir Hudson Lowe's stepdaughters.

3   Count Alexandre Balmain was the Russian commissioner on St Helena from 1816 until 1820.

4   Lord Charles Somerset (1767–1831) was governor of the Cape from 1814 until 1826. An intelligent man but controversial governor, he had to deal with the political repercussions of settling 5,000 British on the turbulent East Cape frontier. In 1820 he went on leave back to Britain, calling on St Helena on the way home.

5   Captain Englebert Lutyens was orderly officer at Longwood from 10 February 1820 until 15 April 1821, just three weeks before Napoleon died. A Captain William Crockat, also of the 20th Regiment, was orderly officer from 15 April until 6 May 1821. See Chaplin, *A St Helena Who's Who*, p. 9.

APPENDIX VI

1   BL, Lowe papers, Correspondence between Lowe and Joseph Luson, EIC agent at the Cape, June 1816, Add Mss 20,227, ff. 1–8b.

2   There are, in fact, 136 entries listed.

Bibliography

MANUSCRIPT MATERIAL

Bodleian Library, Oxford
Trevor Hearl papers, sketches by Captain Guy Rotton, 1821.

British Library
India Office Records:
    General Correspondence, 1602–1859
    Madras Despatches
    St Helena: Consultations, 1676–1817 (Public Consultations, 1817–1836)
    St Helena: Despatches from the Court to St Helena, 1820–1835
    St Helena: Letters from St Helena to the Court, 1698–1836
    St Helena: Factory Records, 1676–1836.

Governor Brooke's Account of St Helena, 1792; *St Helena Gazette*, 10 October
    1808 article 'Botanic Garden'; and 1789 catalogues of plants in New
    Botanic Garden, Plantation House and High Peak in IOR/G/32/163

'A Catalogue of Trees and Shrubs growing in the Honble East India Companys New Botanic
    Garden in Jamses Vally, St Helena, 1789' G/32/163 (Also contains lists for Plantation
    House and High Peak garden: see appendices I, II and III).

Manuscript room:
    Add Ms 33981(60)
    Lowe papers: Ms 20,131; Ms 20,227

Social Sciences room:
    St Helena Almanacs

Irish Architecture Archive
Guinness Collection, J. Corneille, Plantation House, St. Helena, Topographical view showing
the rear of the house, *c.*1780

Jardin des Plantes
Bibliothèque du Phanérogamie, Paris (Botanique livre d'Entré 1864–1900)

Kew: Royal Botanic Gardens Library and Archives
'The botanical gardens St Helena and St Vincent' (James Anderson): Ms 42/2/3
Burchell papers:
    Flora Heleniana manuscripts WJB/1/1
    Flora of St Helena WJB/1/2
    Notes of St Helena and the South Sandwich islands WJB/1/3
    Manuscript of Plant List WJB/1/4

Burchell illustrations of St Helena: One volume of 125 leaves, with mounted pencil and watercolour drawings. Presented to the library of the Kew Herbarium by Sir Joseph Hooker, in January 1878, to whom the drawings had been given by William Burchell's sister, Anna Burchell.

Director's correspondence:
African letters
Vol. 180, North African & Atlantic letters, 1901–1914
Vol. 181, Atlantic Island letters, 1866–1900
Miscellaneous reports, Cinchona, 1868–1898, MR/435
Miscellaneous reports, St Helena, 1836–1913, MR/435
Miscellaneous reports, St Helena, 1813–1928, MR/437
Plant lists:
Record Book, 1793–1809, f. 11
Record Book, 1804–1824, ff. 162, 192 and 232
Outwards Book, 1805–1809, ff. 348 and 352
Inwards book, 1805–1809, ff. 120 and 143

Muséum National d'Histoire Naturelle, Paris

Herbaria specimens of Napoleon's fern: https://science.mnhn.fr/institution/mnhn/collection/p/item/p00301433?listIndex=1&listCount=1719 [Accessed 13 May 2020].

National Library of Australia

Journal of Arthur Bowes Smyth, 1787 March 22–1789 August, Ms 4568: https://nla.gov.au/nla.obj-233672863/view

St Helena Archives

East India Company in-letters from India, China and Cape, 1813–1835
EIC letters from England, 1673–1815; 1804–1835
EIC letters to England, 1706–1835
EIC letters to India, China, Rio de Janeiro and Cape, 1823–1825
EIC St Helena Records, 1678–1824
EIC Public Department, 1824–1836
EIC Secret Department, 1823–1826
Despatches from Secretary of State, 1838–1912
Despatches to Secretary of State, 1836–1909
In-letters, Colonial Secretary, 1839–1908
Out-letters, Secretary, 1805–1814
Out-letters, Colonial Secretary, 1839–1885
Newspapers (published in St Helena): see list below
Flax report, 1907–1923
Harbour Master: Ships arriving and departing, 1815–1818
Proceedings of the Agricultural and Horticultural Society, 1823–1825 (ms)
Official notices, 1840–1844; 1856–1907
Ordinances, 1837–1910
Register of proclamations, 1809–1823; 1835–1898
Records, 120, 1824–182?
St Helena colonial annual reports (Blue Books) from 1836. See also from 1840: https://www.friendsofsthelena.com/page/annual-colonial-reports
St Helena Commission, 1835
Secretary's out-letters, 1805–1814

The National Archives, London

Barrack accommodation, St Helena: Correspondence respecting the transfer of the site of Botanic Gardens in Jamestown, St Helena, for erection of additional barrack accommodation. Confidential. A642. TNA, WO 33/3234.

'St. Helena. Plans of properties', July 1839, G. W. Melliss. TNA, CO 700/STHelena8.

NEWSPAPERS (Including those housed in the St Helena Archives, as noted) and journals

Botanical Cabinet
Botanical Register
Botanist's Repository
Curtis's Botanical Magazine
De Krijgsgevangene (St Helena Archives: 1901)
Maund's Botanic Garden
St Helena Chronicle (St Helena Archives: 1852–1853)
St Helena Herald (St Helena Archives: 1853–1860)
St Helena Gazette (St Helena Archives: 1845–1852; 1858–1867; 1871–1922)
St Helena Guardian (St Helena Archives: 1861–1912)
St Helena Record (St Helena Archives: 1860–1861)
St Helena Sentinel (online)
St Helena Times (St Helena Archives: 1889)
The Bug (St Helena Archives: 1888)
The Floricultural Cabinet
The Monthly Critic and Flashlight (St Helena Archives: 1891–1892)
The Mosquito (St Helena Archives: 1888–1889)
The St Helena Advocate (St Helena Archives: 1851–1853)
The St Helena Church News (St Helena Archives: 1888)
The St Helena Connection
The St Helenian (St Helena Archives: 1895–1896)
Wirebird: The Journal of the Friends of St Helena (online)

CONTEMPORARY MAPS

'Carte de l'isle Ste Hélène', *c.* 1790. Marks the Company garden at Plantation.

T. E. Fowler, 'Map of St Helena' in *Views of St Helena*, London, Day and Son, 1863: marks country house names.

G. W. Melliss, 'St. Helena. Plans of properties', July 1839, The National Archives, London, CO 700/STHelena8: marks properties in Jamestown including public gardens as well as several landed estates.

'Plan de la Forteresse et Bourg de l'Isle de St. Helene', Bellin, *Petit Atlas Maritime*, tome 3, no.124, 1764: shows the juxtaposition of the Company fort with the garden at Jamestown.

'Plan de l'isle Ste Helene' Bellin, *Petit Atlas Maritime*, tome 3, no. 123, 1764: clearly marks the Company garden at Plantation.

Lieut R.P. Read, 'The geographical plan of the island and forts of Saint Helena', 1817. There were two editions: October 1815 and June 1817: marks house names or owners of landed properties. The National Archives, London, CO700/St Helena/c (1818)

St Helena Ordnance Survey, UK for Government of St Helena, scale 1:10,000, six sheets, 1990: marks many surviving old country houses and some ruined ones.

'Sketch map of St Helena, indicating the three zones of vegetation'. First appeared in the 1907 edition of the *Colonial reports—annual:* St Helena.

'South Atlantic Ocean: Island of St Helena from the latest information in the hydrographic Department, Admiralty, 1922': excellent detailed map of St Helena including house names.

'Trigonometrical survey of the island of St Helena situated latitude 15.55 south longitude 5.11 west. Distinguishing the whole of the landed estates Public and Private Property, their boundaries, divisions fences, lines of free or lease lands also the original grants of lease recently converted into permanent tenure, Roads, Telegraphs, Springs Fortifications and Remarkable Places inland. Surveyed between the years 1825 & 1836 by George W. Melliss'. (A copy was made in 1972 by Dr Percy Teale and L.W. Shepherd).

ALMANACS AND ANNUAL REPORTS

St Helena Calendar and Directory for the year 1832, St Helena, 1831.

The St Helena Almanac and Annual Register, St Helena, 1858, 1868, 1883 and 1884. British Library reference: General Reference Collection C.S.C.558/4.

St Helena Archives have almanacs for the years: 1830, 1833–1834, 1843–1845, 1855–1857, 1862, 1864–1865, 1867–1868, 1875, 1884 and 1913.

Census reports for St Helena may be found on the Friends of St Helena website (available to members): https://www.friendsofsthelena.com/modern_report

Dates available:
1814, 1861, 1871, 1881, 1891, 1901, 1911, 1921, 1931, 1946, 1956, 1966, 1976, 1987 (no commentary), 1998, 2008, and 2016 (summary).

Copies of Colonial Annual Reports for St Helena may be found on the Friends of St Helena website (available to members): https://www.friendsofsthelena.com/page/annual-colonial-reports

Dates available:
1845–1850, 1852–1856, 1860–1873, 1875–1882, 1884–1938 (no reports published 1939–1946) and 1947–1951.

SELECTED BOOKS, PAMPHLETS AND ARTICLES

Anyone who does not have access to a good botanical/horticultural library can access many older texts via several excellent websites. These include:
The Biodiversity Heritage Library, https://www.biodiversitylibrary.org/
The Hathi Trust Digital Library, https://www.hathitrust.org/
The Internet Archive, https://archive.org/

ABBOTT, John S. C., *Napoleon at St. Helena: Interesting anecdotes and remarkable conversations of the emperor during the five and a half years of his captivity collected from the memorials of Las Casas, O'Meara, Montholon, Antommarchi, and others*, New York, Harper & Brothers, 1855.

ABEL, Mrs [Betsy], *Recollections of the Emperor Napoleon on the Island of St Helena*, 3rd ed., London, Sampson Lowe, Marston, Lowe and Searle, 1873.

AITON, William, *Hortus Kewensis, or, A catalogue of the plants cultivated in the Royal Botanic Garden at Kew*, 1st ed. Printed for George Nicol, bookseller to his Majesty, 1789; and 2nd ed. Longman, Hurst, Rees, Orme, and Brown, 1810–1815.

ALEXANDER, James Edward, *Narrative of a voyage of observation among the colonies of western Africa, in the flagship Thalia and of a campaign in Kaffir-land, on the staff of the commander-in-chief in 1835*, Vol. 1, London, Henry Colburn, 1837.

ALLEN, David Elliston, *The Victorian Fern Craze, A history of pteridomania*, London, Hutchinson, 1969.

ANONYMOUS 'A botanical station at St. Helena', *St Helena Guardian*, 2 April 1896.

ANONYMOUS 'Intelligence respecting literature etc Africa', [Including a letter from James Anderson in Madras to the St Helena Planters' Society], *The Bee, or Literary Intelligencer*, Vol. 1, 2 February 1791, pp. 194–198.

ANONYMOUS [Beatson/Watson?], *Flora St. Helenica*, St. Helena, pamphlet printed by J. Boyd, 1825.

ANONYMOUS [DUNCAN, Francis], *Description of the Island of St. Helena; containing observations on its singular structure and formation; and an account of its climate, natural history, and inhabitants*, London, Printed for R. Philips, 1805.

ANONYMOUS 'Memoir of Governor Brooke', *The Asiatic Journal and Monthly Register*, Vol. xix, 1836, pp. 181–184.

ANONYMOUS [REID, Eleanor], 'Cursory remarks on board the Friendship', in *The Asiatic Journal and Monthly Register*, Vol. 8, November 1819, pp. 452–453. See also https://joan-druett.blogspot.co.za/2014/02/mary-ann-reid-visits-island-of-st-helena.html [Accessed 20 March 2017].

ANONYMOUS *St Helena, nature's neglected citadel*, pamphlet, *c.* 1891.

ANONYMOUS 'White ants at St. Helena', *Scientific American*, Vol. 32, no. 24, 1875, p. 373.

[ANTOMMARCHI], *The Last Days of Napoleon. Memoirs of the last two years of Napoleon's exile by F. Antommarchi. Forming a sequel to the journals of Dr. O'Meara and Count Las Casas. In two vols*, 2nd ed., London, Henry Colburn, 1826.

ARKIN, M., 'John Company at the Cape. A history of the agency under Pringle (1794–1815), based on a study of the "Cape of Good Hope Factory records"', *Archives Year Book for South African History, 1960*, Vol. 33 no. 2, Elsies River, Office of the Chief Archivist, 1961.

ARKIN, M., 'John Pringle', *Dictionary of South African Biography*, Pretoria, National Council for Social Research, 1968. Vol. 1, pp. 655–656.

ARKIN, M., 'Supplies for Napoleon's Gaolers: John Company and the Cape–St. Helena trade during the captivity, 1815–1821', *Archives year book for South African History*, Vol. 1, 1964, pp. 269–330.

ASHMOLE, Philip and Myrtle, *St Helena and Ascension Island, A natural history*. Oswestry, Anthony Nelson, 2000.

BALDWIN, Edward, Baldwin, 'Replica rock fall fountain', *St Helena Connection*, no. 28, June 2020, pp. 14–15.

BARNES, Capt. John, *A tour through the island of St Helena; with notes of its geology, mineralogy, botany, etc etc collected during a residency of twelve years; with some particulars concerning the arrival and detention of Napoleon Buonaparte*, London, J. M. Richardson, 1817.

Barrack accommodation, St. Helena. Correspondence respecting the transfer to the war department of the site of the Botanic Gardens in Jamestown, St. Helena, for the erection of additional barrack accommodation. Confidential, War Office, 644, *c.* 1899: TNA, WO/33/3234.

BEAN, W. J., *The Royal Botanical Gardens, Kew, Historical and descriptive*, London, Cassell, 1908.

BEATSON, Major-General Alexander, *Tracts relative to the island of St Helena written during a residence of five years*, London, W. Bulmer, 1816.

BELLIN, J–N. *Le petit atlas maritime*, Vol. 3, l'Afrique, Paris 1764, plates 123 and 124.

[BERTRAND] *Napoleon at St Helena. Memoirs of General Bertrand, grand marshal of the palace. January to May 1821. Deciphered and annotated by Paul Fleuriot de Langle. Translated by Frances Hume*, London, Cassell, 1953.

BLACKBURN, Julia. *The Emperor's Last Island, A journey to St Helena*, London, Vintage, 1997.

[de BOURRIENNE] *Memoirs of Napoleon Bonaparte, complete by Louis Antoine Fauvelet de Bourrienne, his private secretary* (ed. R. W. Phipp), Vol. 4, 1891, New York, Charles Scribner's Sons.

BRADLOW, Frank R. *Baron von Ludwig and the Ludwig's–burg Garden: A chronicle of the Cape from 1806 to 1848*, Cape Town, A.A. Balkema, 1965.

BRETSCHNEIDER, Emil, *History of European Botanical Discoveries in China*, Hamburg, Severus, 2011.

BROCKWAY, Lucile H., *Science and Colonial Expansion: The role of the British Royal Botanic Gardens*, New York, Academic Press, 1979.

[BROOKE, Robert], *A letter from Mr. Brooke to an Honorable Member of the House of Commons*, Dublin, printed by B. Dugdale, 1786. [Copy in the National Library of Ireland.]

BROOKE, T. H., *History of the Island of St Helena, from its discovery by the Portuguese to the year 1823*, 2nd ed., London, Kingsbury, Parbury and Allen, 1824.

BRUCE, Ian, 'The soldier and the harbour master [George Randal Bruce]', *Wirebird*, no. 42, 2013, pp. 23–38.

BRUCE, Ian and THORPE, Nick, 'William A. Thorpe, 1842–1918', *Wirebird*, no. 43, 2014, pp. 14–20.

BUCHANAN, Susan, *Burchell's Travels: The life, art and journeys of William John Burchell, 1781–1863*, Cape Town, Penguin, 2015.

CAIRD, D. A. R., 'Brooke, Charlotte (1740?–1793)', *Dictionary of Irish Biography*, Vol. 1, Dublin and Cambridge, 2009, pp. 869–870.

CASTELL, Robin, *Prince's Lodge: Island of St. Helena 1808–2003*, St Helena, Castell Collection, 2003.

CASTELL, Robin, *St. Helena Illustrated (1502–1902)*, Cape Town National Book Printers, 1998.

CASTELL, Robin, *Saint Helena Proclamations*, Fish Hoek, 2004.

CASTELL, Robin, *William Burchell (1781–1863) St. Helena (1805–1810)*, St Helena, Castell Collection, 2011.

CHAMBERS, J. H., *Report on the experiment of establishing the chinchona plant in St Helena: From 7th July 1868, to 17th December 1869*. https://www.jstor.org/stable/60229800

CHAMBERS, Neil (ed.), *Indian and Pacific Correspondence of Sir Joseph Banks*, London, Routledge, 8 vols, 2008–2014.

CHAMBERS, Neil (ed.), *Scientific Correspondence of Sir Joseph Banks, 1765–1820*, Vol. 4, London, Pickering and Chatto, 2007.

CHAPLIN M.D., Arnold, *A St Helena Who's Who: A directory of the island during the captivity of Napoleon*. London, published by the author, 1914.

CLUBBE, C. P., HAMILTON, M. A. and CORCORAN, M. R., 'The role of native species nurseries in mitigating threats from invasive species: case studies from UK Overseas Territories.' *Proceedings of the 4th Global Botanic Gardens Congress, June 2010*, Dublin: Botanic Gardens Conservation International, 2010, pp. 1–13.

CONNOR GEARY, Sheila and HUTCHINSON, B. June. 'Mr. Dawson, Plantsman', *Arnoldia* 40(2), March/April 1980.

CRALLAN, Hugh P. , 'Island of St Helena: Listing and preservation of buildings of architectural and historic interest', report, 1974. http://sainthelenaisland.info/crallanreport1974.pdf

CRONK, Q. C. B., 'W. J. Burchell and the botany of St Helena', *Archives of Natural History*, 15.1 (1988), pp. 45–60.

CRONK, Q. C. B., *The Endemic flora of St Helena*, Oswestry, Anthony Nelson, 2000.

DANDY, J. E. (revised & edited), *The Sloane Herbarium: An annotated list of the Horti sicci composing it; with biographical details of the principal contributors*, London. British Museum, 1958. https://www.biodiversitylibrary.org/item/233790#page/9/mode/1up

DAWSON, Warren R. (ed.), *The Banks Letters: A calendar of the manuscript correspondence of Sir Joseph Banks preserved in the British Museum, the British Museum (Natural History) and other collections in Great Britain*, London, Trustees of the British Museum, 1958.

DEE, Emma, 'If walls could speak: The secrets of Plantation House', *St Helena Sentinel*, 4 August 2016.

DEE, Emma, 'Old Luffkins', *St Helena Sentinel*, 25 August 2016.

DESMOND, Ray, *Dictionary of British and Irish Botanists and Horticulturalist including plant collectors and botanical artists*, London, Taylor and Francis, 1977.

DESMOND, Ray, *Sir Joseph Dalton Hooker: Traveller and plant collector*, Woodbridge, Antique Collectors' Club and the Royal Botanic Gardens, Kew, 1999.

DRAYTON, Richard, *Nature's Government: Science, imperial Britain and the 'improvement' of the world*, New Haven, Yale University Press, 2000.

[DUNCAN, Francis] *A description of the island of St. Helena; containing observations on its singular structure and formation; and an account of its climate, natural history, and inhabitants*, London, R. Phillips, 1805.

du PREEZ, Michael and DRONFIELD, Jeremy, *Dr James Barry: A woman ahead of her time*, London, One World, 2016.

Extracts from the St. Helena Records, (second edition,) and chronicles of Cape commanders, compiled by the late Hudson Ralph Janisch, Esq., C.M.G., governor of St. Helena; with a preface by His Excellency Lt.-Col. H.L. Gallwey, C.M.G., D.S.O. governor and commander-in-chief of St Helena, Jamestown, Benjamin Grant printer, 1908. Reproduced by P. L. Teale, St Helena, W. A. Thorpe, 1981.

[FENNAH, R. G.] 'Discussion: The origin and relationships of insular faunas', *Proceedings of the Royal Society*, B, Vol. 152, issue 949, 12 July 1960, p. 575, https://doi.org/10.1098/rspb.1960.0067

FIELD, Lady, *The history of Plantation House St Helena 1673–1967*, Penzance, Patten Press, 1998.

First report of the commissioners for the exhibition of 1851, to the Right Hon. Spencer Horatio Walpole, &. &. one of Her Majesty's principal secretaries of state, Houses of Parliament, London, 1852.

FORSTER, Georg, *A Voyage Round the World in His Majesty's Sloop, Resolution, commanded by Capt. James Cook, during the Years 1772, 3, 4 and 5.* London, B. White, J. Robson, P. Elmsly and G. Robinson, 1777. http://pacific.pitt.edu/ForsterGeorgComplete.html [Accessed: 8 September 2020].

FORSYTH, William, *History of the Captivity of Napoleon at St Helena; from the letters and journals of the late Lieut.-Gen. Sir Hudson Lowe, and official documents not before made public*, New York, Harper & Brothers, 2 vols, 1855.

FOWLER, T. E., *Views of St Helena*, London, Day and Son, 1863.

FOX, Colin, *A Bitter Draught: St Helena and the abolition of slavery, 1792–1840*, Elveden, Society of Friends of St Helena, 2017.

FOX, Colin (ed. & trans.), 'Henry Russell: A nabob's sojourn on St Helena 1821', *Wirebird*, no. 47, 2018, pp. 26–64.

FOX, Colin, *The Bennett Letters: A 19th century family in St Helena, England and the Cape. The lives of Captain James Bennett H.E.I.C.S. of St Helena (1773–1835) including the mysterious story of Napoleon's coffin and of his son George Brooks Bennett, soldier and botanist (1816–1907)*, Gloucester, Choir Press, 2006.

FOX, Colin, 'Two governors: Robert Brooke and Robert Patton', *Wirebird*, no. 49, 2020, pp. 40–60.

FOX, Colin and BALDWIN, Edward (eds), *A precarious livelihood. St Helena 1834: East India Company outpost to crown colony. The commissioners of inquiry report HR Brandreth and E Walpole*, Elveden, Society of Friends of St Helena. [Original manuscript material: The National Archives, Kew, CO 247/37–39. A manuscript copy of the report also exists in the St Helena Archives.]

FOX, Colin (ed. & trans.) and MABBETT, Bernard (provided letters), 'Governor William Grey-Wilson. Letters to his mother', *Wirebird*, no. 41, 2012, pp. 26–35.

FROST, Alan, *Sir Joseph Banks and the Transfer of Plants to and from the South Pacific. 1786–1789*, Melbourne, Colony Press, 1993.

GALLWEY, H. L., *Extracts from the St. Helena records (second edition) and chronicles of Cape Commanders, compiled by the late Hudson Ralph Janisch, Esq., C.M.G.*, Jamestown, printed by the 'Guardian', 1908. Reprinted by P. L. Teale, Durban, 1981.

GALWAY, Henry L., 'A sojourn in St Helena', *Journal of the Royal African Society*, Vol. 40, no. 160, July 1941, pp. 223–237.

GEORGE, Barbara B. *Names of Places on St Helena*, Jamestown, privately published, 2016.

GEORGE, Barbara B. *The History of the Chinese Indentured Labourers on St Helena 1810-1836 and beyond*, Jamestown, privately published, 2002.

GILL, Mrs [Isobel], *Six Months in Ascension: An unscientific account of a scientific expedition*, London, John Murray, 1880.

GILL, Robin and TEALE, Percy, *St. Helena 500: A chronological history of the island*, Epping, printed by Creda Communications, 1999.

GOODENOUGH, S., 'St. Helena and its endemic plants—a conservation success: The best known unfamiliar land in the world', *Curtis's Botanical Magazine*, Vol. 2, no. 4, 1985, pp. 369–379.

GOSSE, Philip, *St. Helena 1502–1938*, London, Cassell, 1938.

GOURGAUD, General Baron, *Talks of Napoleon at St. Helena* (trans. Elizabeth Wormeley Latimer), Chicago, A.C. McClurg, 1904.

GRANT, Benjamin, *A Few Notes on St Helena and Descriptive Guide*, Jamestown, 1883: http://www.museumofsainthelena.org/wp-content/uploads/2018/03/Descriptive-Guide-benjamin-grant.pdf

GROVE, A. T., 'St Helena as a microcosm of the East India Company world', in Vinita Damedaran, Anna Winterbottom and Alan Lester, *The East India Company and the Natural World*. Basingstoke, Palgrave Macmillan, 2015, pp. 249–269.

GROVE, Richard, 'Conserving Eden: The (European) East India Companies and their environmental policies on St. Helena, Mauritius and in Western India, 1660 to 1854', *Comparative Studies in Society and History*, Vol. 35, no. 2, 1993, pp. 318–351. www.jstor.org/stable/179402 [Accessed 24 July 2020].

GROVE, Richard H., *Green Imperialism: Colonial expansion, tropical island Edens and the origin of environmentalism, 1600–1860*, Cambridge University Press, 1997.

GUMEDE, Sizakele, 'Maldivia House once belonged to the Natal government of South Africa', *Wirebird*, no. 48, 2019, pp. 21–25.

GUNN, Mary, and CODD, L. E., *Botanical Exploration of Southern Africa*, Cape Town, A.A. Balkema, 1981.

HEARL, Trevor W., 'Darwin's island', in *St Helena Britannica: Studies in South Atlantic island history* (ed. A. H. Schulenburg), London, Society of the Friends of St Helena, 2013: https://www.friendsofsthelena.com/upload/files/Darwin%E2%80%99s_island.pdf

HEARL, Trevor W., *St Helena Britannica: Studies in South Atlantic island history* (ed. A.H. Schulenburg), London, Society of Friend of St Helena, 2013.

HEMSLEY, W. Botting, 'Report on the botany of the Bermudas and various islands of the Atlantic and Southern oceans. Second part', St Helena, in Sir C. Wyville Thomson and John Murray, *Report of the scientific results of the voyage of H.M.S. Challenger during the years 1873–76*, Botany Vol. IIB, London, HMSO, 1885, pp. 49–122.

HEMSLEY (compiler), W. Botting, 1882, *The gallery of Marianne North's paintings of plants and their homes, Royal Botanic Gardens, Kew. Descriptive catalogue*, London, Kew Gardens, 1882.

HOOKER, Joseph, 'Insular flora', *Gardeners' Chronicle*, 12 January 1867, p. 27.

HURBURGH, M., *The Royal Botanical Gardens, 1818–1986*, Sandy Bay. Shearwater Press, n.d.

HUXLEY, Leonard, *Life and Letters of Sir Joseph Dalton Hooker O.M., G.C.S.I. Based on materials collected and arranged by Lady Hooker*, 2 vols, London, John Murray, 1918.

JACKSON, Basil, *Notes and Reminiscences of a Staff Officer*, London, John Murray, 1903.

JACKSON, E. L. *St Helena: The historic island from its discovery to the present date*. London, Ward Lock, 1903.

JARVIS, Charles E., '"The most common grass, rush, moss, fern, thistles, thorns or vilest weeds you can find": James Petiver's plants', *Notes and Records: the Royal Society Journal of the History of Science*, 74, 2019, pp. 303–328, http://doi.org/10.1098/rsnr.2019.0012

JARVIS, Charles E., and OSWALD, Philip H., 'The collecting activities of James Cuninghame FRS on the voyage of Tuscan to China (Amoy) between 1697 and 1699', *Royal Society Journal for the History of Science*, published online 24 December 2014, https://doi.org/10.1098/rsnr.2014.0043

KARSTEN, Mia C. *The Old Company's Garden at the Cape and its Superintendents*. Cape Town, Maskew Miller, 1951.

KELLY, James, 'Brooke, Robert (1744–1811)', *Dictionary of Irish Biography*, Vol. 1, Dublin and Cambridge, 2009, p. 877.

KEMBLE, James, *St Helena during Napoleon's Exile: Gorrequer's diary*, London, Heinemann, 1969.

KEOGH, Luke, *The Wardian Case: How a simple box moved plants and changed the world*, Kew Publishing and University of Chicago Press, 2020.

KEYNES, Quentin, *St. Helena: The forgotten island, An article originally published in the National Geographic Magazine in August 1950 with an introduction by Simon Keynes*, Friends of St Helena, 2005.

KEYNES, Richard Darwin (ed.), *Charles Darwin's Beagle Diary*, Cambridge University Press, 2001.

KITCHING, G. C. *A Handbook and Gazetteer of the Island of St Helena including a short history of the island under the crown 1834–1902*, typescript, 1947. Available online: http://sainthelenaisland.info/kitching1947.pdf [Accessed 22 April 2018].

KNOWLES, Sir Lees (ed.), *A Gift of Napoleon; being a sequel to letters of Captain Engelbert Lutyens, orderly officer at Longwood, Saint Helena, Feb. 1820 to Nov. 1823*, London, John Lane, 1921.

KNOWLES, Sir Lees (ed.), *Letters of Captain Engelbert Lutyens orderly officer at Longwood, Saint Helena: Feb. 1820 to Nov. 1823*, London, John Lane, 1915.

KOLBEN [Kolbe], Peter, *The Present State of the Cape of Good Hope*, London, printed W. Innys and G. Smith, 1731, 2 vols.

KUMAR, Deepak, 'Botanical explorations and the East India Company: Revisiting "plant colonialism"', in Vinita Damodaran, Anna Winterbottom and Alan Lester, *The East India Company and the Natural World*, Basingstoke Macmillan, 2015, pp. 16–34.

LAMBDON, Phil (ed. by Andrew Darlow), *Flowering Plants and Ferns of St Helena*, St Helena Nature Conservation Group, Pisces Publications, 2012.

LAMBDON, Phil and CRONK, Quentin, 'Extinction dynamics under extreme conservation threat: The flora of St Helena', *Frontiers in Ecology and Evolution*, Vol. 8, article 41, 10pp.: DOI=10.3389/fevo.2020.0004. URL=https://www.frontiersin.org/article/10.3389/fevo.2020.00041 [Accessed 17 April 2020].

LAMBDON, P. and ELLICK, S., 'A Rare Plant Census of St Helena', Darwin Plus: Overseas Territories Environment and Climate Fund Final Report (DPLUS008), 2014. Available online: https://www.darwininitiative.org.uk/documents/DPLUS008/23470/DPLUS008%20FR%20-%20Edited.pdf [Accessed 19 April 2020].

LAMBDON, P. W. and ELLICK, S., '*Dryopteris napoleonis*, small kidney fern', The IUCN Red List of Threatened Species, 2016.

LATIMER, Elizabeth Wormeley (trans & notes), *Talks of Napoleon at St. Helena with General Baron Gourgaud: Together with the journal kept by Gourgaud on their journey from Waterloo to St. Helena*, Chicago, A. C. McClurg, 1904.

LEE, Ida, *Captain Bligh's Second Voyage to the South Sea*, London, Longmans, Green, 1920. Available online: http://gutenberg.net.au/ebooks12/1204361h.html [Accessed 9 November 2021].

LEFROY, J. H. (ed. A. D. Thiessen), 'The removal of Napoleon's remains from St Helena to France, October 1840', *Journal of the Royal Astronomical Society of Canada*, Vol. 36, 1942, pp. 66–73.

LOCKWOOD, Joseph, *A guide to St. Helena, descriptive and historical, with a visit to Longwood, and Napoleon's tomb*, St Helena, Geo. Gibb printer, 1851.

LORING, Lorna M., 'Voyages of improvement: Ambition and failure in projects of plant transfer and improvement in the late eighteenth–century British Empire', PhD thesis, Washington DC, American University, 2016.

McALEER, J, '"A young slip of botany": Botanical networks, the South Atlantic, and Britain's maritime worlds, c.1790–1810', *Journal of Global History*, Vol. 11, no. 1, 2016, pp. 24–43.

McALEER, John, 'Looking east: St Helena, the South Atlantic and Britain's Indian Ocean World'. *Atlantic Studies*, 13:1, 2016, pp. 78–98.

McALEER, John, *People, Places and the World of the East India Company*, University of Washington Press, 2017.

McCRACKEN, Donal P., 'Beyond the Glynns: The phenomenon of the Giant's Causeway in eighteenth–century Ireland', *The Glynns: Journal of the Glens of Antrim Historical Society*, Vol. 13, 1985, pp. 21–25.

McCRACKEN, Donal P., 'Dependence, destruction and development: A history of indigenous timber use in South Africa', in M. J. Lawes, H. A. C. Eeley, C. M. Shackleton and B. G. S. Geach (eds), *Indigenous Forests and Woodlands in South Africa: Policy, People and Practice*, University of KwaZulu–Natal Press, Pietermaritzburg, 2004, pp. 277–283 and 287–308.

McCRACKEN, Donal P., 'Fraternity in the age of jingoism; the British imperial botanic and forestry network', in Benedikt Stuchtey, *Science across the European Empires, 1800–1950*, Oxford University Press, German Historical Institute London, 1995, pp. 49–62.

McCRACKEN, Donal P., *Gardens of Empire: Botanical institutions of the Victorian British empire*. London and Washington, University of Leicester Press/Cassell, 1997.

McCRACKEN, Donal P., 'Plant hunting and provenance of South African plants in British botanical magazines, 1787–1910', in Mary N. Harris (ed.), *Sights and Insights: Interactive images of Europe and the wider world*, Pisa University Press, 2007.

McCRACKEN, Donal P., 'The indigenous forests of colonial Natal and Zululand', *Natalia*, no. 16, 1986, pp. 19–38.

McCRACKEN, Donal P. and McCRACKEN, Eileen, 'A register of trees, Co. Cork, 1793–1860', *The Journal of the Cork Historical Society*, Vol. 81, 1976, pp. 39–60.

McCRACKEN, Donal P. and McCRACKEN, Eileen, *The Way to Kirstenbosch*, Annals of Kirstenbosch Botanic Gardens, Vol. 18, Cape Town, National Botanic Gardens of South Africa, 1988.

McCRACKEN, Eileen, 'The botanic garden, Trinity College, Dublin', *Garden History*, Vol. vii, no. 1, Spring 1979, pp. 86–90.

McCRACKEN, Eileen, *The Palm House and Botanic Garden, Belfast*, Belfast, Ulster Historical Foundation, 1971.

MACKAY, David, *In the wake of Cook: Exploration, science and empire, 1780–1801*, Routledge, 2018.

MARCHAND, Louis-Joseph, *In Napoleon's Shadow, The Memoirs of Louis-Joseph Marchand, Valet and Friend of the Emperor 1811–1821 including the original notes of Jean Bourguignon Académie Des Beaux Arts and Henry Lachouque,* preface by Jean Tulard, Barnsley, Greenhill, 2018.

MARCHAND, Louis-Joseph, *In Napoleon's Shadow: The Memoirs of Louis-Joseph Marchand, Valet and Friend of the Emperor, 1811–1821*. Greenhill Books. Kindle Edition, 1998.

MASSELIN, E., *Sainte-Hélène ... Dessins de staal d'aprés les croquis de l'auteur*, Paris, 1862.

MAYDOM, Katrina Elizabeth, 'James Petiver's apothecary practice and the consumption of American drugs in early modern London', *Notes and Records: the Royal Society Journal of the History of Science*, Vol. 74, issue 2, published: 1 April 2020, https://doi.org/10.1098/rsnr.2019.0015

MELLISS, J.C., 'The fate of St Helena', *The Standard*, 28 May 1908.

MELLISS, John Charles, *St Helena: A physical, historical, and topographical description of the island including the geology, fauna, flora and meteorology*, London, L. Reeve, 1875.

MEYNELL, Henry, *Conversations with Napoleon at St Helena*, London, Arthur L. Humphreys, 1911.

MONTHOLON, Charles-Tristan, Comte de, *Napoleon's appeal to the British nation on his treatment at Saint Helena. The official memoir, dictated by him, and delivered to Sir Hudson Lowe*, London, William Hone, 1817.

MONTHOLON, M. Le Général, *Récits de la captivité de L'empereur Napoléon a Sainte–Hélène*, Paris, Paulin Libraire, 1847.

MORRIS, Dr D., *Reprint of a report (written in 1884) upon the present position and prospects of the agricultural resources of the island of St Helena*, Colonial Reports no. 38, CD 3248, London. (HMSO), 1906.

MURPHY, David, 'Barry Edward O'Meara', *Dictionary of Irish Biography*, Vol. 7, Dublin, Royal Irish Academy, 2009, pp. 691–692.

NELSON, E. Charles, and McCRACKEN, Eileen M., *The Brightest Jewel: A history of the National Botanic Gardens Glasnevin, Dublin*, Dublin, Boethius Press, Kilkenny, 1987.

O'MEARA Esq., his late surgeon, Barry E., *Napoleon in Exile; or, A voice from St Helena, The opinion and reflections of Napoleon on the important events of his life and government, in his own words, in two volumes*, New York, William Gowans, 1853.

Paxton's Botanical Dictionary: Comprising the names, history, and culture of all plants known in Britain, revised 2nd ed. by Samuel Hereman, London, Bradbury, Evans & Co., 1868.

PAXTON, Joseph, assisted by Professor LINDLEY, *A Pocket Botanical Dictionary; comprising the names, history, and culture of all plants known in Britain; with a full explanation of technical terms*, London, J. Andrews, 1840.

PEARSON, Andrew, 'Waterwitch: A warship, its voyage and its crew in the era of anti-slavery', *Atlantic Studies*, Vol. 31, no. 1, pp. 99–124.

PESSINA, Mattia, 'Labour, environment and empire in the South Atlantic (1780–1860)', PhD thesis, Università Degli studi di Trento (2014–2015).

[Plukenet, Leonard] *Almagesti botanici mantissa : plantarum novissimè detectarum ultrà millenarium numerum complectens, cui, tanquam pedi jam stantis columnae, plus inscribere fas est, cum indice totius operis ad calcem adjecto.* Londini, Sumptibus Autoris, 1700. https://www.biodiversitylibrary.org/bibliography/166144#/summary

POSTANS, Mrs, 'The emperor's grave; a sketch of St. Helena', in *The Oriental Herald and Colonial Intelligencer*, Vol. 4, July to December 1839, pp. 213–218. Reproduced in *The Wirebird*, no. 40, 2011.

PRITCHARD, Stephen F., and BOWIE, James, *An alphabetical list of indigenous and exotic plants, growing on the island of St. Helena*, printed by G. J. Pike, Cape Town, 1836.

Proceedings of the Dublin Society, from November 2d 1780, to August 23d 1781, (1781), Vol. 17.

Report of the St. Helena Industrial Exhibition, for 1874. Presented to His Excellency the Governor, 13th August 1874, Jamestown, 1874.

ROBSON, Thomas, *St. Helena Memoirs. An account of a remarkable revival of religion that took place at St. Helena, during the last years of the exile of Napoleon Buonaparte. In two parts.* 2nd ed. London, James Nisbet, 1827.

ROBINSON, T. F., 'William Roxburgh (1751–1815): The founding father of Indian botany', PhD thesis, University of Edinburgh, 2003.

ROBINSON, Tim, *William Roxburgh: The founding father of Indian botany*, Chichester, Phillimore, 2008.

ROSEBERY, Lord, *Napoleon the Last Phase*, London, Jonathan Cape, 1928.

ROYLE, Stephen A., 'Island history, not the story of islands: The case of St Helena', *Shima*, Vol. 13, no. 1, 2019, pp. 44–55.

ROYLE, Stephen A., *The Company's Island: St Helena, Company colonies and the colonial endeavour*, London, I.B. Tauris, 2007.

St. DENIS, Louis Etienne, *Napoleon from the Tuileries to St Helena: Personal recollections of the emperor's second mameluke and valet*, Harper and Brothers, New York, 1922.

SCHULENBURG, Alexander Hugo, 'St Helena: British local history in the context of empire', *The Local Historian*, Vol. 28, no. 2, May 1998, pp. 108–122.

SCHULENBURG, Alexander Hugo, 'Transient observations: The textualizing of St Helena through five hundred years of colonial discourse', PhD thesis, University of St Andrew, 1999.

SEALE, Robert F. *The Geognosy of the Island of St. Helena, Illustrated in a Series of Views, Plans and Sections; Accompanied with Explanatory Remarks and Observations*, London, Ackermann, 1834.

SMALLMAN, David L., *Quincentenary: A story of St Helena, 1502–2002*, Penzance, Patten Press, 2003.

SMITH, David Baird, 'St Helena in 1817', *Scottish Historical Review*, Vol. 19, no. 76, July 1922, pp. 273–282.

SMITH, Edmund, *The Life of Sir Joseph Banks*, London, John Lane, Bodley Head, 1911.

SMYTH, Jonathan, 'A governor with a 'good heart', *Anglo-Celt*, 6 July 2017, p. 43.

STEINER, Sue, *St Helena, Ascension, Tristan da Cunha*, Chalfont St Peter, Bradt, 2002.

STERNDALE, R. A., 'St Helena in the present time', *Asiatic Quarterly Review*, January 1900, pp. 98–107.

STERNDALE, R. A., 'St Helena in ye olden tyme', *Asiatic Quarterly Review*, April 1899, pp. 345–352.

SWEET, Robert, *Sweet's Hortus Britannicus: A catalogue of plants cultivated in the gardens of Great Britain*, 2 parts, London, J. Ridgway, 1826.

TAVOLACCI, Laura, 'Vegetable gardens versus cash crops: Science and political economy in the Agricultural and Horticultural Society of India, 1820–40', *History Workshop Journal*, Vol. 88, Autumn 2019, pp. 24–46, https://doi.org/10.1093/hwj/dbz028

TEALE, P. L., 'The island of St Helena', *Chartered Surveyor*, December 1874, pp. 127–130.

TEALE, Percival Leslie, *Saint Helena 1502 to 1659 before the English East India Company*, Durban, 2nd ed., privately published, 1981.

TEALE, Percival Leslie, 'St Helena; A history of the development of the island with special reference to building civil and military engineering works', Master of Architecture thesis, University of Natal, 5 vols, 1972.

THISELTON-DYER, W. T., *The Botanical Enterprise of the Empire*, London, Phillimore, 1880.

THOMAS, Adrian Peter, 'Calcutta Botanic Garden: Knowledge formation and the expectations of botany in a colonial context, 1833–1914', PhD thesis, King's College London, 2016.

THORPE, Henry, 'The history and re–development of Rock Rose', *The St Helena Connection*, no. 26, June 2019, p. 18.

TURRILL, W. B., 'On the flora of St. Helena', *Kew Bulletin*, Vol. 3, no. 3, 1948, pp. 358–362.

VAN DE VELDE, Stéphane, 'Chasing the slavers: The establishment of the Vice Admiralty Court of St Helena', *The Wirebird*, No. 40, 2011, pp. 3–14.

VERNON, B. J., *Recollections of Jamaica, with the particulars of an eventful passage home via New York and Halifax at the commencement of the American war in 1812, to which are added, trifles from St Helena relating to Napoleon and his suite*, London, Whittaker, 1848.

WALKER, Rev. John, 'St Helena as I saw it: 1886', *Wirebird*, no. 50, 2021, pp. 69–93.

WALTER, Henry, *Events of a Military Life: being recollections after service in the Peninsular war, invasion of France, the East Indies, St. Helena, Canada, and elsewhere*, 2 vols, London, William Pickering, 1843.

WATSON, G. L.de St., 'Gorrequer at St. Helena', *History*, Vol. 1, no. 3, 1912, pp. 183–188.

WEIDER, C. M. and FORSHUFVUD, Sten, *Assassination at St Helena Revisited*, New York, John Wiley, 1995.

WILLIAMS, Benjamin Samuel, *Select Ferns and Lycopods: British and exotic*, London, Victoria and Paradise Nurseries, published by the author, 1873.

WILLIAMSON, William D., *History of the State of Maine; from its discovery, A.D. 1602, to the separation, A.D. 1820, inclusive*, 2 vols, 1839, Hallowell, published by Glazier, Masters and Smith.

WILSON, Sir Arthur (ed.,) *A Diary of St Helena. The Journal of Lady Malcolm (1816, 1817) Containing the Conversations of Napoleon with Sir Pulteney Malcolm*, New York and London, Harper, 1929.

WOLLASTON, Mrs T. Vernon, 'Notes on the Lepidoptera of St Helena', *The Annals and Magazine of Natural History; zoology, botany, and geology*, Vol. 3, ser. 5, 1879, pp. 219–233 and 329–441.

WOLLASTON, T. Vernon, *Coleoptera Sanctæ–Helenæ*, London, John van Voorst, 1877.

YULE, Marianne A., 'Napoleon on St Helena: Altered plates', *Print Quarterly*, Vol. 28, no. 2, June 2011, pp. 155–161.

ONLINE SOURCES
Attacking the slave trade: http://sainthelenaisland.info/slavetrade.htm [Accessed 28 November 2021].

Bank's *Endeavour* journal: https://collections.tepapa.govt.nz/topic/3642 https://www.joseph-banks.org.uk/garden-plants/ http://nzetc.victoria.ac.nz/tm/scholarly/tei-Bea02Bank-t1-body-d2.html [Accessed 2 December 2021].

James Barry, *Dictionary of Irish Biography* (Bridget Hourican and Frances Clarke): https://www.dib.ie/biography/barry-james-a0442 [Accessed 23 November 2021].

Captain Cook: http://www.captaincooksociety.com/home/detail/the–second–voyage–1771–1776 [Accessed 7 August 2020].

Captain Cook: http://cudl.lib.cam.ac.uk/view/MS–JOD–00020/533 [Accessed 8 September 2020].

Captain Cook and St Helena (Ian Boreham): https://www.captaincooksociety.com/home/detail/captain–cook–and–st–helena [Accessed 8 August 2020].

Chancellor and van Wyhe (eds) Despoblado notebook. EH1.6 [English Heritage 88202326] (6-8.1835, 5-8.1836) . (Darwin Online, http://darwin-online.org.uk/) [Accessed 2 December 2021].

Charles Darwin: http://friendsofdarwin.com/articles/darwin–visits–napoleon/ [John van Wyhe, editor. 2002–. The Complete Work of Charles Darwin Online. (http://darwin-online.org.uk/content/frameset?pageseq=531&itemID=EH88202366&viewtype=side)] [Accessed 9 November 2021].

Charles Darwin: Keynes, R. D. ed. 2001. Charles Darwin's Beagle diary. Cambridge: Cambridge University Press. (darwin–online.org.uk) [Accessed 29 April 2021].

Charles Darwin: Rookmaaker, Kees ed. [Darwin's *Beagle diary* (1831–1836)]. [English Heritage 88202366] (Darwin Online, http://darwin–online.org.uk/).

Charles Villet: http://www.s2a3.org.za/bio/Biograph_final.php?serial=2989

The Great Wall of St Helena: https://sainthelenaisland.info/greatwoodwall.htm [Accessed 4 June 2020].

'Kerr's views in the island of St. Helena', https://bweaver.nom.sh/Kerr/kerr.htm [Accessed 24 March 2020].

Killybeggs House (Brooke): Nicola Jennings, 20 February 2007. Co. Kildare Online Electronic History Journal: http://www.kildare.ie/library/ehistory/2008/02/post_21.asp [Accessed 23 August 2020].

Maldivia House: http://sainthelenaisland.info/maldivia.htm [Accessed 3 July 2020].

Nathaniel Ward: https://www.plantexplorers.com/explorers/biographies/ward/nathaniel-bagshaw-ward.htm [Accessed 14 May 2020].

The Plant List: http://www.theplantlist.org/tpl1.1/record/ifn–21862 [Accessed 14 May 2020].

Saint Helena 15.55 South 5.43 West [Great Wall] http://jcgrimshaw.blogspot.com/search/label/Photographs

Saint Helena, Ascension and Tristan da Cunha [Officials as listed] https://www.worldstatesmen.org/Saint_Helena.htm [Accessed 5 January 2021].

St Helena Council Records, 1678–1681, f. 25 (21 October 1678), https://www.friendsofthelena.com/upload/files/1678-1683_St_Helena_Records.pdf [Accessed 3 December 2021].

Toby, Napoleon and slavery on Saint Helena: https://www.napoleon200.org/events?fbclid=IwAR0qOQnlgEQmzzGOb5rDSMaSYBfxqvSAXzzsQHTYb_bM7D0VU6N40Ri0rMQ [Accessed 3 April 2021].

William Burchell and St Helena: https://thegardenstrust.blog/2019/06/29/william–burchell–and–st–helena/ [Accessed 12 July 2020].

General Index

Extended entries are provided under **Napoleon**, **St Helena** and **St Helena endemic plants**.

Taxonomic Index

Great variations in spelling exists in 18th and 19th century sources, both manuscript and print. Where possible, the modern spelling is used in the index though the quoted source in the text of the book remains as was in the original source.

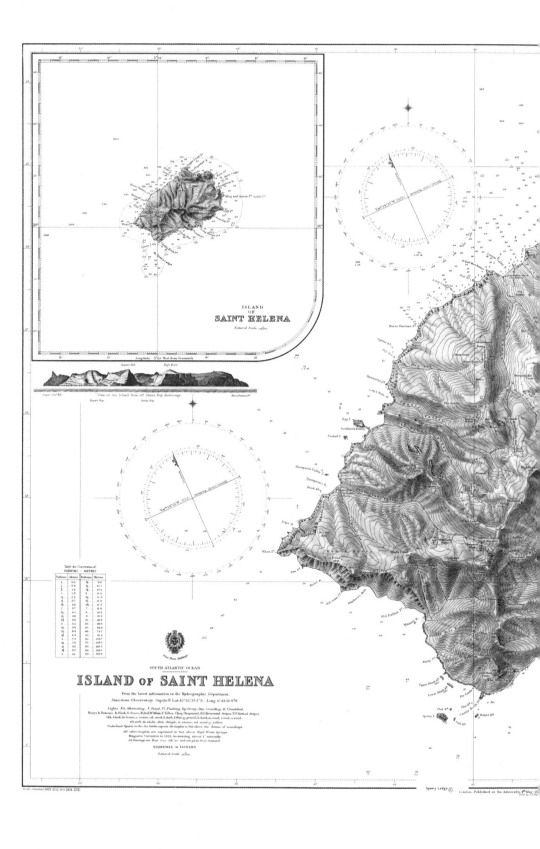

ISLAND
OF
SAINT HELENA

Natural Scale 1:37800

"View of the Island from off Sainse Bay Anchorage."

SOUTH ATLANTIC OCEAN

ISLAND OF SAINT HELENA

From the latest information in the Hydrographic Department.

Jamestown Observatory Cupola ⊕ Lat.15°55'33·3"S. Long.5°43'19·8"W.

Lights. Alt. Alternating, F. Fixed, Fl. Flashing, Gp.Group, Occ. Occulting, (U) Unwatched.

Buoys & Beacons. B.Black, G.Green, R.Red,W.White, Y.Yellow, Cheq. Chequered, H.S.Horizontal Stripes, V.S.Vertical Stripes

bk. black, br. brown, c. coarse, cl. coral, d. dark, f. fine, g. gravel, h. hard, m. mud, r. rock, s. sand,
st. soft, sh. shells, sti. shingle, st. stones, wd. weed, y. yellow.

Underlined figures on the dry banks express the heights in feet above the Bottom of soundings

All other heights are expressed in feet above High Water Springs.
Magnetic Variation in 1922. Decreasing about 1' annually.
All Bearings are True (this 126 etc. etc.) and are given from Seaward.

SOUNDINGS IN FATHOMS

Natural Scale 1:37800

Table the Conversion of
FATHOMS ~ METRES

Fathoms	Metres	Fathoms	Metres
⅛	0·2	5¼	9·6
¼	0·4	5½	10·1
⅜	0·6	5¾	10·5
½	0·9	6	10·9
⅝	1·1	6¼	11·4
¾	1·3	6½	11·8
⅞	1·6	6¾	12·3
1	1·8	7	12·8
2	3·6	8	14·6
2½	4·5	9	16·4
3	5·4	10	18·2
3½	6·4	20	36·5
4	7·3	30	54·8
4½	8·2	40	73·1
5	9·1	50	91·4
		60	109·7
		70	128·0
		80	146·3
		90	164·5
		100	182·8

London, Published at the Admiralty, 4ᵗʰ May

Sperry Lodge